Merleau-Ponty and the Possibilities of Philosophy

SUNY series in Contemporary French Thought

David Pettigrew and Francois Raffoul, editors

Merleau-Ponty and the Possibilities of Philosophy

Transforming the Tradition

EDITED BY
Bernard Flynn,
Wayne J. Froman,
and
Robert Vallier

SUNY
PRESS

Published by State University of New York Press, Albany

Printed in the United States of America

For information, contact State University of New York Press, Albany, NY
www.sunypress.edu

Production by Ryan Morris
Marketing by Anne M. Valentine

Library of Congress Cataloging-in-Publication Data

Merleau-Ponty and the possibilities of philosophy : transforming the tradition / edited by Robert Vallier, Wayne Froman, and Bernard Flynn.
p. cm. — (SUNY series in contemporary French thought)
Includes bibliographical references and index.
ISBN 978-1-4384-2669-3 (hardcover : alk. paper)
ISBN 978-1-4384-2670-9 (pbk.: alk.paper)
1. Merleau-Ponty, Maurice, 1908–1961. I. Vallier, Robert. II. Froman, Wayne Jeffrey, 1945– III. Flynn, Bernard.
B2430.M3764M46825 2009
194—dc22

2009002953

10 9 8 7 6 5 4 3 2 1

Contents

Acknowledgments vii

List of Abbreviations ix

1. Introduction 1

2. Homage to Merleau-Ponty 17
Paul Ricoeur

3. Merleau-Ponty
Beyond Husserl and Heidegger (1989) 25
Paul Ricoeur

4. The Turn of Experience
Merleau-Ponty and Bergson 33
Renaud Barbaras

5. Community, Society, and History in the Later Merleau-Ponty 61
Marc Richir

6. Tracework
Experience and Description in the Moral Phenomenology of Merleau-Ponty and Levinas 79
David Michael Kleinberg-Levin

7. Merleau-Ponty and the Philosophical Position of Skepticism 117
Bernard Flynn

8. The Elemental Flesh
Nature, Life, and Difference in Merleau-Ponty and Plato's *Timaeus* 129
Robert Vallier

9. The Blind Spot 155
Wayne J. Froman

10. Proximity and Distance
With Regard to Heidegger in the Later Merleau-Ponty 165
Michel Haar

11. Chiasm, Flesh, Figuration
Toward a Non-Positive Ontology 183
Véronique M. Fóti

12. Phenomenology of the Icon 197
Jenny Slatman

13. On the "Fundamental of Painting"
Chinese Counterpoint 221
Jacques Taminiaux

14. Variations of the Sensible
The Truth of Ideas and Idea of Philosophy in the Later Merleau-Ponty 237
Mauro Carbone

15. The Body of Speech 257
Françoise Dastur

16. Body, Flesh 275
Claude Lefort

List of Contributors 293

Index 297

Acknowledgments

The editors wish to thank the following publishers for permission to publish translations from texts originally published in French: J. Vrin for permission to publish "The Turn of Experience" by R. Barbaras (trans. by R. Vallier) from *Le tournant le l'expérience* by R. Barbaras (Paris: J. Vrin, 1997); Encre Marin for permission to publish "The Body of Speech" by F. Dastur (trans. by R. Vallier) from *Chair et langage: essais sur Merleau-Ponty* (Paris: Encre Marin, 2000); Les Éditions Gallimard for permission to publish "Body, Flesh" by C. Lefort (trans. by R. Vallier) from *Sur la colonne absente: essais autour de Merleau-Ponty* (Paris: Gallimard , 1978); Éditions du Seuil for permission to publish "Homage to Merleau-Ponty" and "Merleau-Ponty: Beyond Husserl and Heidegger" by Paul Ricoeur (trans. by W. Froman, in consultation with R. Vallier) from *Lectures 2: La contrée des philosophes* (Paris: Seuil, 1992); J. Millon for permission to publish "Community, Society, and History in the Later Merleau-Ponty" by M. Richir (trans. by R Vallier) from *Merleau-Ponty: phénoménologie et experiences*, edited by M. Richir and E. Tassin (Grenoble: J. Millon, 1992).

The editors also wish to express their heartfelt gratitude to Judith Walz, whose ongoing input, encouragement, and steadfastness were simply indispensable in bringing this project to fruition.

Abbreviations

The following abbreviations appear in the text:

BT *Being and Time* by Martin Heidegger, trans. J. Macquarrie and E. Robinson (New York: Harper and Row, 1962)

Hua *Husserliana: Edmund Husserl—Gesammelte Werke* (Heidelberg: Springer Verlag)

HT *Humanism and Terror*, trans. J. O'Neill (Boston: Beacon Press, 1969)

Praise *In Praise of Philosophy and Other Essays*, trans. J. O'Neill by Maurice Merleau-Ponty (Evanston, Ill.: Northwestern University Press, 1988)

Nature *Nature: Course Notes from the Collège de France* by Maurice Merleau-Ponty, complied by D. Seglard, trans. R. Vallier (Evanston, Ill.: Northwestern University Press, 2003)

PhP *Phenomenology of Perception*, trans. C. Smith, 2nd edition (London: Routledge, 2006)

Pri *The Primacy of Perception and Other Essays*, trans. W. Cobb (Evanston, Ill.: Northwestern University Press, 1964)

SB *The Structure of Behavior*, trans. A. Fisher (Piitsburgh, Pa.: Duquesne University Press, 1983)

Themes *Themes from the Lectures at the Collège de France 1952–1960*, trans. J. O'Neill (Evanston Ill.: Northwestern University Press, 1970)

VI *The Visible and the Invisible (Followed by Working Notes)*, trans. A. Lingus (Evanston, Ill: Northwestern University Press, 1969)

1

Introduction

BERNARD FLYNN AND WAYNE J. FROMAN

In lectures in the late 1950s and up until his death in 1961, Merleau-Ponty, who at that time held the Chair in Philosophy at the Collège de France, addressed the topics of Nature and philosophy today. The latter topic would account for his interest in Nature and the direction it would take. The title of one of his courses in 1959–1960 was "Nature and Logos: the Human Body," and the titles of two of the courses interrupted by his death were "Philosophy and Non-Philosophy Since Hegel" and "Cartesian Ontology and Today's Ontology." Merleau-Ponty had discerned a possibility for philosophy in our time. When the work of major proportions with which he was engaged when he died, later published as *The Visible and the Invisible*, was left incomplete, it appeared that the possibility he had glimpsed was simply gone. But the stakes proved too important and the work of delineating features of this possibility and assessing its strength was taken up eventually, as the work in this volume demonstrates.

Although in the course of his work, Merleau-Ponty was a proponent of a certain "primacy of perception," to see in this a reductionist bias is a mistake because it is in perception, which Merleau-Ponty never did stop questioning with regard to what it may be, that Merleau-Ponty discovered certain formidable resources that challenged the long-standing model of perception and so many elements of the philosophical tradition that took this as a secure point of departure. To see in Merleau-Ponty's sense of "the primacy of perception" grounds for neglecting the way in which issues belonging to the history of thought were at stake in his work is tantamount to thinking that nature, on the one hand, and the human world, on the other, are regarded by Merleau-Ponty as mutually exclusive, which is likewise a mistake. Essays in this volume address the import of Merleau-Ponty's thought vis-à-vis Husserl and Heidegger, his phenomenological predecessors, Bergson, a twentieth-century predecessor at the Collège de France, Schelling, a pivotal figure in the history of the previous two centuries, Hume, a precursor figure in the analytic philosophical context, Descartes and the rationalists, major contributions in the opening Greek philosophical period, including the pre-Socratics and Plato, as well as vis-à-vis the more recent philosophical work of Emmanuel Levinas and Jean-Luc Marion, and signal features of major Asian traditions. In the course of this volume, contributors address and assess the import of what Merleau-Ponty says in regard to epistemological issues, ethical issues, ontological issues, the philosophy of logic and language, the philosophy of art, and the philosophy of nature. Specific topics include time, subjectivity, the intersubjective, the bodily, skepticism, the status of nothingness, the relation between seeing and hearing, the relation between spontaneity and receptivity, and the significance of an element that Merleau-Ponty found had no name in any philosophy and that he discussed as *la chair*, the flesh.

The volume opens with two essays from Paul Ricoeur. The first, and the earliest essay in the volume, dates from the time of Merleau-Ponty's death in 1961 at the age of fifty-three. The essay still registers the shock and sense of loss that was felt at the time. Ricoeur discusses how Merleau-Ponty's phenomenological description of perception in *Phenomenology of Perception* became "the touchstone of the veritable human condition" and how the philosophical implications drawn by Merleau-Ponty contain "an entire conception of action, and even an entire politics." The politics, at first, would be understood in terms of how "to continue the young Marx, against the old Marx," but eventually, Ricoeur observes, the disagreement in depth with Marxism altogether weighed more heavily, and Merleau-Ponty concluded that "once the communist nostalgia was conjured away, then everything becomes interesting and new again." The estrangement between Merleau-Ponty and Jean-Paul Sartre dates from that point. Ricoeur expresses doubt that Sartre's development, in *The Critique of Dialectical Reason*, of a conception of history in terms of totalization, even if "detotalizing," could have found favor where Merleau-Ponty was concerned.

Features of *Phenomenology of Perception* that Ricoeur emphasizes as particularly admirable include Merleau-Ponty's constant attention to the relation between the human sciences and philosophy, how Merleau-Ponty brought to bear "the magisterial teaching of the founder of phenomenology, Edmund Husserl, whose published and unpublished work he knew perfectly," in such a way as "[to continue] the movement on his own account, without regard for orthodoxy," and the way in which Merleau-Ponty installed the theme of one's own body in his own reading of the world and of the human being in the world. Still, when Merleau-Ponty died, the basis for this important work had long been put into question in his thinking. With this, themes concerning nature that had been at the forefront of Merleau-Ponty's first book, *The Structure of Behavior*, would reassert themselves, the question concerning language would become more insistent, and the bearing of Heidegger's philosophy of Being and of speaking would become more significant. At the time of his death, the second landing in Merleau-Ponty's work had not yet emerged from the underlying dynamic of his thought.

Paul Ricoeur's second essay, "Merleau-Ponty: Beyond Husserl and Heidegger," was written eighteen years after Merleau-Ponty's death. Here, Ricoeur finds in the chapter of *Phenomenology of Perception* devoted to temporality, the central chapter in the third and final part of that work, a condensed reading of a give and take between Husserl and Heidegger on this issue that was in fact crucial where the interaction between the two of them was concerned. The opening chapter that precedes this is an analysis of the *Cogito*. The import of this topic would itself seem to affirm a Husserlian allegiance. But the analysis of the inseparable character of the reflexive operation and an "active transcendence" suggests both Husserlian intentionality and Heideggerian being-in-the-world. The appeal here to "sedimentation" and the sense of a "temporal thickness" of the *Cogito* do seem to reinforce a Husserlian allegiance. Yet, Ricoeur points up how what Merleau-Ponty says here concerning the priority of a "tacit *Cogito*" moves in the direction of Heidegger's sense of being-in-the-world. "Tacit *Cogito* and original project of the world are one single and same thing. What is the significance of the oscillation here between Husserl and Heidegger?"

Ricoeur turns to the chapter on temporality for an answer. The language of consciousness and intentionality is retained throughout the analysis. But, in the course of the analysis, a subtle reorientation takes place with the introduction of the question of the passage of time in its totality, a question that leads in the direction of Heidegger's analysis of "temporalization." And then, when Merleau-Ponty says, "[B]ut the present (in the broad sense, with its originary horizons of past and future) still has a privilege because it is the zone where being and consciousness coincide," Ricoeur observes that "one thinks that one hears Husserl again." The question here is whether indeed Heidegger's hermeneutics of care succeeded in supplanting a priority of the present with a priority of the future, and to reinforce that question, Ricoeur brings forward Heidegger's own anlaysis, toward the end of the portion of *Being and Time* that was completed and published, of the point where "resolute anticipation" and the revival of received legacies intersect at the moment of repetition. What Merleau-Ponty has discerned, finds Ricoeur, is a "profound relationship between two successive philosophical projects, at a certain period of indecision in each of them." Here, by way of "operative intentionality" and the dynamic of "passive synthesis," Husserl's subjectivism is set on the road to surpassing itself via the phenomenology of time, and Heidegger's analytic of *Dasein*, in *Being and Time*, remains attached to a sense of subjectivity and in so doing demonstrates how that analytic belongs to the *phenomenological* age of ontology. In what Ricoeur calls the "most audacious rapprochement" that Merleau-Ponty attempts, he appeals to Kant's sense of "self-affectivity" in making the point that "the explosion or the dehiscence of the present toward a future is the archetype of the *relation of self to self* and indicates an interiority or an ipseity." Ricoeur concludes that Merleau-Ponty, in revealing a convergence in depth of Husserl and Heidegger goes beyond both, "[b]ecause, to reveal this convergence is *to institute it.*"

In "The Turn of Experience: Merleau-Ponty and Bergson," Renaud Barbaras explores the relationship between the thought of Merleau-Ponty and the philosophy of Bergson. In the process of doing this he reveals an important dimension of Merleau-Ponty's thought, showing that its relationship to Bergson is both complicated and subject to reversal. At the time of the writing of the *Phenomenology of Perception*, Merleau-Ponty makes a sustained critique of Bergson from the perspective of phenomenology. While sympathetic to Bergson's critique of positivism, Merleau-Ponty argues that his critique of spatiality in the name of temporality fails to go to the roots of positivism because it reproduces an opposition between an externality grounded in spatiality and a pure internality that he characterizes as *duration.* In Merleau-Ponty's opinion, Bergson had failed to transcend a realist prejudice because he had not understood "consciousness as intentionality." He conceived of consciousness not as a subject of acts that have the world as their intentional correlate but as a "liquid in which instants and positions melt together." In Bergson's thought, realism and spiritualism do not only coexist but they live off one another.

In Merleau-Ponty's later thought, he characterized phenomenology, at least in its classical form, as a variant of the philosophy of consciousness. Subsequently, he made a strong critique of the philosophy of consciousness and thus one should not be surprised that he reevaluated his relationship to Bergson. In brief, the problem with any philosophy of consciousness is that it will think "being" in the form of an object, thereby viewing positivity as presence. It is as though Merleau-Ponty saw in the philosophy of Sartre the *denouement* of the concept of consciousness conceived of as intentionality, and this critique of Sartre moved him in the direction of Bergson's critique of negativity. Barbaras cites Bergson to the effect that metaphysics arrives at Being only by starting from, by passing through, Nothingness. Being is defined as that which resists Nothingness. Arriving at a similar position, Merleau-Ponty refers to this way of thinking as a "philosophy of something." Nonetheless, in *The Visible and the Invisible* he makes a critique of a philosophy that would escape negativism by a fusion with Being. This could appear to be a critique of Bergson's notion of intuition. However, Barbaras shows that this need not be the case, since Bergson's conception of a "partial fusion" can be read, and was read by Merleau-Ponty, as adumbrating a conception of Being that does not simply refuse Nothingness but integrates it into itself in the form of a necessary distance, an irreducible concealment.

In "Community, Society, and History in the Later Merleau-Ponty," Marc Richir carefully explicates some extremely enigmatic ideas concerning history and society found in the Working Notes of *The Visible and the Invisible.* Evoking the sense of "the experience of the other" in the work of Merleau-Ponty and Husserl, he considers the question of the communalization of our intentional life, in the Husserlian sense of "transcendental subjectivity is transcendental intrasubjectivity" and correlatively, in Merleau-Ponty's sense of the "worldliness of the mind" in the sedimentation of meaning in the visible. Richir cites a working note of 1959, "In the visible there is never anything but the ruins of spirit," ruins in the sense of the ruins of the Roman Forum, the traces of what was once instituting. The field of sedimentated meaning constitutes the articulation of our field of experience, and these sedimentations are essentially communal and unconscious. Merleau-Ponty writes, "intrasubjectivity is very much beyond lived experience," we are always already in an articulated field of meaning. Condemned to meaning, it is the elementary tissue of "the flesh of history" which gathers the community and holds it together.

Richir directs his attention to the notion of a phenomenological community as an incarnated community. In his reflection on the tissue of intrasubjective meaning, he presents some critical comments on Merleau-Ponty. For Merleau-Ponty, originating language breaks the silence of the world and is thus the act of a savage mind. "Savage mind is the mind of the incarnated phenomenological community." Richir's contention is that Merleau-Ponty does not give a satisfactory explanation of the relationship between what Richir calls the "phenomenological symbolic" and the "conventionally instituted symbolic." Richir writes, "[T]hat which goes without saying in its self-evident givenness precedes always from the symbolic institution. And it is only in that which does not go without saying (that which is not self-evident) that the savage mind [and the phenomenological symbolic] puts itself into play again." The savage mind is radically heterogeneous from what is conventionally instituted symbolically. Richir ends by sketching out what a more adequate interpretation of the phenomenological symbolic would look like.

In "Tracework: Experience and Description in the Moral Phenomenology of Merleau-Ponty and Levinas," David Michael Kleinberg-Levin attempts to show that in Merleau-Ponty's reflection development, one on the prepersonal subject of perception, there is implicitly a possible theory of moral that would bring Merleau-Ponty's thought into line with the moral philosophy of Levinas. According to Kleinberg-Levin, Levinas claims that man, at the deepest level of experience, is not fundamentally egotist and that there is a relationship with the other in the form of an intercorporality which could be viewed as subtending, or developmentally protending, the type of ethics elaborated in *Totality and Infinity* and *Otherwise Than Being*, that is, an ethics of the presence of the other. What Kleinberg-Levin attempts to show is that both Levinas and Merleau-Ponty were engaged in a "trace work," a return to the primordial body of experience. They both wished to express, in the language of phenomenology, the articulation of an original assignment of motivations that make possible a stage of moral development beyond that of the "logical subject." Kleinberg-Levin discovers structural similarities in the works of Merleau-Ponty and Levinas, similarities which he contends have not been seen before.

Bernard Flynn's chapter, "Merleau-Ponty and the Philosophical Position of Skepticism," is engendered by an early remark in *The Visible and the Invisible* that concerns Merleau-Ponty's notion of a *pre* or *non*-cognitive relation to Being. His reflections begin with both a presentation and a refutation of Pyrrhonian skepticism, showing that it contains unproblematized presuppositions, for example, a representational conception of consciousness and a conception of "truth in itself." He argues that rather than abandoning the notion of skepticism, one must reformulate the skeptical arguments. He questions *why* there has been, and still is, a continued fascination with skeptical arguments. It would seem there must be something in our experience that offers a basis for this way of thinking, namely, that we believe both that our perceptions present the world as it is and that they are, in some respects, formed by my own body. When these two dimensions of experience are reflected upon, they become contradictory and give rise to skepticism. Flynn evokes Hume as a philosopher who has both elaborated the skeptical position in great detail and who has shown that this position is unoccupiable. Intelligibly compelling as skepticism may be, we are psychologically constituted in such a way that we cannot believe it.

Kant, who was awakened from his "dogmatic slumber" by Hume, elaborates his system of transcendental philosophy against him. Notwithstanding his great respect for Hume, Husserl gives birth to phenomenology by elaborating arguments against psychologistic positions that have Hume as their ultimate source. He does so through his conceptions of the phenomenological and the eidetic reductions. Merleau-Ponty makes a critique of the movement of analytic reflection by which transcendental philosophy is established. He criticizes the possibility of a completed phenomenological reduction and also the "process of free variation" through which the eidetic reduction is established. Having rejected all the arguments brought to bear against skepticism, how does Merleau-Ponty stand in relationship to it? Flynn suggests a certain convergence between an aspect of Hume's philosophy as a "philosophy of belief" and Merleau-Ponty's conception of "perceptual faith" as our noncognitive insertion into the *there is* of Being.

Robert Vallier's chapter, "The Elemental Flesh: Nature, Life, and Difference in Merleau-Ponty and Plato's *Timaeus*," is fueled by two lines from *The Visible and the Invisible* that return us to the Greek context: "Nature is the Flesh, the mother," and, "The Flesh is an element of being." Merleau-Ponty claims that he is using the word *element* in the ancient Greek sense of Earth, Fire, Air, and Water; he does not elaborate any further on this ancient sense of element, but Vallier does. By intertwining aspects of Merleau-Ponty's late work with a reading of Plato's *Timaeus*, he creates a highly imaginative intertext. This is justified by the contention that a meditation on the notion of the element in the *Timaeus* can help to clarify the meaning that this notion has in the work of Merleau-Ponty. After an insightful rehearsal of the basic structures of the *Timaeus*, Vallier arrives at the idea that the elements are effected by an "event cause," and are thus implicated in a circle of "'self-othering,' a negative movement of self-differentiation, such that they can never be 'this' or 'that' but only 'suchlike.'" He refutes the contentions made by some hasty readers of Merleau-Ponty who claim that the flesh functions as a sort of metaphysical foundation in Merleau-Ponty's work, arguing that the flesh is not an "elementary substrate." On the contrary, the flesh is *elementality* and it never appears as such. Through its movement of self-differentiation, things come to show themselves. Vallier offers some striking connections between the thought of the Earth in the *Timaeus* and the Earth in the late work of Husserl.

Wayne Froman's contribution, entitled "The Blind Spot," relates the "irreducible concealment," which was addressed earlier in Renaud Barbaras's comparison of Merleau-Ponty and Bergson, to Schelling's *Naturphilosophie*, which was continually in the background of Robert Vallier's essay. In the experiences of the touching/ touched and the seeing/seen, there is always a moment of noncoincidence in which "the hand that is touching" is not really touching an object in the same way as "the hand touching it." There is a certain "blind spot" whereby what is interior and what is exterior constantly circle around one another. Froman cites Deleuze's claim that Merleau-Ponty shows us the possibility of a horizontal relation between seeing/seen and also creates the possibility of the derived relationship between the exterior and the interior. Deleuze writes, "It is even this twisting which defines 'Flesh', beyond the body proper and its objects." It is this blind spot that anchors "the point of view" in "a being always already there," preconstituted or not completely constituted. Following Merleau-Ponty, Froman connects the blind spot with what Schelling called the "barbarous source," a generality or communality that lies "between the inert essence, or *quidditas*, and the individual located at a point in space and time." The blind spot is the Flesh considered from the point of view of cognition.

Froman seeks to explicate the ontological dimensions of this idea, which on an epistemological level prevents "perspectivism" from spinning off into a vertiginous skepticism (recalling Bernard Flynn's essay), or employing Wittgenstein's metaphor, "a thought which cannot move because it cannot get traction." Merleau-Ponty connects this "barbarous source" to the Stoic idea of a brute unity through which the universe "holds." Developing this idea further, Froman evokes the Heideggerian idea of *physis* and Husserl's conception of an original opinion (*Urglaube* or *Urdoxa)* that is prior to any attitude or point of view. *Urdoxa*, or perceptual faith, does not give us a representation of the world but rather the world itself, and to question this would be a kind of madness that asks questions such as: "Where is the world? Am I alone? Am I the only one to be me?" Froman ends his article by forging a connection between these "philosophemes" and Heidegger's conception of Fate.

In "Proximity and Distance: With Regard to Heidegger in the Later Merleau-Ponty," Michel Haar addresses the relation between Merleau-

Ponty's thought and Heidegger's. Haar contends that Heidegger's thought served in fact as an inspiration, if not a model, for Merleau-Ponty in *Phenomenology of Perception* in regard to the emphasis on the irreducibility of world where phenomenological reduction is concerned and in regard, moreover, to *Phenomenology of Perception*'s challenge to subjectivity. But instead of making the role of Heidegger's thought explicit, Merleau-Ponty associated *Phenomenology of Perception* more closely with Husserl's work, probably by virtue of the crucial role that the world as perceived plays in Husserl's thought. Haar suggests as a reason that Merleau-Ponty did not make the bearing of Heidegger's thought on *Phenomenology of Perception* explicit is that Merleau-Ponty positioned Heidegger's thought next to Sartre's in regard to a heroic assertion to overcome the world in its facticity. The motif that makes it possible eventually for Merleau-Ponty to appeal explicitly to Heidegger's thinking of Being, and in so doing to carry out a "turn " in his thought that is comparable to the "turn" in Heidegger's thought, is how for Heidegger, with the dispossession of "man's properties or faculties," they are "transferred to Being," signaled, in particular, by Heidegger's dictum, in his later efforts to think the question concerning language from the question concerning Being, to the effect that it is not we who have language, but rather language that has us. But Haar finds that the result, where Merleau-Ponty is concerned, amounts to a "quasi-naturalism" and an "abstraction" from what Heidegger means by the "*there is*," the "*il y a*," the "*es gibt*." Haar makes the point that while for Heidegger, what is found at the point where we reach the "there is" has no single name, and accordingly, time, first of all, and then world, truth, history, and language are only "prenames" of Being, for Merleau-Ponty, by contrast, the name for what is found there is "*la chair*," "*the flesh*," and what this signals is Merleau-Ponty's "quasi-naturalism." Haar suggests that this amounts to a relapse into a metaphysical thinking of nature and of life such as we find in the post-Kantian metaphysical works of Schopenhauer, Schelling, and Bergson.

Haar takes aim at Merleau-Ponty's qualifications with regard to the phrase "flesh of the world," which Merleau-Ponty employs only to add that the world is not "flesh" in the same sense in which my body is. Resultant equivocations that Haar delineates here only highlight a hesitation resulting from resistance to a thoroughgoing naturalism, which in fact, although inadequate, is the only means, Haar finds, that Merleau-Ponty has available to follow Heidegger in regard to the "properties and faculties" that are "transferred to Being." With regard to Merleau-Ponty's specification of a "dehiscence" characteristic of the flesh and pivotal to a chiasm of flesh and world, Haar writes:

> The Heideggerian model of the dispossession of man is not applicable to the philosophy of the flesh, for the latter—which, not without analogy with Being, oscillates between the thickness of the element and the differential finesse of "dehiscence"—would not have an initiative, not produce a "destinal sending," that of which it is by the way necessarily incapable because of non-historicality. Man can respond to being thrown because he is historical but how can he respond to the flesh that has no age, and that englobes him?

To any "jointure," or any "identitity" between the "always historical and languagely *world*," and "ageless *life*," Haar counterposes "the prudent Heideggerian limitation of the 'clearing' of Being as this is separated from the 'black of the forest.'" Further, Haar concludes that what Merleau-Ponty says of the flesh closes off another difficulty, and that, for Haar, is how Merleau-Ponty's thought is totally lacking in regard to any principle of conflictuality or strife that would be needed in order to reach Heidegger's radical sense of strife in the intimate relation of earth and world. Ultimately, what is announced by Merleau-Ponty's "abstraction" from Heidegger's sense of the "there is" is what Merleau-Ponty makes of negativity, of nothingness, and Haar assesses this as the "most benign and least redoubtable figure of nothingness in the history of philosophy." In effect, Haar's essay is opposed to the argument that the dispossession of the elements of subjectivity is more radical in Merleau-Ponty's thought than in Heidegger's, and it also denies the association that Wayne Froman draws between the two based on the affinity of Heidegger as well as Merleau-Ponty's thought to Schelling's thought.

In "Chiasm, Flesh, Figuration: Toward a Non-positive Ontology," Véronique Fóti brings forward a movement in Merleau-Ponty's later thought toward an ontology that is "non-positive," and Fóti does so by turning our attention to the role that art, in particular painting, plays for that thought. Her chapter is the first of three that address the import of Merleau-Ponty's interrogation of painting. Tracing the intricacies of Merleau-Ponty's descriptions of the latencies of the flesh and its chiasmatic dynamics, Fóti leads us to the heart of the mirror-play of the carnal and the world. These latencies recall both Leibnizian and Spinozistic motifs and yet, for Merleau-Ponty, what we find here is not to be understood in substantialist terms. Phenomenology does not take Merleau-Ponty to a "pristine positivity," nor to a nothingness understood as its counterpart. Fóti cites Marc Richir in "Le sensible dans le rève," where Richir writes that "Merleau-Ponty better than many others understood that phenomenology has to do with the fundamental non-positivity of all that is, of all that is practiced and of all that can be thought." (Barbaras and Robert, *Notes de Cours* 1959, 239–54). Phenomenology leads Merleau-Ponty to sedimented layers deposited by chiasmatic dynamics and ultimately to a "nucleus of absence," as Merleau-Ponty puts this in a *Working Note* for *The Visible and the Invisible*, in what Fóti specifies as one of Merleau-Ponty's most succinct and daring formulations:

> The invisible is here without being object; it is pure transcendence without an ontic mask. And the "visibles" themselves, they are, in the last analysis, likewise only centered upon a nucleus of absence—(*VI*, 282f; 229)

The "dehiscence" of the flesh, its "bursting forth" (éclatement), Fóti notes, works a "dispossession," and this work must be taken up by philosophy.

The *punctum caecum*, the "blind spot" of visibility (that pertains to a theme discussed by Wayne Froman in this volume), which is emblematic for Merleau-Ponty of sensibility as such, and which in fact makes for the possibility of vision, ordinarily gets obscured by vision in so far as vision prefers the object to Being. The painter, by contrast, refuses both this transcendental illusion as well as the intellectualist illusion according to which vision is, to begin with, derivative from, or mediated by, thought, and by means of figuration the painter brings forth a visible of the second power, an icon, which responds to that which "senses itself" in her or in him. This icon itself may or may not be figurative. It marks, in Heidegger's language, an *Unverbogenheit der Verborgenheit* (unconcealment of concealment), "an originary presentation of what is incapable of originary presentation." The artistic figuration described closely here by Fóti can, Merleau-Ponty found, guide philosophy, and first of all, phenomenology, to the essential unthought of Husserl's late work.

Jenny Slatman's "Phenomenology of the Icon" approaches Merleau-Ponty's aesthetics not merely as a branch of his philosophy, but more importantly as revealing an essential dimension of his thought. She begins by making a distinction between the three terms *idea*, *icon*, and *idol*. The notion of an idea is the traditional conception of a second domain of positivity, an invisible world behind or above the visible one. In the notion of the icon, the essence is revealed not behind but within the visible. Slatman cites Merleau-Ponty's "Eye and Mind" where he argues that in the painting there appears "a visibility to the second power, a carnal essence or icon of the first," along the lines of what

Merleau-Ponty will say of the invisible of the visible. Drawing from Jean-Luc Marion's work, she makes a distinction between the icon and the image. The icon contains within itself a relationship with the invisible and also the reversibility of the visible and the invisible, whereas the idol intends only the visible. The idol has as its correlate a subject conceived within the Cartesian tradition, while the icon is given to a vision and is itself part of the visible. Her explication of the ontology of Merleau-Ponty through a reading of his aesthetics is fueled by the description and consideration of a number of works of art, some of which were dealt with by Merleau-Ponty and others not. Slatman concludes her article by reflecting on Merleau-Ponty's conception of expression and institution in both painting and language, asking what would, or could, it mean for the type of linguistic practice of philosophy itself, suggesting that we reconsider our conception of the relationship between metaphorical and nonmetaphorical language.

In the third chapter to address the import of painting in Merleau-Ponty's thought, "On the 'Fundamental of Painting': Chinese Counterpoint," Jacques Taminiaux takes his point of departure from an exhibition of paintings by the twentieth-century Chinese painter Zhu Qizhan (born in 1892) organized by the British Museum in 1995. Zhu Qizhan's work represents a "transcultural possibility" that contrasts with both the reduction to a lowest common denominator and the subjugation of one tradition to the other. Taminiaux responds with insights gleaned from Merleau-Ponty's interrogation of painting, insights that Taminiaux finds conducive for this "transcultural possibility." Painting in the West, beginning with Cézanne, exhibits a certain "fundamental of painting" more explicitly than did earlier painting in this tradition. No longer governed by the early Byzantine sense of painting that accords with the long-standing Christian Platonic tradition and where painting is to convey us to a heavenly world beyond the image of the world in which we find ourselves (a point that recalls Jenny Slatman's discussion of Merleau-Ponty's understanding of the "iconicity" of painting and how it differs from what Jean-Luc Marion says concerning "iconicity"), nor governed by the Renaissance sense of perspective, which remains allied with an insistence on a transcendent vantage point, beginning with Cézanne, painting more explicitly exhibits our primordial and carnal belonging to the world of multiple perspective and appearance. This marks an affinity with the Chinese tradition of painting that Taminiaux illustrates first in terms of the significance of the fact that "still life" is not one of the classifications found in the tradition of Chinese painting, and then in terms of principal features that are found in Chinese landscape painting.

Furthermore, in Merleau-Ponty's delineation of the reversibility marking the chiasmatic dynamics of flesh and world that are deployed, for example, in paintings by Cézanne of Mt. St. Victoire, where we find how it happens that "essence and existence, the imaginary and the real, the visible and the visible, painting confuses all our categories by deploying its oneiric universe of carnal essences," Taminiaux detects a strong affinity with the sensibility in regard to oppositions found in Chinese painting. This pertains to the oppositions of being and nonbeing, and the visible and the invisible in painting (a point that recalls Véronique Fóti's discussion of Merleau-Ponty's interrogation of painting and its implications for a "non-postive ontology"). Taminiaux points out that this marks an opening for interaction between Merleau-Ponty's thought and both the Taoist and the Confucian traditions that Chinese paintings reflect.

In "Variations of the Sensible: The Truth of Ideas and Idea of Philosophy in the Later Merleau-Ponty," Mauro Carbone turns our attention directly to Merleau-Ponty's last lecture courses where the principal themes are Nature and the possibility of philosophy today. What joins the two is Merleau-Ponty's sense of a mutation in the relation of our selves to Being, a phrase that Merleau-Ponty deploys in "Eye and Mind" to characterize what he detects when he holds classical thought en bloc up against what we find in the work of modern painters. This mutation in the relation of our selves to Being is indicative of an innovative ontology that Merleau-Ponty holds is already implicit in recent scientific work (which, although providing no ontology at all, may yet be philosophically instructive) and in the art of our time as well. Carbone explores this link between the two major themes of Merleau-Ponty's last lectures.

In his work on Nature, Merleau-Ponty drew on the contribution in biology made by Jakob von Uexküll. Von Uexküll developed an understanding of the relation between the organism and its animal environment or *Umwelt* that is neither causalist nor finalist, nor dependent upon a Platonist *eidos*. Rather, what Von Uexküll discerned was a deployment of an *Umwelt* that took the form of a "melody that sings itself." Merleau-Ponty (recovering themes from his early book *The Structure of Behavior*) detected in this a basis for specifying an ontological value for the notion of species. Carbone explains this in terms found in Merleau-Ponty's notes for the lecture course "Cartesian Ontology and Ontology Today" where we find a discussion of seeing as "voyance," ordinarily understood as clairvoyance with its "double vision," but understood here as seeing in so far as it "complies with" the self-showing of the seen, in contrast with the Cartesian context (where, in effect, thought displaces seeing), and indicative, along these lines, of the "Renaissance beyond Descartes." With "voyance," a level of generality opens up and remains open, relating particulars although not given as such in any one, and rendering these particulars simultaneous. This suggests the dynamics of a "melody that sings itself" and the level of generality indicates how an ontological value of species is to be understood. Merleau-Ponty detects "voyance" in literary work by such authors as Valéry, Claudel, and Proust, and Carbone both points out that what Merleau-Ponty says of Proust here (as well as the association he makes explicitly, in the work on Nature, between the "melody that sings itself" and Proust's understanding of melody) helps us elaborate on our understanding of the discussion of Proust in *The Visible and the Invisible*, and makes the point that Merleau-Ponty's concentration on painting should not lead to a neglect of what he says regarding literature. Carbone also relates the discussion to Merleau-Ponty's reference elsewhere to Rimbaud's sense of poetry as "voyance." "Voyance" ultimately indicates a *Wesenschau* that must be understood in terms of the "sensible idea" and the "carnal essence," recasting, in fact, our understanding of the relation between the sensible and the intelligible and pointing us toward what is meant by a phrase from Claudel, commented on by Merleau-Ponty, concerning a "listening eye." Carbone finds a possibility here for the elaboration of the "new ontology" begun by Merleau-Ponty.

In "The Body of Speech," Françoise Dastur addresses Merleau-Ponty's findings in regard to language. Dastur makes the point that as early as *The Structure of Behavior*, Merleau-Ponty challenged the instrumental conception of language as he appealed to the notion of *Gestalt* in analyzing the interaction of an organism and the environment. The sense of *Gestalt* as a "joining of an idea and an existence which are indiscernible" points in the direction of a primordial operation of expression, one that would be understood along the lines of an "inhabitation," a "transcendence in inherence," and eventually a dynamic of "institution." In *Phenomenology of Perception*, where Merleau-Ponty leaves behind "the massive oppositions of reflexive philosophy," his decisive findings in regard to the indissociability of a phonetic and a semantic element of language move directly toward the phenomenon of expression at the same time as they call into question both the logicist element in Husserl's earlier work that would disengage signification from the contingent "clothing" of linguistic signs, and the determination by Heidegger, in *Being and Time*, to the effect that assertion is a derived or a supplemental linguistic mode. Heidegger would later unequivocally reject the priority ascribed here to signification vis-à-vis speaking. We now know that in Heidegger's 1934 course *Logic* he would seek a way to think logic from the same origin as language and that it was in the 1930s that he would turn to poetry as a more originary modality of language where language could be thought in terms of Being. In *Phenomenology of Perception*, Merleau-Ponty had indeed found that the specificity of language as a mode of expression would have to be sought in originary instances of speech.

In *Phenomenology of Perception*, the same finding in regard to the indissociability of a phonetic and a semantic element means that language understood as gesture rules out conceiving of "communication with the other as the operation that would consist in compensating for or getting around the abyss that separates us from the other, and which would thus be similar to that which procures for us the knowledge of beings different from us, [but] on the contrary it would be necessary for us to 'restitute the experience of the other deformed by intellectual analyses,' just as much as the concern is to 'restitute the perceptual experience of the thing' over against the same analyses that see a knowing in perception." Beyond the impasses of realism and idealism, Merleau-Ponty looks to the originary alliance of spontaneity and receptivity that he will designate as "institution" and that brings him into close proximity with Humboldt's indications regarding nature and culture in the origin of language. To find in speech not the "clothing" of thought but rather its emblem or its body requires that we renounce the idea of transparency in language and we recognize language as a specific case of "this irrational power that creates significations and that communicates them."

The volume concludes with an early article (1971), "Body, Flesh," by Claude Lefort, who was Merleau-Ponty's literary executor. This rich text evokes the difference between the role of the body in the *Phenomenology of Perception* and that of the flesh in *The Visible and the Invisible.* In a certain sense, Lefort's chapter concerns itself with Merleau-Ponty's reaction to a line of Husserl cited in the preface to the *Phenomenology of Perception,* which reads, "It is that as yet mute experience which we are concerned to lead to the pure expression of its meaning." It is Lefort's contention that Merleau-Ponty remains faithful to threads of Husserl's unthought, "his shadow," while rejecting his project of a "pure" phenomenology. This rejection is what marks the difference between the *Phenomenology of Perception* and *The Visible and the Invisible*. He argues that Merleau-Ponty's trajectory is a process of learning that "the place from which" the restitution of mute experience to its pure meaning is to proceed is a place that it is *impossible* to occupy. The desire to occupy this place is the "last illusion" of metaphysics. This illusion is a belief in the possibility of returning to a privileged place, a point of origin through which reflection could come to coincide with prereflective experience. In the *Phenomenology of Perception,* the phenomenology of the body is what marks such a place. In the form of objectivism, metaphysics has denied the body by it giving it the status of an object. Thus, the critique of objectivism should reveal the body as the place of the origin. Lefort writes, "Must we not wonder if the body does not leave its author in the prison whose task it was for him to escape?" It is the search for an "original," an ultimate text, that constitutes the last metaphysical illusion. He argues that *The Visible and the Invisible* rejects the conception of a *tacit cogito*, and with it the possibility of reflection coinciding with the prereflective, "the fiction of coincidence by right between being and thinking."

In *The Visible and the Invisible* Merleau-Ponty writes that "the originating breaks up, and philosophy must accompany this explosion, this coincidence, this differentiation." The flesh is the term that Merleau-Ponty uses to indicate a thought that could accord itself to this enigma, a thought that is not one of man, but as Merleau-Ponty says, one of Being. The flesh is not the successor of the body. In *The Phenomenology of Perception*, Merleau-Ponty identifies the body as the subject of perception. He contends that: I should not say that *I* perceive, but rather that one (*on*) perceives, and that this "one" is the anonymous subject of the body. In *The Visible and the Invisible*, he tells us that we should not say that the body perceives, but rather that the body is built around perception, that perception dawns through it. Lefort writes, "The flesh is not a successor of the body, a more elaborate version of mute experience or of the last text that was otherwise discerned through the body. He attempts to view Merleau-Ponty's critique of metaphysics as something other than its reversal, and as other than the expectation of an apocalyptic "new beginning." The flesh (reflecting that originary alliance between receptivity and spontaneity that Françoise Dastur pointed up in what Merleau-Ponty says of language) is both in continuity and in discontinuity with the past.

2

Homage to Merleau-Ponty

PAUL RICOEUR

Great and pure was the consternation of the colleagues, disciples, and friends who had come on that Saturday afternoon to accompany the mortal remains of Maurice Merleau-Ponty to the houses of the dead. When the funereal task was complete, each had been hesitant to take their leave; no discourse had been given, and I believe no one regretted that: this death, more improbable than any, had literally *cut off speech*. At fifty-three years old, the philosopher was gone from us, without having had the time to say that which was ripening in him and which it appears would have been called *The Visible and the Invisible*. The supplemental leaflet that had been inserted in the last collection of articles, entitled *Signs*, tells in a terribly premonitory manner of the state in which the interrupted discourse was stopped and frozen: "Signs, which is not to say a complete alphabet, and not even a discourse followed. But rather signals, as sudden as a glance, which we receive from events, from books and from things." In a single stroke a trait is emphasized, a trait that had had a completely different meaning when he was alive and his speech underway was still inclined toward a future; yes, in a single stroke, the meanings of the calculated inexactitude, the englobing complexity, this sparkling density of Merleau-Ponty's last writings all changed. The void [*creux*] of incompletion will henceforth be imprinted on the same texts that had seduced us and embarrassed us by their surfeit of meaning.

The philosopher had certainly and explicitly professed this incompletion. His 1953 inaugural lecture at the Collège de France, entitled "In Praise of Philosophy," began without slyness with these words:

"The man who witnesses his own research, which is to say, his own internal disorder, can hardly feel himself to be the heir of the accomplished men whose names he sees on these walls. If, in addition, he is a philosopher, which is to say that he knows that he knows nothing, then how could he believe himself justified to assume this chair, and how could he even wish it? Is he able to desire this? The answer to these questions is very simple: What the Collège de France, since its founding, is charged with providing to its audience are not acquired truths, but rather the idea of free investigation" (*Praise*, 3). And a bit farther on: "The philosopher does not say that a final overcoming of human contradictions is possible and that the complete man awaits us in the future: like everyone, he knows nothing of this. He says—and this is something altogether different—that the world begins, that we do not have to judge its future by what has been its past, that the idea of a destiny in things is not an idea but a vertigo, that our relations with nature are not fixed once and for all, that no one can know what freedom may be able to do, nor imagine what the customs [*moeurs*] and human relations would be in a civilization no longer haunted by competition and necessity. He does not place his hope in any destiny, even a favorable one, but precisely in what in us is not destiny, in the contingency of our history, and it is its negation or denial that is position" (*Praise*, 43–44).

The lack of a completion of a philosophy of incompletion is doubly disconcerting.

And nevertheless, Merleau-Ponty's philosophy had from the beginning attained a *landing* [*palier*] where it was provisionally stabilized, before putting itself back en route toward something else. This first landing was the *Phenomenology of Perception* in 1945. We will have to return continuously to this masterwork in order to check the drift of this striking [*foudroyé*] work.

How was a simple description of seeing, hearing, or sensing able to contain such a philosophical responsibility [*charge*]? Ordinarily, the psychologists' books about vision, hearing, and touching do not have these repercussions or effects [*retentissement*], in all senses of this word. What the philosopher proposed by means of this description, and beyond all psychophysiology of sensation, was a manner of seeing the world and of being seen in the world. The description of perception became the touchstone of the true human condition. What is astonishing about perception is that we ceaselessly decipher a sense that is continuously removed from the opacity of the brute and mute presence, without ever being detached itself from the limitation of a perspective, without ever renouncing the inherence of consciousness in a point of view. In the same stroke, perception reveals the properly human level of existence, namely, that we move in *the interim of non-sense and the absolute*, halfway between a phantasmagoria of silhouettes that succeed each other without ever meaning anything and an absolute intemporal truth, which would be the truth of a non-situated discourse, of a science without point of view or perspective.

Many things were admirable in this great book: first, a manner of taking up again the results of the human sciences and enlisting them in a properly philosophical purpose. Merleau-Ponty closely followed work done in physiology, psychophysiology, experimental psychology, and psychopathology; he never stopped reflecting on the relations of philosophy to the human sciences, reflecting not only on the results but also on the methods. On the other hand, in order to provide this liaison, Merleau-Ponty returned to the magisterial teaching of the founder of phenomenology, Edmund Husserl, whose published and unpublished work he knew perfectly. But he did not enclose phenomenology (which claimed to be a descriptive science of what appears) in a Husserlian archaeology or scholasticism: he continued the movement of phenomenology for his own account, without regard for orthodoxy. Finally, with no less liberty and in order to install it in his own reading of the world and of the human being in-the-world, he took up again the theme of the lived body [*le corps propre*] (which had been introduced by Marcel), the living experience of my body, of this body that is neither an object known from without nor a subject transparent to itself. With Merleau-Ponty, the theory of the body is thoroughly a theory of perception: the body becomes the place of the general symbolism of the world.

The findings of the human sciences, the method of phenomenology, and the philosophical aim of existentialism are thus found mixed together in a complex ensemble. The import of this enterprise was considerable from the start: perception appeared as the model of all human operations, with its play of significations that refer one to the other, without ever halting in an object, seen from nowhere and thoroughly known. "In a general manner," he said, "all of our experience, all of our knowledge, involves the same fundamental structures, the same synthesis of transition, the same type of horizons that we believe are found in perceptual experience." "There is meaning. Simply put, rationality is neither a total nor immediate guarantee. It is somehow open, which is to say threatened." "All consciousness is perceptual consciousness, even the consciousness of ourselves."

It is not exaggerated to say that these formulae themselves contain an entire conception of action, and even an entire politics. For if perception is the model of existence, then this means that there is in action no longer an "all or nothing," and that politics is likewise approximate.

From the *Phenomenology of Perception* onward, Merleau-Ponty's philosophical style thus distanced itself from Sartre's. On the basis of such a model of perception, how could one oppose the "in-itself" of things and the "for-itself" of freedom? How could one posit a freedom that nothing could limit, except what freedom itself determined as a limit, by its own initiative? How could human being be the nothingness of things? For Merleau-Ponty, the only concrete and effective freedom is that which takes up some worldly propositions, takes the measure of things, and transforms obstacles into support: "Our freedom does not destroy our situation, but is geared to it: our situation, in so far as we live in it, is open, which implies both that it calls for privileged modes of resolutions, and that by itself, it is impotent to obtain any of them."

We didn't mean anything else when we called this philosophy a philosophy of ambiguity: what is realized in history is never properly speaking wanted or represented; the ends are recognized only at the moment of being attained. There is neither destiny nor absolutely free act; here too, only the double or the in-between is real.

It is an entire philosophy of *praxis*, of effective action in the world, that Merleau-Ponty intended to outline in the prolongation of his philosophy of perception. He thus intended to continue the young Marx, against the old Marx, and especially against Engels: "What Marx calls *praxis* is the meaning that is spontaneously decided at the intersection of actions by which humans organize their relations with nature and with others. It is not at first directed by an idea of total universal history. We recall that Marx insists on the impossibility of thinking the future. It is rather the analysis of the past and present that lets us glimpse in outline a logic in the course of things, a logic that does not regulate it from the outside, but that rather emanates from within it, and which is fulfilled only if humans understand their experience and want to change it" (*Praise*, 50–51).

All of Merleau-Ponty's political writings (*Humanism and Terror* in 1947, *The Adventures of the Dialectic* in 1955, and a number of texts in *Sense and Non-Sense* [1948] and in *Signs* [1960]) are dominated both by the will to "understand," to understand what there is of rationality sketched out in or underway up until the Stalinist "Terror," and by the refusal to grant that some reason governed history. In truth, the agreement with the young Marx concerning always the evolving meaning of intersubjective praxis, weighed less heavily than the profound disagreement with Marxism as a whole: Merleau-Ponty could not believe that there was a *universal class* and that the proletariat was this class. This is why history was for him without an absolute point of view, without a true perspective. *Humanism and Terror* ended in this way: "The human world is an open or incomplete system and the same fundamental contingency that threatens it with discord also takes it away from the fatality of disorder and rules out despairing of it, only on condition that we recall that here the apparatuses are humans, and that we maintain and multiply the relations between humans" (*HT*, 188).

The texts of 1955 are harder: the Marxists' dialectic idea seemed to him to be an obstacle to all historical comprehension, including all knowledge of the U.S.S.R. and all modern critique of capitalism. In his eyes, the dialectical idea is no more than the "point of honor" of an enterprise that it does not animate, the true nature of which is difficult to see under this veil and no doubt escapes the protagonists themselves. The Sartre of the important articles on "The Communists and Peace" is brutally criticized, accused of professing an "ultra-bolshevism," which is to say an entirely voluntaristic communism wherein the Party's choices are substituted for every spontaneous logic of history, in which nobody believes any more. Sartre's reticent sympathy for action without criteria, his presence in absence in the Communist Party represented then, in Merleau-Ponty's eyes, the very model of what the noncommunist Left had to stop doing. He wrote that "once the communist nostalgia is exorcized, then one leaves behind reveries and everything becomes interesting and new again." The end of Merleau-Ponty's and Sartre's collaboration in the direction of *Les temps modernes* dates from this text, a distancing that never assumed the abrupt and unfriendly character of the rupture with Camus. I do not know what Merleau-Ponty thought of *The Critique of Dialectical Reason*, which obviously entirely escaped the reproach of voluntarism. He no doubt awaited the second volume of the work, on the theme of history. It is, however, doubtful that the idea of totalization, even as a detotalizing idea, would have found favor in his eyes, to the extent that it retained what Merleau-Ponty wanted to lose in order to see clearly: the idea of universal history. Be that as it may, this explicitly professed "a-communism" organized Merleau-Ponty's diverse political initiatives, his adherences, and his reserves. The detail in this is, I believe, less important with respect to the principal battle, carried on at the level of reflection, against the ideologies and the mythologies, which according to him prevented leftist intellectuals from passing from an absolute politics (which is a death struggle) to a realistic politics (which is capable of outliving the illusion of the true history carried by a revolutionary class).

I have probably given the impression, in this overview of Merleau-Ponty's philosophical work, that everything follows from the *Phenomenology of Perception*. One can and must understand matters this way in order to assure the unity of this brutally interrupted work. But what makes this interruption tragic is that the philosophical basis of the great 1945 work had for a long time been put back into question, and that this work of the undermining from below had not yet, it seems, let the *second landing* of the work appear.

It must not be lost from sight that from the start, the *Phenomenology of Perception* left apart from itself the results attained as early as 1938 but published only in 1942 in *The Structure of Behavior*. The "existentialism" of 1945 was not able to include the more "objective" notions of form, structure, order (physical, vital, and human orders), despite the philosopher's efforts to recapture every theory of structure in a philosophy of signification. *The Structure of Behavior* is just as much a masterwork as the *Phenomenology of Perception*. One will thus have to return to this initial oscillation between a philosophy of existence and a philosophy of nature.

On the other hand, during the last years Merleau-Ponty had doubted more and more that the manner of being in the world revealed by *mute* perception could effectively serve as a model for the totality of our relations with beings and with being. If the engagement of the human in his flesh and in his history were without distance, how then could reflection be produced and phenomenology itself be articulated? Could a simple phenomenology of perception take account of the philosophical act without recourse to something like the "reduction" of our very presence in the world? Is not language itself the witness of this distance, of this reflection, of this reduction? In fact, the theory of language (which the *Phenomenology of Perception* tried to contain within the limits of a reflection on "the body as expression" and tried to understand as "linguistic gesture") did not stop making the framework of the relation to the world by simple perception explode. The influence of the Heideggerian philosophy of Being and of speech gradually made itself more felt in the more recent writings and in the unpublished courses. *Saying* [*le dire*] is therein increasingly understood as access to the unseen—to the Invisible—of beings. At the same time, the problem of a philosophy of nature was taken up anew, and a difficult convergence was sought between a nature that is always more and always other than the perceived world, and the function of language that is the least "gestural" and the most "symbolic." To the simple idea of the human's incarnation by means of a perceiving body in a perceived world was added (or was substituted) "the idea of a vision, of an operative word, of a metaphysical operation of the flesh, of an exchange where the visible and the invisible are rigorously simultaneous" (according to the expression in *Signs*). To what point these meditations announced a simple prolongation of the initial themes, or a second philosophy markedly different from the first, is what this death prevents us forever from calculating.

3

Merleau-Ponty

Beyond Husserl and Heidegger (1989)

PAUL RICOEUR

In order to discern Merleau-Ponty's originality, at least in the *Phenomenology of Perception*, one often lets oneself be fascinated by the most apparent antinomy that this phenomenology undertook to overcome, the antinomy between the Neo-Kantian intellectualism of a Brunschvicg or of a Lachièze-Rey on the one hand, and the empiricism of behaviorism on the other hand. This approach is not negligible in that it shows Merleau-Ponty effecting a movement of thought that carries him *beyond* the two terms of the alternative. This approach has, however, lost much of its pertinence, in that the two combatants who find themselves thereby dismissed have receded from our horizon of thought. At the same time, the movement effected by Merleau-Ponty ceases to surprise us and to give us something to think about. Another movement *beyond* traverses Merleau-Ponty's phenomenology, one that calls for a sharper discernment, all the more so since the difference between the two positions overcome in the movement is dissimulated. This is the movement *beyond* Husserl and Heidegger. The third part of the *Phenomenology of Perception* constitutes a privileged touchstone for measuring both the divergence between the two positions, and the distance that Merleau-Ponty puts between himself and his two teachers [*maîtres*]. It has seemed to me that the study devoted to *temporality* (*PhP*, 476–503), which is cast as a bridge between the chapters on the *Cogito* and on *freedom*, offered in shortened form the essential innovation that Merleau-Ponty effects in relation to Husserl's *Lectures on the Consciousness of Internal Time* and the second section of *Being and Time*.

The *title* of the third part of the *Phenomenology* already contains a valuable clue: "Being-for-itself and Being-in-the-world." One could say that the first part of the title gestures toward Husserl and the second toward Heidegger. In fact, the analysis of the Cogito affirms the inseparable character of the reflexive operation and the "active transcendence" (*PhP*, 438) that throws and projects consciousness outside of itself. Yet this active transcendence resembles both Husserlian intentionality and Heideggerian being-in-the-world. It resembles intentionality, in that every object is the presumed unity of a multitude of profiles or sketches. And it resembles being-in-the-world, in that "what I discover and recognize through the Cogito is not psychological immanence . . . nor even transcendental immanence, the belonging of all of phenomena to a constituting consciousness . . . but rather it is the profound movement of transcendence that is my very being, the simultaneous contact with my being and the being of the world" (*PhP*, 438–39). The refusal of all constituting consciousness marks a distance from Husserl and brings him closer to Heidegger. But it is nevertheless Husserl, not Heidegger, to whom Merleau-Ponty refers us when he assigns the relation between reflection and the unreflected to an operation of *Fundierung* (*PhP*, 458). Moreover, the first allusion to temporality is advanced in this Husserlian ambiance: it is under the heading of a *sedimented* phenomenon that the intemporal seems to escape from the passage of time; it is, however, only an "acquisition for always" (*PhP*, 457), according to the term that Thucydides applied to the work of the historian. It is indeed to a genetic phenomenology that the genesis of meaning (which makes of reason a "sedimented history" (*PhP*, 459)) must be referred. In any case, it is to the *Formal and Transcendental Logic* that Merleau-Ponty explicitly refers us at this point. What seems to mark the Husserlian allegiance of Merleau-Ponty's phenomenology more than anything else is the very trust maintained in the problematic of the Cogito. The Cogito does not mark the irremediable decline of modern thought. It can still be saved, but at the price of a drastic revision that the consideration of time inaugurates: "In sum, we are restoring to the Cogito a temporal thickness," Merleau-Ponty declares (*PhP*, 464). Would the *Phenomenology of Perception*, then, be a simple variant of Husserlian phenomenology in its last phase? At the very moment that this hypothesis appears to take shape, the analysis of the Cogito suddenly escapes from all Husserlian allegiance and appears to shift once again toward Heidegger. The notion of a "tacit Cogito" (*PhP*, 468) initiates this apparent change of positions: the tacit Cogito is the place of my attachments to the world, anterior to any conscious awareness; it is traversed by "a total project or a logic of the world" (*PhP*, 471), which leads to this decisive affirmation: "The essential point is to take hold of the project of the world that we are" (ibid.). The tacit Cogito and the original project of the world are one and same thing. Is this to say, then, that Merleau-Ponty hesitates and oscillates between Husserl and Heidegger? Or indeed does the *Phenomenology of Perception* already carry its author beyond them both? This is what the chapter on "Temporality" will perhaps make possible to decide.

At first glance, the same balancing of thought between the two poles of phenomenology seems to be pursued in the second chapter of the third part of the *Phenomenology of Perception.* What can surprise and disconcert the reader is the facility with which Merleau-Ponty passes not only from one citation from Husserl to a citation from Heidegger, but also from a Husserlian theme to a Heideggerian theme, all in order to construct his own analysis, incorporated in a phenomenology of perception. In a first approximation, one can consider the very enterprise of understanding subjectivity and time in terms of each other (*PhP,* 476ff) as a purely Husserlian effort. The vocabulary of "consciousness," preserved throughout the analysis, seems to confirm this allegiance: "*there is no time in the things,*" says one of the subtitles of the chapter. In this sense, in order to compare time to the flow of a river, one would have to grant this to a witnessing consciousness. The declaration with which the description opens is equally Husserlian: "It is in my 'field of presence' in the large sense . . . that I make contact with time, that I learn to know its course. . . . Everything sends me back . . . to the field of presence as the originary experience whereby time and its dimensions appear *in person*, with no distance interposed and in ultimate evidence" (*PhP*, 483). The description of temporality as a network of intentionalities marked by the exchanges of protensions, retensions, and a field of presence is above all Husserlian. This description is what permits taking up again (with important reservations that will be discussed later) the unfortunate Husserlian schema, constructed along a horizontal line representing the series of "nows," a representation that the whole analysis precisely contradicts. What one risks not seeing, however, is that from the beginning, what is at stake in the intentional analysis is the *course of time considered as a unique totality*, not as a constituted totality, but at least as an ensemble in the process of formation. One could already notice it in the aforementioned declaration: if one enters the problem of time by way of the notion of the field of presence, it is in order to learn "to know the course of time." Beyond the relations of future, past and present, what needs to be understood is "the very passage of time" (*PhP*, 492). What consequently proves to be more Heideggerian than Husserlian is the primacy given to the question of time as being-a-whole in comparison to the play of intentionalities. As a result of this priority, there is a subtle reorientation of the analyses of protention and retention, which in appearance are most faithfully Husserlian. It is less the case that the relations engender time than that time deploys its "natural and primordial unity" across them. And the subsequent analysis verifies it: the Husserlian diagram, Merleau-Ponty suddenly declares, represented only "an instantaneous cross-section of time" (*PhP*, 486). There are thus not at first discrete instants of time, and then a play of retentions: "[T]here is not a multiplicity of linked phenomena, but one single phenomenon of flow." (*PhP*, 487) The citation from Paul Claudel ("time is the means offered to all that is destined to be, to come into existence in order that it may no longer be" [ibid.]), makes this analysis swing from a phenomenology to an ontology in which the play of intentionalities is firmly subordinated to the grasp of time as passage, as transition, as transit. It is finally the Heideggerian definition of time as *temporalization* that prevails in order to say this "synthesis of transition": "Temporality temporalizes itself as future-that-lapses-into-the-past-by-coming-into-the present." (*PhP*, 488). On the basis of this, we can discern a discreet disavowal of Husserl in the following passage: "What there is, is not a present with the perspectives of past and future, followed by another present where these perspectives would be disrupted, in such a way that an identical spectator would be necessary in order to effect the synthesis of the successive perspectives, but rather there is one single time that affirms itself, that could not bring anything into existence without having already founded it as present and as past to come, and which establishes itself in one single stroke" (*PhP*, 489). In other words, the "cohesion of a life" (another expression borrowed from Heidegger) is given with the ek-stasis of time (an expression that never appears except in the singular, as temporalization itself, even though Heidegger speaks of ek-stases of time). Merleau-Ponty even seems led farther than Heidegger (at least the Heidegger of *Being and Time*) when, following Kant, Merleau-Ponty declares that time, taken as an ensemble, "abides" (ibid.). It is this profound truth, in Merleau-Ponty's estimation, that common sense and myths anticipate when, in order to illustrate this "intuition of the permanence of time" (*PhP*, 490), they personify it. And in effect, "time is someone" (ibid.) because it is subjectivity itself. Since the emphasis is placed on " time in its entirety" (*PhP*, 493), one can, as in the case of Heidegger this time, blur the identities preserved by the very terms of past and of future: the past is only ever a former future and a recent present, and the future, an upcoming past. The continuous unity of time means that each dimension is aimed at as other than itself. Time is this "power that . . . holds together [the exterior events] while distancing them from each other" (*PhP*, 490). The continuity of time is therefore what is to be thought across the play of intentionalities: "Time as indivisible thrust and as transition can alone render possible time as successive multiplicity, and what we put at the origin of intratemporality is a constituting time" (*PhP*, 491). But at the very instant that the analysis appears to lean so strongly to the side of Heidegger despite the vocabulary of constitution, the primacy of the present is reaffirmed: "[T]here is time for me because I have a present. It is by coming into the present that a moment of time acquires the indestructible individuality, the 'once and for all' quality which will permit it henceforth to traverse time and to produce in us the illusion of eternity None of the dimensions of time can be deduced from the others" (*PhP*, 492). One thinks that one hears Husserl again: "But the present (in the broad sense, with its horizons of originary past and future) still has a privilege because it is the zone where being and consciousness coincide" (ibid.).

Do these comings and goings between Husserl and Heidegger betray a lack of perspicacity on Merleau-Ponty's part? It seems to me rather to have brought to light the *profound kinship of two successive philosophical projects, with a certain period of indecision in each of them*. If one still speaks of intentionality, with Husserl, it is no longer a matter of thetic intentionality of the *Logical Investigations*, but rather of the "operative" (*fungierende*) intentionality, which the *Formal and Transcendental Logic* will later elaborate. Now, this "operative" intentionality is not unrelated to the transcendence of Dasein according to Heidegger. Likewise, if one still speaks of "synthesis" in order to state the globality of time, it is not a synthesis of which the subject would be the master, but rather a composition of which the subject is not the author but is instead constituted by it. In brief, it is a "passive synthesis." Yet neither is passive synthesis without relation to the displacement Heidegger effects from a problematic of consciousness to a problematic of Dasein.

In return, Merleau-Ponty's subtle analysis shows to what extent the notion of Dasein remains close to the notion of subjectivity, prior to Heidegger's turn. This analysis reveals, first of all, in the Heideggerian notion of ek-stasis, the heritage of the Husserlian analysis of protention and retention, which is just as much retained as overcome by the Heideggerian analysis. Next, Merleau-Ponty attests that the intertwining of temporal intentionalities comes about ultimately in the present. One can certainly see in this last thesis the resistance that a phenomenology of perception opposes to a hermeneutic of care, spontaneously oriented toward the primacy of the future (and the word *care* does not appear in this chapter, nor, for very good reasons, is the term "being-toward-death," even though consciousness is redefined by the repercussion of the phenomenology of temporality on the phenomenology of subjectivity, in terms of a "global project," as one finds in Sartre). But faced with Merleau-Ponty's reticences and silences, one can also wonder if a hermeneutic of care fully succeeds in replacing the primacy of the present with that of the future. After all, in Heidegger's own work, is it not the case that rendering-present constitutes the intersection of resolute anticipation and the revival of received legacies, in the moment of repetition?

Finally, Merleau-Ponty's genius is, on the one hand, to have glimpsed in the Husserlian phenomenology of time an analysis that subverts all the idealism of the *Sinngebung* and that demands a recasting of the notions of intentionality and constitution in accord with the primacy of being-in-the-world. His genius is, on the other hand, to have recognized in the Heideggerian hermeneutic not so much a rupture with all phenomenology of subjectivity, but rather, the transposition of this phenomenology into an ontological language that prolongs its efficacity. For if time must be thought "as a whole," it is to the extent that "it is someone." The very support that Merleau-Ponty seeks in Heidegger's work for thinking time "as a whole" as passage paradoxically reinforces the right of subjectivity: temporality is subject to the extent that the subject is temporality.

This profound kinship between Husserl's subjectivism (which is en route to being overcome by the phenomenology of time) and Heidegger's analytic of Dasein (which still is secretly dependent on a phenomenology of subjectivity) is expressed in the most audacious rapprochement attempted by Merleau-Ponty, namely, the rapprochement between the notion of *auto-affection* (borrowed from Kant in *Critique of Pure Reason,* B 67), and Husserl's affirmation (in *The Lectures on the Consciousness of Internal Time*) that "the original flux not only is, [but also] must give itself a manifestation of itself [*Selbsterscheinung*]" (*PhP*, 495). What, then, do these two notions have in common? This: in auto-affection, "what affects is time as thrust and passage towards a future; what is affected is time as a developed series of presents" (*PhP*, 494). One thus recognizes, on the side of that which affects, time "in its entirety," and on the side of that which is affected, the transition from one present to another present, which is subjectivity itself. Auto-affection is in this way also auto-manifestation. Merleau-Ponty summarizes the equivalence of the two analyses thus carried to extremes with these terms: "It is essential to time to be not only effective time or time that flows, but also to be time that knows itself, because the explosion or the dehiscence of the present toward a future is the archetype of the *relation of self to self* and traces out an interiority or an ipseity" (*PhP*, 495). It is in this profound sense that temporality and subjectivity mutually interpret one another, in Heidegger's work no less than in Husserl's.

In what sense consequently can one say that Merleau-Ponty's phenomenology situates itself beyond Husserl and Heidegger? In a double sense to which the analysis of temporality attests: on the one hand, this analysis leads the interpretation of the phenomenon of intentionality to the point where its *rootedness* in the *ontological* structure of being-in-the-world is disclosed, and on the other hand, this analysis recalls that the hermeneutic of Dasein still belongs to the *phenomenological* epoch of ontology. By revealing their convergence in depth, Merleau-Ponty moves beyond Husserl and Heidegger, because to reveal this convergence is *to institute it.*

4

The Turn of Experience

Merleau-Ponty and Bergson

RENAUD BARBARAS

Bergson's enterprise, which he himself characterizes as an attempt "to go seek experience at its source, or rather, above that decisive *turn* where, bending itself in the direction of our utility, it becomes properly *human* experience,"[1] influences Merleau-Ponty, whose own project is presented from the beginning as an effort "to return to that world which precedes knowledge, of which knowledge always *speaks*, and with respect to which every scientific schematization is an abstract and derivative sign-language" (*PhP*, x). T. Geraets recalls that the Bergsonian project sustained Merleau-Ponty's enthusiasm very early on, and he goes so far as to say that "this Bergsonian orientation would in large part determine Merleau-Ponty's very selective reading of Husserl."[2] Whether or not this claim is just (and we will return to this), it is true that from the beginning, Merleau-Ponty welcomes both Husserlian phenomenology and Bergson's thought as two essential attempts to return to the things themselves; as such, a confrontation is called for. Just consider the review that Merleau-Ponty wrote of *The Imagination*, a work in which Sartre severely criticizes the theory of images in *Matter and Memory*: "[W]e could think that by presenting the world as an ensemble of *images*, Bergson wanted to underline that the thing must be neither resolved into *states of consciousness* nor sought beyond what we see in a substantial reality. This would be exactly, though in a much less precise language, an anticipation of Husserl's noema."[3] There is no doubt that throughout his work, Merleau-Ponty engages Bergson in a debate the terms of which are fixed from the beginning, and in the course of which Bergson appears more and more as an alternative to phenomenology—i.e., as a perspective irreducible to it, yet without becoming an objective philosophy.

In the first two works, the allusions to Bergson give the image of a thought that is difficult to situate, and which Merleau-Ponty does not manage to integrate easily into his critical apparatus. Consider the rare references to Bergson—always in notes—in *Phenomenology of Perception*, as if Bergson belonged to a parallel universe, possible neither to integrate nor to reject purely and simply. Yet to the extent that Merleau-Ponty moves away from *Phenomenology of Perception*, Bergson's thought becomes more present and the discussion more profound. The courses on *Nature*, where numerous pages are devoted to Bergson, show this more clearly than do other texts from the 1950s, which remain largely circumstantial homages. This *rapprochement* culminates in the form of a confrontation between Husserl and Bergson in the chapter of *The Visible and the Invisible* entitled "Intuition and Interrogation"—a completely edited and revised part of an unfinished text, wherein the question is again to define the authentic meaning of philosophical interrogation, and already, the meaning of being [*sens d'être*] at which it aims. At this stage of the development of Merleau-Ponty's thought, the two philosophers are attributed an equal philosophical dignity, and everything happens as if the concern to clarify the meaning of his philosophical questioning once and for all finally required Merleau-Ponty to take up this always-adjourned confrontation, allowing him consequently to situate himself with respect to his two major heritages. We would like to sketch the terms of this debate while trying to understand the reasons for this increasing proximity to Bergson. Would there not be a truth of Bergsonism, beneath the difficulties that Merleau-Ponty underlines, a truth whose thematization would contribute to the passage to ontology while freeing Merleau-Ponty from the limitations of Husserlian phenomenology, on which he remains incontestably dependent in *Phenomenology of Perception*?

Even if it is probable that the reading of Bergson played a decisive role in Merleau-Ponty's formation, his attitude toward Bergson was nevertheless essentially critical when he wrote *Phenomenology of Perception*. It consists in rejecting Bergson's thought as an introspectionist philosophy which, unable to tear itself away from the realism characteristic of the natural attitude, and therefore incapable of grasping the ontological originality of consciousness, is consequently unable to distinguish it from the thing. Here, contrary to Geraets's thesis, the reading of Husserl organizes the critique of Bergson. The rejection of the

Bergsonian conception of consciousness relies at first on the phenomenological reduction and the discovery of intentionality as the fundamental eidetic trait of psychic reality, even if Merleau-Ponty appeals to *Gestaltpsychologie* in order to denounce what is still idealist in the Husserlian conception of subjectivity (at least in *Ideas I*). However, if phenomenology furnishes Merleau-Ponty with an original determination of the meaning of the being of consciousness, his critique of Bergsonism as such is also strongly influenced by Politzer, already cited in *The Structure of Behavior*.[4] In Merleau-Ponty's eyes, Politzer's thought represents the negative and critical version of an attitude, the constructive aspect of which—singularly absent in Politzer—was incarnated by Husserl. In other words, if Merleau-Ponty finds in Husserl, and probably even more so in Goldstein, a positive determination of what Politzer outlines in his concept of "drama," he nevertheless discovers in Politzer a very precise critique of the realism of Bergsonian psychology, which converges with the phenomenological recognition of psychology's submission to the natural attitude. We know that Politzer's aim is to achieve the process of the "dissolution" of psychology by underlining the scientific sterility of the currents of classical psychology, a project echoed in certain contemporary attempts (behaviorism, *Gestaltpsychologie*, psychoanalysis): psychology cannot claim the status of a science because it is incapable of giving itself a specific object—that is, of properly defining a psychic fact. Psychology is in effect characterized by the unquestioned adoption of the realist attitude: psychic reality is approached as a reality in the third person, comparable to the object of the sciences of nature, and thus accessible to a simple perception. The specificity that confers unto psychic contents their belonging to an "I" is not perceived: they are conceived like atomic contents, ruled by anonymous processes. Whether psychology remains an introspection, or whether it attempts to overcome its arbitrariness by trying to link the psychic event to objective processes (as in the psychophysiological tradition), in each case what is missed is the essence of psychic reality as existence in the first person. Such a realism leads inevitably to abstraction: psychology, far from being able to progress in the determination of its object, can only recognize in it the exemplification of general laws. The access to a concrete psychic reality, that is, to the individual, is forever prohibited. Yet, in certain respects, Politzer's critique is not without echos in the attitude adopted by Bergson in the *Essai sur les données immédiates de la conscience,* which also denounces the complicity of introspection and objectivism, refuses psychical atomism, and criticizes the confusion of existence in the first person and existence in the third person.[5] But for Bergson, the objectivation leads to missing the true signification of the self and must be shifted to a movement of spatialization. His concern is above all to emphasize a line of demarcation *within psychic reality itself*, corresponding to a duality of attitude between the objective and the authentically subjective, between the spatialized course of lived experience and the deep self (the synonym for duration). From then on, rather than leading him to reject interiority under the pretext of its contamination by natural objectivity (as Politzer will do), Bergson's critique of space allows him instead to retrieve the originary sense of interiority. The concern is not to look for the true being of psychic reality beyond the alternative of interior and exterior, but rather to assume the introspective attitude as radically as possible. Naturally, we can wonder, as Merleau-Ponty subsequently does, if by defining psychic reality as duration, Bergson still aimed at a psychological interior opposed to an exterior, or if he does not instead emphasize that which, inside psychic reality, inscribes us in exteriority and opens us to the absolute. Whichever it is, the submission of introspection to the spatial schema reveals a fault in the *manner* that introspection was practiced, but this does not in any way condemn introspection itself. According to Politzer, Bergson remains imprisoned by a psychological realism, giving a more refined version of it: the qualitative is substituted for the quantitative, the fluid or dynamic for the static, intuition for perception—but it is still a reality in the third person that is described. The Bergsonian return to the concrete can consequently deliver only a concrete in general—that is, an abstraction.

Merleau-Ponty easily appropriates this critique of Bergsonism: for him, the realism denounced by Politzer is only the particular form that the natural attitude (as described by Husserl) takes in the field of psychology, an attitude that is at the basis of the naturalism of the positive sciences. Certainly Bergson tries to attain the specificity of psychic reality (and thus of psychology) from over against objectivism by underlining the spatializing tendency of intelligence and by describing consciousness as an original multiplicity, but he does not grasp this objectivism at the root; his critique of space thus does not save him from falling back into realism. According to Merleau-Ponty, it was only on the condition of understanding that spatialization is only a manifestation of a more radical ontological attitude (which consists in allowing for the existence of a world resting in itself) that Bergson could take account of the specificity of psychic reality. Just as "*Gestalt* psychology cannot see that psychological atomism is only one particular case of a more general prejudice: that of the determinate being of the world" (*PhP*, 59n), so too could we say that Bergson does not see that spatialization is only a particular case of the same realism. Briefly, the destiny of every introspective psychologist is also Bergson's: "[W]ith the scientist and with common sense, he presupposed the objective world as the logical framework of all his descriptions and as the milieu of his thought. He was unaware that this presupposition dominated the meaning given to the word '*being*,' forcing him to realize consciousness under the name of 'psychic *fact*,' thus diverting him from a true awareness or from truly immediate experience, and rendering derisory the multiple precautions taken in order not to deform the 'interior.' . . . This is what happened to Bergson at the moment when he opposed the 'multiplicity of fusion' to the 'multiplicity of juxtaposition'. For it is a still a question of two genres of being" (*PhP*, 59).

From this comes both the attempt to respect the phenomenological character of time (in the concept of duration), and the impossibility of doing so. Like Husserl and Heidegger, Bergson discovers the continuity of time as an essential phenomenon; such is the meaning of the notion of the multiplicity of fusion and of interpenetration, in opposition to the multiplicity of juxtaposition proper to exterior things. Bergson attempts to escape the classical perspective of time by understanding it as continuity, as a process of fusion and of qualitative differentiation. He does so by starting with a real multiplicity of distinct instants, and must then appeal to an act of synthesis in order to take account of the unity of duration, of the appearance of instants in one same time. Bergson's goal is thus to escape from the alternative of a series of instants that do not elapse, progress, or change, where time is somehow missed by default, and of a synthetic supratemporal unity where time is somehow missed by excess. But because he is a prisoner of the realist attitude, "he proceeds by dilution. He speaks of consciousness as if it were a liquid in which instants and positions melt together. He seeks in it an element in which their dispersion is really abolished" (*PhP*, 321n47). The proper reality of time is thus inevitably missed. Grasped in the realist mode, temporal fusion cannot be understood as a process or a development; it instead becomes a mixture in which the moments agglomerate and crystallize in immobility: "[I]f in virtue of the principle of continuity, the past is still of the present and the present already for the past, there is no longer neither past nor present; if consciousness snowballs on itself, it is, like the snowball and all things, entirely in the present" (*PhP*, 322n47). In other words, in the realist attitude, we cannot mark a difference between a process of fusion and a thing, or between a continuous development and an aggregate. Even if the Kantian perspective is also a prisoner of the prejudice of real multiplicity, it at least works against Bergson's realism in that the notion of synthesis requires consciousness as the agent of synthesis, which would not be confused with a thing. And so in Merleau-Ponty's eyes, the problem of time can be resolved only on the condition of overcoming the alternative between a synthetic unity that supposes pure multiplicity and a real fusion that abolishes all diversity, or between a consciousness which, exterior to its contents, is the pure power of negation, and a consciousness which, as the penetration of the contents in each other, is deprived of negativity. Between synthetic consciousness and the thing, he must manage to think a mode of unity immanent to diversity, in such a way that this diversity is not abolished. Bergson respects the first condition, but at the price of the abolition of diversity; Kant subscribes to the second condition, but the unity falls under a power of synthesis exterior to the contents. In this way, taking time into consideration leads to overcoming realism, because the temporal flux as unity immanent to diversity cannot be "real"; it requires an original mode of being that, for Merleau-Ponty, following Husserl, can only be that of consciousness itself, but understood in an entirely different sense from Bergson's. There would thus be a tension in Bergson between an acute attention to the specificity of time and the persistence of a realist prejudice, leading to the dissolution of the duration in an immobile element. In other words, by determining duration in opposition to space, Bergson submits himself to an abstract alternative: it does not suffice to denounce spatial exteriority and then by antithesis to construct the duration in order to have access to a true intuition of time.

Merleau-Ponty's 1948–49 course devoted to *Matter and Memory* testifies to the same attitude. If Bergson tries to think perception in terms that bring him close to phenomenology, or at least calls for a comparison, he nevertheless remains incapable, in Merleau-Ponty's eyes, of accessing the authentic meaning of being of consciousness precisely because he remains prisoner to a realist conception of Being. By denouncing the submission of the classical approach of perception to representation, and by trying to think perception starting from the body conceived as the center of action, Bergson "aims at restoring the body to its struggle with the world," beyond the abstract opposition of the sensorial and the motor.[6] To such a Bergsonian determination of perception—i.e., the "reflection" of the object on the brain as the center of indetermination, which draws an appearance of the object directly on the object—there corresponds the characterization of the real as an ensemble of images, "realities" midway between the object and the representation.[7] Merleau-Ponty sees in this the anticipation of the universal a priori of correlation thematized by Husserl—that is, the attempt to interpret the essential relation uniting a consciousness, which is the effectuation of a world, and an object, whose being essentially refers to a subjective givenness. However, Bergson postulates the identity of the *esse* and the *percipi* without somehow supporting it with a constituting consciousness; as a result, the ensemble of images can only be conceived as a reality-in-itself, the perception of which proceeds by negation or subtraction: the primacy of the *esse* over the *percipi* gets the better of their identity. And so instead of wondering to what type of subjectivity an image that is not actually perceived can refer—and more generally, what consciousness understands such images—Bergson produces the ensemble of images and then deduces perceived being from it: "Bergson does not see, does not address the problem of the Cogito: he posits total being and carves out my perspective from it" (*Union,* 88). A real relation is, in the end, substituted for the noetico-noematic correlation: the action of the living explains the apparition of the perceived. In brief, such is the center of Merleau-Ponty's critique, "there is in Bergson, then, a blindness toward the proper being of consciousness and its intentional structure" (*Union,* 89).

This realism is, however, only the counterpart of his spiritualism: "[T]he body does not succeed in being a subject . . . for if the body were a subject, the subject would be body, and this is something Bergson does not want at any price" (*Union,* 91; cf. 96). In effect, our perception is never the simple delimitation of an image right on the world, because it is not produced in instanteneity; the subject finds itself reintroduced as the condition of recognition, and is identified with memory. But because the universe of images is conceived as a real Whole, then memory, which is the negation of it, will itself be understood as positivity: "[R]adically different from objectivity, the subject will at the same time be radically homogenous with it—a simple difference of substance and not of existential modality" (*Union,* 90). Consequently, the articulation effected between two positive and somehow concurrent realities, between action and representation, between the body and subjectivity, remains incomprehensible. This is why the two central chapters of *Matter and Memory* justify two opposed interpretations. Must we say that it is the body that takes the initiative and that, in function of the requirements of action, it calls for memories not having true existence outside of this actualization? Or must we claim on the contrary that the initiative comes from memories, which would be what is essential in perception, so that the function of the body would be only to impede the integral actualization of it? The problem of time is here again at stake: in order to think the true articulation of actual action and of memory, the mode of being of the subject had to be determined in such a way that the *passage* from the present to the past, the essential appeal of one to the other, was thinkable. Yet, as Merleau-Ponty notes, either we are enclosed in a present without temporal horizon, or we remain prisoner of a phantom past which is pure virtuality and has no root in the present. No temporal passage would be thinkable since the subject is traversed by the substantial duality of pure perception and of pure memory, and since "mental life takes on the aspect of a coming and going between two levels of the In-Itself" (*Union,* 91).

In Merleau-Ponty's eyes, it is possible to guarantee the identity of the *esse* and the *percipi* in the image only by thematizing the correlation with the Cogito, that is, by emphasizing the intentional structure of perceptual consciousness: such a perspective is thus led to overcome the duality between motor action and pure representation. This is exactly the program of *Phenomenology of Perception*, the conclusions of which crop up on the surface of and throughout Merleau-Ponty's critical reading of Bergson. But the phenomenological fecundity of the concept of the image is compromised by the realist position of a Totality-in-itself, the perception of which arises by subtraction—a position to which responds the scission between an objective motricity and a contemplative subject, between a movement in the third person and the pure interiority of an ego. As Merleau-Ponty notes already in *The Structure of Behavior*, Bergson cannot articulate perception and action in a satisfactory manner because the latter is restrictively understood as vital action, just as the life of consciousness is conceived as immanence and can include neither the dimension of escape, nor of internal opacity that would allow it to be incarnated in an action: "As a result of a prejudice inherited from Spencer, the human is conceived of as an animal power of action, on which would be a *faculty of distances* pathetically superimposed. Everything which is not animal action falls then to the side of the dream" (*Union*, 94). And so on the one hand, Merleau-Ponty recognizes the force and the originality of the Bergsonian attempt, which he interprets in a strictly phenomenological perspective. With the concept of image, Bergson foreshadows a meaning of the being of the world that escapes from the natural attitude, that is, from the naive distinction of an existence-in-itself and of a correlative appearing of an intraworldly consciousness. The attempt to think perception starting from a motor subject, instead of grounding it in a representation, heads in the direction of a recognition of the a priori of correlation, that is, of the characterization of the body as a "debate with the world." But on the other hand, by failing to criticize realism at its root, that is, to effect the phenomenological reduction—which signifies for Merleau-Ponty the recognition of the incarnated subject—Bergson pushes the images back to the side of the in-itself, thus compromising their constitutive relation to a subjectivity, and in so doing he divides the subject into a duality of an intraworldly, anonymous motricity, and a memorial subjectivity cut off from the world.

Merleau-Ponty's critique is gradually unfurled on the terrain of phenomenology, that is, of the essential articulation between the neutralization of the natural thesis and the intentional mode of existence which is constitutive of consciousness. The divergence is then crystallized around the question of time, capital for the two thinkers. For the Merleau-Ponty of *Phenomenology of Perception*, time names the being of the subject, insofar as it permits articulating the constitutive immanence and the transcendence of it, its self-presence and its self-absence. Bergson, on the other hand, anticipates that insertion in the world and the givenness of meaning, or intentional transcendence and subjective polarity, can be reconciled within time. If it is given for him that perception puts in play both the present of action (which inscribes perceiving in the world) and memory (which assures the dimension of recognition and of the donation of meaning), then Bergson does not possess a conception of duration that allows him to take account of the unity of these two dimensions. If, however, it is true that it is essentially in the name of a philosophy of consciousness that Bergson is criticized, then it would not be surprising that Merleau-Ponty's abandonment of the subject-object polarity goes hand in hand with a rereading and a reevaluation of Bergson's thought, in such a way that his "positivism" reinterpreted could weigh in against the limitations of philosophy of consciousness.

From the beginning, Merleau-Ponty's project is to go back to the perceived world in its native purity, to bring mute experience to the expression of its own meaning. However, by virtue of the teleology of reason—that is, of the movement by which perceptual life occults itself as subjective life—the access to the originary is the least immediate approach, and demands a preliminary methodological reflection. We can call the method allowing access to the meaning of being of the world a "reduction" in an enlarged sense. Since we know from *The Logical Investigations* that perception is an originary meaning-bestowing intuition, the reduction can thus be characterized as the gesture permitting access to the sense of the being of the perceived. This gesture is essentially negative in that the concern is to dismiss whatever is an obstacle to a return to the originary, whatever covers over experience in the native state; moreover, this gesture conforms to the inflection that Husserl gives to the problematic of the reduction in the *Crisis*. The entire difficulty is due to the fact that, in the reductive method, we can never be sure that we haven't surreptitiously introduced categories or presuppositions belonging to the very attitude we seek to neutralize. This is the reason why Merleau-Ponty takes his distance from the Husserlian reduction, as it is explained in the *Ideas* or in the *Cartesian Meditations*. According to a gesture that relates him to the reflexive tradition that Merleau-Ponty never stops denouncing, Husserl presents the reduction as "the return to transcendental consciousness before which the world is spread out in an absolute transparence, animated partially by a series of apperceptions that the philosopher would be charged to reconstitute starting from their result" (*PhP*, xi). In virtue of a circularity characteristic of reflexive philosophy, the natural attitude can appear only as the inverse of transcendental life, because constitutive life has been in some way projected in advance in the definition of the natural attitude; that is, the work of the constituting ego, forgetful of itself, is consequently susceptible to being partially reconstituted starting from acts of the subject. The determination of the world of the natural attitude as the universe of the *blosse Sachen*, and the return to a nonworldy transcendental consciousness that partially constitutes it, are the two faces of the same gesture which in Merleau-Ponty's eyes, Husserl inherits from the idealist tradition.[8] As a result, the transcendence constitutive of the world—that is, the transcendental dimension of constituting consciousness—is not truly respected. Because consciousness posits the world in acts that are given to themselves in immanence, the world cannot be constituted as world, that is, as that whose meaning of being exceeds consciousness. The transcendental consciousness of the *Ideas* takes account of the meaning of being of the world of the *naturalist* attitude, a world in which objectivating reflection had been integrated in advance—but it cannot pretend to deliver the truth of the natural attitude.

Merleau-Ponty's purpose is thus to dig beneath this correlation, entirely ordered by the model of the pure thing, toward the perceptual world properly so-called. The method consists in taking certain results from the psychology of form and from Goldsteinien physiology as a starting point, in order to show that these disciplines are led by their own discoveries to overcome the realist presupposition that ordered their spontaneous ontology. This return to consciousness, which repeats the Husserlian transcendental turn, has the specificity of leading into a new sense of subjectivity, characterized as an incarnated subjectivity. The subject of behavior cannot be confused with the transparent subject of objectivating acts. For the face-to-face meeting between reflexive consciousness and pure object, Merleau-Ponty substitutes the complicity of an incarnated, indistinctly active and perceptive subject with a perceived world, the pole of this still anonymous existence (and consequently irreducible to a pure object). Because incarnated consciousness cannot be transparent to itself, but rather escapes from itself, the transcendence of its object is thus preserved. The Merleau-Pontyan version of the reduction allows for the substitution of the vital coexistence of corporal subject and world as milieu of our life, with the mirrored correlation of reflexive subject and object, which is still dependant on a natural attitude.

However, we know that Merleau-Ponty is gradually led to question these results again, which, as we have seen, organized his critique of Bergsonism. From the beginning of the 1950s, there are signs of the movement that leads into the ontological perspective of *The Visible and the Invisible*, which ruptures with *Phenomenology of Perception* and the categories that govern it: "[T]he problems posed in *PhP* are insoluble because I start there from the consciousness-object distinction" (*VI*, 200; cf. 183). In *Phenomenology of Perception*, Merleau-Ponty is situated fully within the phenomenological perspective of the *consciousness-object* correlation and tries only to overcome the idealist components that persist in the Husserlian perspective. Access to the true sense of the perceived requires a critique of reflexive consciousness that benefits a living subjectivity, which attains itself only by escaping itself, and which is the unity of a presentation and a depresentation. What changes with *The Visible and the Invisible* is that the impossibility of rejoining the meaning of the being of the world (which until then was attributed to reflexive or thetic consciousness) is now judged *inherent to the philosophy of consciousness as such*. It seems henceforth illusory to want to overcome the limitations of intellectualism within the framework of a philosophy of consciousness, including the Husserlian version. Intellectualism is the truth of consciousness because every consciousness, whatever it may be, has in the end a world of *blosse Sachen* for a correlate: we can renounce this world only by renouncing consciousness. We are thus either situated in the framework of a philosophy of consciousness and therefore led back to intellectualism at the very moment when we claim to overcome it, or else we do indeed rejoin the true meaning of the being of the perceived—that is, return to the things themselves—but at the price of renouncing consciousness, and thus at the price of a radical recasting of the terms of the argument. And so, the "concepts such as *subject*, *consciousness*, *self-consciousness*, *mind*, all of which, even if in a refined form, involve the idea of a *res cogitans*, of a positive being of thought—whence results the immanence in the unreflected of the results of reflection" (*VI*, 74). The central difficulty of *Phenomenology of Perception* is due precisely to the fact that it tries to integrate the encroachment of the body and the world within the framework of consciousness, which psychology underlines in its own right. The specificity of perceived being is both recognized in the plan of description and denied by the conceptualization of perceptual life in terms of incarnated consciousness. Paradoxically, the central concept of *Phenomenology of Perception* is also the most poorly formed: *incarnation* (which gestures toward an original meaning of being of the world that Merleau-Ponty will soon name "flesh," of which the lived body is only an eminent case) *is in fact incompatible with the reference to a consciousness*. The concept of incarnated consciousness is an unstable concept that Merleau-Ponty himself eventually criticizes. Either we are attentive to the correlative meaning of being of incarnation (but then an ontological recasting is indispensable, at the end of which the concept of consciousness is abandoned), or we try to refer the perceived world to a subjective pole (but then we are led back to a consciousness whose incarnation remains incomprehensible, and which does not allow for taking the specificity of the perceived into account).

The step taken with respect to *Phenomenology of Perception*—a step that appears as a condition for the passage to ontology—consists in bringing to light an essential correlation between the philosophies of consciousness, be they empiricist or intellectualist, and a certain ontology, always implicit, that Merleau-Ponty qualifies several times as an "ontology of the object." Even though Merleau-Ponty claims in *Phenomenology of Perception* to overcome the natural attitude and to thematize the being of the perceived in the phenomenological framework of the subject-object correlation, he gradually discovers that all philosophy of consciousness (including Husserlian phenomenology) participates in an unquestioned ontology on which he himself was implicitly dependent. The pertinent opposition is no longer that of a philosophy of reflexive consciousness and of a phenomenology of incarnated consciousness, but rather of an ontology of the object (from which both are drawn) and an ontology of a new genre that the reading of Bergson will allow him to explicate. The reduction is therefore given a new signification. Now it occurs by emphasizing the situation (which is both theoretical and historical) that compromises the access to the perceived within a philosophy that claims to go back to the things themselves. It signifies first an awareness of the metaphysical distinction that orders the essential correlation between a philosophy of consciousness and a thematization of Being as pure object—that is, as fully determinable de jure.

This decision is clearly explicated in the chapter entitled "Interrogation and Intuition," as well as in the text published as an appendix by Claude Lefort; this appendix was in fact the first draft of the chapter, and they must be read in parallel. In this part of the text, where the critical moment of the work is completed, Merleau-Ponty tries to effect the phenomenological reduction, that is, he tries to define the conditions of a return to perceptual experience. He is therefore led to perfect his critique of phenomenology. Yet, we can only be struck by the fact that this critique is entirely centered on the notion of essence: Merleau-Ponty shows that even if phenomenology does manage to overcome the natural attitude by converting beings into their meanings, it still commits the error of thinking the being of meaning as essence, that is, as a fullness of determination, accessible de jure by an intellectual intuition, itself made possible by eidetic variation. The stakes of this critique are not to return to the initial phase of Husserl's thought, but rather to show that the founding gesture, as well as the limit, of phenomenology, consist in the decision *to determine Being as essence.* If the truth of phenomenology resides in transcendental subjectivity, then the truth of this subjectivity resides in the eidetic approach to Being. In other words, as Gérard Granel has shown very well, modern or objective phenomenology is characterized, according to Merleau-Ponty, by the determination of the presence of being-present as *pure self-presentation*: to say that a thing is present amounts to saying that it is present *itself* in what it presents. Yet this characterization of presence as presentation calls for the positioning of a subject as a necessary correlate, that is, as the place or the element in which presentation is gathered: "[T]o establish that the phenomenological meaning of Being is Presentation can only be understood, however, on the condition that Consciousness, itself taken in the phenomenological sense, is recognized as Being."[9] In other words, if the presence of being signifies the presentation of its essence, then this presence calls for a consciousness as the *vis-à-vis* to which presentation presents, that is, as that in which the essence is gathered. Inversely, to think experience starting from consciousness is inevitably to determine its object as essence, and, as Merleau-Ponty notes, to allow it "the immanence into the unreflected of the results of reflection." The determination of the transcendental as re-presentation, that is, as Subject, responds to the determination of Being as presentation of essence.

It is at this exact point that Merleau-Ponty's path crosses Bergson's, because if the truth of phenomenology rests in essence, then the truth of essence rests in a metaphysical decision that Bergson explains in *Creative Evolution* and that Merleau-Ponty takes up into his own account. The construction of a philosophy that sees in duration the very stuff of reality requires understanding why philosophy has always tended to consider Becoming as a lesser being. Yet, "the hidden spring, the invisible motor of philosophical thought" resides in the notion of *nothingness.* The proper character of metaphysics is, in effect, to approach Being starting from nothingness, that is, to define all existence as what emerges from nonbeing and that consequently requires a sufficient reason. And so, "the disdain of metaphysics for all reality that endures comes precisely from the fact that reality arrives at being only by passing by 'nothingingness,' and from the fact that an existence that endures seems to it not strong enough to conquer non-existence and itself to posit itself."[10] The proper character of logical being is *necessary being*, that is, being such that it cannot not be; having thus not been able to begin to exist, the question of the reason for its existence cannot even be posed. And so, metaphysics does not think Being starting from Being as such, but rather starting from that which in Being resists nothingness. Being is then gradually *what it is* because the least insufficiency of being would make it fall to the side of nothingness: if it were not fully what it is, then it would not be at all. In brief, "[I]f we pass (consciously or unconsciously) by the idea of nothingness in order to reach at the idea of Being, then the Being to which we come is a logical or mathematical essence, therefore non-temporal."[11]

Such is the determination of metaphysics that organizes Merleau-Ponty's critique of phenomenology and makes the passage to ontology possible. The essential reproach that Merleau-Ponty addresses to the Husserlian eidetic consists in the fact that in order to take full possession of the *eidos*, and to have a positive intuition of it, one would have to be situated in the point of view of nothingness, which contradicts the essential rooting of all thought, and thus the very necessity of passing by a variation of it: "[I]n order truly to reduce an experience to its essence, we should have to take a distance from it, that would put it entirely under our gaze with all the implications of sensoriality or of thought that play in it, to bring it and to bring ourselves wholly to the transparency of the imaginary, think it without the support of any ground, in short, withdraw to the bottom of nothingness" (*VI*, 111). The determination of the transcendental as consciousness, the determination of being as essence, and the recoil into nothingness are the three faces of the same metaphysical decision. The chapter published as an appendix—where Merleau-Ponty tries to open up an access to the thing of perception, that is, to the "something" which is not yet an object—largely confirms this. The passage by nothingness, which would be preliminary to all existence, is denounced as the root of objectivism, and thus as the essential obstacle to a restitution of the perceived world: "[S]tarting with the things taken in their native meaning as identifiable nuclei, but without any power of their own, we arrive at the thing-object, at the In-itself, at the thing identical with itself, only by imposing on experience an abstract dilemma which experience ignores . . . the thing thus defined is not the thing of our experience, it is the image that we obtain of it by projecting it in a universe where experience is tied to nothing, where the spectator would be distracted from the spectacle—in short, by confronting it with the possibility of nothingness."[12] And so the approach to Being starting from the principle of sufficient reason is the ultimate ground of its determination as essence, and thus, at least in the eyes of Merleau-Ponty, of the philosophy of consciousness. In this sense, doubt as the *epokhe*, repeating in some way the metaphysical event by which Being emerges from nonbeing, fully assumes that which organizes the very possibility of consciousness, that is, the power to step back from the ground of nothingness. Similarly, we could note that Sartre's philosophy, to which Merleau-Ponty devotes numerous pages in *The Visible and the Invisible*, is like the purified and subjectivated performance of the spontaneous and essentially unconscious movement of ontology: the subject is there defined as a nothingness that only a Being fully identical to itself can fill up or preserve in its absolute difference.

Whatever the case, the rereading of Bergson goes together with an inflection of the meaning of the phenomenological reduction. Merleau-Ponty understands that the search for a consciousness that can get lost in perceptual originality is in vain, since all consciousness is essentially dependant on an objectivist understanding of Being. The reevaluation of Bergsonism thus allows Merleau-Ponty to grasp the root of the natural attitude. The natural attitude cannot consist simply in the naive position of a world in itself: this position of a world fully determinably de jure, that is, granted a priori to the requirements of reason, is itself subtended by the attitude consisting in approaching Being on the ground of nothingness. Naivety is overcome by taking into consideration the Bergsonian discovery of the metaphysical foundation of the essential solidarity between nothingness and essence. Consequently, the reduction, as the leading-back to the true meaning of the being of the perceived, requires approaching Being directly, without a detour through nothingness. Here, Merleau-Ponty's method is closest to Bergsonian intuition: "[W]e must accustom ourselves to think Being directly, without making a detour, without appealing first to the phantom of nothingness that interposes itself between it and us."[13] The specificity of Merleau-Ponty's method does not consist so much in the return, within a philosophy of consciousness, *from* an objectivating consciousness *to* an incarnated consciousness, as it does in the passage, within ontology, *from* a philosophy that profiles Being against the ground of nothingness—which is the proper attitude of a philosophy of consciousness—*to* a philosophy that begins with Being—in short, from a philosophy of the thing to a philosophy of "something." To go back to the things themselves no longer means to return to subjective acts in which the world as it is for us is constituted, but rather to think Being directly "without addressing ourselves to the phantom of nothingness that interposes itself between it and us." The reduction is no longer the neutralization of the thesis of existence, but rather the neutralization of nothingness itself as preliminary to the thesis of existence.

We find ourselves confronted by a situation that is, to say the least, unique. On the one hand, the essential point of the critique that Merleau-Ponty addresses to Bergson consists in denouncing his positivism in the name of a philosophy of a transcendental inspiration. But on the other hand, the Bergsonian characterization of metaphysics allows Merleau-Ponty to bring to light the ultimate ground of the eidetic constitutive of the phenomenological gesture. Phenomenology itself, in the name of which Bergson's thought had first been criticized, is now convicted of positivism, with the absolute negativity of nothingness having the absolute positivity of essence as a counterpart. We must thus reevaluate the Bergsonian "realism" insofar as it proceeds from a critique of metaphysics, and thus from the concern to approach Being without interposing nothingness. In effect, this realism, grasped in its authentic signification, could reveal itself to be the *contrary* of a positivism, and could therefore deliver the true meaning of negativity.

Merleau-Ponty reproaches Bergson several times for not having drawn the consequence that imposed themselves from valid premisses: "Bergson was right in his critique of nothingness [*le néant*]. His error is only not saying nor seeing that being [*l'être*] which fills nothingness is not a being [*l'étant*]."[14] Thus, from the claim that Being does not stand out against nothingness, it does not effectively follow that Being is an absolute positivity; what follows is rather that *Being tolerates nothingness within itself.* What justifies the determination of Being as essence is the necessity of resisting nothingness, of "co-appearing" in front of it: the positivity of Being corresponds exactly to the negativity of nothingness from which it frees itself. Inversely, grasped directly and without nothingness interposed, Being no longer requires the positivity that only nothingness imposed, and it can thus include a dimension of negativity. Naturally, the nothingness interior to Being has an entirely different sense from the nothingness against which metaphysics made Being co-appear: the critique of absolute nothingness opens the way for an adequate determination of nothingness as the dimension interior to Being.

Bergson's "non-consequence" is due to the orientation of *Creative Evolution.* The question in this work is to understand why metaphysics turns out to be incapable of thinking duration, and why it falls back on nonbeing. Bergson is thus above all attentive to the fact that the Being which overcomes the menace of nothingness is characterized, like a logical essence, by immutability and eternity, such that the refusal to pass by nothingness will consequently have the recognition of what is neither immutable nor eternal, that is, of what *becomes*. Because the concern is to ground the *reality* of becoming, Bergson emphasizes the dimension of immutability among the classical determinations of Being. Contrary to Merleau-Ponty, he does not thematize the fact that essence resists nothingness in virtue of its *positivity*, or in brief, that immutability and eternity themselves proceed from the nucleus of the classical conception of Being, namely, the plenitude of determination and the absence of negativity. Consequently, and contrary to what Bergson claims, the neutralization of nothingness does not lead to becoming in opposition to an immutable essence, but to a meaning of being that includes the negative by opposition to full positivity. Such is the line of demarcation, both narrow and deep, that separates Merleau-Ponty's thought from Bergson's. The latter tends to accentuate the positivity of becoming, against the classical perspectives that relegate it to nonbeing. Merleau-Ponty on the other hand generalizes the Bergsonian analysis of nothingness, sees a modality of the positive in the immutable, which is like the essence of essence, and draws from this the consequence that the Being that does not have to resist nothingness can accept negativity within itself. This is why Merleau-Ponty will see in the Bergsonian duration the anticipation of an original meaning of being, integrating negativity without knowing it. Nevertheless, there is indeed a Bergsonian positivism in that Bergson tends to displace the positivity of essence to becoming, and thus to substantialize the latter, instead of conferring on Becoming the negativity that essence lacks. Merleau-Ponty's analysis here rejoins G. Lebrun's: "Bergson probably recognizes that true mobility—duration—is self-difference, but it is in order to give it access to the substantial dignity for which Hegel felicits Xeno for having delivered movement. Bergsonism is thus less a critique of metaphysics than a displacement of its topic: Being only has to change content."[15] Bergson attributes to Becoming the privilege that metaphysics grants to essence, thus entering into a sort of contradiction. This explains why Merleau-Ponty could criticize Bergsonism while at the same time sharing his fundamental positions: "The open, in the sense of a *hole*—that is Sartre, that is Bergson, is negativism or ultrapositivism (Bergson)—indiscernible" (*VI*, 196). In effect, to think duration as an entity is inevitably to be given nothingness as that which duration fills in by its substantiality. If it is true that the Bergsonian conception does not move beyond a modification of the "content" of Being, the meaning of which remains intact, then what goes for essence will be valid for duration. There can thus be no doubt that, in Merleau-Ponty's eyes, Bergson does not escape from a certain positivism, but now his positivism is grasped in a different depth than it was at the time of *Phenomenology of Perception*. From this, the Bergsonian characterizations of intuition as contact or fusion with the things: the possibility of coincidence is well ordered by the characterization of that which is as positivity.[16]

Nevertheless, Merleau-Ponty's approach to Being at the time of *The Visible and the Invisible* proceeds entirely from the concern to get at Being without nothingness interposed, and to draw all the consequences from it. There is here a convergence between the phenomenological analysis and the speculative deduction: "against the philosophy of the thing and the philosophy of the idea. Of philosophy of 'something'—something, and not nothing" (*Nature*, 238). Such is the shared line between objectivist ontology and Merleau-Ponty's phenomenological ontology: one thinks Being as thing, that is, as idea (as essence, i.e., as consciousness); the other limits itself to previous Being, which does not come to fill in nothingness, and of which all that one can say is that it is "something" by the fact that it is not nothing. This is what Merleau-Ponty specifies in an unpublished note, the first part of which we have already cited: "this 'not nothing' gives eminent Being only if (Bergson) we think starting from nothing. We must think starting from *not nothing*: from non-hidden Being."[17] To limit oneself to Being without passing by nothingness is to recognize that what is around us is nothing more than the negation of nothing, a negation that somehow retains this nothingness negated in itself, insofar as it does not overcome itself toward the affirmation of a fully positive being. To say that Being is not nothing is to say that there is the "impossibility of the ontological void," that is, a preliminary ground of presence which does not go as far as full Being in which all nothingness would be absent. Being is that which cannot be nothing, but which as tacit presence interiorizes this nothingness, and which in principle it excludes as the abyss from which it surged forth. Paradoxically, even though essential Being deprived of the indetermination of negativity hides by its fullness the abyss of nothingness from which it emerges, the presence of perceived being that rests on nothing other than itself, on the contrary, presents by its distance and its indetermination a nothingness from which it does not emerge. To say that Being does not emerge from nothingness is to understand that it remains at a distance, transcendent, not in the sense of a distancing that could be overcome, but rather as transcendence that makes its being—i.e., that it thus presents itself as a sort of effacement or retreat. Being is fully present only in being present tacitly, visible only insofar as it contains a dimension of invisibility: even though the abstract plenitude of essence is defined by the exclusion of nothingness, the plenitude proper to the perceived requires on the contrary a share of negativity. Such is exactly the Merleau-Pontyan sense of sensible Being: "[T]he sensible appearance of the sensible, the silent persuasion of the sensible is the sole means for Being to manifest itself without becoming positivity, without ceasing to be ambiguous and transcendent" (*VI*, 214). An immediate approach to Being, far from excluding all negativity, thus imposes the recognition of a certain nothingness that no longer designates the other of Being, but is rather its dimension of irreducible transcendence: "true nothingness, nothingness which is true, is Being as distant and as *non-hidden* (that is, also hidden)."[18]

Beyond the abstract alternative of pure Being and absolute nothingness, phenomenal being (which is not nothing and nothing more, and which thus is retained in the absence that it pushes away) is characterized by an originary "mixture" of Being and nothingness, synonymous with its constitutive distance. Perceived being is a being that is not posited, that cannot be the object of a remainderless [*sans reste*] appropriation, and that thus draws back under the gaze. An immediate grasp of Being without nothingness interposed, which respects its true meaning, can thus be attained only at a distance, and excludes coincidence by principle. If intuition signifies a bestowal of Being conforming to its true meaning of being, then it must no longer be opposed to mediation. Such is the essential conclusion at which Merleau-Ponty arrives at the end of the chapter on "Interrogation and Intuition": "[T]he immediate is at the horizon and must be thought as such; it is only in remaining at a distance that it remains itself," so much so that this distance "does not prevent us from knowing it . . . [but] is on the contrary the guarantee for knowing it" (*VI*, 123; 127). The symmetry that Merleau-Ponty organizes between Husserl and Bergson is also understood in this way: a philosophy of intellectual intuition can claim to appropriate Being in the figure of essence only because it retreats into the ground of nothingness. But what prohibits identifying Being and essence, namely, the impossibility of grasping it on the ground of nothingness, is also that which impedes us from thinking experience as factual coincidence, and intuition as fusion. In effect, to begin with Being is to recognize a negativity constitutive of it, which is not different from the distance of the effacement proper to the perceived.

If it is true, however, that Bergson uses the vocabulary of coincidence and of fusion in order to accentuate the necessity of approaching Being without nothingness interposed, then it would be incorrect to conclude from this that he understands the intuition as effective contact, or that this distance interior to Being is foreign to it. Careful above all to ground the reality and duration over against a tradition that ignores them, Bergson tends incontestably to draw from the critique of nothingness the affirmation of a wholly positive Becoming, which would then justify the vocabulary of coincidence. But the conclusions that Merleau-Ponty draws from the critique of metaphysics could not escape Bergson; the revindication of positivity and of fusion "express less what Bergson had to say than his rupture with received doctrine when he began his research" (*Praise*, 13). In reality, and in an altogether consequential manner, even if this consequence is not thematized in the chapter devoted to nothingness in *Creative Evolution*, Bergson rehabilitates nothingness as the ingredient of Being by conferring on it the renewed meaning that Merleau-Ponty will thematize later on. In other words, the theory of intuition as coincidence is the polemic and still only approximate form in which is expressed the discovery of the conditions for a return to the things themselves in Bergson. In any case, such is Merleau-Ponty's conviction, and thus the deepest justification of this confrontation: "[T]he true meaning of Bergsonian philosophy is not so much to eliminate the idea of nothingness as to incorporate it in the idea of Being."[19] If it is true that Bergson begins by installing himself in the positive, then "the progress of his analysis dislodges him from it" (*Themes*, 145). By thus making contact with Being according to the method that he himself established, Bergson rediscovers the negative component that his analysis of nothingness had not allowed him to deduce immediately. And as Merleau-Ponty notes, "[T]o rediscover the dialectic despite himself is maybe a more sure way to take it seriously than is to begin by it, to know of it in advance, the formula or the schema of it, and to apply it everywhere" (*Themes*, 145).

From here, we proceed to the reevaluation of the theory of images in the texts of the 1950s. We would not exaggerate by saying that from the beginning, the theory of images in chapter 1 of *Matter and Memory* represents for Merleau-Ponty the indication of the true sense of perceived being, which phenomenology has to understand as a task. Witness the way in which he presents the signification of the Bergsonian theory of perception: "[T]he visible things around us rest in themselves, and their natural being is so full that it seems to envelop their perceived being, as if our perception of them is formed in them."[20] He expresses this even more carefully in an unpublished note of February 1959: "to show the value of 'images' as expressing the being *von selbst*, the identity of *Seyn* and *Vernehmen*." For Merleau-Ponty, there is thus a perfect coherence between the Bergsonian critique of metaphysics and the determination of the meaning of the being of *what is* in terms of images. The whole problem is to interpret perception correctly, because a contradiction remains between the true ontological status of images (which the critique of metaphysics contributes to clarifying), and the interpretation that Bergson gives of perception in *Matter and Memory*. Can the image, as identification of a being and an appearing, be achieved in a pure perception, where the givenness of the thing is produced directly on the thing, by reflection on the center of indetermination which is the brain? In effect, Merleau-Ponty notes, "the moment my perception is to become pure perception, thing, Being, it is extinguished; the moment when it lights up, already I am no longer the thing" (*VI*, 122). At first blush, Merleau-Ponty's critique seems here to rejoin that of older texts: there is a contradiction between the discovery of images and the attempt to think perception as limitation within an objective Whole, that is, to economize conscious activity, and the divergence inherent to experience. But the accent is different here. Merleau-Ponty at first indicates that, rather than understanding perception as the coincidence of a consciousness and a real being, the image instead reveals an original meaning of the being of the perceived, beyond the distinction of consciousness and the object. Contrary to what emerged in the early texts, it is no longer a matter of denouncing the positivity of the universe of images in the name of a philosophy of consciousness, but rather of making a contradiction appear between the idea of real coincidence present in the theory of pure perception and the meaning of the being of the image. This implies a native *negativity* which is not a divergence susceptible to reduction but rather the proper character of perceived being as being-at-a-distance. Far from defining perception by coincidence, the theory of images shows that there is perception *only* if there is *not* coincidence. This is again more clear concerning pure memory: "and likewise, there is no real coincidence with the being of the past: if pure memory is the former present preserved, and if, by remembering, I truly become again what I was, it becomes impossible to see how it could open me to the dimension of the past. And if, in being inscribed with me every present loses its flesh, if the pure memory into which it is changed is an invisible, then there is indeed a past, but not a coincidence with it" (*VI*, 122). The impossibility of pure memory thus does not refer to a factual impotence to coincide with the past; it signifies rather that there is memory, that is, the givenness of the past as such, only at a distance. The status of the past here delivers the truth of perceived being: the perception of the past implies a divergence, not because we will be separated from the past by an assignable and irreducible distance de jure, but rather because this distance takes part in its being. Such is the authentic sense of the negativity interior to being, out of which arose the critique of nothingness.

However, if Bergson begins by postulating pure perception as perception of the object directly on the object (perception where, according to Merleau-Ponty, the coincidence of the perceiving and the perceived compromises the very dimension of experience), he adds that it is a matter of a perception de jure, corresponding to a pure unthinkable instant, perception that is never realized de facto, since we are in time, and since after all, every duration, however short, can be divided. The always-present dimension of memory in fact unties perception from the perceived object, just as in return the dimension of incarnation distinguishes consciousness from pure memory by inscribing it in the present. And so even if Bergson uses the word *coincidence* concerning perception, he is also led to recognize that there is only *partial* coincidence.[21] The force of Merleau-Ponty's critique is thus entirely different from the texts of the period of *Phenomenology of Perception*: even though he limited himself then to the theory of pure perception and pure memory, which he interpreted as manifestations of a naive realism and thus of a substantial dualism, he now emphasizes the tension between the horizon of a coincidence and the fact of a distance, the very movement that leads Bergson from a de jure coincidence to a de facto divergence. The mode of the articulation of perception and of memory can thus be understood in a manner rigorously *opposed* to how it had appeared in *Phenomenology of Perception*. To say that all perception is memory is to recognize that there is coincidence only at a distance; but to say there is no pure memory, or that mind inscribes itself in matter via its body, is equally to claim that distance envelops the horizon of a coincidence, that it is the givenness of a world. Far from expressing a "coming and going between two levels of the In-itself," the articulation of perception and of memory would instead reveal the originary unity of a distance and a proximity, which the Bergsonian formula names partial coincidence.

Whichever it is, only on the condition of being understood in this way does the Bergsonian theory of perception seem to conform to the ontological status of the image, and in any case, to the critique of metaphysics. To begin with Being is to understand that there is an intuitable reality only in an irreducible distance, that a thing is attained in person only in and by a distancing, or in brief, that there is only a partial coincidence. It is true that Bergson does not go this far since he begins with pure perception, which he says exists "de jure": the reference to the order of the de jure can be understood here as the mark of the persistence of a positivism within a perspective that denounces it, of a tension between the myth of coincidence and the fact of intuition at a distance. For as Merleau-Ponty notes, "[T]he difficulties of coincidence are not only factual difficulties which would leave the principle in tact. . . . If the coincidence is only ever partial, we must not define the truth by total or effective coincidence" (*VI*, 124). In other words, if the de jure of pure perception expresses only a horizon of impossible coincidence, then the de facto of perceptual distance has the force of law. Always—and such is the force of the Bergsonian position—to renounce the horizon of a coincidence would be to accept the irreducible duality of the perceiving and the perceived, and consequently to fall back into the rut of classical philosophy. The reference to pure perception as possible de jure has the merit of valorizing the fact that the distance that characterizes appearing being is not a reducible divergence between a subject and an object, but rather a negativity interior to it, which is synonymous with its essential retreat and thus does not appear to pose an alternative to coincidence. We must understand coincidence not as fusion or contact, but as the index of a non-difference, in the sense of the zero-degree of difference, that is, of an in-division which, situated on this side of duality, cannot be reabsorbed in identity: "[W]hat is a coincidence that is only partial? It is a coincidence always past or always futural, an experience that remembered an impossible past, anticipates an impossible future, that emerges from Being or that will incorporate itself into Being, which is *of it* but is not it, and is therefore not coincidence, a real fusion, as of two positive terms or two elements of an alloy, but an overlaying, as of a hollow and a relief that remain distinct" (*VI*, 12–23). Despite a vocabulary that sometimes remains lagged behind his central intuition, the critique of metaphysics leads Bergson to grasp a negativity at the heart of being, which is the condition of its appearance, or rather, which is the appearance itself *as* partial coincidence, the difference of the identical. To approach Being without nothingness interposed (and thus without deporting it to the side of essence) is thus to bring to light a new sense of negativity: it is no longer pure negation nor the positivity of the positive, but rather is synonymous with the perceptual presence insofar as it contains an essential distance, which is its own distance. Nature in Bergson "is not the perceived fascinating thing of actual perception, but is rather as a horizon from which we are already distant, a primordial and lost indivision, a unity that the contradictions of the developed universe negate and express in their manner" (*Themes*, 146; cf. *Nature*, 58).

When one gets used to thinking Being directly, Bergson says, "then the Absolute is revealed very near to us, and to a certain extent, in us. It is of a psychological essence, and not mathematical or logical. It lives with us. Like us, but in certain aspects infinitely more concentrated and more gathered up in itself, it endures."[22] This rehabilitation of duration out of which the critique of nothingness arose can certainly be interpreted as a simple displacement of the topic of metaphysics, or as the replacement of a logical positivity by a psychological positivity. But we cannot be indifferent to the fact that the psychological is defined as duration, the specificity of which is probably not sufficiently taken into account in this present interpretation. The question is in effect to know either if, in thinking the Absolute as duration, Bergson is content to confer a psychological content to it, which would thus maintain it on the plane of positive being, or if, on the other hand, he discovers within the psychical a dimension of being that exceeds it, thus placing the determination of Being as positivity and of intuition as coincidence into question. For Merleau-Ponty, there can be no doubt that "duration is simply only change, becoming, mobility, it is being in the vital and active sense of the word. Time is not put in place of being, it is understood as being born, and it is now the whole of being which must be approached from the side of time" (*Signs*, 184; 190–91). Bergson's philosophy does not aim at substituting becoming for immutable Being, but rather, through the concept of duration, to qualify the meaning of the being of Being insofar as it escapes positivity. Duration is what assures its continuity only by the incessant development of heterogeneous moments; it remains itself only in always becoming other: it is the Unity of the Same and the Other.[23] A separated Absolute would be cashed out in appearance because it does not maintain itself as such, and accomplishes its unity thanks only to its finite manifestations. It is rather the element wherein is accomplished the identity of the Absolute and the finite. As Merleau-Ponty writes, "[T]his recourse to temporality is another way of explaining that there is no separated absolute" (*Nature*, 48). Bergsonian Being, to which the duration initiates us, is thus not a positive Being, not of a preexistent order from which we would be separated and vis-à-vis which coincidence would be possible de jure. It is itself only by indefinitely mediating the renewal of its finite negations, which are the actualizations of it. It is its own future, always both younger and older than it is. Therefore, the idea of coincidence turns out to be deprived of meaning: to say that the Absolute is in us is not to determine Being as psychological positivity, but on the contrary to recognize that in being ourselves, we are in the Absolute, and that our psychological finitude is alone what can initiate us to an Absolute that is not positive. If duration is indeed the unity of the Absolute and the finite, then the intimacy of my relation to it, far from signifying the closure of a psychological ego, instead makes possible an opening to exteriority. Bergson gives as a principle to philosophy "not an *I think* and its immanent thoughts, but a Being-self whose self-cohesion is also its tearing away from itself" (*Signs*, 184). Duration is what resides indistinctly in us and outside of us, that which we contain only as what contains us: "[I]n one sense, all is interior to us, and in another sense, we are in the Absolute" (*Nature,* 48). Duration is not of a psychological nature rather than ontological; it is the articulation of the psychological on the ontological, or rather, that which makes possible the passage from one to the other. Grasped in its most radical sense, duration allows for thematizing this identity of coincidence and divergence, of being-for-myself and being-at-a-distance which we recognized in the Bergsonian analysis of perception, conferring on it an ontological status.

We have recalled that Bergson defines his own enterprise as an attempt to go seek experience at its source, "or rather on this side of this decisive *turn* where, being inflected in the meaning of our utility, it becomes proper *human* experience." Such is the Bergsonian version of the reduction, which, in a certain way, Merleau-Ponty takes into account: the concern is to come back from this side of construction, of the sedimentation and its deformations deposited by the development of knowing and by the *praxis* that corresponds to it, toward the experience of a pure state. However, the possibility of grasping the true signification of a return to the things themselves depends on the precise comprehension of the status of this turn. Must it be understood in the already metaphorical sense of a rupture separating a before and an after, that is, of a line of demarcation between two circumscribed territories? The properly human experience—dominated by action, and consequently by intelligence and space—would both recover and structure another relation to Being, which, contrary to what the classical transcendental perspective claimed, would itself be accessible only at the price of a sort of torsion of thought on itself. The *this-side* of the turn would then be understood as a positive ground. Bergson's philosophy lends itself in part to this reading, and this justifies Merleau-Ponty's persistent reticence: "Bergson is one of those who seek to find in the experience of man what is at the limit of this experience, whether it be the natural thing or life. He wants 'to seek experience at its source, or rather above that decisive *turn* where, bending itself in the direction of our utility, it becomes properly *human* experience.' But this philosophical and necessary effort is compromised by taking sides with positivism which makes of the pre-human a being with which we coexist" (*Nature*, 58).

Nevertheless, would not the deepest truth of Bergsonism, as Merleau-Ponty emphasizes, consist in the attempt to think *this turn as the very meaning of human experience*? This, in any case, is how Merleau-Ponty understands perceptual life. The turn would not only be an adventure advening on experience, an inflection that would remain exterior to it, but also what characterizes the essential dynamism of it. The proper character of the turn is that it has always already begun—in a way that a positive coincidence with a pre-human is deprived of all meaning—and which however, as a turn, refers to a *that-side*, to something like an origin or an *arche*. To say that there is a turn of human experience, in the sense that experience is not other than the turn itself, is to recognize *both* that it does not manage to recover a positive ground that would precede it, *and* that it refers nevertheless to a more originary dimension—or in short, that experience contains a dimension of transcendence in its heart, which does not rest on a positivity, an invisible hither-side that it both expresses and occults. In effect, to the extent that it has always already begun, the turn is never achieved, so that the origin perdures in what covers it, and whatever denies or negates it is just as much its work or its expression. Rather than being referred to assignable criteria, humanity is consumed with the very movement of covering over a pre-human, a covering-over that would be at the same time an unveiling of it. Because the turn is a never-achieved rupture, advanced and always retained in what it covers over, the distance from the origin would be at the same time the quest for it, its distance-proximity. By confusing itself with the turn, human experience should be understood as the originary unity, both the separating and the unifying, of itself and its other. The pre-human would not be an existence with which it would be possible to coincide, but rather the ground of transcendence from which experience and action are nourished, because "the light would clarify nothing if nothing made a screen for it."[24]

NOTES

1. Henri Bergson, *Matter and Memory*, trans. N. M. Paul and W. S. Palmer (New York: Zone Books, 1988), 184.
2. Theodore Geraets, *Vers une nouvelle philosophie transcendentale* (Dordrecht: Nijhoff, 1971), 6.
3. Merleau-Ponty, "Sartre's *The Imagination*," trans. M. B. Smith in *Merleau-Ponty: Texts and Dialogues*, ed. H. Silverman and J. Barry Jr. (Atlantic Highlands: Humanities Press International, 1992), 113.
4. *Structure*, 164. The passage concerns Politzer's *Critique des fondements de la psychologie* (1928) and *La fin d'une parade philosophique: le bergsonisme* (1929), published under the pseudonym François Arouet.
5. Politzer recognizes this at least once in the *Critique*, 90.

6. Merleau-Ponty, *The Incarnate Subject: Malebranche, Maine de Biran, and Bergson on the Union of Body and Soul*, ed. A. Bjelland and P. Burke, trans. P. Milan (Amherst, NY: 2001), 87. Hereafter the references to this text will be given in the body of the essay as *Union*, followed by the page number.
7. See Frédéric Worms's commentary on this work in "Les Grands Livres de la Philosophie," (PUF, 1997).
8. On this point, see especially the "The Philosopher and His Shadow," in *Signs*.
9. Gérard Granel, Le sens du temps et de la perception chez Husserl (Paris: NRF, 1968), 145–46.
10. Bergson, *Creative Evolution*, trans. A. Mitchell (Boston: University Press of America, 1911 and 1983), 276.
11. Ibid., 298.
12. *VI*, 162. In an unpublished note from January 1960, Merleau-Ponty is even clearer: "As to eminent Being, it always supposes essentialist thought according to which there is something that makes Being arise in the last resort, a necessary ground i.e. essential for the il y a, a nail that pegs and grounds Being as absolutely opposed to nothingness. Being eminent Being, there is at bottom negative ontology, like negative theology: the definition of Being as what overcame or denied nothingness. This *not nothing* gives eminent Being only if (Bergson) we think starting from nothing." Translation mine.
13. Creative Evolution, 298.
14. Unpublished note from February 1959. In another note from the same month, Merleau-Ponty specifies, concerning Bergson, that "he was right to refuse an idea of nothingness, he was wrong only in not seeing that the being which resists the neg-intuition of nothingness is not "positive" being, that it is *Seyn*."
15. G. Lebrun, *La patience du concept* (Paris: NRF, 1972), 240. This echoes another of Merleau-Ponty's unpublished notes: "The rehabilitation of *Werden* in Bergson: it can only be *ergänzend Abstraktion* that tries vainly to correct substantialized being." (February 1959).
16. See for example, *Praise*, 10–15.
17. Unpublished note from January 1960.
18. Unpublished note from October 1959.
19. *Nature*, 66. Cf also *Praise*, 21: "If true philosophy dispels the vertigo and anxiety that come from the idea of nothingness, it is because philosophy interiorizes them, because it incorporates them into being and preserves them in the vibration of the being that makes itself." Translation modified. Wild and Edie translate the last

words "*de l'être qui se fait*" as "of the being that is becoming," which while valid, risks the surreptitious reintroduction of the thought of being opposed to becoming.

20. *VI*, 122. Compare *Signs*, 185; *Nature*, 53–58; and *Praise*, 16–17.
21. Bergson, Matter and Memory, 218–23 passim.
22. Bergson, *Creative Evolution*, 298–99.
23. Bergson, *Matter and Memory*, 197. See also *VI*, 266–67.
24. *Themes*, 84. "La lumière n'éclairerait rien si rien ne lui faisait écran." O'Neill translates this as "light would not illuminate a thing unless there were something to screen it."

5

Community, Society, and History in the Later Merleau-Ponty

MARC RICHIR

INTERSUBJECTIVITY AND INCARNATION

Instead of taking up again the whole question of a doctrine that is only gradually becoming well known, we will approach it in its ultimate version, as glimpsed in some of the "working notes" published by Claude Lefort as an appendix to *The Visible and the Invisible*. We know that it is in the nooks and crannies of Husserl's work that Merleau-Ponty, who probably never stopped meditating on it, patiently and progressively inscribes his own problematic of the "Flesh." Merleau-Ponty owes a lot to Husserl concerning the question we are going to treat here (and many others as well), not so much for the positive content of the doctrines of phenomenology's founder as for the very *terms* with which Husserl first begins phenomenological interrogation. This is particularly true of the problematic of the intersubjectivity of society, and even of History, as we shall see.

In what follows, we must presuppose that the reader is already familiar with the Husserlian doctrine of the apperceptive appresentation of the other [*autrui*] by means of *Einfühlung*, but when necessary we will briefly recall it for the sake of understanding. Let us say right away, in order to initiate the problematic and to eliminate any misunderstandings issuing from its equivocal formulation in the fifth *Cartesian Meditation*, that the appresentation of the other is first the apperception of a *Leib*—a body-of-flesh—by another *Leib*, in which the "life" of the other appears to me without any "reasoning" and without being given itself "in presence," and in such a way that it is *mine*, at least in appearance. There is an *immediate* apprehension in the apperception of the other that "I see *my* life" and not the other's. But I am not a *solus ipse* closed in on itself, but rather an *ipse* phenomenologically open in its life and its time to the other's life and time. The other is also present—*leiblich*—in its flesh, which is already beyond the separation of soul and body; this presence is paradoxical, however, since it is the coherent presence of a certain absence that I immediately sense myself to be. There is thus in this experience a sort of intentional encroachment [*Ineinander*] and a transgression [*Überschreiten*] of two presences—one which is made here and now in me, the other which is made over there in a "now" that is always lagged or out of synch [*déphasé*] with respect to my own. This originary "desynch" of presence in relation to itself is *already language*, according to certain texts published in the *Husserliana* (Bd XIII, XIV, XV). By means of it, I understand the mimicries, gestures, or manifestations of the other's "humors" [*Stimmungen*], without having learned them. In these texts (and not as one wrongly believed in the logic-eidetic purification of the first *Logical Investigation*), we will see the true Husserlian concept of language show up on the surface.[1]

Merleau-Ponty approaches the questions of the other and of intersubjectivity in a working note dated February 1959. He writes:

> [I]n fact what has to be understood is, beyond the "persons," the existentials according to which we comprehend them, and which are sedimented meaning of all our voluntary and involuntary experiences. This unconscious is to be sought not at the bottom of ourselves, behind the back of our 'consciousness' but in front of us, as articulations of our field. It is 'unconscious' by the fact that it is not an object, but it is that through which objects are possible, it is the constellation wherein our future is read. . . . It is between them as the interval of the trees between the trees, or as their common level. It is the *Urgemeinschaftung* of our intentional life, the *Ineinander* of the others in us and of us in them.
>
> It is these existentials that make up the (substitutable) meaning of what we say and of what we understand. They are the armature of that 'invisible world' which, with speech, begins to impregnate all the things we see—as the 'other' space, for the schizophrenic, takes possession of the sensorial and visible space. . . . Not that it ever becomes a visible space in its turn," in the visible there is never anything but ruins of the

> spirit, the world will always resemble the Forum, at least before the gaze of the philosopher, who does not completely inhabit it. (*VI*, 180)

At first, it is clear that Merleau-Ponty situates himself beyond the dualist encounter of self and other, and thus *in* what Husserl named transcendental subjectivity, precisely in order to understand the transcendental nature of it, including the apparently solitary experience that I may have of objects and things. The question is that of the "communitization" [*Urgemeinschaftung*] of our intentional life, of the chiasm [*Ineinander*] of others in us and of us in them—that is, of *how* it is the case that "transcendental subjectivity is transcendental intersubjectivity" (as Husserl's poorly thought out formula puts it). In the same movement, the concern is also for that which results in the "*Weltlichkeit du Geist*," or "worldliness of spirit," by which we understand that the visible (and not simply "seen") world is only ever a field of ruins like the Roman Forum. What Merleau-Ponty seeks to think here is thus what we call the *phenomenological community.*

The key concept of this research is that of the existential. The concept is somewhat paradoxical, because it is imported from a different context in *Being and Time*, wherein for Heidegger it concentrates the cohesion of the structures of existence, that is, the characters or modes of the being of Dasein according to which Dasein is always already referring in its being to that which it questions, and is thus always already *taken by* or *thrown into* that which it questions in projecting itself. The situation is indeed that of transcendental subjectivity as transcendental Intersubjectivity, but the paradox here comes from the fact that the existentials "are the *sedimented* meanings of all our voluntary and involuntary experiences"—since sedimentation is a properly Husserlian concept, falling under the originary passivity of consciousness. Consequently, what appears in Merleau-Ponty as a very rich idea is that the Heideggerian "facticity" of Dasein is understood by means of sedimentation, at least as *historical*, even though in Heidegger the historicity of Dasein could reveal itself properly only as destiny [*Schicksal*] in the opening of resoluteness. Furthermore, by appearing as historical, facticity becomes *communal*, since it is the sedimented deposit in which the meaning of human experience is enclosed (so to speak), just as much in the course of individual experience as in collective experience.

What we must understand, then, is that by its very constitution (which is sedimentation), the existential structure explodes into a multiplicity of existentials, in which the sedimented communal meaning itself explodes into a constellation of sedimented meanings structuring our experience of the world in advance; in this sense, they are transcendental structures. This constellation of an exploded facticity of Dasein—necessarily unconscious since it proceeds from the passivities of consciousness by means of its sedimentations—is also, Merleau-Ponty says, the "articulation of our field," on the inside of which alone can a project or projects have meaning according to the existential structures, that is, where "our future can be read." Merleau-Ponty specifies that this is the "interior armature" of the invisible. These sedimentations are thus of a very strange nature, since they are not the visible (or maybe the all too visible) sedimentations of terms, signs, beings, or entities (as in Husserl), but rather are sedimentations (themselves invisible) of *meaning* and not of signifiers and signifieds. This unconscious thus does not have a positive content; it consists in the plural sedimentations of the plural and indefinitely multiple experiences of meaning. Made up of empty places or voids, "it is like the interval of trees between the trees," and it makes up the depth of experience, "the common level" of trees, which anchors them in what Husserl distinguished (as early as the *Philosophy of Arithmetic*) as the "sensible multiplicities" borrowed from passive synthesis. In this sense, this already properly phenomenological "unconscious" is, for Merleau-Ponty, the transcendental condition of the possibility of the *experience* of objects and things. As if there were, through the communitarian historicity of these sedimentations of a new kind, a communal historicity *hidden* in the very structuration of *passive* syntheses (or of *ontological* modes of the facticities of Dasein)! Let us underline in passing the extraordinary novelty of such a thought in which what Heidegger had begun in *Being and Time* finds its most concrete prolongation.

But that's not all: Merleau-Ponty adds right away that it is somehow in the hollows of these articulations or of these invisible constellations of the invisible that what he calls the (substitutable) meaning for what we say and hear—i.e., speech—resides. Rather than consisting in the temporal unfurling of ready-made significations, speech is the profoundly communal manner of bringing the substitutability of meanings into play between the existential structures and the already sedimented invisibles of meaning, even when I speak or write or think alone. This is nearly impossible to understand, and remains to be thought, but it is what seems to *impregnate* all of the visible. A *mute* and *invisible* form of impregnation, in a sort of *logos endiathetos* which is both a resource for the *logos prophorikhos* and as we might have guessed, also the place of new possible passive (and thus unconscious) sedimentations of *meaning* in another form of the same historicity. A mute and invisible impregnation which also makes the visible world (which is much more than the "seen" world) appear as the ruins of spirit, that is, of *meaning*. But Merleau-Ponty adds a phrase that relaunches this interrogation: this is the case "under the gaze of the philosopher" who "does not live entirely in the visible." From whence comes this philosophical sense for meaning—i.e., the sense for the invisible? What is this invisible that is not merely the intelligible, since it goes so far in its unconscious dimension as to structure what Husserl had taken up as passive syntheses? If passive syntheses fall under what we call the *phenomenological* unconscious more profoundly than under the symbolic unconscious of psychoanalysis, would there then be both an unconscious and a properly phenomenological *historicity*?[2] Would there consequently be an irreducible worldliness, not only of transcendental subjectivity and Intersubjectivity, not only of Dasein and *Mitsein*, but also of *Geist*? In this sense, would there thus be a communal and historical *Weltgeist*, and thus also a *Zeitgeist*?

Such is the extraordinarily fecund difficulty that Merleau-Ponty leads us to think. He writes, still in February 1959, that "Intersubjectivity, the *Urgemein-Stiftung*, is very much beyond lived experience." We must come from this to the apparently most simple experience of the encounter with the other, in order to understand it better. Let us limit ourselves to some citations from the working notes, in the guise of a recall.

> What the other says appears to me to be full of meaning because his lacunae are never where mine are. Perspective multiplicity. (*VI*, 187, May 1959)

> The other, not as a 'consciousness,' but as an inhabitant of a body, and consequently of the world. Where is the other in this body that I see? He is (like the meaning of a sentence), immanent in this body (one cannot detach him from it to pose him apart) and yet, more than the sum of the signs or the significations conveyed by them. He is that of which they are always the partial and non-exhaustive image—and who nonetheless is attested wholly in each of them. *Always in process of an unfinished incarnation*. . . . Beyond the objective body as the sense of the painting is beyond the canvas. (*VI*, 209–210, September 1950; emphasis added)

> Being is this strange encroachment by reason of which my visible, although it is not superposable on that of the other, nonetheless opens upon it, that both open upon the same sensible world. And it is the same encroachment, the same junction

> at a distance, that makes the messages from my organs (the monocular images) reassemble themselves into one sole vertical existence and into one sole world. (*VI*, 216, November 1959)

> The Weltlichkeit of minds is ensured by the roots they push forth, not in the Cartesian space, to be sure, but in the aesthetic world. The aesthetic world is to be described as a space of transcendence, a space of incompossibilities, of explosion, of dehiscence, and not as objective-immanent space. (Ibid.)

> It is necessary to rediscover as the reality of the inter-human world and of history a surface of separation between me and the other which is also the place of our union, the unique Erfullung of his life and my life. It is to this surface of separation and of union that the existentials of my personal history proceed, it is the geometrical locus of the projections and introjections, it is the invisible hinge upon which my life and the life of others turn to rock into one another, the inner framework of intersubjectivity. (*VI*, 234, January 1960)

> The invisible is a hollow in the visible, *a fold in passivity*, not pure production. (*VI*, 235, February 1960; emphasis added)

> The mind quiet as water in the fissure of Being . . . there are only structures of the void. But I simply wish to plant this void in the visible Being, show that it is in the reverse side. (Ibid.)

All these texts—and we would be able to sate ourselves just by following through on these citations—show that the other is for Merleau-Ponty (as for Husserl)[3] the site of the revelation of our *incarnation*, of a *living* incarnation, to the extent that the incarnation is never achieved lest it fall either into an de-anchoring of the flesh with respect to the body-of-flesh [*Leib*] (this de-anchoring tends to be produced in the schematizing and productive imagination [*Einbildungskraft*]), or into a total incorporation of the flesh into a body-of- flesh closed in on itself and consequently turned into a *Körper*, a cadaver. For Merleau-Ponty this incarnation clearly means that in the apperception of the other's body-of-flesh, the other is "appresented" as an *incarnated meaning* of which the visible manifestations (mimicry, gestures, physiognomy) are the indefinitely fluent "signs," which Husserl very significantly related to "clues" or "indices" while specifying that these clues are an integral part of the temporalization of the other *in language*. This meaning itself is, just as the *rapprochement* with the meaning of a painting indicates, an "aesthetic" meaning in the Kantian sense, or a meaning that can be rigorously reflected only *without* a (a priori or empirical) *concept,* since every concept in reality aims at "reifying" the other or at least at identifying the other, and consequently at leading the other back to the Same. Yet this meaning comes to be by the "desynch" and the mutual encroachment of two visibles, which themselves are not superposed on one another to the point of coincidence. It thus comes to be, as invisible, in an originarily intersubjective temporalization in which presence is temporalized as the very divergence that tries to catch up with itself by placing the lacunae of the other in my own. We must understand lacunae here in the sense of the lacunae of the visible (and not the seen)—i.e., in the sense of principally invisible lacunae, *irreducible* to the visible. Just as there is something about the life of the other that will always and forever escape me, so too do I come to understand through the other that there is something of my own life that will always forever escape me, though not in the same way. Intersubjective encroachment is thus not at every intersection of two wholly positive ensembles, but rather at a "junction at a distance," in such a way as to rejoin itself somewhere, in the invisible (the meaning) as *existential.* And this encroachment is already "in me" since for Merleau-Ponty, it makes the "aesthesiological worlds" of my diverse senses regroup in one sole sensible mass, and thus constitutes it as an "aesthetic world." Transcendence, incompatibilities (which transgress the principle of noncontradiction), explosion, dehiscence are thus all generalized, and we know that the traits that characterize what Merleau-Ponty discovers as the flesh are found in this. The flesh is in effect what enigmatically holds all this together as an elementary tissue—or as Levinas says, an "elemental" of an inextricable complexity—a tissue that is supposed to have a "metaphysical structure" for Merleau-Ponty. And he tries to think this tissue, with a "surface of separation" (which is also a surface of juncture) between me and the other, as the tissue around which my life and the lives of others pivot, crossing and weaving into each other in the "lining of intersubjectivity." Even if the image of "geometrical site" is clumsy (here we refer to an unpublished working note), it allows us to understand that the Dasein's existentials (i.e., the invisible constellations of the invisible that allow us to *orient* ourselves with respect to meaning) are anchored in the multiple and "perspectival" crossing, which means that this possibility is *ontological* in the Heideggerian sense (the possibility of something and the world *ek-sisting* in the transitive sense), and furthermore as originarily intersubjective—which was not the case in *Being and Time.*

By the sad necessity of his premature death, it will always be difficult to think rigorously what remains inchoate in Merleau-Ponty. This does not prevent his thought of meaning as incarnate existentials from opening not only onto a new thought of incarnation, but also onto an entirely new conception of meaning and of the intelligible as not always already given in the "universe of significations," or in what he named the universe of "things said." He even goes so far as to risk this proposition in a note already cited from February 1960: "[S]edimentation is the only mode of being for ideality" (*VI*, 235).

First of all, what is this new thought of incarnation in virtue of which what we have called *phenomenological* community is in reality an *incarnated* community? It is entirely contained in the difficult concept of encroachment or the chiasm, of juncture-at-a-distance across the void or the invisible. And correlatively, the invisible is not a reservoir of the visible, but rather its irreducible reserve—not originarily presentable, and even unrepresentable—which pushes philosophical language to its limits. In this regard, we must go a bit farther than Merleau-Ponty himself does in order to understand it, and we must *add* the trait of *absence* to those he assigns to it—i.e., *originary* absence, in that its character as the nonpresentable and the unrepresentable authorize it, given that the notions of presentation and representation lead to thinking it in the first place. This gives a stronger and greater consistency to the notion of flesh. It also allows us to grasp the entire dimension of non-presence, of the absence of the other's life from mine in our encounter, and the manner that this absence is distributed both in the lacunae of the meaning we make *together* and in the holes of absence in presence, which give to meaning the phenomenological horizons of its depth. But this leads us, on the other hand, to distinguish what was still confused in Merleau-Ponty, namely, that which is the *presence* of meaning in its temporalization into presence and the holes of absence in it which also just as originarily *spatialize* it from *within*, by constituting what Merleau-Ponty names the "folds" of passivity (of present time flowing between its presentations and retentions). Finally, along the same line, this allows us to grasp the dimension of the flesh in the imagination, not as "the faculty of representation" (which is a sort of metaphysical abstraction, or today, technology), but rather as the free schematizing power of contact with the given, and in this sense, an "existential," structuring a priori the proof of things and given objects as Merleau-Ponty understands it. If we have a critique of him, as little authorized as this may be given the incomplete status of his work, it would be to say that his conception of the invisible is perhaps too *mas-*

sive, and thus dissolving, as if the visible were only the decoration of a gigantic and inextricable obverse side, and thus despite what he says of it, quasi-positive. This dissolving or excessively "fluidifying" power is furthermore due only to a very equivocal indecision with regard to the distinction (which must nevertheless be made) between presence [*Anwesen*, not *Vorhandenheit*] and absence [*Abwesen*]. This again opens the possibility, already opened by Merleau-Ponty, but which we must explore, of thinking *Wesen* consequently between *Anwesen* and *Abwesen*, rather than as *Sein*, *Seyn*, or Being. This possibility leads us into what we call proto-ontology.

This is not valid without next rebounding on the conception of ideality. Merleau-Ponty's proposition ("Sedimentation is its sole mode of being") appears to us a bit risky. Because it again risks englobing in indifference what we had at first discerned as his strong thought of an existential sedimentation of facticity or of an originary and ontological passivity (which had been the Husserlian thought of sedimentation as the occultation of ideality, behind which there is a but its *blind* signifier). Once again, the concern here is for modes of temporalization: that of ideality is exactly to appear at the *same* time (in the "same" time of spatialization and temporalization) as the *effacement* of its conditions of temporalization, which opens (better than any other meaning temporalizing itself into presence) to its "setting" [*prise*: in the sense that wet concrete "sets"], and to its re-setting in sedimentation, to the reversal of the light that there is in illumination when it temporalizes itself (in what Husserl called originary *Sinnbildung*) back into the obscurity of a signifier (the Husserlian *Gebilde*) in which no horizon of meaning lives, and which thus literally places itself *outside the world*. In other words, there is an irreducible hiatus between the incarnated phenomenological community of meaning and meanings, and the true, blind system of signifiers that we call the symbolic *Gestell*, which unties itself from lived experience, incorporates itself, and thereby disincarnates itself by placing itself outside of the world. And there is correlatively a similarly irreducible hiatus between the ontological passivity folded and structured by the invisible as radical absence (the passivity that we have named the *phenomenological* unconscious) and passivity itself encoded by the mechanical repeatability of blind signifiers (which falls under what we call the symbolic unconscious). If we are to understand better what Merleau-Ponty understands by what we have called the incarnated phenomenological community and ontologico-existential (and historical) passivity, there still remains the task of understanding what he means by "savage mind."

SAVAGE MIND, SOCIETY, AND HISTORY

We find an explication of savage mind in a note from February 1959:

> [L]anguage realizes, by breaking the silence, what the silence wished and did not obtain. Silence continues to envelop language, the silence of the absolute language, of the thinking language. . . . But . . . these developments must . . . issue in a theory of the savage mind, which is the mind of praxis. Like all praxis, language supposes a *selbstverstandlich*, an instituted, which is *Stiftung* preparing and *Endstiftung*, the problem is to grasp what, across the successive and simultaneous community of speaking subjects, wishes, speaks and finally thinks. (*VI*, 176)

In other words, according to Merleau-Ponty's terms in the same note, the concern is to "restore the very presence of a culture," that is, of "this intersubjectivity which is not perspectival but vertical, which is, extended into the past, existential eternity, savage mind [*esprit sauvage*]" (*VI*, 175). According to this vertical view of mind, it is "one sole movement . . . that one coins out in judgements, in memories, but that holds them in one sole cluster as a spontaneous *word* contains a whole becoming, as *a sole grasp* of the hand contains a whole chunk of space" (*VI*, 236). In this *Weltlichkeit*, which we've seen is the flesh or incarnated, the mind is not "insular" but "the milieu where there is *action at a distance* (memory)" (*VI*, 242).

Savage mind is thus the mind of the incarnated phenomenological community. This constitutes both the (living) present of a culture or of the *Lebenswelt*, and the existential immemorial eternity of the community of flesh, by being historical in the sedimentation of the existentials wherein the facticities of Dasein are incarnated. There is thus hidden in it an implicit historicity, which unfolds itself behind the explicit historicity (which we've called symbolic) of events, of the life and death of "civilizations" or rather of cultures. In other words, it is the "verticality" (or rather maybe the "transversality") intrinsic to savage mind that makes their common humanity, and which allows us to recognize human beings rather than animals. And this verticality is well beyond the perspectivalist views, wherein one relativizes the points of view of one culture with respect to another. It is even that which makes all verticality of movements one and the same movement, which one senses is not only temporalizing (opening unto memory, Merleau-Ponty says), but also spatializing and co-extensive with a "transcendental geography," itself to be understood in a horizon of a "transcendental geology."

But why, in the end, is this mind a "savage" or "wild" mind? Why not be content with characterizing it as "transcendental"? Merleau-Ponty's starting point in the cited note from February 1959 is that of language, or rather the praxis of language, as englobing in itself a praxis of silence, from which language first appears. This praxis is what Merleau-Ponty names elsewhere as "praxis of speech" or "operating speech." And here in a striking way, he opposes a first *Stiftung* that goes without saying (which we call a *symbolic institution* of language) to the very movement of speech that "realizes" something of the silence, something of the *mute* apperception or the apprehension of the world, by breaking it. Even if this *Stiftung* or symbolic institution prepares an *Endstiftung* or final institution (which is a new institution), we anticipate that this novelty cannot be already inscribed, unless by contradiction, in the initial *Stiftung*, but rather that it will be the sedimented "result" of a movement of making meaning, an eminently "praxical" movement, because it is adventurous and not predetermined. It is this very movement that constitutes the *savageness* of mind, since in its praxical adventure, it owes to symbolic *Stiftung* only the relative determination of its starting point, but which at first blush escapes it in that it constitutes exactly the *selbstverständigkeit* part of it. What goes without saying in its self-evidential givenness proceeds always from symbolic institution, and it is only what is not obvious that savage mind puts itself in play again. The savageness of mind comes from its heterogeneity, in hiatus with respect to the obviousness of the symbolically instituted. That does not mean that it could not change places and appearances at the wish of the symbolic re-elaboration subtended by it by passing from a *Stiftung* to an *Endstiftung*. If there is consequently a historicity of the savage mind, or something like an intrinsic diachrony, then it is by means of these changes of places and appearances resulting from the intracultural symbolic re-elaborations, without this preventing that it remain *inexhaustible* in a historicity that Merleau-Ponty will call "vertical." It remains to be seen if this historicity is itself intrinsically savage.

Our perplexity increases when we notice that Merleau-Ponty is seeking to think both the synchrony and the diachrony of wanting, speaking, and thinking a community. This is the whole question of a *Weltgeist* which would also be a communal *Zeitgeist*, and which would be *that which* wants, speaks, and thinks, and of that which the discernible wantings, speeches, and thoughts would be like total parts. This is a difficult question, whose Hegelian anchorage we know, and about which we wonder if it is not based on an abstraction, at least at this level. If it is more or less easy (and it is already a great difficulty) to grasp something like a *Weltgeist* through the articulations and symbolic institutions of cultures (and it is at this level of the problem that we would situate Hegel), if there is an incontestable ground of legitimacy for historical periodization—if for example Imperial France is already profoundly different from Revolutionary France—then it is a lot more difficult, if not impossible, to grasp "what" properly "wants, speaks, or thinks" through these different periods without making something like a subject out of the "substance" of savage mind, exactly as Hegel does (though mind is understood in a sense different from Hegel's). In virtue of its savageness, is the savage mind not intrinsically *an-archic* and *a-teleological*? Do we not find here, at the very heart of Merleau-Ponty's thought in the making, a true antinomy, even an irreducible aporia? Can existential eternity, which is, in his words, the immemoriality of the flesh of the spirit, accommodate a savage and intrinsic historicity without contradiction? If there is historicity, is it not increasingly symbolic, or ceaselessly "re-alimented" in its internal drift by the savage movement of the savage mind? And this, in the irreducible inadequation of every *Endstiftung* with respect to every initial *Stiftung*?

It is not the case that this line of Merleau-Ponty's thought is insistently present throughout his working notes. We read in a note entitled "*Wesen* of history": "[T]he being society of a society: that whole that reassembles all the views and all the clear or blind wills at grips within it, that anonymous whole which through them *hinauswollt*, that *Ineinander* which nobody sees, and which is not a group-soul either, neither object nor subject, but their connective tissue, which *west* since there will be a result" (*VI*, 174). But does this whole exist, and in the same way as all the existential sedimentations of the historical facticity of Dasein? And if it makes only *Wesen*—that is, beyond *Sein*, similarly beyond *An-wesen* and *Ab-wesen*, as the invisible chiasm [*Ineinander*] of invisible chiasms, and in this sense like the "connective tissue" of the group—then is it not to "resubstantialize" it and above all to "resubjectivize" it by considering it like a whole that furthermore is declared or announced in collective wanting [*hinauswollt*]? Or again, if Merleau-Ponty aims incontestably at what we called a "phenomenological common sense" as the meaning of the incarnated phenomenological community, and if, as history has shown many times, this meaning is capable of *resisting* or *refusing* this or that symbolic institution of science, this or that social *Stiftung* (supposedly always already recuperated in its *Endstiftung*), then is it capable of wanting, and of wanting something? Do we not find the already old political aporia of the "general will," the phenomenological root of which would be the impossibility of the *sensus communis* to want *something*, because it is simply a-teleological (and an-archic)—or in other words, because if it wanted something, this something could only be *selbstverständlich*, which would no longer allow for understanding in what way history is ceaselessly the place of conflict, and which finally would reduce the community to the plane of an integrally symbolically instituted society in the clarity or explicitness of what is obvious?

All this leads us to think that the whole aimed at by Merleau-Ponty is a *transcendental illusion*, from the phenomenological point of view. In relation to this *apeiron*, the whole can only be a regulative idea, the symbolic horizon of an infinite task—which, in Husserlian terms, is a teleological horizon of meaning without a phenomenological *arche*. Merleau-Ponty owes much more to Husserl than one generally believes, as is particularly clear since the publication in 1974 of the *Nachlass* on intersubjectivity (the essential analyses of which Merleau-Ponty probably did not in fact know) in *Husserliana* XIII–XV. But on the point that concerns us, if Husserl seems often less profound than Merleau-Ponty, he nevertheless appears more rigorous. Husserlian teleology is the means of phenomenologically thinking the *contingency* of the *selbstverständlich* givenness of every symbolic institution.[4] It is in order to appear to misconstrue the originary and irreducible duality (which is architectonic and in no way metaphysical) between the phenomenological and symbolic dimensions of experience that Merleau-Ponty becomes snared in the trap of the transcendental illusion—the price that he continued to pay to Marxism, which we know long haunted him. There is too much materialism, here refined to an extreme and fecund point, of an existential sedimentation of the multiple facticities of Dasein, and not sufficient attention paid to everything that makes up the symbolic dimension of life in society. Finally, in order to take up again the terms of the working note, there is only the symbolic that "gathers" the clear or blind views or wills, and we know thanks to Claude Lefort, that in the social field, the symbolic is always ipso facto political.

Having indicated these reservations, which are not without importance, it remains for us to envisage what Merleau-Ponty tells us in a beautiful working note concerning the problematic of the historicity of savage mind and its geographical or geological inscription. What we approach here concerns not only its temporalization but also its spatialization:

> For history is too immediately bound to individual praxis, to interiority, it hides too much its thickness and its flesh for it not

> to be easy to reintroduce into it the whole philosophy of the person. Whereas geography—or rather: the Earth as *Ur-Arche* brings to light the carnal *Urhistorie* (Husserl, "*Umsturz* . . ."). In fact it is a question of grasping the nexus—neither 'historical' nor 'geographic' of history and transcendental geology, this very time that is space, this very space that is time, which I will have rediscovered by my analysis of the visible and the flesh, the simultaneous *Urstiftung* of time and space which makes there be a historical landscape and a quasi-geographical inscription of history. Fundamental problem: the sedimentation and the reactivation. (*VI*, 258–59, June 1, 1960)

In other words, the depth or thickness of the flesh of history, which alone is supposed to make the internal historicity of savage mind, of the mind in its *Weltlichkeit*, must not be a pretext to reintroduce a philosophy of the person (as if persons alone were proper to the incarnation of history, even though they risk incorporating it, which is not at all the same thing) but on the contrary must be understood as such, starting from Husserl's famous unpublished text on the Earth, under the horizon of the transcendental earth as unmoveable soil of all experience. It is consequently the originary spatialization of carnal *Urhistorie* that is in question, not so much as Husserl explicitly thought it in the unpublished texts on intersubjectivity (e.g., *Hua* XV), but rather as the spatialization of the human group on a territory, which as temporalization/spatialization in a "landscape" can only be a "landscape of the world" and thus a "transcendental landscape." Consequently, the "carnal" or "savage" history can only be a "transcendental geography" by savage (or transcendental) temporalization, and cannot fall under an archeology that itself, in its transcendental dimension, would suppose an *arche*. In this context, the fundamental problem is that of sedimentation and reactivation. But in a sense, it is already no longer Husserlian, since it no longer concerns the sedimentation and reactivation of particular formations of meaning (e.g., logical as in *Experience and Judgement* or as geometrical in "The Origin of Geometry") but rather those by which we have begun, namely, the existential sedimentations constitutive of the facticity of Dasein, which alone are likely to constitute the "landscapes of the world" and be in themselves *invisible* structures of the invisible.

Here we return to the mystery of our staring point, to that kind of second-degree sedimentation that is supposed to constitute the intrinsic historicity of savage mind and which no doubt is both a new thought and a strong thought in Merleau-Ponty, from which we must eliminate the idea of a kind of collective will or mind, in that what it tries to think is much deeper and even more mysterious. As to the problematic that we are outlining concerning the encounter of the savage phenomenological dimension and the symbolic cultural dimension proceeding from symbolic institution and from experience, Merleau-Ponty sketches at the end of the last of his *Themes from the Lectures at the Collège de France (1952–1960)* the following question: "What could be the relation between this tacit symbolism or indivision and the artificial or conventional symbolism, which seems to be privileged, to open us to ideality and to truth?" (*Themes*, 199). The question is posed in the context of an interrogation of the materials of psychoanalysis, which leads him to the "idea of the human body as natural symbolism" (*Themes*, 199). If there is a carnal *Urhistorie* through the existential sedimentations of facticities, then it can be only the *meeting* of this "natural symbolism" that we call phenomenological and a properly so-called symbolism, which is co-extensive with the symbolic institution of culture. And this encounter would itself be sedimented in the fixed and unconscious entanglement of the two—even if we must go farther than Merleau-Ponty's restrained and somewhat abstract conception of a "second" symbolism as "artificial or conventional symbolism." This opened way (and Merleau-Ponty in his *Theme* of 1960 explicitly announces a follow-up to it) is what we have systematically explored in our *Phénoménologie et institution symbolique*, by rigorously distinguishing an always inchoate phenomenological symbolism from a "symbolic" symbolism, itself *instituted in rupture* with the first, in what constitutes the blindness of symbolic unconscious, a machine-like blindness—in *Gestell*—referring to no "artifice" nor any "convention." But as Merleau-Ponty glimpsed, it is indeed by the properly symbolic field of symbolic institution that we seem to open ourselves, if not immediately to ideality, then at least to truth.

It is no doubt because he did not clearly measure for himself all the consequences of his distinction between the "tacit symbolism or indivision" and what we will call a "symbolism of division" (which is no less tacit than a "conventional symbolism") that Merleau-Ponty comes to transpose the Husserlian sedimentation in the first degree to an existential sedimentation of the second degree, in an indistinction of the two that make one incarnated phenomenological community, society and history implode in the other, in a short-circuit of symbolic and *eo ipso* of political institution of society and history. The concern here is for that to which the transcendental illusion bears witness, namely, an *architectonic error* as Kant says, which Merleau-Ponty did not commit in the passage from the *eidos* to savage mind. In this context, what he had audaciously thought as "existential sedimentation" is probably nothing more than the very characteristic "setting" [*prise*] of the phenomenological symbolism of indivision *by* and *in* the "symbolic" symbolism of division, of blind coding and cut-ups. For as Kant might say, they are spontaneously but blindly *determinant*. It thus does not seem to us for the reasons indicated that the Merleau-Pontyan idea of a carnal and originary history of savage mind is completely tenable. Historicity comes rather from what constitutes the concrete tenor of our life and our experience (i.e., from what is inextricably interwoven in its savage, inchoate, undivided, and indeterminate phenomenological dimension) and from its symbolic dimension *giving* us beings, things, their qualities, and their relations of structure as always-already-made. If the motor of historicity is indeed savage mind in its nonadherence to cultivated mind, its *motif* is nevertheless always already taken up by symbolic institution. Existential sedimentation is thus not only to be taken *from* savage mind, as Merleau-Ponty invited us to do, but also from symbolic institution, or at least from the inclination that is the natural tendency of this latter to *autonomize* itself in relation to the phenomenological, to machinize itself in a blind symbolic *Gestell* of every question of meaning—and in this regard there is indeed a sort of kinship between the first-order Husserlian sedimentation and this second-order existential sedimentation. For the rest, it is in virtue of this kinship that something remains profoundly just in the Husserlian conception of history as teleology of meaning: the originary meaning of the *Sinnbildung* is forever on the way to losing itself, exactly because it does not have an *arche*, and it is thereby called upon to be tirelessly taken up again or reactivated in line with a symbolic historicity as symbolic drift taking it from its capture and taken again in what can appear only as the symbolic re-elaboration within the same tradition. It is also true, *mutatis mutandis*, for the second-degree sedimentation—since it is by the phenomenological reopening of the existential, beyond its "setting" [*prise*] in symbolic existentiality that the first-degree sedimentation can be conjured—that the question of the meaning of such a *Sinnbildung* under the horizon of the question of meaning in general can be reactivated. That this latter has been subsumed by Husserl under the name "Reason" is a factual given, if not a factical "setting," which must not be obsessed: if we take philosophers at their word, they would always be wrong, because they would be enclosed in the mechanical inertia of their "system." It is this that after Heidegger made so many others less grand, but also less redoubtable than he. Let us keep on doing this with respect to Merleau-Ponty, and try, as we hope to have done here, to take up his questions as living questions again, situating them there where they situate themselves, without pretending that he speaks like an oracle. The fidelity to the tradition, to the question of its meaning, does not work without the ineluctable infidelities to its ancestors. Such is the very life of mind.

NOTES

1. This is the case of Jacques Derrida's *Speech and Phenomenon*, trans. D. Allison (Evanston: Northwestern University Press, 1973).
2. See our works *Phénoménologie et institution symbolique* (Grenoble: Jérôme Millon, 1988), and *La Crise du sens et la phénoménologie* (Grenoble: Jérôme Millon, 1990).
3. See our study "Le problème de l'incarnation en phénoménologie," in *L'Ame et le corps* (Paris: Plon, 1990), 163–84.
4. See our work, *La Crise du sens et la phénoménologie*, op. cit.

6

TRACEWORK

Experience and Description in the Moral Phenomenology of Merleau-Ponty and Levinas

DAVID MICHAEL KLEINBERG-LEVIN

INTRODUCTION

Are moral values merely our creations, or do they derive their authority from the very nature of things? For more and more people in the technologically advanced countries of the Western world, the grand narratives regarding the ontological, metaphysical origin of morality in an absolute and ultimate ground are no longer convincing. We of today have lost our ancient authorities and must turn elsewhere for our moral sources. Are the phenomenologies of Merleau-Ponty and Levinas motivated by nostalgia for the lost metaphysical ground of the moral law? Are they attempting to retrieve and restore for present moral living an experience of the origin? Are they in search of an intuitively immediate, complete, and self-evident experience of the originary moment? Are their phenomenologies attempts at a hermeneutical revelation of the originary event in which the moral law was first given to, or imposed on, human beings? Such a reading of their projects would be altogether mistaken. But they are engaged in a hermeneutic process of rememoration and retrieval, attempting to approach, without any illusions of intuitive possession, the affective-conative sense of a certain preoriginary appropriation by the moral law, an appropriation that is felt to have claimed our flesh in a time which memory cannot recover, and that, at least for Levinas, brings out the paradox at the very heart of Kant's formulations of the moral law, namely, that it is a universality that commands its own transcendence, its own supercession, for the sake of the absolute priority of the other, an individual whose singularity constitutes a supererogatory responsibility that infinitely exceeds the universal prescription. In question, then, is the tracework of an event or impression by which our bodies would have been wrought in their exposure to the other and bound in a responsibility that takes absolute precedence over egoism and its freedoms. Thus, it is not, for these two philosophers, a question of our *appropriation of* the metaphysical origin, but rather a question of letting ourselves be *appropriated by* the moral claims on our lives that the existence of others make. And yet, beyond our natural capacity for sympathy, beyond the spirit determining the disposition of our flesh, conditions which social practices and institutions can of course either promote or damage, there are no other sources for our moral responsibilities in relation to the other. It is accordingly to the intricate tracework of our flesh that Levinas and Merleau-Ponty turn their attention.

In brief, then, I would like to draw on the phenomenology of Merleau-Ponty, first, to flesh out and make sense of Levinas's claim that there is a preoriginary assignment of moral responsibility; and second, to bring out the significance of Levinas's characterizations of the ego and the self, showing their distinctive roles within a process of moral development that his ethics would seem to require but does not thematize and elaborate.

TRACEWORK

Levinas

As is well known, a principal concept or trope in Levinas's later phenomenology is the trace: the unrepresentable trace, namely, of an unrepresentable alterity. In both *Totality and Infinity* (1961), and later in *Otherwise than Being, or Beyond Essence*, (1974), it is in terms of the human face that Levinas formulates his moral phenomenology.[1] This point is explicitly avowed in "Diachrony and Representation," where he wrote that he had "attempted a 'phenomenology' of sociality starting from the face of the other person."[2]

In *Totality and Infinity*, the face of the other is described as an absolute singularity, infinitely transcendent, beyond essence, beyond being, beyond the positivity of presence: "absence from the world" (*TI*, 74–75). But in the later work, this absence, this radical alterity, is brought into language in the figure of the trace, emphasizing its paradoxical status in withdrawal from the reifications, the violence, of being; emphasizing its peculiar relation to a morally disposed desire which seeks to retrieve for moral life its affective-conative significance. In effect, his phenomenology becomes what I will call a "tracework": an attempt to approach and describe the unapproachable, which seems to withdraw from apprehension the closer and more intensely it is approached (*OB*, 116, 166). But how can there be a phenomenology of that which is indescribable, that which never directly appears, that which never gives itself to immediate intuitive apprehension, that which resists representation? How can anything be said about a trace that can be located neither "in" me nor "in" the other—a trace that operates in the between-us that is otherwise than being? How can we say anything at all about a trace that is supposed to be "less than nothing," when anything we might say would inevitably make it into something present?

My experience of the face of the other as a moral commandment is not that of a presence reducible to the present; it belongs, rather, to a paradoxical temporality: in the face of the other whom we encounter there is revealed the singular event or impression by which the moral law lays claim to us, takes hold of us, commanding responsibility. But what is revealed of this event or impression is nothing but the trace of a trace, a relation to the other irreducible to the present and beyond the serial orders of conventional time. Levinas writes of "the trace of the utterly bygone, the utterly past absent,"[3] "before the present, older than the time of consciousness that is accessible to memory" (*OB*, 93, 106). Describing the face of the neighbor, Levinas says that "he [*sic*] loses his face as a neighbor in narration. The relationship with him is indescribable in the literal sense of the term, unconvertible into a history, irreducible to the simultaneousness of writing, the eternal present of a writing that records or presents results" (*OB*, 166). Levinas wants to argue, moreover, that even *before* the time of my first "actual" encounter with another—in an immemorial time before any order of time we can conventionally calculate, I have somehow already been deeply touched and marked by, and prepared for, the encounter: thus, there is at work, before the encounter, the "trace of a passage" (*OB*, 91) that is also the passage of a trace, the passage of an event belonging to a time I cannot possibly bring into memory, but which nevertheless calls for rememoration. As Levinas notes, "a trace lost in a trace, less than nothing in the trace of an excessive, but always ambiguous trace of itself . . . the face of the neighbor obsesses me with his [*sic*] destitution" (*OB*, 93). Taking into account the logic of supplementarity that Derrida discusses in his critique of Husserl,[4] I would like to suggest that we might think of the trace that is in question here as virtually nothing—*unless we make something of it.* But the significance of this formulation will perhaps become intelligible only later, when it can be thought in terms of a reflexive process of moral development. For now, let us return to Levinas's references to "obsession." This "obsession" is to be recognized as a moral responsibility, a responsibility already inherent in my exposure, my capacity to be responsive to the welfare of the other, and already importuning, claiming and appropriating me, even before I am able to recognize its claim on my existence: "The face of the neighbor signifies for me an unexceptionable responsibility, preceding every free consent, every pact, every contract" (*OB*, 88). The responsibility to which Levinas is referring precedes consent, precedes every pact, every contract. It therefore precedes socialization; but in this precedence, it constitutes the condition of possibility for all socialization.[5] It is as if I were being touched and moved from afar by the categorical force of a moral imperative: a claim on my responsibility for the other coming from "an immemorial past, a past that was never present" (*OB*, 88). But this past is not entirely lost, for, as I shall argue, it haunts the moral sense, which imagines it as preserved in the intricate tracework of the flesh, in the intrigue of an archi-writing.

This is neither mysticism nor metaphor. But without a sufficiently elaborate account of the role of the flesh, the concept of the trace makes no sense. What I think Levinas needs therefore to thematize and explain is the thesis that obligation takes hold of us bodily in a time that is prior—not just as past, but right now, and at each and every moment—to thematizing consciousness, prior to reflective cognition, and therefore prior, not just as past, but right now, and in each and every moment, to the ego's construction of a worldly temporal order. Morality, for Levinas, is not—or not first of all—an obligation mediated, as for Kant, by the formal and procedural universalization of maxims; nor is it grounded in a "good conscience" constructed through processes of socialization. Instead, morality is first of all a *bodily affected and bodily carried* sense of obligation,[6] an imperative sense of responsibility felt at first below the level of ego-logical consciousness, in the responsiveness of an elemental flesh that is anonymous, prepersonal and pre-egological: a bodily responsiveness that, unless severely damaged by the brutality of early life experiences, the I cannot avoid undergoing again—at least to some extent—when face to face with the other.[7] But even *before* beholding the other, the I is already rendered beholden; thus, in the normal case, when the I actually beholds the suffering and destitution of another face to face, there *can be* an "immediate" response. (Although in one sense "immediate," in another sense, of course, this response figures as a repetition mediated by the operation of a preoriginary responsiveness.) But there could also even be, deepening and strengthening this response, a process of rememoration, a certain *anamnesis*, attempting to lift into bodily felt awareness the I's originary sense of beholdenness. Thus, it would be through the reflective retrieval of this originary sense of beholdenness that the universal claims of justice could be brought to bear on the way we as individuals live our lives.

Searching for traces of this originary beholdenness and responsiveness, affecting me and commanding me "unbeknownst to myself, 'slipping into me like a thief'," Levinas speaks of my "pre-logical subjection"[8] to the other and my "involuntary election" by "the Good" (*OB*, 11, 15, 18). Although the recovery of these traces is impossible, what Levinas says here shows that the search is nonetheless not futile, not entirely in vain, since the very effort, the very attempt itself, carries enormous moral merit.

Thus, in spite of the impossibility of thematizing, representing, or narrating the "prehistory" of the traces of the other's claims on me, on my responsibility and obligation, Levinas nevertheless undertakes to *describe* the register of these traces. This provokes numerous questions. What is the status of Levinas's descriptions? How can he avoid the violence of an ontologizing discourse? Are the "traces" that he declares to be registered as an infinite responsibility for the other in the depths of my flesh discoveries of memory or fabulations of the imagination? Is it possible that they are nothing but the wishful projections of certain norms, values, and ideals, cast onto "human nature" in order to give them the force of nature? What kind of "reality" is to be attributed to them? If neither discoveries nor inventions, could they be, ambiguously, paradoxically, and like everything that partakes of the hermeneutical, both and neither? Hermeneutics works with an intricate rhetoric and a "supplementary" logic, a dialectic between languaging and experiencing in which there is an intricate "supplementary" interaction, by no means straightforward, between the implicit and the explicit, the virtual and the actual, the "always already" and the "not yet." A certain "supplementary" work of imagination is always involved, of course; but it is not a matter of mere invention ex nihilo. For the trace weighs on us, importunes and insists, and despite the fact that it belongs to a temporality that precedes the time of memory, it calls on us urgently to remember. Belonging to a temporality not of the present and appealing to us through the auspices of memory, it carries the weight of a past to be remembered—but the past in question is older than every accountable past, and the memory-work we are called upon to enact is in search of that which is immemorial, beyond the reach of memory.

Then are these traces figures of the moral imagination schematizing an ideal of moral relationships in terms of a deep topography of the intersubjective body—a body not just mine, but the other's, a body belonging as much to preceding and future generations as to those living in the present? Could it be said that the traces of the other's claims on me have no reality other than the role they play in my trace-work—the tropological staging of my self-development as a moral subject, provocatively figured as a reflexive turn, or rather return, attempting to retrieve traces of motivation and guidance from the gift of a primordial incarnation, a body imagined as already graced with a moral predisposition? In this case, it is not that traces of the moral inscription are already there, present in the flesh, simply awaiting the time of a reading, but rather that the traces are a tropological production, markings on a fabulous topography of the body, legible, if at all, only in and as the very movement that would make the flesh reveal its moral appropriation, its moral assignment—legible, as it were, only by the heart that seeks them as signposts of encouragement along the stages of its moral journey.[9]

The desire to retrieve traces of our originary moral disposition therefore cannot succeed; but the effort itself and as such nevertheless opens us, precisely in the moment of failure, to that which we never have possessed and never can possess: breaching the ego's defensive walls, it opens and exposes us to the claims, the welfare of the absolutely other.

Merleau-Ponty

Midway through the *Phenomenology of Perception*, readers encounter an important comment on the radically altered self-knowledge toward which it is hoped that phenomenological reflection will have conducted them; there Merleau-Ponty notes that "we have relearned to feel our body; we have found underneath the objective and detached knowledge of the body that other knowledge which we have of it . . . by virtue of the fact that we are our body . . . [and] are in the world through our body" (*PhP*, 206). The self-knowledge toward which Merleau-Ponty's work directs us is not possible without our learning to feel our body, learning to make contact—again—with the body's own felt sense of existence.

Although one can easily overlook it, there is a certain tracework already organizing the construction of the *Phenomenology of Perception*.[10] The figure of the trace—and that of the peculiar work it calls forth—are made explicit for the first time in the *Phenomenology*, in a passage where Merleau-Ponty says that "when I turn toward perception, and pass from direct perception to thinking about that perception, I re-enact it, and find [*je la ré-effectue, je retrouve*] at work in my organs of perception a thought older than myself of which those organs are merely a trace" (*PhP*, 351–52).[11] A few pages later, the figure of the trace is once again invoked; here, however, he gives it some phenomenological specification. As we shall see, the traces for which he is searching are, for him as for Levinas, traces of the other, traces of alterity:

> [I]t is precisely my body which perceives the body of another person, and discovers in that other body a miraculous prolongation of my own intentions, a familiar way of dealing with the world. Henceforth, as the parts of my body together comprise a system, so my body and the body of the other are one whole . . . and the anonymous existence of which my body is the ever-renewed trace henceforth inhabits both bodies simultaneously. (*PhP*, 354)

But is this trace the trace of a merely phantom body? As the "product" of a peculiar "turn" of thought, a peculiar reflexivity, would not this tracework body be, like the tracework that Levinas invokes, a tropological, "supplementary" generation? How can he "know," or claim to know, so much about a dimension of our bodily existence of which we can obtain only a trace? What is the significance for our moral life of this (trace of a) prolongation—what later will be described or represented as an intertwining—of bodily intentionalities? These are questions for which we will at most find oblique and metaphorical answers in Merleau-Ponty's writings. For, as Merleau-Ponty repeatedly insists in reference to Heidegger, "One cannot make a direct ontology": one can approach the metaphysical—this tracework, this originary relation to the other—only by way of an "indirect method" (*VI*, 179). Incapable of achieving intuitive immediacy, incapable of achieving a coincidence between reflection and its object, we confront the limits of our knowledge, our freedom, our egoism (*VI*, 122–23, 127, 147). In this failure, though, there is a blessing in disguise: for rather than appropriating the origin of the moral law, we find ourselves strangely appropriated by it.

Many years later, when Merleau-Ponty was writing the material posthumously assembled under the title *The Visible and the Invisible,* the figure of the trace briefly—but again significantly— recurs: here it is introduced in the context of a phenomenological meditation on vision, on the visible and the invisible, as a question, then, of the "tracework nature" of the flesh, an elemental being "of which my vision is a part, a visibility older than my operations or my acts" (*VI*, 123), a being that is "eventually" to be thought, perhaps—and at this point he allows himself to speculate freely, wildly—*comme dentelles*: as if it were organically differentiated like "laceworks" (*VI*, 270; see also *VI*, 101). This thought of tracework as in search of a lost lacework is already in fact prefigured, first when he writes of the "intentional threads" that run out from my body, from my arms and legs, projecting the trajectories of my motility in a vectorial field and compose a reality of intertwining identities [*entrelacs*] (*PhP*, 130); and it is prefigured again later when he says, continuing the same trope, that "my body is the fabric into which all objects are woven" (*PhP*, 235).[12] These "intentional threads" are the traces of an alterity that is implicated in the formation of my ego-logical body; consequently, it would be reasonable to expect that a reflexive return to retrieve them could significantly alter whatever identity emerged from the ego-logical incorporation.[13]

It is noteworthy, in light of Levinas's phenomenology of the trace, that Merleau-Ponty likewise ascribes to the trace a peculiar temporality: it is "a thought older than myself," "a visibility older than my operations or my acts." Yet what is brought forth by phenomenological reflection in a time much later is a "supplement," substituting for the inaugural moment that cannot be made present, cannot be made accessible, cannot be made to appear. The trace, however, is not merely older in relation to the linear temporality of my life; it is an "origin" before any "origin" to which we may accede, an anarchic *arkhé* that precedes the temporal order as we know it. Since we always inhabit a present that is not totally present to itself, it is the trace of "an original past, a past which has never been present" (*PhP*, 242); but as not yet fulfilled, as still only latent, the *arkhé* can only come *after* the temporal order as we know it, altering the temporal order posited by the ego and laying down the radically other temporality constitutive of the moral self. This is a thought which, in spite of its seeming paradoxicality, Merleau-Ponty certainly could acknowledge as congenial, for he holds that "the body is solidified or generalized existence and existence is a perpetual incarnation" (*PhP*,166). We will return to this point when we consider the methodological problematic of language and description.

But does the peculiar status of the trace mean, then, as Derrida contends, that the language of phenomenology is "inadequate." Perhaps so—but perhaps only if this language is committed to a metaphysics of presence. And it is not at all clear, and not beyond vigorous debate, that phenomenology—Merleau-Ponty's in particular—perpetuates such a commitment.[14] Merleau-Ponty himself points to the uncanniness of the trace—the fact that we can no more retrieve it for an intention-fulfilling presence than we can preserve the shadow when bringing it into the light (*PhP*, 359). And yet, how are we to interpret the task of radical reflection, which in some way, some sense, is unquestionably committed to retrieving or recovering the traces inscribed in the flesh of our bodies by a certain secret archi-writing belonging to a "prepersonal time" beyond consciousness, beyond memory, beyond ego-logical time, time as we know it (*PhP*, 84)?

MERLEAU-PONTY'S RETRIEVAL OF A PREPERSONAL TRACEWORK

In one of the texts published in *The Visible and the Invisible*, Merleau-Ponty reminds us that "we are interrogating our experience precisely in order to know how it opens us to what is not ourselves. This does not exclude the possibility that we find in our experience a movement toward what could not in any event be present to us in the original and whose irremediable absence would thus count among our originating experiences" (*VI*, 159). There is no possibility—Merleau-Ponty insists on this point again and again—of a "coincidence" between prereflective experience and the reflection that seeks it out (*VI*, 122–24, 127, 147). But the process of rememoration, of reflection, is nonetheless essential to our moral development.

Eager to pursue thoughts that Husserl began to articulate only in his late manuscripts, Merleau-Ponty proclaimed "a new conception of intentionality" (*PhP*, 243) and attempted to show the working of "an operative intentionality [*fungierende Intentionalität*] already at work before any positing or any judgment" (*PhP*, 429; cf. also *PhP*, 418). His phenomenology thus undertook the retrieving of this intentionality, a radically "passive" functioning of embodiment ("radically passive" because it is "deeper" than the passivity posited by traditional systems of thought as in opposition to "activity") that occurs without consciousness and apart from volition (*PhP*, xviii). As presented in the Preface, this project might seem to confirm his fidelity to the program of

Husserl's transcendental metaphysics; but the work does not in fact sustain the Husserlian conception of origins. Nor does it proceed to retrieve them, as the passages already quoted sufficiently demonstrate, in the way Husserl thought possible and necessary.

The intentionality that fascinates Merleau-Ponty and to which he wants to draw our attention, constitutes "all the latent knowledge of itself that my body possesses" (*PhP*, 232). There is a "deeper intentionality" at work "beneath the intentionality of representations" (*PhP*, 121), and it is to the explication of this concealed intentionality, a functioning of the body the traces of which phenomenology must somehow retrieve, that Merleau-Ponty turns, thereby transforming the Husserlian inheritance without entirely realizing what he accomplished. It is not until, many years later, he returned to the question of intentionality that he understood the radicality of his appropriation (cf. *VI*, 35, 238–39, and 244) for the elaboration of the world-opening characteristics of an intentionality preceding the subject-object structure). But already in the *Phenomenology,* he will be calling attention to the generously "erotic" character of this "originary intentionality" (*PhP*, 157).

However, it is not just a question of retrieving traces of this primordial intentionality. Merleau-Ponty wants to *describe* in as much concrete detail as possible the intricacies of an originary dimension of our experience of embodiment of which we are for the most part unaware. There is, he claims, an "anonymous life," an "amorphous existence" which "preceded my own history" (*PhP*, 347): that is the deeper experience of embodiment whose traces he sets out to retrieve. Because I am an embodied being, I belong not only to the time of culture and its representative, the ego, but to another time, a time much older, older even than the a priori of metaphysics, that is, to "a time which pursues its own independent course, and which my personal life utilizes but does not entirely overlay. Because I am borne into personal existence by a time which I do not constitute, all my perceptions stand out against a background of nature" (*PhP*, 347). "My personal life," he continues (and one should note, here, the ambiguity in the next word),

> must be the resumption [reprise] of a prepersonal tradition. There is, therefore, another subject beneath me, for whom the world exists before I am here, and who marks out my place in it. This captive or natural spirit is my body, not that momentary body which is the instrument of my personal choices and which fastens upon this or that world, but the system of anonymous "functions" which draw every particular focus into a general project. (*PhP*, 254)

There is, preceding the personal, "beneath the personal" (as he explains it, using a certain metaphorics), a prepersonal dimension and stage of bodily existence, an anonymous and generalized existence (*PhP*, 84, 330–31, 352–53), a bodily way of being in the world that is not yet structured according to the conditions of subject and object. This primordial level, global, syncretic, bodily felt (*PhP*, 215, 227), is, he says,

> on the horizon of all our perceptions, but it is a horizon [origin] which cannot in principle ever be reached and thematized in our express perception. Each of the levels in which we successively live makes its appearance when we cast anchor in some "setting" which is offered us. This setting itself is spatially particularized only for a previously given level. Thus each of the whole succession of our experiences, including the first, passes on an already acquired [level of] spatiality. (*PhP*, 253)

The same may be said, mutatis mutandis, for the stages and "strata" of embodiment constituted by the prepersonal and personal forms of experience. According to Merleau-Ponty, "the stages passed through are not simply passed; they have called for or required the present stages. . . . The past stages continue therefore to be in the present stages—which also means that they are retroactively modified by them" (*VI*, 90). Notice how, in this passage, the stages become strata, levels, or dimensions. What is "earlier" is also described as "underneath," because it is an experience that has been suppressed or forgotten, silently sublated, but not abolished, and can later, to some extent, be retrieved—in and as a bodily felt sense of the moral claims of the other. To remind us of this point, I suggest that we think in terms of both stages and dimensions: considered structurally and synchronically, it is a matter of dimensions; considered dynamically and diachronically, however, it is a matter of stages or faces. Every stage or face of moral self-development therefore constitutes a vital dimension of embodiment. This passage, written late in his lifetime, deserves to be treated as a point of the utmost importance—and we shall accordingly, in the context of our present reflections, do just this, proposing a story that continues and elaborates the one that I take Merleau-Ponty to have begun. In this story, then, the child's prepersonal experience, never fully present in the presence of awareness, is, however, soon sublated, *aufgehoben*, in the formation of a personal embodiment. In other words, this "prepersonal existence" (*PhP*, 330) is virtually lost to memory, buried in a past that was never present, never possessed. As the elemental body of the child is increasingly subject to socialization and the civilizing forces of culture, it gradually becomes an ego-body, a body ruled by ego-logical processes. But the possibility of attempting to retrieve traces of this earlier, prepersonal sense of embodiment nevertheless persists: at least a trace of this sense can, according to Merleau-Ponty, be realized, brought to consciousness, at any moment. Thus: "Rather than being a genuine history, perception ratifies and renews in us a 'prehistory'" (*PhP*, 240).

In "Reflection and Interrogation" (*VI*, 2), Merleau-Ponty calls this prepersonal level of embodiment our "natal bond" with the world. Thus, in perception—vision, for instance—we always enter into a certain prepersonal engagement with the world, "a kind of primordial contract" (*PhP*, 208, 216) that is prior to the Levinasian "social contract," an initially "sympathetic relation" (*PhP*, 214), whatever trials and misfortunes our subsequent life-experience may heap upon us. There is in the gaze, he writes, a "perceptual genius underlying the thinking subject which can give to things the precise reply that they are awaiting in order to exist" (*PhP*, 264). A prepersonal "Eros or Libido" is at the origin of perception, constituting an "erotic 'comprehension' not of the order of [conceptual] understanding" (*PhP*, 157). At the prepersonal level, "every perception is a communication or communion" (*PhP*, 320; cf. also *PhP*, 212). As he says in "Interrogation and Dialectic" (*VI*, 76), "things attract my look, my gaze caresses things, it espouses their contours and their reliefs; between it and them we catch sight of a complicity" (cf. also *PhP*, 209, 227).

Such perception is "a communication with the world more ancient than thought," prior to the structure of subject and object, and therefore to a certain extent "impenetrable to reflection" (*PhP*, 254). But the inherent impenetrability and irretrievability of the prepersonal dimension of perception does not entirely account for the neglect of this experience:

> The fact that this may not have been realized earlier [by philosophers] is explained by the fact that any coming to awareness of the perceptual world was hampered by the prejudices arising from objective thinking. The function of the latter is to reduce all phenomena which bear witness to the union of subject and world, putting in their place the clear idea of the object as in itself and of the subject as pure consciousness. It thereby severs the links which unite the thing and the embodied subject, leaving only sensible qualities to make up our world. (*PhP*, 320)

This union of subject and world takes place not only in the prepersonal dimension of our perception; it also takes place in our gestures. Therefore, "we shall have to rediscover [*redécouvrir*], beneath the objective idea of movement, a pre-objective experience from which it borrows its significance, and in which movement, still linked to the person perceiving it, is a variation of the subject's hold on his world" (*PhP*, 267).

Moreover, "communication or comprehension of gestures comes about through the reciprocity of my intentions and the gestures of others, of my gestures and intention discernible in the conduct of other people. It is as if the other person's intention inhabited my body and mine his" (*PhP*, 185). This passage shows, I believe, that the later concept of a chiasmic intertwining, an *entrelacs*, was already prefigured in the "embodiment" articulated in the *Phenomenology*. And what the passage asserts is that, prior to reflection, to knowledge and the possibility of skepticism, there is between myself and the other a prepersonal (experience of our) interconnectedness, an existence in alienation, hostage—as Levinas says—to the other. However, in the context of his early work, the significance of this experience for our moral life is not sufficiently registered. In this work, the phenomenological hermeneutics that discloses the prepersonal primarily serves to deconstruct the metaphysical constructions of "objective thought." It is only later that this experience is articulated in a way that contributes to what I call a moral phenomenology.

In the *Phenomenology*, what consumes Merleau-Ponty is the daunting task—already by itself requiring the most extreme exertion—of breaking the spell of the "projections" of metaphysics and attempting to articulate what the subject-object structure conceals and would consign to a certain oblivion, were it not for the possibility of an "involuntary memory" or a difficult act of "radical reflection":

> Radical reflection is what takes hold of me as I am in the act of forming and formulating the ideas of subject and object, and brings to light the source of these two ideas. . . . We must retrieve [*retrouver*], as anterior to the ideas of subject and object, the fact of my subjectivity and the nascent object, that primordial layer at which both things and ideas come into being. (*PhP*, 219)

Consequential though this is for epistemology and metaphysics, what concerns us here are the implications for moral phenomenology. What would be the significance for moral phenomenology "if," as he supposes, "I find [*trouve*] in myself, through reflection, along with the perceiving subject, a pre-personal subject" (*PhP*, 352)? Would this redemption of prepersonal subjectivity, of an embodiment bearing the traces of the other that were involved in its very emergence as a subject, remind us of our shared, common humanity? In "The Philosopher and His Shadow," Merleau-Ponty asserts, still using the Husserlian language of constitution but making with it a point that Husserl would never have made, that "[t]he constitution of others does not come after that of the body; others and my body are born together from an original ecstasy" (*Signs*, 174). It is in the traces of this originary "ecstasy" that the traces of a normative alterity are to be retrieved.

Thus, I want to argue here that what is to be retrieved for moral life, insofar as this be possible, are traces of an originary intercorporeality, because the ecstatic intercorporeality that is functioning in the prepersonal stage and dimension of our embodiment is already a form of communion, already a form of communication with the other. This gives a second, much deeper significance to Merleau-Ponty's assertion, that even "refusal to communicate is still a form of communication" (*PhP*, 361).

When, years later, Merleau-Ponty resumes his reflections on the body, he is equipped with some provocative new conceptual configurations, new figures of thought. Now what his thought wants to elicit is the primordial dimension of what we might quite appropriately call "moral experience": the structure of intersubjectivity—the subject's encounter with another subject. Penetrating the secrets of our being flesh, our "*être charnel, comme être des profondeurs*" (*VI*, 136), he brings to light an "intercorporeal being" for which our flesh is the elemental medium (*VI*, 143, 139–47). Attempting to articulate further the nature of this intercorporeality (which had in fact already been adumbrated in the *Phenomenology*, but without the later emphasis that carries it forward into the proximity of a moral phenomenology), he suggests that the self and its other belong to and participate in an intertwining [*entrelacs*] of shared flesh, such that "there is here no problem of the *alter ego* because it is not I who sees, not *he* who sees, because an anonymous visibility inhabits both of us, a vision in general" (*VI*, 142). And there are "motor echoes" that follow the gestures we make in the presence of others—echoes "by which we pass into one another" (*VI*, 144). A related point appears in "The Indirect Language," another late text, where he observes that "it is characteristic of cultural gestures to awaken in all others at least an echo, if not a consonance" (*PW*, 132).

For the most sustained reflection on intercorporeality, wherein he begins explicitly to bring out the moral implications of his phenomenological tracework, we must turn to "The Child's Relations with Others,"[15] wherein what still concerns him is the possibility of a compelling phenomenological answer to solipsism, to skepticism about the existence of other people. The term *prepersonal* does not figure in this text—it seems, indeed, that after the *Phenomenology*, Merleau-Ponty no longer made use of this term; but the absence of the term does not mean that the experience to which it referred is no longer at stake. We know already that in his later thinking, he had other ways of referring to that same dimension of our embodied experience.

In "The Child's Relations with Others," Merleau-Ponty carries forward Husserl's account of intersubjective intentionality, but without retaining his originary transcendental egology, arguing that the child is from the very beginning oriented toward others by a sociable predisposition. The child enters the world already inhabiting an "anonymous collectivity, an undifferentiated group life" and an "initial community" (*Pri*, 119). Touched and moved by others according to a "syncretic sociability" (*Pri*, 135), the child is already responsive to others in a way that shows (to others) that she already, at the deepest level of bodily feeling, and thus prior to thematic consciousness, is enjoined by a rudimentary sense of her shared kinship with the others—a sense that of course can be and needs to be appropriately solicited and developed further. From the very beginning of life, the infant—as he argues, referring, for example, to the "contagion of cries" in the nursery—is engaged by an "initial form of sympathy": a *passively enacted* sympathy with others that comes, at this stage of psychosocial development, from the absence of a self, a boundaried identity, a certain fusion and confusion in relation to others, and that, while entirely different from the "genuine sympathy" (*Pri*, 120) of the mature adult, which is at least volitional and deliberate, if not also motivated by reflectively constituted moral principles, nevertheless provides something—call it an initial predisposition—upon which the mature form may eventually be constructed, provided that all the necessary conditions are sufficiently favorable. In other words, I am arguing that Merleau-Ponty's recognition of this "initial form" of sympathy implies that there is a stage and dimension of our embodied life *prior* to the mirror-stage of narcissism: a stage of passivity, asymmetry, heteronomy, alterity, and being-for-the-other that correlates with the moment of passivity, asymmetry, and heteronomy in the phenomenology of Levinas. Thus, the assumption of an irreconcilable difference between the phenomenologies of Merleau-Ponty and Levinas, according to which the former articulates only symmetry and reciprocity, whereas the latter articulates the more radical asymmetry of alterity, overlooks the fact that there is, in Merleau-Ponty's phenomenology as in Levinas's, a radical asymmetry, heteronomy, and alterity preceding the formation of a personal ego—a stage of intertwining and reversibility that precedes both the mirror-stage of narcissism and also, of course, the symmetry and reciprocity constitutive of the sense of justice carried by the mature, critically reflective moral individual.

Implicitly, Merleau-Ponty sets this phenomenology into a dialectic of developmental sublations, such that the mature adult still in some way dwells within, and is capable of retrieving, or at least attempting to retrieve, if only in the figure of traces, the attunement of that early childhood "precommunication" wherein, as he says, "the other's intentions somehow play *across* my body while my intentions play across his" (*Pri*, 119). Even the adult can therefore say—if appropriately self-reflective: "I live in the facial expressions of the other as I feel him living in mine" (*Pri*, 146). Here we see how a hermeneutical phenomenology can contribute to moral education and moral self-development, bringing out a proto-moral disposition of the flesh—what, in "The Intertwining—The Chiasm," he will call "an ideality not alien to the flesh" (*VI*, 152). It is a question of approaching an affective-conative sense given unbeknownst to the body, carried in a tracework of the flesh: a sense so deep and recessive, so elemental and autochthonous, that it cannot even be said to be mine, and every attempt to grasp and possess it only finds it receding, ever more inacessible in its origin. This "sense" is radically different from the "moral sense" conceptualized, for example, in the moral psychology of Hume and the philosophical anthropology of the Enlightenment philosophers. But I cannot argue this point here.

In "The Concept of Nature," Merleau-Ponty extends the phenomenological articulation of intercorporeality even further, virtually drawing it into the realm of the political, evoking and invoking "an ideal community of embodied subjects, of an intercorporeality" (*Themes*, 82). In the light of this thought, one might well project, therefore, a certain moral-political imaginary grounded in—or say born of—the reversibility and reciprocity of a shared flesh, the redeemed experience of intercorporeality and the intertwining it involves.

But the accounts that Merleau-Ponty gives in these texts are not without their perplexities. Let me briefly indicate, here, some of the matters that call for further thought. (1) Is there a contradiction between, on the one hand, the claim regarding the child's intersubjective and possibly protomoral predisposition (e.g., initial sociability, primordial sympathy), and on the other hand, the claim that "the experience of the other is necessarily an alienating one, in the sense that it tears me away from my lone self and creates instead a mixture of myself and the other"? If the child's encounters with others are from the very beginning manifestations of an inherent but originally latent sociability, why does Merleau-Ponty follow Husserl, Sartre, and Lacan, holding that "my alienation of the other and his alienation of me" (*Pri*, 118) is what "makes possible the perception of others" and describing the I's original experience of social encounters in terms of "alienation," "transgression," and "encroachment" (*Pri*, 154)? How are these two accounts to be reconciled? Analogous questions must be broached with regard to Levinas's terms for the experiencing of the other: "trauma," "wound," "obsession," "persecution," "hostage," "subjection," "subordination." In the following section, I will attempt to show that Levinas's terms suggest a way to understand how the originary sociability that Merleau-Ponty's phenomenology recovers can be described as an "alienation," a moment in which one is passively subject to the other's "encroachment" and "transgression."

(2) But is there not some problem with the phenomenology of intercorporeality as it is elaborated in "The Intertwining—The Chiasm" and the working notes? How are we to understand the assertion (again made after a reading of Lacan) that in the reversibilities of the flesh is effected a "mirror phenomenon" (*VI*, 255) and that it therefore constitutes a "fundamental narcissism" (*VI*, 139)? How fundamental is this narcissism? And how persistent is it as a structuring of the self? Is there not also the inevitability of a double-crossing of narcissism precisely in this chiasmic reversibility of intersubjective positions? On the one hand, Merleau-Ponty contends that the visual relationship between myself and an other is subject to the fate, the condition, of a chiasmic intertwining of flesh, radically reversing our positions and deconstructing any narcissistic ego-formation, while on the other hand he describes this reversal as the turning-back distinctive of the stage of narcissism through which the child must pass. Why does he not see that although the reversibilities of the mirroring stage do induce a narcissism, they ultimately effect a powerful double-crossing of this tendency? Indeed, one might even imagine that this mirroring by the other could effect the most extreme antithesis: an extremely frightening alienation from oneself, a terrifying transfer of one's identity to the other. Reflecting on a hand feeling itself touching itself when touching the hand of another, and on the mirroring whereby the gaze of the other is said to reflect and return my gaze to and upon myself, he says that

> there is vision, touch, when a certain visible, a certain tangible, turns back upon the whole of the visible, the whole of the tangible, of which it is a part, or when suddenly it finds itself *surrounded by* them, or when, between it and them, and through

> their commerce, is formed a Visibility, a Tangible in itself, which belong properly neither to the body as fact nor to the world as fact—as upon two mirrors facing one another . . .

"Thus," he says,

> since the seer is caught up in what he sees it is still himself he sees: there is a *fundamental narcissism* of all vision [and all touching]. And thus, for the same reason, the vision he exercises, he also undergoes from the things, such that, as many painters have said, I feel myself looked at by the things, my activity is equally passivity—which is the second and more profound sense of the narcissism: not to see the outside, as the others see it, . . . but especially to be seen by the outside, to exist within it, to emigrate into it, to be seduced, captivated, alienated by the phantom, so that the seer and the visible reciprocate one another and *we no longer know who sees and which is seen*. (*VI*, 139 and 141; italics mine)

This point about the deconstruction of ego-logical boundaries at the prepersonal level of our intercorporeal intertwining is repeated later, this time in reference to communication: "One no longer knows who speaks," he says, "and who listens" (*VI*, 264–65). If reversibility "defines the flesh" (*VI*, 144), why would it not ultimately deconstruct the narcissistic privileging of the ego-position? If I see myself reflected in your eyes, would I not also see myself responding to you—to you in a way that recognizes you both as an absolutely irreducible other and as an other very much, in some morally crucial respects, like myself? And in seeing my response to you reflected back to me from you, would I not also, therefore, be indirectly seeing you *in myself*? "To touch," he says, "is to touch oneself" (see *VI*, 254–56). But just as surely this proprioceptive phenomenon does not prevent me from actually touching you and sensing your very being—how you are at this very moment: having vigorously repudiated theories of vision that posit a sense datum and then conclude that the sense datum eclipses my sighting of the object, he would not wish to maintain that my kinesthetic sensations of being myself touched while shaking your hand somehow interfere with the alterity of the contact.

Merleau-Ponty himself throws into question the priority and persistence of the narcissistic moment precisely in those numerous passages—including the one just cited—where he interprets the reversibility of the chiasmic intertwining more radically, deploying the most provocative tropes—a reference, for example, to *tourbillons ouverts*, opening vortices—to register its destabilization of the boundaries constitutive of identity and its deconstruction of the egocentric position. When he declares that there is a point where, "by a sort of *chiasm*, we become the others and we become world" (*VI*, 160), is this the deluded omnipotence of an arrogant narcissism? Or is it an expression of moral self-overcoming or transcendence—i.e., of humility, recognition, sympathy, and solicitude? Could it even be, perhaps, the thematization of an originary substitution—the moment of my moral subjection to the other, none other than the moment that Levinas wants to evoke? Perhaps in a narrative of moral development, these would represent phenomenological thematizations of different stages.

Could a developmental dialectic such as Merleau-Ponty formulates in *The Visible and the Invisible* reconcile the narcissism of mirroring, of a certain kind of reflection, with the intertwinings and sympathies of subjectivities that take place at the stage or level of prepersonal bodily experience by showing how they are related according to a logic of developmental stages (see *VI*, 90)? In articulating a moment of "initial sympathy" in the infant's life, Merleau-Ponty is implicitly recognizing that, preceding the narcissistic stage, there is a stage of passive alienation, a stage of heteronomic subjection to the other. Could the mimetic reversibility constitutive of a primitive sympathy be associated with the earliest, prepersonal, pre-egological phase of development, while the reflexive reversibility of the mirror-stage, which encourages a certain narcissism (in touching you I touch myself, in seeing you I see myself), would be associated with the early formative stages of the personal ego? The "radical reflection" that Merleau-Ponty practices, a phenomenology that attempts to recuperate our prepersonal experience, would then come on the stage *after* the ego has formed, representing the maturity of an ego that is motivated to strive for moral perfection by attempting, as a "practice of the self," to strengthen its moral character and retrieve for present living something of (what I will call) the mimetic "confluence of identities" peculiar to the prepersonal?

An elaboration of the logic of the developmental dialectic suggested by these would explain Merleau-Ponty's use of terms such as "alienation," "transgression," and "encroachment" to describe my experience of intertwining in relationship to the other (*Pri*, 118, 136). What these terms accurately describe is the way that the ego-logical subject experiences the other: they tell the phenomenological truth about the ego's experience of intertwining and intercorporeality. But this is not the whole truth, since the ego is capable of a higher, more mature existence—and indeed is *called upon* by conscience to overcome itself, to transform itself into a moral self. For such a moral self, however, the experience to which these terms refer would bear a totally different meaning. Crucial for the possibility of such a transformation is the ego's deliberate attempt to retrieve through radical reflection what the memory-voice of conscience calls the remaining traces of the prepersonal relationship with others, constructing for itself the normative ideality of a representation, a simulacrum, of the primordial sympathy and community it imagines itself to remember enjoying once upon a time. Thus, "alienation" and "transgression" *also* refer to the infant's experience of the other in a stage of moral development preceding the formation of an ego—a stage in which the proto-moral self would have submitted, passively and asymmetrically, without volition, to a sympathetic, heteronomic mimesis in relation to the other.

In representing the character of intercorporeality, Merleau-Ponty speaks of reversibility and of reciprocity, suggesting an equality or symmetry of substitution. And in representing the character of the prepersonal, predominant in the child but still always functioning "beneath" the subsequently instituted ego, he will speak of a stage and dimension of experience in which the boundaries that constitute my sense of myself in relation to the other are almost fluid—certainly weaker, looser, more permeable, less determinate, and more open than they are when the culturally constructed ego has established its relatively fixed identity and is allowed to rule unchallenged. But in the light of Levinas's work, we must understand this stage and dimension in terms of the most extreme subjection to the other: reversibility not as symmetry, not as reciprocity, not as equality, but as unilateral substitution, substitution in the sense of my responsibility for and my assumption of the suffering that falls on the other. For the time being, it may suffice to say, briefly, that, if we set the their seemingly divergent phenomenologies within a four-stage process of moral development, we may see that, for both, there is (stage 1) a certain asymmetry and heteronomy in the originary condition, followed by (stage 2) a different asymmetry and heteronomy in the ego-logical stage, and (stage 3) autonomy, symmetry, and reciprocity at a stage of moral development beyond the egoism. This will be the stage required by social justice, by the presence of the "third party." But, for Levinas, there must also be a *fourth stage* of moral development: one where the self would voluntarily become selfless, choosing anonymity in service to others, once again subject to an asymmetrical, heteronomical responsibility.

(3) We must carry forward the phenomenology Merleau-Ponty began, articulating our experience of embodiment in such a way that the nature of the prepersonal, the corporeal intertwining of subjectivi-

ties and the reversibilities set in motion through the element of the flesh, can be articulated in relation to the ideals of moral-political life, ideals such as mutual recognition and respect, equality, reciprocity, autonomy, and justice. In "The Intertwining—The Chiasm," Merleau-Ponty states that "[w]e will have to recognize an ideality that is not alien to the flesh, that gives it its axes, its depth, its dimensions" (*VI*, 152). But he does not attempt to investigate the moral-political significance of his hermeneutic explication of the nature of the flesh. How are the asymmetrical reversibilities that are set in motion through the intertwinings of the flesh in which I and the other participate eventually (to be) connected to the symmetrical reversibilities necessary for the possibility of justice? How do the intertwinings of our intercorporeality set the stage—or how could they—for the possibility of mutual recognition and respect? How could this phenomenology assist moral education in recognizing and realizing the latent normative "ideality" already inscribed—as if it were a gift, as if by benevolent design—in the tenderness and vulnerability of the flesh? How could the *techné* of moral education work with and "build" on this potential, this preliminary stage of development already set by the graceful if ultimately contingent order of nature? If there is a "proto-moral" predisposition already ordering the nature of the body, then the task of moral education, its "civilizing" work, will not need to be impositional, forcing on the body an order that is entirely alien; it can afford to work hermeneutically, bringing forth and developing a potential intimated by the traces. The phenomenological retrieval of a proto-moral disposition of the flesh is therefore a project of the utmost significance.

LEVINAS'S PHENOMENOLOGY OF RESPONSE AND RESPONSIBILITY

Whereas Merleau-Ponty continued working with the concept of intentionality, but called attention to its engagement in the prepersonal dimension of embodiment, thereby making explicit a more primordial—and differently functioning—mode of intentionality than anything recognized by Husserl, Levinas rejected intentionality and attempted to practice phenomenology without it. For him, the concept of intentionality inevitably subverts the moral work of phenomenology, because it requires—so he thinks—an adequation, correspondence, or correlational equivalence between a subject and its object (where, in the cases that concern him, the "object" would be another subject) that can only deny the absolute transcendence or infinite height of the other. Intentionality is an appropriate concept for the task of "disclosure" or "representation," where it is a question of our objective knowledge in regard to things such as houses, trees, and musical instruments, and where to "disclose a thing is," as he puts it, "to clarify it by forms: to find for it a place in the totality" (*TI*, 74). But it becomes an instrument of violence when used to articulate the phenomenology of the intersubjective, which absolutely requires of us the moral recognition of the humanity of the other, i.e., a recognition of the radical alterity of the other.

To avoid such violence, we must recognize that "the welcoming of the face and the work of justice—which condition the very birth of truth itself—are not interpretable in terms of disclosure" (*TI*, 28). Here the question is not one of "disclosure," but rather of "revelation": a phenomenology that lets the other, that enables the other, to be, beyond identity, beyond essence, beyond categorization, beyond being (*TI*, 46; 65–66). In this regard, Levinas argues that "truth, which should reconcile persons, here exists anonymously. Universality presents itself as impersonal, and this is another inhumanity" (*TI*, 46). Thus, although the justice of the moral law makes a universal claim on each and every one, what it commands is paradoxically its own transcendence, the absolute ethical priority and exceptionality of the singular individual.

The phenomenology of moral experience must not only be descriptively truthful, but also must itself be a morally responsible, morally respectful mode of comportment, causing no injury to the other, and serving the moral character of the intersubjective relations it describes. Thus, he holds that "intentionality, where thought remains an adequation with the object, does not define consciousness at its most fundamental level" (*TI*, 27). Intentionality can only constitute a superficial intersubjectivity; the moral relation requires a deeper, higher register: the other's gaze, he claims, "must come to me from a dimension of the ideal," and this means that I must learn to "catch sight of the dimension of the height and the ideal in the gaze of him [*sic*] to whom justice is due."[16]

Like Merleau-Ponty, Levinas is in search of a stage and dimension of our experience that is more "fundamental," indeed more primordial, than the level of ordinary, conventional experience, namely, the thematic, ego-logical level he calls "consciousness." The imagined topography of this "new dimension" is perhaps most explicitly articulated in *Totality and Infinity*, where he says that it "opens forth from the human face" (*TI*, 78) and "opens in the sensible appearance of the face" (*TI*, 198ff). This level can be understood, however, only in terms of embodiment. How else can we make sense of the thesis that morality can be traced back to an originary responsibility to and for the other which takes hold of us in a temporality before before the time of memory, and that, in traces of this taking hold, we can approach this originary moral commitment? The fact of "incarnation," he says,

> far from thickening and tumefying the soul, . . . exposes it naked to the other, to the point of making the subject expose its very exposedness. . . . The concept of the incarnate subject is not a biological concept. The schema that corporeality outlines submits the biological itself to a higher structure. (*OB*, 109)

This "higher structure" is the moral law—and it lies *beneath* the biological as well as, in a different topological sense, above it. But in a parallel gesture, Levinas likewise removes this "higher structure" from ontotheology. Thus, somewhat later, he explicitly introduces the question of the categorical imperative into our thought of embodiment:

> The fact that immortality and theology could not determine the categorical imperative signifies the novelty of the Copernican revolution: a sense that is not measured by being or not being; but on the contrary, being is determined on the basis of sense. (*OB*, 129)

"Sense" here refers to the body's sense and sensibility, enjoined by the inherent directionality of the moral law. We might think of this moral assignment that is registered in the flesh as a "gift of nature." This gift, however, constitutes a radically paradoxical givenness, for it is given only as the assignment of a task: the *Hingabe* assigns an *Aufgabe*. But it can only be a question, here, of a gift that is not, and cannot possibly be, fully or totally received, retrieved, or recuperated—a gift, moreover, that does not in any way diminish the fact that the assignment is, as Levinas says, "against nature" (*OB*, 197): against nature in the sense that, while the obligation comes over us, is given to us, and takes hold of us only by grace of the very nature of the flesh, it nevertheless makes the most rigorous, most impossible demands on us, calling on us from a time before consciousness, before memory, before time, before volition, to resist the temptations of desire that easily possess us in the time of our egoism. And because the moral assignment that takes hold of our embodiment makes demands that are *against* nature and function in a time before volition, Levinas will argue that what he is trying to articulate cannot and can never be adequately represented in terms of some "natural benevolence" or "divine instinct" (*OB*, 124).

Like Merleau-Ponty, Levinas is calling attention to "a pre-original reason that does not proceed from any initiative of the subject, an anarchic reason" (*OB*, 166). It is, he says, "a reason before the beginning, before any present, because my responsibility for the other commands me before any decision, before any deliberation" (ibid.). And it is constitutive of the very existence and formation of the subject as such. This tracework reason, the anarchic origin of moral law more original than whatever we are able to contact and represent as the "origin," is recognized as more original only after the event, *après coup, nachträglich*, in rememoration—a belated reading of our responsibility, too late for any immediate, intuitive apprehension of the metaphysical ground of our moral experience. Thus, Levinas will speak of the "posteriority of the anterior" (*TI*, 54). "This recurrence" to an incarnate moral reason, he argues,

> would be the ultimate secret of the incarnation of the subject; prior to all reflection, prior to every positing, an indebtedness before any loan, not assumed, anarchical, subjectivity of a bottomless passivity, made out of assignation, like the echo of a sound that would precede the resounding of this sound. (*OB*, 112)

The peculiar "presence" of this categorical imperative, taking hold of us, as he imagines it, "beneath the level of prime matter" (*OB*, 110), transforms the very substance of our bodies from mere "matter" into a spiritualized "flesh." In this transformation, the flesh is commanded, called upon it to realize its glorious moral vocation.

Of course, something of this transformation is not unrecognizable within the phenomenology of Merleau-Ponty's late thought. For in a late text, he emphatically calls attention to a certain spiritual appropriation and destination of the flesh when, in a context that recalls Spinoza, whose "intellectual love of God" must surely be correlated to a glorious transfiguration of its embodiment, he writes of a "glorified body" (*VI*, 148). As for Levinas, he writes that the "incarnation of the [moral] self . . . [must be understood as] a passivity prior to all passivity at the bottom of matter becoming flesh [*la matière se faisant chair*] (*OB*, 196). The inscription of the categorical imperative, absolutely transforming our corporeal substance, forbids violations of the flesh, a flesh that must never be reduced, as the Nazi branding of number tattoos on the arm attempted, to mere biology, mere organic life. Here, then, in matter becoming flesh, we can begin to construct the narrative that Levinas sets in motion: As "passivity incarnate" (*OB*, 112), the flesh of our bodies receives an assignation, "an extremely urgent assignation" (*OB*,

101), an "exigency" (*OB*, 112) that takes hold of our flesh and renders us beholden, facing the other in the condition of subjection, "hostage" to the other, responsible to and for the other. If it has not suffered fatal trauma in the early years of its passage through the world, but on the contrary is recognized and appropriately nurtured, the impression of this categorical imperative, our incarnate moral assignment, can give crucial support and guidance to moral deliberation, moving and disposing us according to its commandment.

Using some of the same tropes, the same figurative topography as Merleau-Ponty, Levinas says that the

> logos that informs prime matter in calling it to order is an accusation, or a category. But obsession [which takes hold of us in the form of a moral predisposition] is anarchical; it accuses me beneath the level of prime matter. . . . Western philosophy, which perhaps is reification itself, remains faithful to the order of things and does not know the absolute passivity, beneath the level [of the traditional dualism] of activity and passivity. (*OB*, 110; notice the perplexing "or": "accusation or category")

The embodiment of the categorical imperative cannot be understood, therefore, until our way of thinking about the body undergoes a radical revision: "The body is neither an obstacle opposed to the soul, nor a tomb that imprisons it, but that by which the self is susceptibility itself. Incarnation is an extreme passivity . . . exposed to compassion, and, as a self, to the gift that costs" (*OB*, 195). This suggests that we should give some thought to Levinas's previously noted use of the word *assignation*, because it already assigns to the body, in the form of a certain "sign," the *inscription* of a moral obligation, the urgent and "traumatic" claims of the moral law. Thus, it is not surprising to find a passage where this inscription in the flesh, this moral *logos* (*OB*, 121) is actually made explicit. Even before the ethical relation set in motion by the "approach" or "proximity" of the other, "there is inscribed or written [*s'inscrit ou s'écrit*] the trace of infinity, the trace of a departure, but trace of what is inordinate, does not enter into the present, and inverts the *arkhé* into an-archy, that there may be . . . responsibility and a [morally disposed] self" (*OB*, 117).

This passage is fascinating and demands considerable time, but here a few brief comments must suffice. First of all, it suggests a remarkable proximity to Merleau-Ponty's observation that "my flesh itself is one of the sensibles in which an inscription of all others is made" (*VI*, 259–60). And secondly, of course, we must recall the Book of *Numbers*

15:31, wherein it is written that "[o]ne who has broken God's commandment is one who profanes the covenant inscribed in the flesh." This must be the authority behind the argument that the tracework is inscribed on (or is cut into) the flesh, thereby appropriating it for the moral law and forever rejecting the reduction of the *bios* of the human body to mere *zoé*, mere natural, organic life. In other words, the inscription's moral binding of the flesh categorically forbids what took place, for example, in the Hell of Auschwitz: the reduction of the human being to the condition of *bloßes Leben*, a bare life abandoned to the unconditional power of death, abandoned to sheer violence, protected neither by the power of divine law nor by the authority of a political-juridical law, a life "exposed," therefore, as Giorgio Agamben says, "to a death that no rite and no sacrifice can redeem."[17]

Thirdly, the topology becomes a topography, since the flesh becomes a site, a *topos*, where the *logos* gets inscribed. Fourthly, this passage implicitly weaves together three distinct functions. For the moment, let us call them description, inscription, and prescription. The first two are obvious; the third, which I might prefer to call "performative" or "enactment," is less so, but in the final analysis, I think it is quite indisputable. Finally, we must note that in the rhetoric of tropes, in his "turns" of speech, Levinas speaks of the inscription as nothing more than a "trace," or rather a trace of a trace, because we cannot possibly return to the originary moment of the inscription, and in any case, even if, *per impossibile*, we could, we still would not get at it, because it belongs to a past that never was fully present to itself, a past event that withdrew, leaving only a trace of its self-effacement, the tracework of its absence; because it continues to withdraw the more it is approached; and because, in spite of this, it remains the responsibility of the philosopher to attempt the impossible "return," a rememoration of the trace, and to experience affective "contact" with the moral assignment it is imagined to register.[18] But how can affectively contacting the body's carried sense of this inscription—somehow managing to read it, despite its peculiar illegibility—alter our affective-conative disposition? How can such contacting or reading empower us to heed the command of "the Good"? Does it matter that it remains beyond contact, beyond apprehension?

Though its claim on the body is beyond our comprehension, beyond our powers of possession, the moral imperative nevertheless is always already (imagined or remembered as) predisposing us in certain ways prior to the ego-logical time in which we are able to become conscious of its functioning. He says that "responsibility for my neighbor dates from before my freedom in an immemorial past . . . more ancient than consciousness."[19]

The sensibility of the human body is "extended" or, to repeat Merleau-Ponty's word, "prolonged," by the sense of alterity it bears within it. "Sensibility is exposedness to the other" (*OB*, 75). In this sense, the flesh—as "sympathetic" intercorporeality—may be said to bear the intertwining of myself and the other in its element. The reversibilities in this intertwining set the stage for the later-developed forms of reversibility, symmetry, and reciprocity involved in the politics of mutual recognition and justice; but for Levinas—and also, I would argue, for Merleau-Ponty, who writes in "The Child's Relations with Others" of the "contagion of cries" (*Pri*, 124) in the nursery, whereby the crying of one infant will arouse a responsive crying in the other infants—the reversibilities of the flesh also manifest the origin of responsibility in a moment of asymmetry: my originary subjection to the welfare of the other. For both, the responsibility comes from a primordial bodily responsiveness—an originary disposition to be responsive, that it is our social responsibility to develop. I want to argue, however, that, for Levinas, this disposition directs us toward a stage of moral development beyond that which concerned Merleau-Ponty: "[T]he subjectivity of sensibility, taken as incarnation, is an abandon without return . . . a body suffering for another, the body as passivity and renouncement, a pure undergoing" (*OB*, 79). Although, for Levinas, the justice of the moral law makes a universal and symmetrical claim on each and everyone, what it commands is, paradoxically, its own transcendence—my submission to the absolute ethical priority of the other, the singular individual whose welfare I must at all times put before my own. But why does Levinas use words such as "persecution," "accusation," "wound," "trauma," "sacrifice," "hostage," and "obsession" to describe the experience of responsibility and obligation that one feels—or should be able to feel—in seeing another human being? In what sense is the moral law a "trauma"? At least part of the answer is suggested by the distinction he makes between the ego and the moral self. These terms would be accurate phenomenological descriptions of the ego's point of view with regard to the moral experience of the other. But in fact, the moral self could also use these terms to describe its experience of the moral relation. However, the grounds for its use of these terms, and therefore what it would mean by them, would be the very opposite of the ego's. In *Difficult Freedom*, Levinas gives us an important clue, arguing that the more just we are, the more harshly we are judged—first, and most of all, by ourselves.[20] Something that Freud remarked in *Civilization and Its Discontents* may further clarify the point. He remarks that "the more virtuous a man is, the more severe and distrustful is his conscience, so that ultimately it is precisely those people who carried saintliness furthest who reproach themselves with the deepest sinfulness."[21] So these extreme terms could also be used to describe the experience of the moral self, aware that its responsiveness to the other is always too late and always too little. The traces, we might say, are therefore lacerations claiming the flesh for ethical life, the life of the spirit.

Perhaps invoking for the imagination the tracework of a rudimentary and preliminary moral disposition, illegible as such, but nevertheless intimating some initial moral direction and motivation, Levinas asserts that "in the 'prehistory' of the ego posited for itself there [nevertheless] speaks a responsibility. The self is through and through a hostage, older than the ego, prior to principles" (*OB*, 117). This passage is exceptionally provocative, because it suggests that the moral "self" appears in two distinct stages or faces: a stage or face—could we not call it, following Merleau-Ponty, prepersonal and anonymous?—which is earlier than the (personal) ego, and in which the flesh, subject to its binding by the moral law, is already passively held responsive to the alterity of the other, and second, a post-egological stage or face which is only an existential or "elective" possibility, and which always depends on the commitment of the (personal) ego for its realization—depends, that is, on the ego's personal assumption of responsibility for the development of our capacity to be responsive to the other. It is, thus, a question of the development of a moral self from the traces, or ruins, of a prepersonal responsiveness and attunement to the registers of alterity, a moral self ideally rooted in, and in good contact with, a vital *sense* of this responsiveness.[22]

It should, however, be noted here that, if we are inclined to think of the tracework as (re)marking a potential for the development of a deeply inscribed moral *disposition*, we must be prepared to concede that it can register its "accusation" of the flesh only by way of a certain radical dispositioning or dis-placing of the presumed topography, for the dispositional tracework could become legible only obscurely, marginally and with the greatest of difficulty within the purview of the subject-object, subject-subject and ego-alter structures recognized by the traditional discourse of metaphysics. Moreover, the "trauma" of the moral law obeys the logic of "supplementarity," a deep structure of belatedness, a temporality which this metaphysics cannot possibly absorb.

Earlier, I referred to the fact that in his discussion of the child's experience of the other, Merleau-Ponty resorts to the words *transgression*, *encroachment*, and *alienation* in order to describe the child's experience. These words suggest that he is thinking of the prepersonal dimension and stage of intercorporeality as an experience not unlike what Levinas describes with words such as *trauma*, *persecution*, *hostage*, and *accusation*. In the context of Merleau-Ponty's phenomenological demonstration regarding the mimetically "sympathetic" dimension of intercorporeality that from the very beginning endows the child with a certain sociability and a certain proto-moral disposition, the use of those words might at first seem unjustifiable, contradictory: if at the anonymous, prepersonal level of embodiment, the child is always already enjoined, already directed by a primitive form of sympathy, a primitive form of communication, to acknowledge the other as both other and same, this ready sociability would seem to preclude an experience appropriately describable in those words. However, words such as "alienation" and "transgression" *are* appropriate ways to describe (1) the mimetic submission to the moral presence of the other that Merleau-Ponty discusses with regard to the earliest stage of infancy, *and also* (2) at a later stage of development, the narcissistic ego's *rejection* of this primal disownment, this originary mimetically induced substitution for the other. The same holds true in Levinas's case, where the use of words such as "trauma," "persecution," "hostage," and "accusation" is required, since otherwise he cannot indicate how the ego and the moral self, each in terms of its own concerns, must experience the moral binding of the flesh.

This discussion of words for the bodily dimension of the ethical relation suggests that something needs to be said about my assumption that Merleau-Ponty's terms for describing the primordial, prepersonal dimension of our embodiment—in particular his use of the term "anonymous"—may be transferred into the context of Levinas's thought and used to describe the earliest stage and dimension of embodiment wherein the tracework of alterity, the moral assignment of responsibility for the other, is inscribed. How is it possible that this responsibility takes hold of me in my absolute singularity and yet also in my anonymity? There is certainly a difference between Merleau-Ponty and Levinas with regard to what they are trying to show us; but there is also an important sense in which the transfer of this terminology proves to be illuminating. In the contexts of Merleau-Ponty's phenomenology, this term, *anonymous*, is used to emphasize that there is a dimension of embodiment in which a mode of experiencing is taking place prior to the emergence of the personal ego-subject; whereas, in my reading of Levinas's texts, this term may be used to point to the fact that the ethical relation first takes hold of one, not in the nominative, but in and as the accusative. The nominative comes later. Thus, to describe the calling of the "accusation," this accusative, as taking hold of the flesh "anonymously" does *not* undo the singularity of the accusation, since the accusation still singles one out. But it singles one out secretly, as it were, at the level of one's primordial embodiment, one's deepest passivity—"prior to all memory and all recall," "unconvertible into a memory" (*OB*, 104–105), and prior to the recurrence to the self through which one would hear one's proper name called in accusation. According to Levinas, the identity (singularity) of the oneself "can indeed appear in an indirect language, under a proper name, as an entity. . . . But it is first a non-quiddity, no one, clothed with purely borrowed being, which masks its nameless singularity by conferring on it a role" (*OB*, 106). For Levinas, "in responsibility for another subjectivity, there is only this unlimited passivity of an accusative which does not issue out of a declension it would have undergone starting with the nominative" (*OB*, 112). We are always already, he says, touched and affected, accused, at a level of our embodiment that calls us in our singularity. But this calling takes place, takes hold of us, in a time before we have taken over our name: "[T]he hypostasis is exposed as oneself in the accusative form before appearing in the said proper to knowing as the bearer of a name" (*OB*, 106). With regard to the experiencing of accusation, obsession, the way that obligation takes hold of us in and through our embodiment, Levinas says that "these are not events that happen to an empirical ego, that is, to an ego already posited and fully identified" (*OB*, 115). Thus, "in the accusative form, which is a modification of no nominative form, in which I approach the neighbor for whom I have to answer, the irreplaceable one is brought out [*s'accuse*]" (*OB*, 124). There is accordingly a sense, perhaps, in which I only receive a proper name by virtue of my attempting to retrieve traces of the accusation, traces of the obligation, that has already singled me out, already claimed me, already taken hold of me through the medium of an embodiment that is still anonymous, still without a true name. In a crucial sense, then, I receive a proper name only when I let myself be appropriated by the accusation, acknowledging that I can never give enough of myself and never do enough for the welfare of the other. "No one," he writes,

> can substitute himself for me, who substitutes myself for all. Or, if one means to remain with the hierarchy of formal logic—genus, species, individual—it is in the course of the individuation of the ego in me that is realized the elevation in which the ego is for the neighbor, summoned to answer for him. (*OB*, 126)

This is an especially significant passage, because in it Levinas seems to position the ego within a process of individuation or self-development, suggesting that this is a process through which the moral self—"the self in the ego"—would emerge from the stage of the ego (ibid.). The ego, of course, is "already a self" (*OB*, 123), in the sense that it is always possible for the ego to become a self, sacrificing itself for the other. But of course, in another sense, the ego in its "imperialism" is *not yet* a moral self. What then is the moral self? It would seem that, for Levinas, it is, in this diachrony, both "older" than the ego, coming immemorially before it as the dimension of our embodiment which, in its absolute passivity, first receives the accusation, the trauma of responsibility, the mark of alterity, the moral appropriation and assignment (*OB*, 128); but the self must also be thought of as infinitely "later" than the ego (*OB*, 113, 117), in the sense that it can only come after it as a possibility dependent on the moral dedication of our use of freedom to taking up this anarchic moral assignment and making of it the guiding principle, the *arkhé* of our relations with others. The moral law, felt in some sense to be *given* to nature, but given, nevertheless, as *against* nature, is thus always a task for the future. The moral self would thus be a possibility that one can begin to realize only *after* the formation of the ego—as the self-effacing sacrifice, never sufficient, which the ego must willingly make, using its freedom for the sake of the other person. If, for Levinas, the highest stage of moral development would be a self that willingly sacrifices itself for the other, even to the point of sacrificing its proper name—for example, in anonymous deeds of charity, I suggest that this stage can be recognized as already prefigured by the anonymity and self-estrangement distinctive of the prepersonal stage and dimension which Merleau-Ponty's early phenomenology has described.

Despite references to anachronism and diachrony, Levinas's discussion of ego and self is inexplicably static and synchronic. There is in Levinas's work no sustained discussion of the process of individuation or self-development as such; nor does he give much elaboration to the relationship between ego and self in terms of such a process. But the process I have schematized is a fair representation of what remains implicit in his phenomenological account. And if this be the case, then there are significant points of correspondence between the process implicit in Levinas and the process implicit in Merleau-Ponty, whom I read as suggesting the desirability for phenomenology to attempt a hermeneutical retrieval of the prepersonal, the traces of which constitute the primordial dimension of our embodiment. And if one puts the *Phenomenology of Perception* together with "The Child's Relations with Others" and the texts of *The Visible and the Invisible*, it becomes possible to show just why the attempt to retrieve traces of the prepersonal would be desirable. From a moral point of view, this attempt would be desirable because it is in the prepersonal dimension of our embodiment that we first experience the sympathetic interconnectedness with the other within the tracework of which a primitive form of responsibility for the other first claims and takes hold of us.

It is to be regretted that Merleau-Ponty never gave much thought to the ways in which we might be transformed, if we were to begin this tracework in earnest as a personal commitment. But neither philosopher forgot the paradoxes into which their thinking drew them. For Merleau-Ponty, the hermeneutic nature of reflection means that the attempt to bring the originary into language is an attempt at a coincidence of thought and being that cannot escape the hermeneutical circle and can only end in a repetition—that is, in aporetic failure. The originary lies forever beyond metaphysical recurrence, beyond the logic of identity and synchronicity, withdrawn into a past that was never fully present. Similarly, for Levinas, the body's affectively carried sense of an "originary source" of our subjection to the alterity of the moral law, which phenomenological rememoration is given the task of recovering, is not the originating event or moment itself, brought back into intuitive immediacy, but instead a later repetition, an impression separated from it forever by the passage of time. The retrieval of the trace, withdrawn from the presence of ontology, is an absolutely impossible task—and yet, in spite of this, morally imperative. But perhaps this is not as paradoxical as it seems, because what matters, ultimately, is not mastery, not knowledge, but the moral character constitutive of the self. What matters, therefore, is the desire to live a moral life—a desire expressed by the attempt, the effort, the undertaking of the recuperative process. Accordingly, it will only be in virtue of the most rigorous exertion, the most binding commitment of our freedom to submit to this ultimately impossible task of self-examination, self-discovery, and self-invention, that the moral self emerges and consummates the life of the ego.

THE BODY OF MORAL KNOWLEDGE

Nearing the end of our present reflections, I would like to return, briefly, to Merleau-Ponty's *Phenomenology of Perception*. Giving thought, in this work, to the process of incarnation that he hoped he was setting in motion, he wrote:

> We are relearning to feel our body; we have found underneath the objective and detached knowledge of the body that other

> knowledge which we have of it. . . . [And] by thus remaking contact with the body [of primordial, prepersonal experience], we shall also rediscover ourself. (*PhP*, 206)

In the final analysis, then, he must concede that the method of phenomenology, as he puts it into practice, cannot possibly be merely descriptive, since its reflexivity is inevitably a transformative intervention. But even when he calls attention to the transformative effect of phenomenological reflexivity, and even when he notices the connection between the capacity for moral judgment and body's upright posture, he still does not fully recognize the significance of this process for our moral life, although he does suggest that the transformations of our incarnation that would make a difference in our moral existence are not prescribed by any teleology of nature, so that a certain existential commitment to engage in the practice of phenomenological reflexivity becomes necessary for the realization of that gift of nature we call embodiment:

> [I]t is no mere coincidence that the rational being is also the one who holds himself upright. . . . On the other hand, everything in man is contingency in the sense that this human manner of existence is not guaranteed to every human child through some essence acquired at birth, and in the sense that it must be constantly reforged in him through the hazards encountered by the objective body. Man is an historical idea and not a natural species. In other words, there is in human existence no unconditioned possession, and yet no fortuitous attribute. Human existence will force us to revise our usual notion of necessity and contingency, because it is the transformation of contingency into necessity by the act of carrying forward [*par l'acte de reprise*]. (*PhP*, 170)

In light of Levinas's hope for the incarnation of a "metaphysics" beyond ontology, beyond essence and being, I would like, finally, to read again a passage in which Merleau-Ponty defines "metaphysics"—defines it, in fact, precisely in relation to nature. Very close in spirit to Levinas's thought, it attributes to metaphysics what can be described only as a sublime vocation: "[M]etaphysics—the coming to light of something beyond nature—is not localized at the level of knowledge: it begins with the opening out upon 'another'" (*PhP*, 168). The difference between ontology and metaphysics, then, is ultimately a question of this opening. Requiring for its recognition that we follow the logic of "supplementarity," the gift of the moral law inscribes and prescribes an arduous moral task. In the work of Merleau-Ponty and Levinas, we see that the task for phenomenology has therefore become tracework, the impossible but necessary attempt to articulate the traces of a long-forgotten dream, a dream belonging to our embodiment, and in which we received the gift of nature as a metaphor recalling this opening.

Let us, in concluding our reflections, cite a passage in *Of Grammatology*, where Derrida explains the moral significance of the tracework. This passage condenses the argument of this essay. Derrida writes, there, that "the arche-writing is the origin of morality as of immorality. The nonethical opening of ethics. A violent opening."[23] The tracework is nothing but an opening, the impression of an inscription of the moral law that does not at all preclude evil. Evil is still always possible. For this arche-writing is not the imposition of fate, but only the always uncertain destiny of a promise.

The moral law remains imperative, commanding respect and obedience, precisely because its hold on us comes from another temporality, the temporality, in fact, of the other: it cannot be reduced to the totally present, an object of possession and knowledge, but demands of us an interminable effort to ground our lives nonetheless in an experience of its paradoxical order—a universality that commands its own transcendence in the name of the absolute singularity of the other. It is only this effort that ultimately matters, for the desire to make immediate contact with the origin of the moral law is, despite—or rather, one might say, precisely because of—the fact that we never have possessed it and never can, that which breaks down the ego's walls, exposing and opening us to the singular moral existence of the other.

The traces of a moral assignment inscribed in the flesh constitute, prior to the recognition of the moral law, our sense of appropriation by a certain moral disposition; but these traces are indeed virtually nothing—unless, as I suggested before, we make something of them. Our "moral sources," which we imagine to be buried beyond recall in the forgotten depths of the flesh, are thus always with us, carried like our death, and making us at least *capable* of sympathetic responsiveness to the suffering and destitution of the other, demanding of us the virtue in an interminable effort to approach and realize the meaning of their assignment, their forever secret promise.

NOTES

1. Emmanuel Levinas, *Totality and Infinity: An Essay on Exteriority* trans. A. Lingis (Pittsburgh: Duquesne University Press, 1969); and *Otherwise than Being, or Beyond Essence* trans. A. Lingis (Dor-

drecht, London, and Boston: Kluwer, 1991). Hereafter these texts will be cited in the body of the essay as *TI* and *OB*, respectively.

2. Emmanuel Levinas, "Diachrony and Representation," in *Time and the Other* (Pittsburgh: Duquesne University Press, 1987), 109. Also, see note 5 below on the social anthropology research reported by Adam Reed.
3. Levinas, "Meaning and Sense," in *Collected Philosophical Papers,* trans. A. Lingis (Dordrecht: Martinus Nijhoff, 1987), 102ff.
4. Jacques Derrida, *Speech and Phenomena and Other Essays on Husserl's Theory of Signs* (Evanston: Northwestern University Press, 1973).
5. It is worth noting here that Merleau-Ponty also wrote of a "contract" preceding socialization, a "primordial contract" between myself and the world that is sealed by the nature of embodiment (cf. *PhP,* 241, 251).
6. See Edith Wyschogrod, *Emmanuel Levinas: The Problem of Ethical Metaphysics* (The Hague: Martinus Nijhoff, 1974) on "affective intentionality."
7. See "Anticipating Individuals: Modes of Vision and Their Social Consequence in a Papua New Guinea Prison," 15, an unpublished manuscript by Adam Reed (Department of Social Anthropology, Free School Lane, Cambridge University). Reed's research would seem to confirm Levinas: he found that prison inmates "state that they do not wish to live 'face to face'. To view another face is to provoke a response or invite a particular relational obligation. Inmates complain that in prison, they do not have the resources to fulfil these obligations. . . . To exchange gazes is therefore to acknowledge a relation and be compelled to act on its basis."
8. See Levinas, "Humanism and An-archy," *Collected Philosophical Papers*, 134–36.
9. Derrida's thought of the "supplement," influenced by Freud and Lacan, can be useful in making the logic of the trace more understandable As Derrida explains, supplementarity produces *après coup* that to which the supplement would otherwise have simply added itself. In other words, it is not added to a stratum which preexists, but produces that which would otherwise have preceded it. Hence it is an originary supplement, produced there where the origin we seek is not to be found present, substituting for the missing, absent origin. See Derrida, *La dissemination* (Paris: Seuil, 1972), 11–12, and *De la grammatologie* (Paris: Minuit, 1976), 208, 442. Also see Jacques Lacan, *Écrits* (Paris: Seuil, 1966), 256, 684, 839, especially on trauma and *Nachträglichkeit.*

10. There is unquestionably an astonishing difference between the *Phenomenology of Perception*, an early work, and the much later writings, such as "The Chiasm—The Intertwining," assembled in *The Visible and the Invisible*. However, in my opinion, all the startling new conceptual configurations of the later texts—for example, "flesh," "chiasmic intertwining," and "reversibility"—are already prefigured by Merleau-Ponty's phenomenological descriptions of the "prepersonal" dimension of perception in the earlier work. In other words, the later conceptual configurations can be found, already implicitly articulated in the early work; but it is also nevertheless true that, without the later texts, the later concepts would not now be legible in the earlier ones: their implicitness is legible only now, only after the fact; they could not have been anticipated in any straightforward way. Thus, we must recognize the late texts as representing a major new development in Merleau-Ponty's thinking.
11. Note the French words. Should we assume that this word *retrouver* is used in opposition to "invent" or "project"? Is it meant to exclude the work of the "creative imagination"? And what is this peculiar "thought" that he "finds"? Or is the matter more intricate than the assumption of such an opposition would imply? In this case, the meaning of the English word *find*, which translates a word marked with the prefix that indicates a certain repetition, would be more ambiguous than it seems, hovering with deliberate undecidability beyond the grasp of metaphysics, *between* the "opposites" of finding and inventing, remoration and imagination.
12. The trope might have been suggested by a reading of Diderot's *Le Rêve d'Alembert*, wherein Diderot describes the body as "a network which takes form, grows, extends, and throws out a multitude of imperceptible threads." See Denis Diderot, *D'Alembert's Dream* (New York: Penguin Books, 1966), 183.
13. In other words, it might be a question of thinking the mature "moral self" in terms of stage-levels beyond the narcissistic ego. This would entail not only a transition from what Habermas would call a conventional, heteronomous appropriation of morality to what he would call a post-conventional, truly autonomous appropriation, but even a movement beyond this, to a stage of moral existence where one is truly selfless, self-sacrificing even to the point of a higher anonymity: an anonymity prefigured, perhaps, in what Merleau-Ponty calls our prepersonal existence.
14. On this question, see Bernard Flynn, "Chair et textualité: Merleau-Ponty et Derrida," *Les Cahiers de Philosophie* 7 (1989): 187–209.

15. Merleau-Ponty, "The Child's Relations with Others," in *Pri*, 96–155.
16. Levinas, "Philosophy and the Idea of Infinity," *Collected Philosophical Papers*, 55–59.
17. See Giorgio Agamben, *Homo Sacer: Sovereign Power and Bare Life* (Stanford: Stanford University Press, 1998), 100. Regarding this *bloßes Leben*, see Walter Benjamin's "Critique of Violence," in *Reflections: Essays, Aphorisms, Autobiographical Writings* (New York: Schocken, 1986). In Giorgio Agamben's *Homo Sacer*, there is a thought-provoking discussion of this concept, which he translates into Italian as *la nuda vita*. One should also consider Adorno's bitter comments in *Negative Dialectics* (New York: Continuum, 1973), 365; one could raise many issues here, but this is not the context in which to engage with Adorno.
18. See Levinas, "The Trace of the Other," in *Deconstruction in Context*, ed. Mark Taylor (Chicago: University of Chicago Press, 1986), 345–59.
19. Levinas, "Ethics as First Philosophy," in *The Levinas Reader*, ed. Sean Hand (Oxford: Basil Blackwell, 1989), 84.
20. Levinas, *Difficult Freedom: Essays on Judaism* (Baltimore: The Johns Hopkins University Press, 1990), 78.
21. Sigmund Freud, *Civilization and Its Discontents* (New York: Doubleday, 1965), 80. Translation modified.
22. I very much agree with Bernhard Waldenfels, "Response and Responsibility," in *Ethics as First Philosophy: The Significance of Emmanuel Levinas for Philosophy, Literature, and Religion*, ed. Adriaan Peperzak (Routledge, 1995), 39–52.
23. For more on this concept of "carrying forward," see the second edition of Eugene Gendlin, *Experiencing and the Creation of Meaning* (Evanston: Northwestern University, 1997) and David Michael Levin, ed., *Language Beyond Postmodernism: Saying and Thinking in Gendlin's Philosophy* (Evanston: Northwestern University Press, 1977). Merleau-Ponty's phrase, "acte de reprise," does not cast much light on the transformative potential in this interaction—the potential, that is, to carry experiencing forward.
24. Derrida, *Of Grammatology*, 140.

7

Merleau-Ponty and the Philosophical Position of Skepticism

BERNARD FLYNN

It has often been contended that Hume's skepticism is the final outcome of a representational theory of consciousness. Against Hume, both Kant and Husserl instituted philosophical gestures meant to overcome Hume's skeptical conclusions. Merleau-Ponty effects a profound critique of those aspects of both thinkers that would ensure us against skepticism by exacting a premium more onerous than the loss they indemnify against, that is, the loss of our relationship to Being. I would like to explore this aspect of Merleau-Ponty's thought and ask myself, and you, where, on the hither side of his critique of phenomenological idealism and transcendental reflection, does Merleau-Ponty stand in relationship to skepticism?

Habitually, when we refer to a *position* in philosophy, we use the word *position* as a transparent metaphor designating a number of positions affirmed or denied. I propose to take the notion of position more seriously, viewing it as "something" that cannot be occupied and distinguishing it from "position" thought as a number of propositions to be defended or rejected. I would like to do something analogous to what Foucault did in his reading of Descartes' *Meditations*, that is, to distinguish between the dimension of a text as "a system of propositions" logically and discursively connected in which the subject is not implicated, and "the work" of the text which creates or forecloses the position of the subject. As for example, when Descartes proposed and quickly withdrew the hypothesis that I might be mad, a hypothesis that would disqualify the position from which the meditation is effective. Even if one follows Heidegger in distinguishing between Greek skepticism and a modern skepticism based on a problematic of representation, skepticism is as old as philosophy itself. Of course, in the popular culture of modern democracies, skeptical relativism is virtually the epistemological coin of the realm. For a philosophy that begins as a first-person reflection on experience, the possibility of skepticism poses itself with particular urgency. Descartes extricates himself from the solipsism of a representational filled mind by his detour through the veracity of God. Somewhere, Aron Gurwitsch once said: "Hume is Descartes without God." The remark is illuminating, but inadequate to the complexity of Hume's position.

Permit me to linger awhile with Hume and to consider the question of skepticism. In the recent secondary literature on Hume, there has been a prolonged debate on the extent of his skepticism. This might appear odd since traditionally Hume has been represented as the arch-skeptic. After all, it was he who advanced arguments against: the rationality of the belief in causality; the existence of the external world; the continued existence of any object, including the identitary existence of the self over time. Nevertheless, if we make the type of distinction that I have proposed above, we see that Hume also argues that it is impossible for any subject not to believe in causality, the outside world, and so forth, whether or not they have a rational foundation for it. He claims that although there is no discursive argument justifying our belief in causality, it is impossible not to believe what has been "established by constant conjunction"; which is to say, in the sciences of facts and also in our ordinary life, the foundation of "first principles" is our psychological incapacity not to believe them, or to believe their contrary. Hume's way out of a total and debilitating skepticism is through what Husserl will call "psychologism." In Husserl's thought, things are quite the contrary since for him far from leading us out of skepticism *psychologism* is the cause of skepticism. Perhaps no philosopher in the twentieth century has been more troubled by, and vigilant against, the specter of skeptical relativism, and his reasons for this are more than purely epistemological. As we can see in his later writings, there is both a moral and a political dimension to Husserl's defense of "the project of objectivity" even if he views this project as an *infinite task*. His worst fears are realized in both the universities and in certain juridical procedures in America today, where on a regular basis a hasty rejection of all pretention to objectivity is used to legitimate the pure assertion of power or group identity.

Husserl's critique of psychologism is a leitmotiv of his entire work from its beginning to its end. In his early writings he attacks any attempt to base the laws of logic on psychology; he does this in terms of its consequences for, and its misunderstanding of, the nature of the ideal sciences. On the one hand, psychologism results in a relativization of the laws of logic; for if the law of noncontradiction is only an empirical generalization regarding the ability of an empirical species, man, to believe or not to believe something, then its validity becomes merely probable as is the case for all such generalizations. Husserl considers this relativization of the laws of logic an absurdity. On the other hand, he argues that this psychologistic reduction does not understand the content of logic. Logic is not about the psychological ability or inability to believe contradictory propositions. It is about the ideal relations that hold between propositions: as mathematics is about numbers and is not concerned with the psychology of counting as Husserl had previously supposed. In his 1910 essay, "Philosophy as a Rigorous Science," he expands his critique of psychologism to a critique of all types of naturalism, defined as "the naturalizing of consciousness, including all intentional imminent data of consciousness, and . . . the naturalization of ideas, and, consequently, of all ideals and norms."[1] Naturalism would make *consciousness* a part of nature, while frequently Husserl will argue that nature is the correlate of intentional acts of consciousness. For him the "naturalization of consciousness" leads to skeptical relativism. He also claims that a certain *misinterpretation* of phenomenology itself could lead in this same direction, namely, the interpretation of phenomenology as introspective psychology. If the descriptions that the phenomenologist offers are faithful to his experience, then on what grounds may they claim more than an idiosyncratic truthfulness? How can they pretend to universality?

In the beginning of his *Cartesian Meditations*, Husserl tells us that "[p]hilosophy, wisdom, is the philosopher's quite personal affair." But it must not be "merely the private concern of the philosopher."[2] Of course, it is the technique of free variation and its attendant essential insight which liberates the phenomenological description from the status of idiosyncratic musings and generates its claim to universality. Let us briefly evoke Husserl's practice of free variation and Merleau-Ponty's critical response to it in order to situate Merleau-Ponty more clearly within our problematic of skepticism. In section 34 of the *Cartesian Meditations*, Husserl writes, "We, so to speak, shift the actual perception into the realm of non-actuality— the realm of the *as if*, which supplies us with pure possibilities, pure of everything that restricts to this fact, or to any fact whatsoever" (*CM*, 70). Thus, a real objective perception, the table, is transformed into an instance of *possible* perception. If I say of my factual perception of a table that it presents itself to me one side at a time, one profile at a time, this statement is valid for this particular table. However, if by free variation the object of perception is transformed from a table, to a house, to a chair, and so forth, then I see that the perspectival character of this perceptual object is not a particularity of the "table" perception, rather it is an essential characteristic of any object of perception. "Perception, the universal type acquired—floats in the air, so to speak—in an atmosphere of pure fantasizableness. Thus removed from all factualness, it has become the pure *eidos* perception, whose ideal extension is made up of all possible perceptions of a purely fantasizable process" (Ibid.). Given Husserl's conception of the parallelism between *noesis* and *noema* within noetic and noematic description, we see that the object is transformed from a real object of perception into a "merely possible" instance of the *eidos*, the perceptual object "floating in the air"; correlatively, the ego, the subject of perception, is transformed into the *eidos* ego. "With each eidetically pure type, we find ourselves not, indeed, inside the *de facto* ego, but inside an *eidos* ego; and constitutive of one actual pure possibility among others carried with it implicitly as its outer horizon, a purely possible ego, a pure possible variant of my de facto ego" (*CM*, 71). Through fictive variation, which is an action of the imagination, the object is transformed into an instance of pure possibility and the factual ego is likewise transformed into an instance of a purely possible ego. The "personal affair" of the philosopher is saved from being his merely private affair by our ascent into the domain of universality.

Let us now turn to Merleau-Ponty's reflection on free variation. According to him, it is through the process of free variation that the contingency of the given is subtended by the necessary structure of the possibility of its appearance. It is a movement from contingency to necessity; and since doubt and possible skepticism are inextricably linked to the contingent, the process of free variation is a movement from the dubious to the certain. For Merleau-Ponty, free variation is a "labor of experience on experience that would strip it of its facticity, as though it were an impurity" (*VI*, 112). This labor, he argues, is an "impossible labor." It is impossible to the extent that it believes itself capable of discovering "the essence as a positive being"; it also claims that this realm of essence is a second order of positivity which both founds and subtends the contingently given. Nevertheless, he does not dismiss "free variation" as a procedure for the clarification of experience. Rather, he puts into question its pretension to discover an intelligible structure that would be independent of the contingently given, since this would presuppose a subject capable of detaching itself absolutely from the field of experience and its contingency; "it would require a spectator without secrets, without latencies," a subject co-extensive with its own upsurgence. He writes:

> Under the solidity of the essence or of the ideal, there is the fabric of experience, the flesh of time, and this is why I am not sure of having penetrated into the hard core of being. My incontestable power to give myself leeway to disengage the possible from the real does not go as far as to dominate all the implications of the spectacle, and to make of the real a simple variant of the possible. On the contrary, it is the possible worlds and possible beings that are variants, and are like doubles of the actual world and actual Being. (*VI*, 111–12)

I have the power to give myself leeway, to move from the actual to the virtual, yet I do not have the power to complete the cycle by transforming the real into a variant, or instance, of the possible. According to Husserl, the *eidetic* and *phenomenological* reductions are linked in an extremely intricate manner. For now let us merely note that, according to Merleau-Ponty, it is the intractability of our contingent insertion into the "there is" of the world and of nature that both forestalls the completion of the *epoche* and precludes the knowledge of essences via the technique of free variation.

We can designate *two* other moments when Merleau-Ponty's critical reflection on a philosophical initiative has taken the form of showing that in order to effect the announced project the subject would be required to extricate itself from its inherence in Being, an inherence whose recalcitrance would thwart the possibility of the very project itself. In the *Phenomenology of Perception* he shows us that the *truth* of the phenomenological reduction is the fact that it cannot be completed; also, in "The Philosopher and His Shadow" he writes, "[A]ll reductions are only a test of primordial bonds—a way of following them into their final prolongations" (*Signs*, 175). Then, in *The Visible and the Invisible* we see that Merleau-Ponty's critical stance toward transcendental philosophy, analytical reflection, is based on his contention that transcendental philosophy in its project to follow backward the path of constitution to its origin in the unity of the subject; it "dissimulates from itself its own mainspring," that is, the domain of experience which is *prior to* reflection. He claims that, given the contingency of its starting point, reflection cannot coincide with itself, that it is "in principle delayed behind itself" (*VI*, 34). The *given* cannot be seen as simply the product of constitution because it both precedes and guides any reflective analysis that would pretend to account for it "without remainder," to use the phrase of Adorno. In each case, our insertion into the "there is" resists the project of moving from the contingent to the certain. As we shall see below, the same *philosopheme* is what prevents any kind of relativizing skepticism.

Now let us reflect on exactly what it is that resists both the movement in the direction of immanence and certainty and the movement toward total exteriority and contingency. Certainly it is not the case that Merleau-Ponty argues for "the irrationality of the given" and here indeed any analogy with Hume breaks down. For Hume what is *given* are atomic units of sensations, that is, impressions that require the associationist apparatus to produce anything resembling a perceived object. We shall not rehearse his arguments given in *The Structure of Behavior* and *The Phenomenology of Perception*; let us simply recall that Merleau-Ponty puts the *Gestalt* in the place of empiricism's "wandering troupe of sensations." If as Heidegger tells us each philosopher thinks but one thought, and if for Merleau-Ponty that one thought is his notion of the Flesh, then it seems to me that the itinerary of thought which will lead to the Flesh begins in *The Structure of Behavior* with his meditation on the notion of the Gestalt. Indeed in a "working note" of *The Visible and the Invisible*, he asks: "What is a Gestalt?" In *The Structure of Behavior* he sympathetically presents the research of the Gestalt theorists, including their critique of behaviorism and their positive achievements, up to the point where they respond to the question, "What is a Gestalt?" When they respond that the Gestalt is a part of nature, a real being, it is at this point that Merleau-Ponty becomes critical of them. His criticism focuses on the fact that the Gestaltists, in their own research, have transgressed not only the atomic unit of sensation but have also unwittingly thrown into question the entire ontology which has, by and large, been inherited from Descartes, an ontology later referred to as the ontology of the "great object," the ontology that subtends the scientific project.

Since the *Gestalt* cannot be thought of as a being *partes extra partes*, its mode of being must necessarily escape any objectivist ontology. One might say that in a turn of phrase Merleau-Ponty almost catches Koehler who wishes to interpret the Gestalt as a natural being. Quoting Koehler who writes, "[A] form rests on the fact that each local event, one could almost say, 'dramatically knows' the other events," Merleau-Ponty continues, "[A] unity of this type can be found only in an object of 'knowledge'"(*SB*, 143). It has the unity of a perceived object and thus "perception is not an event of nature"(*SB*, 145), at least not of nature viewed as a system of causality spread out in objective space. However, if the Gestalt is not an object, it is also not a concept; or if it is a concept, it is one in the sense of Merleau-Ponty's approving citation from Hegel, "the concept is only the interior of nature" (*SB*, 162). This formulation portends the notion developed in *The Visible and Invisible*, that is, the notion that the invisible, or ideal, does not transcend "the fact" but rather it is mounted on the axis, the pivots, of the visible. At this point in the work, Merleau-Ponty vacillates in his notion of the *ontological status of the Gestalt*: against objectivism he argues that it is an idea, against idealism he claims that it is nature. At this time in his thinking, there is also a similar ambiguity in his conception of nature itself. When he rejects the ontology of the "great object," he shows that any scientific conception of nature must borrow its concepts from the perceived world, thereby precluding any attempt to view this perceived world itself as the causal product of the *real* world. The perceived world is a world that exists for-consciousness; however, undercutting the apparent idealism of this position is his contention that the conscious subject is situated within the *human* order. As he argued in *The Structure of Behavior*, this subject is not an autonomous subject; rather it is the outcome of a dialectic of physical and vital structures.

Thought is a "sublation" of vital structures; one needs only to read John Searle's recent work, *The Rediscovery of Mind*,[3] in order to have an updated version of the research dealt with in *The Structure of Behavior*. Stated briefly: computers do not *think* for the same reason that they do not eat or have sex, the reason being that they are not alive and being alive is inextricably linked to thinking. Merleau-Ponty shows that thought is intrinsically tied to physical and vital structures, structures that are in their turn accessible only through thought. For him nature is not simply the object, the accessory of consciousness in its relationship with knowledge. It is an object from which we have arisen, in which "our beginnings have been posited, little by little, until the very moment of tying themselves to an existence which they continue to substain and align." Notwithstanding the fact that Merleau-Ponty reads the second and third volumes of Husserl's *Ideas* in such a way as to authorize his own conception of the relationship between consciousness and nature, and to counter Husserl's earlier contrary assertions (the absolute character of consciousness and the relative character of nature), it would seem that he is far from the dominant strains of Husserl's phenomenological idealism. If we specifically look at Husserl's critical treatment of skepticism as we have done above, then we discover that for him the crux of the skeptical position is "its naturalization of consciousness which includes all intentional imminent data of consciousness." Merleau-Ponty, on the other hand, wishes to view consciousness as arising from, and being sustained by, nature; thus, his rejection, or severe transformation, of the phenomenological reduction along with the practice of free variation, a rejection which, in general, is based on his contention that the perceived world cannot be reduced to "an intentional imminent data of consciousness." Husserl also rejects naturalism on the basis that it misunderstands the nature of mathematics and logic, that is, their ideality and their transcendence of fact, a position that is not at all shared by Merleau-Ponty. In his article, "The Philosopher and His Shadow," he writes, "Logical objectivity derives from carnal intrasubjectivity, on the condition that it has been forgotten as carnal intrasubjectivity, and it is this carnal intrasubjectivity itself which produces this forgetfulness by binding its way towards logical objectivity" (*Signs*, 173).

Awoken from his dogmatic slumber by Hume's skepticism, Kant forged his transcendental philosophy, arguing that the fundamental tenet of his transcendental thinking is the opposition between the *phenomenal* world of nature as a system of appearances and the *noumenal* world of the *things-in-themselves.* Nature as a system of appearances is viewed as being constituted by the synthetic activity of the transcendental ego, a position that Merleau-Ponty rejects. If he has rejected the resources provided by modern philosophy to overcome skepticism, does this imply a return to a position similar to that of Hume? In one sense, it is an implication that is too absurd even to discuss. Merleau-Ponty has certainly not adopted an empiricism based on atomic sensation and the laws of association. Rather, my question is the following: If Hume's position can be characterized as "a philosophy of belief," then to what extent does this resonates with both the theme of *perceptual faith* in *The Visible and the Invisible* and with Merleau-Ponty's retrieval of Husserl's concept of *ur-doxa.* Perhaps the mere fact that he is able to claim that skepticism is thinkable, but nonetheless not a position that one can occupy, shows that there is a certain echo of Hume's thought in Merleau-Ponty's thinking.

Let us glance at Merleau-Ponty's explicit treatment of skepticism in the first chapter of *The Visible and the Invisible.* He first considers a form of skepticism which he readily dispatches, namely, Pyrrhonism, which is a form of skepticism that begins with the priority of doubt. It is a way of thinking that harbors within itself an idea of "the truth in itself" and by means of this idea it terrorizes all of our actual experiences. Between its conception of "being in itself" and our inner life filled by representations, it does not even catch sight of the problem of the world. Merleau-Ponty criticizes this form of skepticism in a traditional manner, that is, he finds within it unacknowledged and unproblematized presuppositions, for example, a "representational theory of consciousness" and of an idea of "truth in itself." Nevertheless, this is not the end of the issue as it does at times seem to be within the thought of Heidegger, for example, when he writes with regard to Leibniz's windowless monads, "We need no windows; we are already out of doors." For Merleau-Ponty the problem posed by skepticism does not evaporate when we make a critique of a representational theory of consciousness; rather, he argues that we must "reformulate the skeptical arguments." His reason for the necessity of reformulating them is the following: having foreclosed both the phenomenological reduction and the eidetic reduction, and also having discarded Kant's contention that nature as appearance is constituted by the transcendental ego, we are faced with the fact that at least in some respect the perception of the world is mine, perhaps even in all its historical forms. It is this anomalous situation that skepticism gives voice to. In *The Visible and the Invisible*, Merleau-Ponty writes,

> The natural man holds on to both ends of the chain, thinks, at the same time, that his perception enters into the things, and that it is formed this side of his body. Yet, coexist as these two convictions do without difficulty in the exercise of life, once reduced to thesis and to propositions, they destroy one another and leave us in confusion. (*VI*, 8)

Beginning with Plato the tradition has attempted to exorcise this confusion by the upward movement of transcendence, which would demonstrate that what I truly perceive is already at least quasi-universal and that the soul that perceives it is itself, as Plato argues "of the race of the ideas." Merleau-Ponty's thought is an attempt to erode the uniqueness, the propriety, the ownness of the one who perceives. According to him, we cannot say of the perceiver what Heidegger says of Dasein, namely, that it always has the character of mineness (*Gemeinigkeit*). He argues that the subject of perception is the *one*; it is not an "I" that perceives but rather that *one* perceives through me. In the *Phenomenology of Perception,* he writes, "I ought to say that one perceives in me, and not that I perceive." As Rudolph Bernet has shown, "[T]his one of perceptual life is not a personal subject that melts into the anonymity of the masses—it is a subject interwoven with the natural world."[4] Merleau-Ponty concludes that "there is, therefore, another subject beneath me. It forms a world which exists before I am here, and it marks out my place in it" (*PhP*, 254). If one were to ask who is this other subject, Merleau-Ponty would answer that "this captive or natural subject is my body," indeed not my personal or momentary body but rather my "habitual body." In the *Phenomenology of Perception*, there remains a sufficient ambiguity that would permit one to say of the body what has classically been said of the subject, that is, to speak of it as a "body-subject," a sort of carnal *cogito*. No doubt it is this very ambiguity, the ambiguity that allows one to speak of a "body subject" that Merleau-Ponty is referring to when he makes an overly harsh auto-critique which claims that the *Phenomenology of Perception* was organized on the basis of subject and object thinking. All such ambiguity is resolved in *The Visible and the Invisible* where he writes, "My body does not perceive, but it is as if it were built around the perception that dawns through it." In this text there is no longer a question of our fundamental insertion into Being being the correlate of an intentional act of a subject, even a "body subject." Perception is seen as a fold in the field of the visible, sometimes wandering, sometimes reassembled. The dimension of Being that is beneath not only our personal life but also beneath history and symbolic institution is what Merleau-Ponty refers to as "wild being." In the context of his reinterpretation of Husserl, one could call this "the earth." This is the dimension that subtends the dimension in which experience can be properly said to be *mine*. In his lecture on "Husserl's Concept of Nature," he writes, "The earth is our stock, our *ur-heimat*, our originary insertion." Farther on, he adds that this is the universe of sensation; and a little later, in the same lecture, he refers to it as "a world of doxa."[5] This later formulation should alert us to the fact that Merleau-Ponty does not conceive of the "first universal" as a definitive overcoming of the problematic of skepticism. There is no question of founding a universal philosophy that would be based upon this dimension of "wild being" as a domain prior to all interrogation and ambiguity, that is, a ground of certainty. Any return to some sort of *first* immediacy or to a presence prior to difference is neither possible nor desirable. He writes:

> What we propose here is not to return to the immediate, the coincidence, the effect of fusion with existence, the search for an original integrity. . . . If coincidence is lost, this is no accident. If being is hidden, this is, itself, a characteristic of being, and no disclosure will make us comprehend it. (*VI*, 122)

Philosophy, in its attempt to overcome skepticism, cannot situate itself prior to the originary division of sense that renders skepticism possible. Merleau-Ponty shows that "the originating breaks up, and philosophy must accompany this breakup, this non-coincidence, this differentiation." There is no way under this originary non-coincidence that would secure us a place immune from doubt and ambiguity. Only with considerable circumspection can we speak of a primordial layer as a bedrock of experience. It is in *Signs* that he writes, "Each layer takes up the preceding one again, and each encroaches upon those that follow. Each is prior and posterior to the others, and thus to itself" (*Signs*, 176). Later, in *The Visible and the Invisible,* paradoxically he says that "the immediate is at the horizon and must be thought of as such. It is only by remaining at a distance that it remains what it is." If our insertion into Being thwarts the reflective turn by which the world would become a correlate of consciousness, it also precludes the possibility of a *radical* skepticism in which we would only be imprisoned in phantasms. Merleau-Ponty argues that "everything comes to pass, as though my power to reach the world, and my power to entrench myself in phantasms, come one with the other" (*VI*, 8). The intractability of our relationship to the earth lays the foundation for a weak universalism, employing the word *weak* in the sense that Vattimo uses it. Not a universal that could "once and for all" be achieved, but rather a universalism that precludes the closure of any particular system of signification; a universalism in which any constituted system of meaning would trail off into the domain of the nonconstituted, the earth. As Merleau-Ponty observes, one cannot think two earths. There are two pieces of the same earth, one single humanity. For humankind, there is nothing except humankind. "The most singular, the most carnal, is the most universal. It is eradicable, one cannot get rid of it."

We have seen that Merleau-Ponty has effected a profound critique of the resources that modern philosophy employed to overcome skepticism, but we have also shown that he has not done this in order to rejoin Hume's skepticism. If naturalism is defined as the reduction of the ideal to nature, then we can truly say that Merleau-Ponty's position is neither naturalistic nor antinaturalistic, since he has both deconstructed the opposition between fact and essence and adumbrated a concept of nature that would displace the opposition between the visible and the invisible, viewing them instead in terms of an intertwining between them. This being said, in one respect, however, his position does resonate with that of the Third Book of Hume's *Treatise.* Here Hume, the moralist, claims that what we believe is not simply a function of what we may think but of what we are, which is expressed by Merleau-Ponty as perceptual faith and not as secured knowledge. It appears that they both are arguing that we are of "the flesh of the world" inserted into wild being which neither guarantees certainty nor precludes objectivity. We might say of our relationship to truth what, perhaps Hume but definitely Merleau-Ponty, says of philosophy, "Its center is everywhere, its circumference nowhere" (*Signs*, 128).

NOTES

1. "Philosophy as a Rigorous Science," in *Phenomenology and the Crisis of Philosophy*, trans. Q. Lauer (New York: Harper and Row, 1965), 80.
2. Edmund Husserl, *Cartesian Meditations*, trans. D. Cairns (The Hague: Martinius Nijhof, 1960), 2.
3. John R. Searle, *Rediscovery of the Mind,* (Cambridge: MIT Press, 1992).
4. Rudoph Bernet, "The Subject in Nature: Reflections on Merleau-Ponty's Phenomenology of Perception," in *Merleau-Ponty in Contemporary Perspective* (Boston: Kluwer, 1993), 58.
5. "*Husserl et la notion de Nature,*" in *Merleau-Ponty, Parcours deux, 1951–1961*, (Paris: Editions Verdier, 2000), 230. It is not quite correct to say that Merleau-Ponty "writes" this text, as it is the transcript of notes taken by Fr. X. Tilliette when he was an auditor in Merleau-Ponty's 1956 course at the Collège de France.

8

The Elemental Flesh

Nature, Life, and Difference in Merleau-Ponty and Plato's Timaeus

ROBERT VALLIER

INTRODUCTION: FLESH, MOTHER, ELEMENT

This communication is oriented by two remarks in *The Visible and the Invisible*, the first of which appears in a working note dated November 1960, wherein Merleau-Ponty describes his task as a "psychoanalysis of nature: it is the flesh, the mother" (*VI*, 267). The text in which this remark appears gathers a number of diverse threads that Merleau-Ponty was weaving into the fabric of his last project, and thus merits considerable attention. Our interest here is not with what a psychoanalysis of nature might mean, but rather with the invocation of the mother, and with the apposition of the mother to the flesh.[1] That Nature should be apposited as "the flesh, the mother" suggests that Nature must be understood in two parallel modes, first as the flesh, to which Merleau-Ponty's own discourse would bear witness. We must always remember that with the term "the flesh, *la chair*," Merleau-Ponty *re*-translates the Husserlian term *Leib* (a lived body as opposed to a *Körper*, a corpse or mere physical body), and is thus both marking a difference from his earlier translation of this term as "*le corps propre*, the proper body," and also re-marking the manner in which he interrogates *the problem of life*, an interrogation that is present throughout, and gives unity to, his entire philosophical effort. The project of a psychoanalysis of Nature would thus, on the one hand, unfold as a phenomenology of the flesh, and thus as an ontology of life. But on the other hand, the apposition of "the mother" to the flesh suggests that such a project concerning Nature would also unfold in a second, complementary mode, to which *another* discourse would testify, and because this apposition is not simply a dead metaphor (e.g., "Mother Nature"), we must therefore ask in what such a discourse would consist. Given the context, it may well be that of *psychoanalysis*, in either its Lacanian or Kleinian variant, which, with its emphasis on the terrible mother, was very much at the center of Merleau-Ponty's attention in the last years of his life. Or it may be a *Romantic* discourse, articulated in part by Schelling, which plays an important role in the development of Merleau-Ponty's thought in the 1950s, particularly in the courses on "The Concept of Nature."[2] Although each of these possibilities could serve to generate a rich and complex reading of Merleau-Ponty's last efforts, we will not pursue them here. Instead, we will argue for a third possibility, a third discourse of the mother, namely, a *choric* discourse, for one of the names by which *khôra* is called in Plato's *Timaeus* is "the *mother*" of all becoming.[3] Can the choric discourse at the very center of Plato's dialogue shed any light on the significance of the flesh and the problem of life? What would such a discourse disclose about the nature of Nature?

This possibility and the questions to which it gives rise may, at first blush, seem arbitrary, but they gain some philosophical weight when we consider our second orienting remark, taken from a passage in the fourth chapter of *The Visible and the Invisible*. By the time the reader encounters the passage in question, Merleau-Ponty has already elaborated the chiasmatic structure of the "exemplary sensible" (*VI*, 138), of the touching touch, extending it from the noncoincidental "always imminent and never realized" (*VI*, 147) reversibility of the flesh of my body, to the relation between self and other, to a generalized structure of the world, a structure that "encroaches," but yet does not efface, the difference between the orders of the subjective and objective, between my body and that of the other, between myself and the world. What he has called "the flesh" is thus no longer simply the structure of the exemplary sensible that is my lived body; rather, the flesh, and all the differences that it entails, must be thought as the "*differentiations* of one sole and massive *adhesion* to Being" (*VI*, 270). The flesh is thus the differentiation of what adheres, and as such, it is prior to difference, both the holding-together and the discriminating of difference. As an in-difference, it is not yet subject or object, mind or body; it is prior to their difference, prior to the orders of consciousness that would allow us to represent it and determine it. For this reason, "there is no name in traditional philosophy to designate it" (*VI*, 139). This then brings us to the passage in question, our second orienting remark: "[T]he flesh is not matter, is not mind, is not substance. To designate it, we should need the old term *element*, in the sense it was used to speak of water, air, earth, and fire, that is, in the sense of a general thing, midway between the spatio-temporal individual and the idea, a sort of incarnate principle that brings a style of being wherever there is a fragment of being. The flesh is in this sense an *element* of Being" (*VI*, 139). While it is true that in his appeal to the ancient notion of the element in his non-definition of flesh, Merleau-Ponty names no ancient thinker in particular, both the appeal itself and that for the sake of which the appeal is made can nevertheless gain specificity if we consider *elementality* in light of the treatment it receives by the Syracusan astronomer in the *Timaeus*. The reference to the mother in the working note, and the appeal to the elements in chapter 4 of *The Visible and the Invisible* thus constitute an invitation to situate Merleau-Ponty's thinking of the flesh as a choric thinking.

Aside from the common use of a few key terms such as "element" and "mother," what reason would compel us to accept this invitation and claim that a reading of the *Timaeus* would be instructive, especially if Merleau-Ponty nowhere, to our knowledge, explicitly comments on it? An answer to this question requires that we consider how Merleau-Ponty reads the historical tradition to which this text belongs. The flesh is the differentiating matrix that lets being stand forth in difference as meaningful. Insofar as Being is an adhesion of differentiations, it is *not* a positive term, not a full plenitude or pure in-itself, not an identity, and as such does not have an exterior dialectical term standing in opposition to it. With the flesh, Merleau-Ponty is seeking to articulate a new conception of Being by interrogating the metaphysical conception of Being as pure identity and plenitude excluding all becoming and negativity, a conception that dominates the tradition from Parmenides to Husserl, and that Merleau-Ponty characterizes as an "ontology of the object" (*Nature*, 125–27). Merleau-Ponty's initial and clandestine partner in this critical interrogation is Bergson, for whom the defining feature of metaphysics is the priority of nothingness over Being, that is, Being is that which emerges from and overcomes, "fills in," nothingness, and only that Being that admits of no negativity whatsoever would be fully what it is, a positivity.[4] In effect, metaphysics as Bergson understands it is concerned with the timeless being and objectivity of pure thought (e.g., mathematics, logic), while human beings, precisely because we are mortal and finite (and hence contain a degree of negativity) are considered secondary, even irrelevant by metaphysics. Now, Merleau-Ponty accepts Bergson's critique of the metaphysical illusion of the priority of nothingness, but rather than concluding with Bergson that the illusion of nothingness has been overcome and then arguing for a positive Becoming, Merleau-Ponty shows that "the meaning sense of Bergsonian philosophy is not so much to eliminate the idea of nothingness *as to incorporate it into Being*" (*Nature*, 66). Thus, Merleau-Ponty, inspired by Bergson, seeks to articulate a conception of negativity that is not exterior to Being (as in Sartre), nor is the simple vanishing of Being into Nothing (as in Hegel), but rather is a constitutive "dimension" of Being, "the invisible of the visible" that aliments and sustains it, lets it come to pass as visible.[5] This dimension of negativity internal to Being would therefore constitute its capacity to differentiate itself and thus to appear. In that the flesh is an adhesion of differentiations, then this internal negativity would be constitutive of the flesh itself.

Even though the tradition is dominated by the ontology of the object, there are nevertheless intimations within the tradition of another, more originary sense of being, intimations that are strategically repressed by the tradition in order to maintain the purity and privilege of the conception of being as positive object. This other sense of being, onto which the Bergsonian critique opens, reveals being to be not an object that stands in front of us in a plenitude of determination and that we would approach directly, but rather that which "englobes" and is all around us, the "soil" that sustains and carries us, and that shows itself through the differences, gaps, hiatuses inscribed by the work of its operative negativity (*Nature*, 4). We can therefore approach only by means of an "indirect ontology," starting from our belongingness to it. Merleau-Ponty characterizes the discourse of this other sense of being as an "ontology of the existent," (*Nature*, 127–29) because the existent is the kind of being that contains negativity, but that we could equally characterize as an "ontology of the element."[6] If he wants to liberate this other sense of being, he must do so by interrogating the repressive strategies deployed by the tradition (the very tradition to which we belong) in order to disrupt them and call into question the privilege of the ontology of the object. We thus can and should read the *Timaeus* as Merleau-Ponty would, as a classic text in which the tension between the two ontologies is clearly marked, in order to interrogate and displace the strategies that obscure the ontology of the element. By letting this other ontology come to the fore, we can thus shed light on the flesh.

We can, in other words, read the *Timaeus* as an exercise in the style of hermeneutics practiced by Merleau-Ponty. We will no doubt fail in our efforts, first and foremost because the Platonic text resists an exhaustive interpretation, but demands the effort of one, a demand that is beyond the scope of our present concern. We will thus not gainsay the recent chorological contributions of Derrida, Margel, Brague, or, most recently, Sallis; quite the contrary, what we offer here presupposes and is indebted to those analyses.[7] Our aim is much more modest: by reading this classic text in a way informed by Merleau-Ponty's understanding of the tradition and by his later texts, and oriented by our two clues, we will be able to clarify the sense of Being that Merleau-Ponty was attempting to articulate as the flesh, the "element" of Being, the Mother. Indeed, we will certainly fail to provide the rigorous reading that is demanded of such a rich and complicated text, and fail to meet the demands of Merleau-Ponty's hermeneutic. But we can at least circumscribe the issues at stake, and thus ground the reasons for bringing Merleau-Ponty into communication with choric thought. There are good *philosophical* reasons immanent to Merleau-Ponty's style of reading and his project, particularly as it bears on questions of life, nature, and flesh; but more importantly, there are *elemental* reasons issued from the very nature of thinking, which is itself the enabling-favoring element by which Being comes to pass, as Heidegger says, for thinking, like the flesh, is also an element of Being.[8] Having thus oriented ourselves to the problem at hand, let us turn now to Plato's choric text.

CHORIC ELEMENTALITY: ON PLATO'S *TIMAEUS*

We all know the story of Plato's *Timaeus*, a text in which the threads of memory and writing, of supplementarity and inscription, of fiction and testimony, are all woven into an account of the origin of the universe and the generation of all the things in it. In light of Sallis's recent extraordinary and close reading of this infinitely remarkable dialogue, there is no need to rehearse the story in full here; but a few indications will, nevertheless, be helpful to situate that which is fundamentally unsituatable, namely, the elements, or more precisely, the *elemental* and mother *khôra*, and thus also the flesh as an element of being.

After an account of the impossibility of giving such an account, Critias, with Socrates' enthusiastic support, nonetheless invites the Syracusan astronomer to recount the generation of the cosmos (27a). Confidently, boldly, Timaeus begins his tale only to discover midway through it that it will have been inadequate, necessitating a new effort. In his second attempt, Timaeus proceeds more cautiously, even suspiciously, telling "a likely story" (40d) governed by "a bastard reasoning" whose logic is at best oneiric. Despite his cautions, his second discourse is nonetheless audacious, opening upon an aporia from which he will recoil. Our first question must therefore ask what in his first account necessitates that Timaeus begin again.

Timaeus begins his first account by repeating a rigorous distinction between two kinds, namely, the eternal self-same and the ephemeral self-different, or the paradigmatic, ungenerated model and the mimetic, generated copies (including, obviously, the cosmos). "In my opinion," he claims at 27d, "there is first to be distinguished the following. What is that which is always being, having no genesis, and what is that which is generated but never being? On the one hand, that which is comprehended by intellection with *logos*, being always according to the same, on the other hand, the opinable grasped by opinion by sense without *logos*, being generated and perishing, never being in the manner appropriate to being." Now, these two kinds of being are heterogenous, and this simple dualism generates all sorts of problems, not the least of which is generation itself: paradigmatic self-same being is always what it is and "has no genesis," but how is the cosmos fabricated out of the kind of being that admits of genesis, is always other than itself, and as such is "disorderly and discordant" (30a)? Timaeus will try to respond to these questions, but because his opening argument is *only an opinion* about the way things seem—an opinion uncritically received from "men of wisdom" (29e) rather than well reasoned—his responses will likewise be equally shady. Timaeus nevertheless feels compelled to defend this opinion; his defense—and thus the entire first account—is a wholly *technological* discourse, and it will turn out to be governed by what Merleau-Ponty called the ontology of the object, as we shall see. Now, Timaeus explains that "everything generated is *of necessity* generated by some cause" (28a; emphasis added), implying that necessity imposes itself from the beginning as a condition of the cause. But tellingly, Timaeus will not address the question of necessity until his *second* speech, trying desperately to contain its operation by reducing it to just a "small part" of the mixture (47e). To what cause does Timaeus initially assign the generation of the cosmos?

The *demiurge* is both "its maker and its father" (28c). The demiurge stands in relation to the two kinds of being as a painter does to his model and the canvas. The demiurge studies the model, comprehends that which is always what it is with *nous*, sees it noetically, and puts his *techne* to work on generated being to construct a copy; his skill and action as a maker constitutes *the intelligible cause* of the cosmos (29a). With his mind's eye on the model, the demiurge uses his *techne* to bring the disorderly and discordant matter into order, declaring that such a state is good and beautiful; analogously, the state of rationality is preferred over irrationality, and reason belongs to soul (30a). Hence, the product of his artifice, the cosmos, will have a body and a soul, and therefore will "come into existence as *a living creature*" (30b-c; emphasis added). The demiurge thus fabricates a *natural* being, the kind of being not normally (at least in the days before cloning) made with *techne*. The demiurge is both "maker and father" (28c), but Timaeus has cautiously and problematically bracketed the question of the erotic necessity of paternity—and with it, questions of the mother, sexual difference, and reproduction—focusing only on technical production. He maintains this narrow focus by speculating about the material operation of this production.

The cosmos as a living creature has a body and a soul. A body is visible and tangible, and as Timaeus tells us, "[W]ithout *fire* nothing could ever become visible, nor tangible without *earth*" (31b). The *elements* are thus arranged by the demiurge in the fabrication of the body; but this implies that the elements have *already* been generated, so we will have to wonder from whence they came. The demiurge is a frugal gourmet with the elements, using all of them without remainder (32c) and according to recipes unknown to us to make the one sole body of the cosmos, which imitates the goodness, and beauty of the model (30d–31b). Without a soul, this body would be a mere corpse, and the soul is also manufactured by the demiurge, but not with the elements (as none remain). Of this second recipe, Timaeus does let slip some of the chef's secret: "[I]n the middle between the being that is indivisible and is always according to the same and that which is divisible and is generated in connection with bodies, [the demiurge] blended from both a *third form of being* . . . from the nature of the same and of the different; and in this way he compounded it in the middle between [them]." The demiurge blends these three ingredients together to form the soul, sets intelligence within it, then subsequently sets it in relation to the body as an ordered whole, that is, the cosmos as a living being.

Commenting on this, "the most perplexing passage in the whole of the dialogue,"[9] Sallis offers an important and instructive insight: some proportion of the kind of being that is supposed to be indivisible and self-same is blended together with some proportion of the kind of being that is divisible and self-different. This means, consequently, that self-same, indivisible being, *must be not what it is*: in order both to be blended in to the third kind of being and to remain as paradigm, it must divide itself within itself, or, more succinctly, be what it is *not*. In the very heart of self-same indivisible being, there must be already a negative principle by which it duplicates, divides, or otherwise differentiates itself. It is this inner principle of negativity that differentiates self-same Being, allows it to be mixed with what is not it in order to form soul, and thus lets living beings come to pass; as such, it is the very condition of life. This then raises important questions about the ontological status of self-same being, and effectively undermines the opinion held by Timaeus at the outset by revealing its insufficiency—if there were such an inner principle, then the difference between the two kinds of being would turn out to be no difference at all; there cannot be, yet there must be. These questions do not give Timaeus pause; rather, he continues to describe how, starting from these initial claims, the entire cosmos and everything in it is constructed, animated, and set into temporal motion. But having marked out the some essential difficulties, we will not follow him farther into the details of his initial effort.

These difficulties, which Timaeus has glibly passed over, will eventually necessitate a new beginning (at 47e), so let us enumerate them summarily. First, Timaeus's technological account presupposes both a familiar distinction and an external point of view for the technician; his model is the kind of being that is what it is because it cannot be otherwise as it has no genesis, and copies this by applying his *techne* on an "inappropriate" kind of being that is inherently discordant, making order of disorder, that is, making it into something, an existence, a living creature. This *kosmostheoros* is exactly what Merleau-Ponty, with the assistance of the Bergsonian critique of the metaphysical illusion of nothingness, decries as the ontology of the object that has dominated the tradition since Parmenides, and it is in effect rooted in a technological practice. Timaeus uncritically receives the traditional opinion and "begins" with self-same Being as a positive object because he cannot begin with nothing; there is thus an unspoken precedence of nothingness over being. But notice, second, the questions that Timaeus has tried to suspend: (1) he has said that the demiurge is *both* maker *and* father, but has not spoken of the erotic necessity of paternity in particular (and already this begs the question of the mother and of a sexual difference before the birth of the cosmos), or for that matter, of *the work of necessity* in general, even though necessity is there from the very beginning as a condition, focusing instead on the technology of material production; (2) the body of the cosmos is made, at least in part, with the *elements*, but their preliminary generation is not considered; finally (3) self-same being has to become other than what it is via an internal negativity and thus also differentiate itself from within itself, in order to be mixed with generated being to form the soul of the cosmos, and as such, on the one hand, this negative principle of differentiation internal to Being is a condition for the life of the cosmos, and on the other hand, this undermines the rigorous distinction upon which the entire account depends. With these difficulties weighing on him, Timaeus recognizes that he has to begin again, farther back, "before the birth of the heavens," prior to the work of the intelligible cause, and describe the work of necessity, which is bound up with the erotic, elemental difference, generation, reproduction, and life. But more importantly, the undermining of the ontological distinction from within also calls into question the inviolability of the ontology of the object, bespeaking the possibility of another, more originary sense of Being, which will unfold as an ontology of the element. Within the text of the *Timaeus*, there irrupts a tension between the ontology of the object and the ontology of the element, and the astronomer employs various strategies to neutralize the latter in order to preserve the integrity of the former. It is this tension that would attract Merleau-Ponty's eye in his attempt to interrogate the ontological tradition, and that we must look to now by considering—again, all too hastily—Timaeus's second discourse in our own attempt to think the flesh as both element and mother. Thus, before returning to Merleau-Ponty, we will consider this tension and its concomitant strategies employed by Timaeus in his second discourse.

Assessing the results of the first account, Timaeus tells us that "the foregoing part of our discourse, *save for a small portion*, has been fabricated by the demiurge through the operations of intellection; but now we must furnish an account of what is borne of *necessity*" (47e), because, he says, the coming into being of our world is the result of a "mixture of intellection and necessity" (48e). For the most part, the technological first account shows how intellection dominates necessity "by persuading it" (48a) to be orderly. There is, however, that "small" portion, resistant to the persuasive operations of intellection, that nevertheless is an essential ingredient in the recipe of the cosmos, and that "small" portion is necessity itself. If we thus want to describe the way in which necessity works, "if we really want to say how the world was born, we must make the species of the errant cause intervene in this tale, and describe the nature of its proper movement" (48a-b). But in what way will we describe this movement? Timaeus tells us that in order to do so, we will have to gain a view of the *real nature* of fire and water, air and earth, as it was before the birth of the heavens" (48b; emphasis added), that is, we will have to consider the generation of the elements *before* they are elements in any orderly, rational sense, *before* they can be called anything such as "substance" or "matter" or "extension," let alone "fire" or "earth," and we will thus have to consider how they *differentiate* themselves. To consider the real nature of the elements—or rather, let us say the *elemental*—is thus also to consider the errant cause, namely, the work of necessity. His first strategy—and we will follow him here—is to ask about this *planomenes eidos aitias*, but it is accompanied by another: he tells us that "it is difficult to explain our views while keeping to our present method of exposition," that is, the relatively straightforward technological exposition of the first account (48c). This strategic caution is multiplied throughout the second speech, first by invoking the gods to "bring us safely through this novel and unwonted exposition" (48d-e), indicating that he will be saying something risqué, maybe a sacrilege, via a "likely account" based in likenesses that appear "as in a dream," indicating further that what follows is something dangerous that is best left unsaid. Timaeus was, after all, a somewhat prudish Pythagorean, so it is not surprising that he might be a bit worried here.

In his professional life, Timaeus was an astronomer who no doubt spent many a night watching Venus chase Mars, and Saturn Jupiter, across the Mediterranean sky, graphing their movements with respect to the rest of the stars. Whereas the cluster of stars known as constellations appear to move collectively and with apparent regularity as the year advances, some stars, which today we know as *planets*, move erratically, not in an annual pattern, not even in a mensual pattern; rather, in virtue of their belonging to our solar system and of their then-unknown elliptical solar orbits, their paths would have appeared "out of synch" with the rest of the stars in the night sky. The path that they traced out would have been a meandering, irregular path that would have defied the calculable, logical, strictly and straightforwardly linear paths of the other stars. There is nonetheless one regular aspect in their observed irregularity, namely, that these stars moved between two fixed points in the sky, but never by the same path. Indeed, the movement itself comes to define the two points as points, joining and separating them, inscribing a difference between them and allowing a meaningful structure (a pattern) to stand out, rather than, inversely, the points existing preliminarily as the limits of the movement. In similar fashion does Merleau-Ponty, borrowing from Husserl's analyses in *Ideas II*, describe the motility of the lived body: as an absolute here or zero point of insertion, the lived body, through its movement or its indicative gestures, inscribes a difference between this absolute "here" and an "over there," and only through this inscription of difference does the original "here" of the body have any meaning (*sens*) or any orientation (*sens*) to elsewhere at all.[10] Most remarkably, in *The Visible and the Invisible*, Merleau-Ponty characterizes the body and its motricity as "a visibility sometimes wandering sometimes reassembled" (*VI*, 137–38), or in the language of his earlier work, as a *transcendence-as-inherence.*[11] Like the movement of the body, the errant cause is a wandering, a meandering, an alteration that consequently differentiates two points and thus gives place to an opposition by defining a polarity, that is, it marks out space, differentiates it, just as the wandering stars differentiate the night sky, marking out the spaces into which astrological significance is assigned. The movement of the errant cause is thus a movement of differentiation, and only on the basis of this inscription of difference is meaning possible, or, said otherwise, through this difference, the world gives itself to us as meaningful. Consider Merleau-Ponty again, when, in "The Philosopher and His Shadow," he writes that "the perceived world endures only through the reflections, shadows, levels, and horizons between things (which are not things and are not nothing, but on the contrary mark out by themselves the fields of possible variation in the same thing and the same world)."[12] The world presents itself in a meaningful way only through the differences between things, themselves inscribed though the differential motility of my body, which, as "a remarkable variant of the flesh" (*VI*, 141), is oriented by the things in such a way that one can no longer easily discern a priority of subject over object, can no longer "say if I look at things or the things look at me" (*VI*, 133). Now, if Merleau-Ponty assigns a privilege to the agency and the motility of the body in *Phenomenology of Perception* in order to think the way in which differences are inscribed, he undermines this in *The Visible and the Invisible* by making the body into a *variant* of the flesh; consequently, it is no longer the body as such that differentiates, but rather a principle "internal" to the flesh itself that differentiates, an elemental principle.

But let us return for a moment to the *Timaeus*. Only now, after the introduction of the errant cause, does Timaeus attempt to speak of the elements and their generation, issuing a correction with regard to the first account: "[W]hereas then we distinguished only two forms, we must now declare another third kind" (48e). The third kind is called "the receptacle and as it were the nurse of becoming" (49a), will be likened to the mother, and eventually named the untranslatable *Khôra*. We will say more about the significance of these images in a moment, but first note that whereas the third kind is introduced in order to take account of the work of necessity, its introduction is itself conditioned by the necessity "to discuss first the problem of fire and its fellow elements" (49b) before they become the elements that we recognize as such. What are these elemental problems that give pause? What is the real nature of the elements, knowledge of which is necessary if we want to understand the errant cause and the work of necessity in the generation of the cosmos?

We assume we know what fire is when we call it an element; but what is meant by "element"? The Greek word used by Timaeus in this context in *stoikheia* (48b), which has the sense of elementary particles, both physical and, more commonly, linguistic (e.g., syllables, letters); there is an ambivalence between a natural and an artificial sense, but both point to elemental *parts* with which one constructs a *whole*. This is a view that Timaeus explicitly rejects; whatever the elements may be (and this is precisely what he wants to clarify), to liken them to natural or linguistic particles is an inappropriate reduction, violating their originary sense, as "the man with even a grain of sense" knows (48c). A grain of sense must have been implanted in Timaeus, since he himself was guilty of such an assumption in his first discourse, having presupposed fire and earth and elaborated a technological notion of the elements as composite parts of a constructed whole. Insofar as he wants to exposit the generation of the cosmos as a living creature, the condition for which is an originary difference that cannot be accommodated in the logic of the first account, he must move away from a conception of the fire and earth as elementary particles, and toward another conception of the elements as a difference that sustains life.[13] Although he does not explicitly say it, this more originary conception is close, on the one hand, to the sense of Empedoclean (and, perhaps differently, Deleuzian?) *rhizomata*, the elemental *roots* that nourish organic growth; as such, this nonparticular conception would be bound up with the manner in which all non-technologically produced living things, including human beings, come to pass.[14] On the other hand, we must recall that we are examining the real nature of the elements before the cosmos was given order, and as such, this more originary sense of the elements is closely bound up with *chaos*. Here we take up again an important acquisition from the earlier meditation on the errant cause: this latter does not proceed in a straightforwardly linear, "mechanical" fashion, but rather errantly wanders. Its errant movement marks out a difference that lets a meaningful structure stand forth, and thus brings order. Similarly, chaos is constantly, diremptively acting on itself, constantly becoming other than what it is, and through this, regulates or organizes itself in the process of which it generates various products, including the cosmos and everything in it. Chaos is anterior to the differentiation of beings but produces difference in virtue of its being a self-differentiating and auto-regulating phenomenon; as such, it is the furnace of life. From this, three consequences immediately follow: first, it implies that the ordered cosmos is the *contingent* product of the work of necessity; second, chaos can never be completely mastered, its activity has no terminus, for otherwise there would be no life; third, since it is unmasterable, it can, despite our best effort, irrupt or intervene at any time in our otherwise well-ordered lives, for example, as the erotic or the mortal. In this regard, elemental chaos is both productive and potentially, ultimately destructive, reclaiming what it generates. Thus, the sense of the element that Timaeus is about to elucidate is more originary than the particular, technological conception, implying a continuous differentiation that sustains life, lets beings appear, and dissolves what appears in its flux.

This is consistent with Timaeus's first claim in his description of the real nature of the elements: they pass into one another in a constant cycle of genesis, never resting in some pure, stable state, always becoming different (49c-d). In a famously difficult passage that has generated much debate,[15] we learn that the individuated elements can never be called "this" or "that" with any determinacy, but only "suchlike," precisely because they are constantly fleeting and passing into one another (49d–50a). There is always a divergence between the name and what is named; the former comes too late, the latter has left the scene. The elemental flees from discourse, and yet, in constantly cycling around and differentiating itself, marking out difference, so that it can stand forth, if only fleetingly, as a sign so that we can discriminately say that this which we are at this moment apprehending is "firelike" or "earthlike." The individuated elements thus lack any determinacy, but *the elemental* remains always what it is precisely in constantly differing from itself, that is, in being this continuous cycle of generation. The receptacle is that which receives and sustains what flees from determinacy; it is that *in which* the differential cycling takes place and *out of which* differentiated beings emerge (50c). Timaeus says that of the third kind, which recall is what is approached and clarified in this preliminary discussion of the elemental, "the same account must be given" (50b), that is, what has been said of the elemental is also, analogically, appropriate to the receptacle, which would thus be both self-same and self-differing, and yet, as third, neither one nor the other, a contradiction that will call into question the ontological status of all three kinds, radically problematizing yet again the ontology of the object. We also observe here that this third kind must in fact be first, anterior to the ontological difference between the self-same first and the self-othering second kinds of being, and would give place to this very difference. It is no wonder that this "third" kind is "baffling and obscure" (51b) for Timaeus, because it cannot be grasped in terms of the traditional oppositional structures that it in fact makes possible.

Now, although Timaeus says that the same account must be given of the receptacle, what follows is *not* the same account. As a natural scientist, he possesses a certain degree of competence (a *techne*, but also an eidetic insight that allows him to exercise his *techne* well) that permits him to speak of the elements. But now, he continues to provide a likely account by likening the paradigm to the father, the receptacle to the mother, and the copy to the offspring (50d). The introduction of the sexual likenesses means that Timaeus has moved beyond his technical competence and has taken up the question of the erotic. Moreover, we must remember that these likenesses, as well as that to which they refer, are "baffling and obscure," and perceived "as in a dream." Timaeus is thus a dreaming man, only half-awake, who easily confuses images of being for the truth of being, and this is no doubt why he has such difficulty proceeding.[16] The oneiric images are introduced to take hold of something dreamlike, unclear, and difficult, namely, that part of necessity that resists the ordering power of intellection, and therefore these images are not mere metaphors. Rather, they come to supplement intellection and bring us close to what is baffling. In simpler terms, if the cosmos is indeed a living being, then what is being thought with the aid of these images is the originary difference that sustains life.

On one level, these erotic dream images are appropriate, since the living cosmos cannot be merely manufactured, but must rather be engendered by erotic necessity, implying an original sexual difference. Timaeus, who as a Pythagorean would normally be somewhat prudish in his comportment, risks being carried away by these sexual dream images, which are anticipated with the claim that the receptacle-mother "from its own proper quality . . . never departs at all; for while it is always receiving all things, nowhere and in no wise does it assume any shape similar to any of the things that enter into it. . . . [She is] *moved and marked* by the entering figures, and because of them it appears different at different times" (50b-c). The receptacle thus both remains what it is and appears to be different. She is "shaken" (53e) by what penetrates her, impregnated with images of the paradigm "in a wondrous manner" (50c) that Timaeus promises to explain later, and gives birth to offspring. Because she is entered or penetrated by the paradigm, she is moved. Penetrated by many different figures, she is "filled with potencies [*dynamis*] that are neither similar nor balanced, so that in no part of herself is she equally balanced, but sways unevenly in every part, and is herself shaken by these and shakes them in turn" communicating movement to the offspring, namely, the continuous differentiating movement of the elemental cycle of generation (52e–53a). And it is an imbalance of dynamic capacities, a state brought about by her own capacity for reception, that produces this generative movement. Because of this dynamic imbalance, she throws off the offspring, which, "as they are moved, fly off in various directions are dissipated" (a phenomenon that Timaeus also explains by immediate recourse to another technical example, the winnowing basket at 52a), settling into their place as a fleetingly individuated element, which, likewise shaken and dynamically imbalanced, "dissipates" into the flux of the generative cycle, which is not the reinstatement of the same, but the repetition that engenders the different. Differential generation is thus thought from out of *dynamis*, capacity, potentiality; we have been trying to take hold of the work of necessity, which we now see is understood in terms of *possibility*. The creation of the cosmos could indeed be read as a sexual act, which we already suspected earlier when it was named a living being, but we must remember that the sexual images function to bring to light something difficult and obscure. Recall that what is at stake is an indwelling negative principle of difference that lets beings come to pass and that is the condition for life. The erotic likenesses allow us to grasp this principle as an image.

But with these images, Timaeus has moved decidedly away from the technological recipe of compositional admixture of the first account and toward a *tiktological* sexuality of procreation in the second; as Heidegger notes, the Greek word for sexual engendering is *tikto-*, the root from which *techne* is ultimately derived.[17] But the tiktological is perhaps too much for poor prudish Timaeus to bear; he describes the whole affair as "embarrassing." And indeed, on another level, the likening is wholly inappropriate for someone like Timaeus. Indeed, if, as we said a moment ago, the Third must in fact be First, prior to and making possible the distinction that governs the first discourse, then the mother would have to precede both Father and Offspring, giving place to both; monstrously incestuous relations, indeed, the whole Pandora's box of the erotic, begin to announce themselves. But Timaeus doesn't want to hear about it, and this no doubt is why he returns to technologically based images (e.g., the analogy of fragrant ointments and their odorless base, and of the winnowing baskets).

All of this might give him it might give him a nervous *tik-* . . .[18] So it's not surprising that at this, the stickiest moment of *tiktos*, the moment of sexual reproduction and difference, Timaeus abandons these questions by means of two strategies: first, he abandons the sexualized images and proceeds to a discussion of the *Khôra*, which the third kind is now called. And second, having gotten through this "unwonted" exposition concerning necessity, generation, and difference, he returns to the question of the elements postcoital, that is, after they are generated, in a more physical and material sense, as bodies in the sense that Husserl defines them qua *Körper*, bodies that possess depth and extension, exist in the plural, have sensuous *quale* and objective sense, and are bounded by a surface that can be described geometrically as a rectilinear plane composed of triangles. From *tiktos*, Timaeus slides back to *techne*. We will say a few words about these two strategies before returning to Merleau-Ponty and concluding.

Timaeus is just as prudent as he is prudish, so rather than being carried away by the sexual images, he soberly maintains his discourse by assessing what he has thus far established, summarizing the series of images he has deployed regarding the third kind with one, untranslatable name, *Khôra*. But as the foregoing argument has tried to show, the very structure of the summary is undermined by (or at least inadequate to) what it summarizes. The passage on the *Khôra* is only twenty-five lines long, a text that merits a long and cautious elaboration, one that we cannot undertake here, in order to expose what is most radical.[19] The word is often translated as "place" or "space," but in the context of the passage in question, such a translation misses what is thought; it is derived from the verb *khoreo-*, *khorein*, signifying a movement that inscribes ("choreography") space but does not occupy it. To translate *Khôra* as space is thus to hypostatize it, localize it, make it determinate as something, and in doing that, we would grasp it with the oppositional conceptual categories (subject, object, etc.) that it subsequently makes possible by giving place through its originary differentiating movement to the dualism that was necessarily presupposed at the beginning. We have seen that insofar as the third is what it is by constantly differing from itself, by never coinciding with itself, it is at once both intelligible, ungenerated, self-same being and sensible, generated self-differing being, both first and second before first and second are differentiated, *and yet* neither one nor the other; it oscillates between the two orders, thus inscribing them *as* orders and as an opposition. Hence every attempt to conceptualize it, and therefore any translation of it, is always effected as a retrospective illusion, a reduction *après coup*, and a neutralization. In effect, every attempt to conceptualize it reduces it by objectifying it and therefore folds it back into the ontology of the object. That Timaeus has to offer many oneiric images is thus not at all surprising, because in a dream, or in "bastard reasoning" that is "hardly trustworthy," the orders of logic break down and get muddled, so that one can begin to have an intimation of what is beyond and before logic; but likewise in a such a dream, "we are unable to say the truth" (52c) but neither "do we speak falsely" (51b).

What is the truth that we must struggle to say? "That as long as one thing is something and another is something else, neither of the two will ever come to be in the other, so as to become, at once, both one and two." That is, as long as the dualism of the first account, the ontology of the object, remains presupposed and operative, we will never be able to understand either how it is that self-same being is able to differentiate or duplicate itself, or how the second kind of being is generated. *Khôra*, and the images that allow us to approach it, gives place to the elemental movement of differentiation that is internal to being, allowing us to hold the opinion that it is of two kinds; the third kind thus turns out to be neither "third" nor a "kind" of being, but rather prior to and making possible both distinctions, and only insofar as it remains the same by continually differentiating itself via a receptive capacity of an enabling movement proper to it. *Khôra* is both one and two at the same time in such a way as to be neither one nor two, and thus we could call it the undifferentiated differentiation of difference. Only the "thought" (if one can call bastard reasoning and the dreamwork by this name) of the *Khôra* allows us to approach the inner negative principle of differentiation, and while it "should always be called by the same name," it is called by several, none of which are ultimately appropriate—"it has no name in traditional philosophy," as Merleau-Ponty says of the flesh, because it is prior to the orders of naming.

The structure of the summary in which Timaeus assesses what he has acquired in his interrogation is thus undermined by that which it summarizes, precisely because he still maintains the oppositional dualism of the first account and adds to it the third kind, which we have now seen makes possible the dualism in the first place, as if Timaeus has not grasped the radical implications of his own discourse; he is, after all, a dreaming man, only half-awake. But that Timaeus should continue to maintain the priority of this oppositionality amounts to a strategy that marginalizes and contains the radically other sense of being that he allows to irrupt. At the most radical moment, when the outline of an ontology of the element sketches itself out oneirically, at the most aporetic moment of the dialogue when another sense of being comes to the fore, Timaeus retreats from the edge of the abyss, and returns to the language and logic of the technological account, rooted in the ontology of the object. This strategic retreat is marked not only by his reductive, dualist-based summary of the three kinds in which he seems to ignore the radicality of his own insights, but also, at the close of the passage, Timaeus announces quite clearly that, having "provided a reasoned account of the matter summarily stated" (52d), he will now explain how the individuated elements interact as compositional particles to produce various bodies and substances by means of a "technical method" (53c), apparently altogether forgetting the inappropriateness of conceiving them as elementary particles and the more radical sense as *rhizome* or as chaotic primal matter. Amazingly, yet almost predictably, the individuated elements are describable *geometrically*, in terms of scalene and isosceles triangles arranged as surfaces of a solid, crystalline molecule (the icosahedron is the geometrical structure of a molecule of water, the tetrahedron fire, the octahedron air, and the cube earth, "the most stable" [53d–55c]; the shaking motion of the *khôra* sends them flying to their regions, but en route, molecules interact, break up into their constitutive triangles, and regroup, forming "an indefinite number of intermediary bodies"). This geometrical account of the individuated elements unmistakably marks his definitive return from *tiktos* to *techne*, from the ontology of the element to the ontology of the object.

We could say much about this elemental geometry, but we will limit ourselves to just one observation. Of the four elements, earth seems to have a singular privilege, because whereas the other elements can be decomposed and recomposed as another form (water when interacting with fire can be broken down into one molecule of fire and two of air), fragments of cubic earth molecules "always reunite and become earth again, for surely earth will never change into another form" (56d). Earth is always reborn and sediments or falls back to the ground as earth, and consequently all bodies produced with an earth molecule, including human beings, remain fundamentally terrestrial, grounded on and by (the) earth. To an extent, then, earth is the privileged element by which beings come to pass and to which they return, it is the root from which stems all life. Thus, even in the technical geometrical account of the elementary particles, there is a trace of the notion of the elemental as *rhizome*, a trace that Timaeus seeks strategically to displace and oppress. Moreover, the cubic molecule of earth is the most stable and "difficult to move" (55e); Timaeus thus anticipates, if somewhat inaccurately, the sense of the earth that Husserl will take up as *Boden* and as *Stamm* in his attempt to overturn the Copernican doctrine during the *Krisis* period,[20] and that Merleau-Ponty views as an image of *tre brut* and the "soil of our experience" or a "living stock from which all objects are engendered . . . a general type of being that contains all ulterior possibilities and serves as a cradle for them" (*Nature*, 77). But we cannot here engage in the lengthy analysis of Husserl's text and its influence on Merleau-Ponty, so let us instead turn to our conclusion.

CONCLUSION: THE ELEMENTAL FLESH

After this passage through the *Timaeus*, one in which our attention was directed to the questions of the element, the mother, difference, and life, we can begin to clarify the meaning of both of our orienting clues. The conception of being that Merleau-Ponty wants to articulate through a critical interrogation of the traditional ontology of the object, and which bears the name "flesh" even though there is no name to designate it within the tradition, is one that contains an indwelling dimension of negativity, which is also an internal principle of differentiation. What has the investigation of the elemental receptacle in the *Timaeus* taught us about the flesh?

First, if we need the old word *element* to designate it, we have learned that the term itself designates nothing precise, but rather a continual movement of differentiation, an on-going inscription of difference that enables and favors the world and living beings, indeed all things, lets them show themselves, makes them be in a manner appropriate to them. This is what Merleau-Ponty means when he says that the element is "*a general thing* [but a thing that is no thing at all], midway between the spatio-temporal individual and the idea, a sort of incarnate principle that brings a style of being wherever there is a fragment of being" (*VI*, 139). Moreover, as with the element, when we use a word to designate the flesh, we do not designate a "this" or "that" in any definitive or determinate sense, precisely because the flesh is a "style of being" that orders fragments of being into meaningful visibles, letting them be "suchlike," bespeaking their belongingness to a cycle of generation. Moreover, the flesh is not a "this" or a "that" because its structure is one of noncoincidence; as such, like the elemental, the flesh always differs from itself, and in differing from itself, remains what it is.

"We must think the flesh," Merleau-Ponty tells us, "not starting from substances, body and mind, for then it would be the union of contradictory terms," that is, it would not be prior to and could not take account of difference, but would be the dialectical resolution of an already standing difference; rather, we must think it "like the element, as a concrete emblem of a general manner of being" (*VI*, 147). Indeed, in that the flesh, like the elemental, is an in-difference prior to and making possible difference, there is no name to designate it because, as we have seen, it is prior to the differentiated orders of subject and object that makes names possible; any attempt to name it, like any attempt to translate *Khôra*, would neutralize it, objectify it, and thus miss it. What we designate when we use the word *flesh* is the elemental, which never appears as such but is the condition for the possibility of all appearing, allowing beings to show themselves; it is thus a "connective tissue that sustains and nourishes, a possibility, an incarnate principle" (*VI*, 132).

While Timaeus seems to want to repress the ontology of the element at the very moment it emerges in order to maintain a technological discourse of the elements as the particles composing some constructed whole, Merleau-Ponty, in thinking the flesh as element, comes close to the Empedoclean sense of the elements as *rhizome*, the roots that sustain life. He comes even closer to the Heideggerian sense: the elementality of the flesh is a *possibility* or a *latency*, a *potentiality* of becoming, the enabling-favoring of Being, a may-be, a *Mög-liche*, which as we saw in our discussion above, reveals necessary being to be but a modality of possibility.[21] Thus, just as the continuous cycling movement of the elemental, that is, the excitation of the *Khôra*, transmits or communicates its movement to the individuated elements, letting them appear as elements and enter into reaction with one another to produce any number of differentiated visible bodies, so too is the flesh, the differential matrix, a movement, "sometimes wandering [or errant] sometimes reassembled," that inscribes differences, that differentiates and thus makes the world appear.

This passage through the *Timaeus* also teaches us something more about the flesh as a "massive adhesion of differentiations to Being." *Adhesion*, in French, has the sense of a force opposed to the separation of bodies in contact, as in intermolecular attraction, a force that both joins and separates what is different, holding them together while maintaining their difference, not resolving that difference in a dialectical synthesis. Moreover, the verbal form, *adhérer*, describes the action one undertakes when one joins a political party or union, which is composed of *adhérents*. This last sense is particularly telling: the party or the union exists only in and through the adhesion of its different adherents, without whom, it would be nothing. And yet, the party or the union is also more than the mere summation of its adherent members, and its position cannot be the result of an inventory of the opinions or beliefs of its members; inversely, the adhesion of its members and the differences among them may redefine the meaning and orientation of the party. What is differentiated thus adheres in being in such a way that does not efface difference; they are held together in being as an in-difference, an indwelling difference. Like the elemental-mother-*Khôra*, whose operative *dynamis* allows for the differentiation of being, so too is the flesh the differentiation of this "massive adhesion," the connective tissues that both unites and differentiates (and by now it should be clear that "massive" does not refer to size but rather to masses of differentiations, which, in a political party or union, would be its members). Not only is there in this thought the possible basis from which one may begin to approach *the political dimension of the flesh*, but also, there is a critical engagement with the problem of the dialectic of parts and whole, many and one, a problem that, in the second course on Nature, during an interrogation of Kantian and post-Kantian philosophic and scientific theories of the organism, he says "is the question at the center of this course on the idea of Nature, and maybe of all philosophy" (*Nature*, 145). In that the elemental choric flesh refers to a negative operation of differentiation internal to being, then it continues to interrogate that central question, constituting perhaps a "hyperdialectic." The encounter with the *Timaeus* has provided material to engage in this meditation on the dialectic of whole and parts. In this regard, emphasizing the operative *dynamis* as that possibility that allows for differentiation, we agree with the conclusion of Renaud Barbaras: *the flesh is a pure dynamism*.[22]

Finally, recall that the first orienting clue that gave impetus to this reflection was Merleau-Ponty's own description of what he wanted to do: "a psychoanalysis *of Nature*: it is the flesh, the mother." The image of the mother in the *Timaeus* is only a dream-image that comes to the aid of intellection in order to grasp what cannot be conceived. Through it and its associated images, especially the elemental, we take hold of "the third kind," or rather, an ontology of the element begins to articulate itself. What it discloses is a sense of being that differentiates itself from within, that contains a dimension of negativity. By its dynamic capacity, by its differentiating activity, it inscribes difference and lets the world stand forth as a meaningful structure, but cannot be retrospectively captured by these structures without being violated; moreover, this internal principle of differentiation is the condition for life. Only when we have a sense of being that contains negativity within it can we take account of *life* in its phenomenality and its generative, productive, self-organizing aspect. The images of the mother and the elemental thus disclose a sense of *living* being that resonates with what Merleau-Ponty calls Nature: "Nature is what has a meaning without it having been posited by thought. . . . Nature is not instituted by man, it is opposed to custom and discourse. Nature is the primordial, that is, the non-constructed, the non-instituted . . . it is an object that is not altogether an object; it is not entirely in front of us. It is our soil, not what is before us, but rather what carries us" (*Nature*, 4). Its first and fundamental sense derives from the Greek *physis*, which refers to an originary indwelling principle that differentiates and nourishes. In this regard, our passage through the *Timaeus* constitutes a contribution to the study of the variations of the concept of nature that Merleau-Ponty undertook in the first course on Nature in 1956–57. Nature is "the flesh, the mother," and we see now how certain aspects of the flesh become manifest when complemented by a choric investigation of the mother. With this, we have some sense of the object of Merleau-Ponty's project, namely, nature; and we understand what he means when he argues for the significance of the philosophical study of nature but in what way this project should be articulated as a "*psychoanalysis* of Nature" remains to be specified, but we will of course not take that up here, and instead, bring this communication to its end.

NOTES

1. On a "psychoanalysis of Nature," see the articles by J. Slatman, D. Olokowski, P. Burke, and R. Vallier in *Chiasmi International* 2 (2000), ed. M. Carbone (Milano: Associazione Culturale Mimesis).
2 See *Nature,* 36–50; see also R. Vallier, " *tre Sauvage* and the Barbaric Principle: Merleau-Ponty's Reading of Schelling," in *Chiasmi International* 2 (2000), op. cit.
3. Plato, *Timaeus*, 50d. I have consulted, but often modified, the Loeb translation prepared by R. G. Bury. It will become apparent that these three possible discourses are mutually imbricated.
4. Bergson makes this argument in chapter 4 of *Creative Evolution*. For a full comprehension of this argument, I am indebted to, and the reader will benefit from, Renaud Barbaras's analysis in his "The Turn of Experience: Merleau-Ponty and Bergson," which appears in translation in this volume.
5. *VI*, 246–47. On the dimension of negativity and the invisible of the visible, see Henri Maldiney, "Chair et verbe dans la philosophie de Merleau-Ponty," in *Merleau-Ponty: Le psychique et le corporel*, ed. A.-T. Tymieniecka (Paris: Aubier, 1988), 55–83.
6. Here once again we refer to the work of Renaud Barbaras, and in particular his essay entitled "De l'ontologie de l'objet à l'ontologie de l'élément," collected in *Le tournant de l'expérience* (Paris: J. Vrin, 1998), 201–24. Following a clue from G. Simondon, Barbaras argues that the sense of "element" that Merleau-Ponty had in mind was an Ionian sense.
7. See Jacques Derrida, *Khôra* (Paris: Galilee, 1993); Remi Brague, *Du temps chez Platon et Aristote* (Paris: PUF, 1982); Serge Margel, *Le Tombeau du dieu artisan*, préfacé par J. Derrida (Paris: Editions de Minuit, 1996); and most recently, John Sallis, *Chorology: On Beginning in Plato's 'Timaeus'* (Bloomington: Indiana University Press, 1999), among others. Contrast these thoughtful and hermeneutically careful works with analytic accounts, of which Luc Brisson, *Le même et l'autre dans la structure ontologique du Timee de Platon*, 2nd edition (St. Augustin: Academa Verlag, 1994), is a classic example. The problem of *khôra* has long been on our minds,

since a graduate seminar in 1993 in which Professor Sallis presented work that would eventually be incorporated into his monograph, which appeared, fortuitously, at the moment when we were engaged in a close reading of Barbaras's collection of essays on Merleau-Ponty.

8. Martin Heidegger, *Letter on Humanism*, tr. F. Capuzzi with J. G. Gray, in *Basic Writings*, ed. D. F. Krell (San Francisco: Harper, 1977), 196.
9. This is the assessment of A. E. Taylor in his *Commentary on Plato's Timaeus*, (Oxford: Oxford University Press, 106). Sallis tackles this difficulty with incisive hermeneutical caution and rigor, thus responding to Taylor, in his *Chorology*, op. cit., 65–66.
10. For a very summary account of the body as absolute here and zero-point of orientation, see *N*, 75; see also Maurice Merleau-Ponty, *Phenomenology of Perception*, trans. C. Smith (London: Routledge, 1962), part one, chapter 3.
1. This phrase is Françoise Dastur's, derived from and consistent with Merleau-Ponty's analysis, which she takes up and examines in her "The Body of Speech," which appears in translation in this volume.
12. Maurice Merleau-Ponty, *Signs*, trans, R. McCleary (Evanston: Northwestern University Press, 1964), 160.
13. One can argue that Merleau-Ponty's entire intellectual trajectory, from *Structure of Behavior* to *The Visible and the Invisible*, is concerned with negotiating the dialectic of whole and parts. Wanting to think the phenomenon of life, for example, Merleau-Ponty seeks to avoid falling into a realist or materialist position, in which life would be reducible to its *partes extra partes*, out of which a living creature could not be reassembled, and he seeks to avoid an idealist or intellectualist position, in which life becomes an idea represented to a constituting consciousness, which in his view misses life as such. It thus seems clear that from the very beginning, Merleau-Ponty rejects a constructionist account of the elements, favoring instead the kind of conception that is beginning to irrupt in the margins of Timaeus's account. Merleau-Ponty's critique of a constructionist account of life is nowhere more forceful than in his reading of Coghill's experiments with axolotl lizards, in *Nature*, 140ff.
14. This is the sense of the elemental that Sallis seeks to articulate in his *Force of Imagination: The Sense of the Elemental* (Bloomington: University of Indiana Press, 2000).
15. For a succinct presentation and able negotiation of the debate, see Sallis, *Chorology*, 101–106. I am following his instructive analysis very closely in this present passage.

16. See Plato, *The Republic*, 476c. See also the commentary of Sallis in *Chorology*, 120–22, as well as the chapter on the *Republic* in his *Being and Logos: Reading the Platonic Dialogue,* 3rd edition (Bloomington: Indiana University Press, 1996).
17. Martin Heidegger, "Building Dwelling Thinking," trans. A. Hofstadter, in *Basic Writings*, op. cit., 337.
18. We (un)fortunately cannot claim credit for this terrible pun; we owe it to David Krell, who first dared utter it in his graduate seminar on the *Timaeus* at DePaul University in Winter 1993, and it subsequently appeared in his *ArcheTicture* (Albany: State University of New York Press, 1997).
19. Here I reproduce the translation attempted by Sallis, which appears in his *Chorology*, 118–19. After having reasserted the priority of the first two kinds, Timaeus adds, at 52a-d: "Moreover, a third kind is that of the *khôra*, everlasting, not admitting destruction, granting an abode to all things having generation, itself to be apprehended with nonsensation, by a sort of bastard reasoning, hardly trustworthy; and looking toward which we dream and affirm that it is necessary that it be somewhere in some place and occupy some *khôra*; and that that which is neither on earth nor anywhere in the heaven is nothing. As for all of these and others akin to them and concerning wakeful and truly underlying nature, under the influence of this dreaming, we are unable to awaken, to distinguish these, and to say the truth: that for an image, since not even that itself on the basis of which it comes to be generated belongs to the image but it is brought forth as the phantom of something other—because of this it is appropriate for it to be generated in something other, clinging to being at least in a certain way, on pain of being nothing at all; whereas to the aid of that which *is* in the manner appropriate to being there comes the precise logos: that as long as one thing is something and another is something else, neither of the two will ever come to be in the other, so as to become at once, one and two." The attentive reader will note that the *khôra* is neither sensible nor intelligible, yet somehow partakes of both, and will note further the extent of the difficulties one confronts when working with this passage.
20. Edmund Husserl, "Foundational Investigations of the Phenomenological Origin of the Spatiality of Nature," in *Husserl: Shorter Works*, ed. P. McCormick and F. Elliston, trans. F. Kersten (South Bend: University of Notre Dame Press, 1981), 222–33. See also Merleau-Ponty's course notes from 1959 in *Husserl and the Limits of Phenomenology*, trans. L. Lawlor with B. Bergo (Evanston:

Northwestern University Press, 2001). For an excellent study of Husserl's text on the Earth, and Merleau-Ponty's reading of it, see Anthony Steinbock, "Reflections on Earth and World: Merleau-Ponty's Project of Transcendental History and Transcendental Geology," in V. Foti (ed.), *Merleau-Ponty: Difference, Materiality, Painting*, ed. V. Fóti (Atlantic Highlands, NJ: Humanities Press International, 1996), 90–111.

21. This emphasis on the modality of possibility puts us directly in dialogue with Heidegger, and indeed, this is precisely one of the themes that Merleau-Ponty takes up in the reading of Heidegger that he effects in one of his last lecture courses at the Collège de France, the *Theme* of which is aptly titled "The *Possibility* of Philosophy Today." This course is not yet translated, but appears in French as "La philosophie aujourd'hui" in Merleau-Ponty, *Notes des Cours au Collège de France*, ed. C. Lefort and S. Ménasé (Paris: Gallimard, 1996), 33ff.
22. See R. Barbaras, "De l'ontologie de l'objet à l'ontologie de l'élément," in *Le tournant de l'expérience*, op. cit., 223.

9

The Blind Spot

WAYNE J. FROMAN

In his 1990 *Memoirs of the Blind: The Self-Portrait and Other Ruins*, Jacques Derrida had made mention of "a program for an entire rereading of the later Merleau-Ponty."[1] He included only a few indications, for lack of space. In particular, Derrida associated his understanding of a "quasi-transcendental," or a sense of "transcendentality," in the context of his discussion of the relation between vision and blindness, with what Merleau-Ponty, in one of the Working Notes for *The Visible and the Invisible*, specified as "transcendence without an ontic mask." Derrida cited the Working Note:

> January 1960. Principle: not to consider the invisible as an other visible "possible," or a "possible" visible for an other. The invisible is there without being an object, it is pure transcendence, without an ontic mask. And the "visibles" themselves, in the last analysis, they too are only centered on a nucleus of absence—
>
> Raise the question: the invisible life, the invisible community, the invisible other, the invisible culture.
>
> Elaborate a phenomenology of "the other world," as the limit of a phenomenology of the imaginary and the "hidden"—. (*MB*, 52; cf. *VI*, 229)

Derrida further cites the following Working Notes:

> [May 1960] When I say that every visible is invisible, that perception is imperception, that consciousness has a "punctum

> caecum," that to see is always to see more than one sees—this must not be understood in the sense of a contradiction—it must not be imagined that I add to the visible . . . a nonvisible . . . .—One has to understand that it is visibility itself that involves a nonvisibility. (*MB*, 52; cf. *VI*, 247)

> What [consciousness] does not see it does not see for reasons of principle; it is because it is consciousness that it does not see. What it does not see is what in it prepares the vision of the rest (as the retina is blind at the point where the fibers that will permit the vision spread out into it). (*MB*, 52; cf. *VI*, 248)

> To touch oneself, to see oneself . . . is not to apprehend oneself as an object, it is to be open to oneself, destined to oneself (narcissism)— . . .
> The feeling that one feels, the seeing that one sees, is not a thought of seeing or of feeling, but vision, feeling, mute experience of a mute meaning—. (*MB*, 53; *VI*, 249)

And Derrida adds:

> The aperspective thus obliges us to consider the objective definition, the anatomico-physiology or ophthalmology of the "punctum caecum," as itself a mere image, an analogical index of vision itself, of vision in general, of that which, seeing itself see, is nevertheless not reflected, cannot be "thought" in the specular or speculative mode—and thus is blinded because of this, blinded at this point of "narcissism," at that very point where it sees itself looking. (*MB*, 53)

That *Memoirs of the Blind,* wherein Derrida tells us that "the *point of view* will have been our theme" (*MB*, 126), prompted the call for an "entire rereading of the later Merleau-Ponty" should not have come as a surprise. The "point of view," in fact, was very much at stake for Merleau-Ponty. When Merleau-Ponty, in *The Visible and the Invisible*, specified his point of departure as the way in which perception gives us access to the world while, at one and the same time, removing us to a margin of the world, and everyday perception manages to make these two go together while philosophy, in trying to account for the matter, finds itself caught up in various contradictions, he was restating the result of his *Phenomenology of Perception.* There, the standard understanding of perception as the bringing together of a concept and a sensory manifold had been "de-structed," in a Heideggerian sense. That standard sense of perception, Heidegger found, had long served as the model for the standard ontology, and that means for metaphysics. The results of this "de-struction" were paradoxical. It turned out that the vantage point from which Merleau-Ponty carried out his analyses of the perceptual dynamic was itself generated by that dynamic. It would appear then that the "point of view" undid itself in the void left by an exhaustion or a dissolution of metaphysics.

In *The Visible and the Invisible*, Merleau-Ponty addresses the apparent impasse in terms of the dynamic of "reversibility," a feature of perception that Husserl had addressed in *Ideen II*, and that Merleau-Ponty had pursued, after *Phenomenology of Perception*, in terms of the overlap of motor projects and vision in the art of painting. In my touching, I touch myself as touching. In my seeing, I see myself as seeing. Consequently, "everything comes to pass as though my power to reach the world and my power to entrench myself in phantasms only come with the other; even more: as though the access to the world were but the other face of a withdrawal and this retreat to the margin of the world a servitude and another expression of my natural power to enter into it" (*VI*, 8). While in touching, I touch myself as touching, and in seeing, I see myself as seeing, I do not do this in the same manner in which I touch other tangibles or see other visibles. There is always a certain lapse such that what is always imminent is not actualized, a certain *punctum caecum* then, a "blind spot" in consciousness. The perceptual clue to "reversibility" and to that "blind spot" is the character of the world, and to begin with my body, as all already there, always. This led Merleau-Ponty to *la chair*, the flesh, and its "doubling" quality, or torsion, whereby I see myself in seeing and touch myself in touching. We find here an externality and an internality constantly circling or turning around one another. This finding with respect to how one who touches is *of* the tangible, and one who sees is *of* the visible, is put well by Gilles Deleuze in his book on the work of Michel Foucault:

> It was Merleau-Ponty who showed us how a radical, "vertical" visibility was folded into self-seeing, and from that point on made possible the horizontal relation between a seeing and a seen.
>
> An Outside, more distant than any exterior, is "twisted," "folded" and "doubled" by an inside that is deeper than any interior, and alone creates the possibility of the derived relation between the interior and the exterior. It is even this twisting which defines "Flesh," beyond the body proper and its objects.[2]

The pertinence of "the blind spot" to flesh points us in the direction of Merleau-Ponty's advancing interrogation of nature. In the pre-Socratic sense of *physis*, Heidegger had found an understanding of an always rising lighting that inclines itself toward, or cannot be dissociated from, a hiding or a hiddenness that does not pertain to anything that could be seen if one were elsewhere. That sense of *physis* comes to life in *The Visible and the Invisible*, as does the pre-Socratic sense of "element," which is precisely how Merleau-Ponty characterizes flesh. That in his late lectures on nature, Merleau-Ponty should endorse a call for a return to "the spirit of Heraclitus" found in Husserl's last phase, should not come as a surprise.

Moreover, Heidegger had found that it was with Schelling's work that something new enters philosophy, and what enters philosophy had been overlooked, or forgotten, as a possibility from the outset. In the lectures on nature, Merleau-Ponty turns to Schelling's sense of nature, and in particular to the sense of a "barbarous source." It is here, I find, that the direction of Merleau-Ponty's thinking in regard to "reversibility" and "the blind spot" of consciousness shows up. We find the following in *Themes from the Lectures at the Collège de France, 1952–1960*:

> [For Schelling, the] *erste Natur* is an ambiguous principle, or, as he puts it, a "barbarous" principle which can be transcended, but will never be as though it had never existed, and can never be considered secondary even in relation to God. (*Themes*, 75)

And then:

> In principle . . . nature in Schelling never gives rise to a second science or a gnosis which would objectivate and absurdly convert into a second causality the relations of existing nature as we glimpse them in the "ek-stasis" of intellectual intuition. There is only the effort to take account of the weight of the existing world, to make of nature something else than an "impotency" (Hegel) and an absence of the concept. Luckács gives Schelling the honor of having introduced "the doctrine of the reflection (*Wiederspiegelung*) into transcendental philosophy, but regrets that he gave it an "idealist" and "mystic" twist. What Luckács considers irrational is doubtless the idea of an exchange between nature and consciousness within man, an internal relation between man and nature. It is clear, however, that the "doctrine of the reflection," or the mirror, leaves

> nature in the state of an object which we reflect, and that, if philosophy is to avoid immaterialism, it must establish a more strict relation between man and nature than this looking-glass relation, since nature and consciousness can only truly communicate in us and through our incarnate being. (*Themes*, 76–77)[3]

The "barbarous source" must first be understood along the lines of what Merleau-Ponty, in *Themes from the Lectures*, calls "*general reality*," an order of possibility understood "not as another eventual occurrence, but as an ingredient of the existing world itself" (*Themes*, 98). In a Working Note to *The Visible and the Invisible*, Merleau-Ponty endorses an understanding of the "unicity" of the world that he found in Husserl's last phase:

> [T]he unicity of the world means not that it is actual and that every other world is imaginary, not that it is itself and every other world for us only, but that it is at the root of every thought of possibles, that it even is surrounded with a halo of possibilities which are its attributes, which are *Möglichkeit* and *Wirklichkeit* or *Weltmöglichkeit*, that, taking on the form of the world of itself, this singular and perceived being has a sort of natural destination to be and to embrace every possible one can conceive of, to be Weltall. Universality of our world, not according to its "content" (we are far from knowing it entirely), not as recorded fact ("the perceived") but according to its configuration, its ontological structure which envelops every possible and which every possible leads back to. (*VI*, 228–29)

In other Working Notes, Merleau-Ponty characterizes the generality as "anonymity" (*VI*, 201), and he writes: "in sum a world that is neither one nor two in the objective sense—which is pre-individual" (*VI*, 262). This is, in fact, the "chiasm" as Merleau-Ponty understands this in *The Visible and the Invisible*: "[T]he chiasm binds as obverse and reverse ensembles unified in advance in process of differentiation" (*VI*, 262). The torsion of internal and external, or the doubling characteristic of flesh, first indicated by the "blind spot" without which consciousness would not be consciousness, displays this very "unicity."

All this provides a clue as to how Merleau-Ponty thought to pursue a number of concerns that he included under the heading of the problem of passivity, including the nature of forgetting, the nature of the unconscious, and the passivity of action. Here too, according to the final paragraphs of the chapter "The Intertwining—the Chiasm" in *The Visible and the Invisible*, where Merleau-Ponty touches on the question of "ideality," is where we are to look for a way to inquire into "[the] miracle [whereby] a created generality, a culture, a knowledge, come to add to and recapture and rectify the natural generality of my body and of the world" (*VI*, 117). Here is where we are to look for the "intertwining," as Merleau-Ponty puts it, of animality with humanity. Merleau-Ponty's advancing interrogation of nature and its point of departure in the "blind spot," without which consciousness would not be consciousness, is where phenomenology had led Merleau-Ponty. In the study of Husserl's work called "The Philosopher and His Shadow," Merleau-Ponty calls attention to what Husserl had written in regard to "a primordial faith and original opinion (*Urglaube, Urdoxa*) which are not even in principle translatable in terms of clear and distinct knowledge, and which—more ancient than any 'attitude' or '*point of view*' [emphasis mine]—give us not a representation of the world but the world itself." Merleau-Ponty points out that this is in fact intrinsic to the "natural attitude," which only becomes "an attitude—a tissue of judicatory and propositional acts . . . when it becomes a naturalist *thesis*" (*Signs*, 163). Here is Merleau-Ponty's description of that *Urglaube*, that *Urdoxa*:

> Reflection cannot "go beyond" this opening to the world, except by making use of the powers it owes to the opening itself. There is a clarity, an obviousness, proper to the zone of the *Weltthesis* which is not derived from that of our theses, an unveiling of the world precisely through its dissimulation in the chiaroscuro of the doxa. When Husserl insistently says that phenomenological reflection begins in the natural attitude . . . this is not just a way of saying that we must necessarily begin with and go by way of opinion before we can attain knowledge. The doxa of the natural attitude is an *Urdoxa*. To what is fundamental and original in theoretical consciousness it opposes what is fundamental and original in our existence. Its rights of priority are definitive, and reduced consciousness must take them into account. (*Signs*, 164)

These definitive "rights of priority" recall the definitive priority of the "barbarous source" understood along the lines of the order of generality intrinsic to the world in its "unicity." As to how reduced consciousness is to take those rights into account, Merleau-Ponty would find only indicators in the last phase of Husserl's work: "pre-givens" (*Vorgegeben-*

heiten) that are "kernels of meaning about which we and the world gravitate" (*Signs*, 165). Of these "kernels of meaning," Merleau-Ponty writes: "[W]e may with equal truth say that they are always 'already constituted' for us or that they are 'never completely constituted'—in short, that consciousness is always behind or ahead of them, never contemporaneous" (*Signs*, 165). In other words, here is the lapse, the "blind spot," without which consciousness would not be consciousness.

If the "reversibility" of perception with its "blind spot," from which consciousness is indissociable, points up the "doubling" or the "torsion" of flesh, understood along the lines of a "barbarous source" as specified by Schelling, such that it reawakens a sense of physis as an always-rising or lighting that inclines itself toward, or is inseparable from, a hiddenness that pertains to nothing that could be seen from elsewhere, which Heidegger found in Heracleitus, the "pre-givens," always already constituted but equally never completely constituted, around which we and the world gravitate such that consciousness is always behind or ahead of them, recall a comparably old sense of Fate. We are again in the vicinity of a Heideggerian concern. It first shows up prominently in *Being and Time*, where, in the chapter "Temporality and Historicality," which promises a more radical approach to the existential analytic than that governed by mortality to the neglect of natality, Heidegger associates *der Augenblick*, an authentic moment, a glimpse or "moment of vision," with *das Schicksal*, fate. Later, Heidegger would find in the pre-Socratic sense of moira, fate, that which sends all things on their way, while at one and the same time, setting limits to all things. In the following passage from *The Visible and the Invisible*, the phrase "constellations of the world" suggests Merleau-Ponty's association of what consciousness is always behind or ahead of with Fate:

> [W]e have with our body, our senses, our look, our power to understand speech and to speak, metrics for Being, dimensions to which we can refer it, but not a relation of adequation or of immanence. The perception of the world and of history is the practice of this measure, the reading of their divergence or of their difference with respect to our norms. If we ourselves are in question in the very unfolding of our life, it is not because a central non-being threatens to revoke our consent to being at each instant, it is because we ourselves are one sole question, a perpetual enterprise of taking our bearings on the constellations of the world, and of taking the bearings of things on our dimensions. (*VI*, 103)

If we would question the very measurants—the reference events and landmarks, as Merleau-Ponty proceeds to call them, we would find that they refer us to others, and that by itself satisfies us only because we leave it unattended, because we think, Merleau-Ponty observes, that we are "at home." But the

> question would arise again and indeed would be inexhaustible, almost insane, if we wished to situate our levels, measure our standards in their turn, if we were to ask: but where is the world itself? And why am I myself? How old am I really? Am I really alone to be me? Have I not somewhere a double, a twin? These questions, which the sick man puts to himself in a moment of respite—or simply that glance at his watch, as if it were of great importance that the torment take place at a given inclination of the sun, at such or such hour in the life of the world—expose at the moment that life is threatened, the underlying movement through which we have installed ourselves in the world and which recommences yet a little more time for itself. (*VI*, 104)

This quite remarkable passage, I find, can help us to make sense of Working Notes where Merleau-Ponty suggests a "re-doubling," where he writes that the "blind spot," of which we cannot say where it is, nevertheless "is there with a presence by investment in another dimensionality, with a 'double-bottomed' presence" (*VI*, 255), and where he writes in the Working Notes of an "auto-inscription," a "subjective correlate" (in Merleau-Ponty's quotation marks) that belongs to the field of the imaginary and of Being (*VI*, 267), as well as an "*Unverborgenheit* of *Verborgenheit*," an unhiddenness of hiddenness, an "*Urpräsentierbar* of the *Nichturpräsentierbar*," an originary presentation of the originary nonpresentable (and which cannot be found by removing oneself elsewhere) (*VI*, 254). Moreover, the passage concerning an exposure of the underlying movement by which we have installed ourselves in the world and which recommences yet a little more time for itself can be of help in understanding the Working Notes that concern *Stiftung*, institution (cf. *VI*, 192, 224), about which we find the following in the report from the lecture course Institution in Personal and Public History from *Themes from the Lectures*:

> [W]hat we understand by the concept of institution are those events in experience which endow it with durable dimensions, in relation to which a whole series of other experiences will

> acquire meaning, will form an intelligible series or history—or again those events which sediment in me a meaning, not just as survivals or residues, but as the invitation to a sequel, the necessity of a future. (*Themes*, 40–41)

The blind spot without which consciousness would not be consciousness, understood along the lines of a "barbarous source" that makes for the doubling of "general reality" or generality, thereby rendering consciousness always behind or ahead of the "metrics for Being," makes as well for the questions wherein the movement through which we have installed ourselves in the world is exposed while recommencing yet a little more time for itself. We find here, I think, a vital element of Merleau-Ponty's late work.

In contact with "the prehuman world," humanity becomes, as Merleau-Ponty puts it, bewitched (*Themes*, 101). Intervening decades have borne out his description and it is worth citing at length:

> With regard to the relations between men, even those thinkers who found no natural harmonies in this area did not, prior to our times, believe that society was condemned to chaos. . . . [The] core of universality around which history was to organize itself has disintegrated. It may properly be asked whether violence, the opacity of social relations and the difficulties of a world in which such questions are the order to the day and where such doubts are unavoidable (even to those who post up complete certitudes) secretes of itself a violence and a desperate counterviolence. History has exhausted the categories in which conservative thought confined it, and it has done the same with those of revolutionary thought. But it is not just that the human world is illegible, nature itself has become explosive. Technology and science range before us energies which are no longer within the framework of the world but are capable of destroying it. They provide us with means of exploration which, even before having been used, awaken the old desire and the old fear of meeting the absolute Other. What for centuries had, in the eyes of men, possessed the solidity of the earth now appears fragile, what was once our predestined horizon has now become a provisional perspective. But equally, since it is man who discovers and fabricates, a new prometheism is mixed with our experience of the prehuman world. An extreme naturalism and an extreme artificialism are inextricably associated, not only in the myths of everyday life, but also in the refined myths

which arise, for example, out of the theory of information or neo-Darwinism. (*Themes*, 102–103)

When the "point of view" undoes itself in the void left by the exhaustion or the dissolution of metaphysics, no expedition to master the impossibility of immanence or adequation, the conundrum of internal and external, finds a point of departure. Rather, what we find is a perplexity that all of this has in fact happened. What memory, older than any point of view, do we have of that? Would not such memory render what has happened a possibility and thereby provide for a free relation to it, and would not such a relation come from the anonymous doubling characteristic of generality, of the elemental, of flesh? The questions that turn up in the heart of Merleau-Ponty's ongoing work are intimations of a possibility specified by Husserl, a possibility that Merleau-Ponty was to endorse, namely, that philosophy may yet be reborn from its ashes (*Themes*, 100).[4]

NOTES

1. Jacques Derrida, *Memoirs of the Blind: The Self-Portrait and Other Ruins*, trans. Pascale-Anne Brault and Michael Naas (Chicago: University of Chicago Press, 1993), 52.
2. Gilles Deleuze, *Foucault*, trans. S. Hand (Minneapolis: University of Minnesota Press, 1988), 110.
3. Merleau-Ponty here cites Georg Lukács, *Die Zerstörung der Vernunft* (Berlin: Aufbau, 1955), 110.
4. Merleau-Ponty here cites Edmund Husserl, *The Crisis of European Sciences and Transcendental Phenomenology*, trans. D. Carr (Evanston: Northwestern University Press, 1970).

10

Proximity and Distance

With Regard to Heidegger in the Later Merleau-Ponty

MICHEL HAAR

If we were to judge by the large number of (certainly elliptical, but never critical) references to Heidegger in the "Working Notes" in the unfinished work *The Visible and The Invisible*, notes dated from January 1959 to March 1961, then it would seem that the later Merleau-Ponty grew considerably closer to the author of *On the Way to Language*, a text on which he commented in his last courses. However, this *rapprochement*, to which one of the first of the posthumous fragments (dated January 1959) testifies, leaves us perplexed: "this perceptual world is at bottom Being in Heidegger's sense" (*VI*, 170). Since Merleau-Ponty was not unfamiliar with the radical Heideggerian rejection of "the primacy of perception," which he himself had partially called into question, what then can be the meaning of this method of reappropriating the ontology of the later Heidegger? Why does Merleau-Ponty feel so close to Heidegger that he multiplies the often forced and sometimes sibylline (or at least allusive) convergences? And having assimilated Heideggerian language for himself, why does he constantly speak—on almost every page—of "Being" (with a capital) and of "the being of which language is the house" (without scare marks), writing that the visible is "not visible, but *unverborgen*" (*VI,* 247), and on several occasions going so far as to invoke "a universal dimensionality which is Being (Heidegger)" (*VI*, 265)? This latter definition, borrowed from Heidegger, is but a modification of what Heidegger expressly rejects at the beginning of *Being and Time*: being as "the most universal concept." The word *concept* is clearly replaced by *dimensionality*, a vaguely spatializing metaphorical expression that signifies "the dimension of all dimensions" and enigmatically designates the "universal" field of the Sensible as it is given to perception. Why borrow from Heidegger this thought of the universality of the Sensible, of the "primordial *il y a*" of the Visible, of this "element" of all elements, or in short, of "savage or brute Being," of the *flesh of the world*? Merleau-Ponty cannot ignore that "the thought of being,"—and moreover the doctrine of the History of Being—is basically incompatible (because of the insertion of being in History, and because of the rupture with the metaphysical ideal of natural totality) with the universalism of the flesh and with this central intuition that postulates that "my body is made of the same flesh as the world" (*VI,* 248).

Merleau-Ponty evidently needed a powerful motif to renounce his initially critical attitude toward Heidegger, and as we will see, this motif is nothing other than his partial rallying to Heidegger, beginning with the admiration for one of the essential themes of the last phase of his thought, namely, the *dispossession* of man's *properties* or *faculties*, which are transferred to being—an idea that helps Merleau-Ponty to criticize the notion to which he was so attached, the notion of the propriety of the "proper body," and thus to accomplish his own "turn." We must add to this the Heideggerian idea of truth as *Unverborgenheit*, adopted by Merleau-Ponty but with an important distortion or divergence, stemming from the fact that what is in retreat—the invisible of the visible, for example—can indeed be named.

This *rapprochement* with Heidegger is made late, probably ten years after *Phenomenology of Perception*, which itself demonstrates no such recognition, either unjust or reappropriating (as is ultimately the case), even though it was *Being and Time* that had served, if not as a guarantee or a model, at least as an obvious inspiration for the renunciation of the Husserlian *Epokhè* and for positing the world as irreducible. Merleau-Ponty probably took account of the distance between the Heideggerian definition of the world as a network of equipmental references and his own definition: "The world is that which we perceive"; "the perception of the world is what forever grounds our idea of truth" (*PhP*, xi). Here he is obviously close to Husserl. And if he cites *Being and Time* several times in the chapter on "Temporality," it is in order to criticize it and to maintain "the privilege of the present," defined as "the zone in which being and consciousness coincide" (*PhP,* 492), over against the primacy of the future, thus reproaching Heidegger for a thesis that he never supported, namely the possibility for Dasein to access authentic temporality "definitively":

> Heidegger's historical time, which flows from the future and which, thanks to its resolute decision, has its future in advance and rescues itself once and for all from disintegration, is impossible within the context of Heidegger's thought itself; for, if time is an ek-stase, . . . how could we ever cease completely to see time from the point of view of the present, and how could we completely escape from the inauthentic? (*PhP*, 496–97)

It seems that what pushed Merleau-Ponty to reject Heidegger during this period was that he situated him with Sartre on the side of a heroic solipsism trying to extricate itself from a world conceived as the place of facticity and as an obstacle to overcome. Even though nothing is more foreign to Heidegger than this idea of a combat of the for-itself against the in-itself, the model of this quasi-fusional philosophy of radical elemental immanence and of monistic physicalism of a new style toward which Merleau-Ponty himself was heading is also not found in Heidegger.

What Merleau-Ponty seeks is a way of getting out of the primacy of perceiving consciousness and of delivering phenomenology from the heavy mortgage of the post-Cartesian metaphysics of subjectivity, the survival of which was so strong in Husserl in the form of the transcendental, omnipositional, "constituting" Ego. Perceptual consciousness is always *preceded* by perceived-being, the fundamental structures of which it discovers—e.g., depth, thickness, the pregnancy of *Gestalt* as form that makes meaning stand out, the perspectivist deformations, the logic of intersensorial equivalences (for example between seeing and hearing) given by the "corporal schema," the relation between this schema and kinesthesis, etc. But rather than these being posited by a consciousness, they instead impose themselves on it. We must not draw from this the conclusion that what the phenomenology of perception had attributed to subjectivity as the properties of the "lived body" [*corps propre*] are in truth *the* most general traits of Being. In this decentering of the subject—where the subject receives from Being the essence of its capacities and sees itself dispossessed of its old "faculties," and even of every initiative—the entire work of the later Heidegger played an incontestable role as a model. Witness this typically Heideggerian formulation (almost to the point of a cliché—"shows itself and hides itself") of the operation of displacement: "[I]n truth, movement, rest, distance, apparent size, etc., are only . . . different expressions of that coherent distention across which Being shows and hides itself" (*VI*, 230). What this model helps to overcome is anthropocentrism. The concern is not to adopt the Heideggerian critique of the primacy of perception (to which we will return later) but rather to show that this critique is prepared *in being*, or on the side of things, in a *logos endiathetos* that emerges in man in the form of *logos prophirokos* (*VI*, 168–69; 179). This is why Merleau-Ponty's "new ontology" is on the whole very far from the "thought of being" even though it is inspired by it, not only because it seeks to bring to light a "savage being" whose essence is *natural* and which would be common to *all beings* without exception (do we not fall here into a new metaphysics, in that this discourse [is] applicable to totality, in which case man ceases to be the interlocutor or the privileged recipient of the "sendings of being" or of the *Seinsgeshick?*), but also because History, and the function of the *epokhè*, are totally absent from this ontology of nature.

Would there not be, however, another proximity with Heidegger in the way he describes not only the relation of language to human being ("that language has us and that it is not we who have language" [*VI*, 194]), but also the relation of language to a silence before words, to a secret Voice, "a speech before speech" (*VI*, 201). Let us say right away—and it remains to be shown—that even if there were a vague similarity between Heidegger's and Merleau-Ponty's positions, they nevertheless are in fact strongly separated.

Merleau-Ponty's ontology seems to have retained from Heidegger's only the regulative schema of the priority of Being over the human, and implicitly rejects what for it is *abstraction* (e.g., "the clearing of being") while also affirming its "universal" corporeity. But are not the ideas of a universal "sensible in itself" and of an ahistorical surplus itself themselves abstract, precisely in being situated in the absolute concreteness of "being as the pure *il y a*"(*VI*, 139)?

THE ANTI-ANTHROPOCENTRIC TURN: TOWARD AN ONTOLOGY OF THE "SENSIBLE IN-ITSELF

For Heidegger, perception is not an original relation to being. Instead of conceiving perception starting from the prejudice of objectivity as the wholly exterior relating of an acosmic subject-in-itself to an object existing in-itself, Heidegger showed—with regard to Kant in *The Fundamental Problems of Phenomenology*—that to perceive a thing supposes a preliminary understanding of what this thing could be, that is, of the domain to which it may belong, whether it be pure extant being (for example, nature) or beings available for use (an instrument, a tool, in the broad sense of what Dasein uses). "The mode of the possible uncoverability of the extant in perception must already be prescribed in the perceiving itself; that is, the perceptual uncovering of the extant must already understand beforehand something like extantness."[1] "Already beforehand" (*im vorhinein schon*), there must be an understanding—and as Heidegger specifies, a *preconceptual* understanding—of the difference between the extant and the available in order that a thing may be perceived. Not only is there not brute, factual perception, but all perception also presupposes that both a *world* is given and understood, with its meaningful references, and so too is a mode of givenness or a *meaning* of the Being of beings that one can encounter in the world. But there are not only the preconceptual grasp of the world and the understanding of being (or of the ontological difference) that precede the claimed "primacy of perception"; there is also a *Stimmung*. "Mood has always already disclosed being-in-the-world as a whole, and first makes it possible directing oneself towards something" (*BT*, 129). This directing or "turning towards," namely, the intentionality according to this or that specific mode (perception, imagination, memory, etc), and under which a being presents itself, is made possible by the mood or "affective disposition" that opens it to the world. There could not be any "givens of meaning" or "sensible impressions" in general if being-in-the-world were not already opened by means of attunement to this or that possibility of being touched by beings. "Indeed, we must ontologically in principle leave the primary discovery or the world to 'mere mood'" (*BT*, 130). In order for something to be perceptible, there must already be a disclosure, just as much as by primordial affectivity as by the relation to the world and by the understanding of being. Even though at first glance perception seems to be born in the eye, it is nevertheless *derived*, is a *latecomer*.

Throughout his work, Heidegger shows that what is given to us in visual or aural perception is essentially inscribed in the relation to being, which is itself always dependant on an epoch of History, which first prescribes or preforms the eidetic of the visible or the audible, thus deciding "the meaning of the senses" [*le sens des sens*]. "What the ear perceives and how it perceives will already be attuned and determined by what *we* hear."[2] "What speaks to us only becomes perceivable through our response."[3] In other words, perception is defined by the meaning of what we perceive, and not the inverse. Understanding—that is, the disclosure of meaning that results from its "correspondence" to being—precedes and makes possible the look and hearing. The signification of a visual form is given by the historical world to which it belongs: and thus, Heidegger says, the Greeks were able to recognize Apollo in the statue of a young boy.

When the later Merleau-Ponty relativizes the primacy of perception, it is not in virtue of a primacy of *meaning*, but rather in virtue of a primacy of the *Sensible*: between the body that sees and the thing seen, the flesh of the world extends the thickness of one and the same texture, one and the same thickness to which they both belong. "The thickness of the flesh between the seer and the thing is constitutive for the thing of its visibility as for the seer of his corporeity" (*VI*, 135). The human, just like the thing, becomes a *variant* of one and the same carnal Being that englobes them both as the unique and universal englobing. The human is no longer at the center, but is rather *de-centered*, not in relation to Being the giver of meaning or truth (as in Heidegger), but rather in relation to Being conceived as "corporeity or visibility in general" (*VI*, 149). This is why it is a question of ontology and not anthropology.

> When we speak of the flesh of the visible, we do not mean to do an anthropology, to describe a world covered over with all our own projections, leaving aside what it can be under the human mask. Rather, we mean that carnal being, as being of depths, of several leaves or several faces, a being of latency, and a presentation of a certain absence, is a prototype of Being, of which our body, the sensible sentient, is a very remarkable variation. (*VI*, 136)

Instead of being the center of the analysis, which no longer refers to it as a "lived body," the body becomes the particular case of a separation or spread [*écart*], of a differentiation operating everywhere throughout the world. And although Merleau-Ponty says it would be an "absurdity" to attribute the same properties as those of the body to the thing (i.e., to be "a color that sees itself, a surface that touches itself"(*VI*, 135)—an absurd thesis supported by Michel Henry in his idea of a universal *auto-affection*)—there is nevertheless a *visibility in itself*, a *tangible in itself*, a *sensible in itself* (and by "in itself" one must hear evidently *not objective*, but everywhere present *in a latent manner*), which are marked by the relation-to-itself of the sensible and of its different aspects, or by the self-difference of the sensible. "[T]here is a relation of the visible to itself that traverses me and constitutes me as a seer, this circle which I do not form, which forms me, this coiling over of the visible upon the visible" (*VI*, 140). The body is the site where a scattered relation of visibility in general (which no longer essentially or exclusively belongs to the body) is gathered.

The body is, however, also no longer placed in a position of inferiority. There is between the body and the flesh a total reciprocal participation, an exchange or "crossing over" or reversibility that is designated by the concept of the *chiasm*. The chiasm is a rhetorical figure that places two terms or two series of terms "in relation," in symmetry with each other in a phrase: body and flesh are reflected in each other according to a multitude of symmetrical images "as upon two mirrors facing one another where two indefinite series of images set in one another arise which belong really to neither of the two surfaces, since each is only the replica of the other, and which therefore from a couple, a couple more real than either of them" (*VI*, 139). This is a strange metaphorical model, for whence come the *images* in this slide show of reflections? In other words, what is the common reality that is reflected in the two mirrors, and to what does it belong? Merleau-Ponty evidently means that each of the two terms is reflecting-reflected, that the body is the indefinitely multiplied image of the flesh, and the flesh the indefinitely multiplied image of the body. But this notion of image or of replica poorly translates or introduces a coefficient of unreality into the idea that it intends to illustrate, namely, that the *couple* body-flesh is "more real" that either of the two terms. How can the "mutual insertion and intertwining" give way to a "chiasm"? The competition of these two figures—one of fusion, intrication, or intertwining, the other of external symmetry, the chiasm—makes manifest the difficulty of making two types of relations between body and flesh coincide. On the one hand, there is co-substantiality, even though the flesh is not "substance" in the metaphysical sense, but rather an "element of being" (i.e., there is a radical monism). On the other hand, there is only "kinship," which means a participation at a distance of my body in the visible, in a universal "anonymity, but to which it is difficult to lend precisely this "mineness," or any ordinary sort of activity (can we conclude from my passivity, by its insertion in the flesh, that there is an activity of things: "I feel looked at by the things." I can be "looked at" by an animal, but by a tree or a stone? Isn't this schizophrenic?). In other words, the symmetry of the chiasm is a problem: on the one hand, we have a specific sensible-sentient, and on the other, we have a "sensible in general" that has "in front of" it a "sentient in general." Even if it is relatively easy to justify the idea of a universal sensible, whether or not it supposes an indetermination and a polysemy of the notion of "sensibility" (if we include here the photosynthesis of plants, then should we call the subatomic processes a "sensibility"?), the idea of a sentient-in-general nevertheless seems to imply the idea of a "nature in general," the name and principle of which is refused: there is "not some huge animal whose organs our bodies would be" (*VI*, 142). If the "sentient in general" is restricted to sensorial intersubjectivity or to human intercorporeity, then the appeal to an "anonymous visibility" that lives simultaneously in me and in the other amounts to positing expressly "a vision in general, in virtue of that primordial propriety that belongs to the flesh . . . being an individual, of being also a dimension and a universal" (*VI*, 142). If the flesh sees, "thinks"—as the body "thinks," that is, realizes meaningful syntheses (for example, the understanding of forms, excluding or including, orienting itself spontaneously according to the higher and the lower, the front and the rear, etc.)—where then does the flesh stop since it is *universal*? Does it include matter or does it stop at the living? The notion of a "sentient in general" would lead back, if we follow it through to its ultimate consequences, to a disheveled Romantic pythagorism, as in Nerval:

> Everything is sensible . . .
> To matter itself a verb is attached . . .
> And like a newborn eye covered by its eyelids
> A pure mind grows under the crust of stones.[4]

Yet there is not a verb in matter, nor is there a sentient in general, because intercorporeity can be achieved, can attain its full meaning, only by the exchange of words. If I look at a prairie at the same time as another person looks at it, there can be, Merleau-Ponty says, an agreement between her green and mine only because "I speak of it with somebody" (*VI*, 142).

If Heidegger effects a radical reversal of the primacy of the subject in order to give priority to being as language, world, time, History, this operation is nevertheless not possible in Merleau-Ponty without the risk of positing the absolute primacy of a natural in-itself, a naturalism that would be in contradiction with every phenomenological demand. The sensible itself could be "universal" only if we possess an "intellectual intuition" that would take us beyond the limits of our finitude. We have no means of knowing if the in-itself is sensible or not, if the essence of the flesh, "the dehiscence of the seeing in the visible and of the visible in seeing" (*VI*, 153), is or is not limited to our corporeity. We have no means of knowing if this "dehiscence," as perpetual internal difference or non-recovering between the sensing and the sensed, is or is not universalizable, or if there is or is not a "natural generality of my body and of the world" (*VI*, 152). The Heideggerian model of the dispossession of man is not applicable to the philosophy of the flesh, because this latter—which, not without analogy with being, oscillates between the thickness of the element and the differential finesse of "dehiscence"—would not have an initiative, not produce a "destined sending," which it is necessarily incapable of producing because of its non-historicality. The human can respond to being-thrown, because the human is historical, but how can the human respond to the flesh that has no age, and that englobes him?

DE-CENTERING THE "PERCEIVING SUBJECT" AND THE "FLESH" AS THE UNIQUE NAME OF BEING

There is not in Merleau-Ponty a radical questioning of subjectivity, in the sense that there is not a "deconstruction" of the subject that brings to light its metaphysical presuppositions and which is explained with the tradition within which it is constituted, namely the mutations of *hypokheimenon* into *substantia* and then into *subiectum*. The subject is admitted as self-evident, and thus in total blindness with respect to its historical provenance. It is simply criticized starting from the primacy of the body, and then affirmed—as it is already in Nietzsche and Husserl—over against the "intellectualist" primacy of objectivating consciousness, of judgment, and of reflection. Such a critique cannot arrive at a complete recasting of the traditional concept of man, as does the Heideggerian critique, which leads to the new concepts of being-in-the-world and Dasein.

Even if there is not a deconstruction of the subject, there is nevertheless a radicalization of the principles discovered in the *Phenomenology of Perception*, and notably of the theme of the "generality" and anonymity of perception: "[E]very perception takes place in an atmosphere of generality and is presented to us as anonymous," to the point that there is, for example, neither a subject confronting an object or a sensorial quality, nor a primordial mineness (*PhP*, 250).The same holds for the lag between the sensing and the sensed, or for the non-recovering of the touching hand and the touched hand, which anticipates an essential property of the "flesh of the world," more universally called *dehiscence*. The radicalization consists in attributing—by means of a jump from regional ontology to a universal Ontology—the properties decried on the perceiving body to a "sensible in general" designated as Being. The body in *The Visible and the Invisible* is both the prototype of sensible Being in general and "a very remarkable variant" of this Being to which it originally gives access. This circle, which repeats Heidegger's hermeneutic circle in *Being and Time*, also differs from it to the extent that the meaning of Being in Merleau-Ponty implies an access to

Being-in-itself, and to the point of view of all points of view (no matter what he says), from which we see a total appropriation of the subject by Being. It is in effect a question of transferring to or transposing into Being all the properties of the subject: "Replace the notions of concept, idea, mind, representation by the notions of dimensions, articulation, level, hinges, pivots, configurations" (*VI*, 224). These multiple dimensions, formerly reserved to the subject, now belong to the unique "dimensionality of Being, i.e. as universal" (*VI*, 257). The principal difficulty is that this positing of Being as the dimension of all dimensions, which encloses "the expression of *every possible being*" (*VI*, 218), englobes dimensions as diverse as organic life, perception, thought, and language! How to admit that it is Being (i.e., the flesh) that thinks, and not us! Heidegger does not encounter such a difficulty, first because he excludes or separates life from being, and second because he does not support that Being thinks, but that it calls us to thinking: "what gives us to think . . . is not anything that only we are instituting."[5]

On the contrary, Merleau-Ponty effects, by brusque and rapid cuts, a de-centering that leaves us in a total aporia, to the extent that the essence of this de-centered subjectivity (which no longer has the initiative of perceptual synthesis, nor of speech or thought, just as it does not give itself life) remains totally unthought. The formula, at first glance impressive—"[I]t is not *me* who makes myself think anymore than is it *me* who make my heart beat" (*VI*, 221; emphasis added)—leaves altogether uninterrogated the essence of this passive *me*. Is it in both cases the same "me" in question? What would be the ontological definition of a subject that would be both the theater of a thought that it watches, and the center of an organic life? In order to give meaning to a "thought *of* the flesh" (subjective genitive), it does not suffice simply to affirm the *inverse* of thought as self-consciousness: "'[T]hought' . . . is not an invisible contact of the self with self, that it lives outside of this intimacy with oneself, *in front of* us, not in us, always ex-centric" (*VI*, 234). How are we to conceive that a thought situated *outside* and *in front* of us is something other than objective automatism?

The formula "it is not we who . . . ," which insistently recurs like a catchphrase in its generalization of all human faculties, has the air of a denial, of a simple refusal that the traditional human-subject be placed at the center. But the concern is to rethink and redefine the human: "[I]t is not we who perceive, it is the thing that perceives itself yonder—it is not we who speak, it is the truth that speaks itself at the depths of speech" (*VI*, 185). "The things have us . . . it is not we who have the things . . . language has us . . . it is not we who have language . . . it is being that speaks within us and not we who speak of being" (*VI*, 195).

But who is this "us"? It is evidently another human, a different species of humanity, otherwise linked to Being-flesh. But presented as such, in the brutal inversion of activity into passivity, this "us" would be a marionette, a toy, or a medium of the Power that lives in it, and there would no longer remain any attribute proper to it. Heidegger showed clearly that "to speak is to respond to language," and if a long analysis (which we don't find in Merleau-Ponty) allows that in a certain way "language speaks," he says more rarely that "Being speaks." But it speaks "through every language" and not as a universal sensible in-itself that would be, against every evidence, mysteriously endowed with speech. Moreover, a word directly inscribed in and directly carried by the flesh would necessarily be non-epochal, that is, a "natural language" that would say only the "quasi-eternity" of the sensible, in order to take up Merleau-Ponty's famous expression concerning the body. It would be the Speech-in-itself of a Being-in-itself! Yet, as Heidegger recalls, "there is no such thing as a natural language in the sense that it would be the language of a human nature occurring of itself, without a destiny. All language is historical."[6] What "speaks in us" perhaps plunges obscurely into a natural ground, but as soon as it emerges from it in the language of a people—at a determinate moment of its history—it is dated, it becomes an event that escapes from intemporality and the eternal repetitions of nature.

What is unthinkable in Heideggerian terms is the point of jointure or *identity* of the always historical and linguistic [*langagière*] *world*, and of ageless *life*, silent in its principle, which postulates *both* the transcendental and empirical unity of the flesh:

> The openness to the world such as we rediscover it in ourselves and the perception we divine within life, a perception that at the same time is spontaneous being (thing) and being-self ("subject") . . . intertwine, encroach upon, or cling to one another. (*VI*, 193)

Is such a subject not closer to post-Kantian metaphysics of nature and life (Schopenhauer, Schelling, Bergson, who here is cited several times in admiration for his idea of a "consciousness at once spontaneous and reflexive") than to the prudent Heideggerian limitation of the "clearing" of being as this is separated from the "black of the forest"? The sensible-in-general may well be designated as *Being* because it reveals itself to every position and every positivity, remaining always ambiguous, and forming the contrary of an op-position. But if it is true that "it is being that speaks in us" and that every expression is "but the trace of a total movement of Speech, which goes unto Being as a whole" or comes back from it (*VI*, 211), then how can it be defined both as "this possibility to be evident in silence, to be understood implicitly" (*VI*, 214), and as the very seat or source of language? Certainly insofar as language belongs to the invisible (*VI*, 258) and as "the visible is pregnant with the invisible" (*VI*, 216). But must we not then admit that if the difference between silence and language coincides with the difference between the visible and the invisible, the flesh itself is then inhabited by an apparently insurmountable difference, and that opens a *wholly other* gaping hole, it seems, than dehiscence thought merely as *silent* difference of sensing and sensed?

The movement that leads Merleau-Ponty to an ontology consists first in recognizing these differences and in showing that they pass into one another according to an unattainable, trembling chiasm, that is, without an effective possible recovering of one by the other (and thus: visible-invisible, silence-language, seeing-visible, touching-tangible, body-mind, nature-culture). The movement consists second in positing the flesh as the unique *il y a*, in which the relations of a "failed" reciprocity between the two sides of the chiasm are enclosed and "completed": "The essential is *the reflected in offset*, where the touching is always *on the verge* of apprehending itself as tangible, misses its grasp and completes itself only in a *il y a*" (*VI*, 260).

The Merleau-Pontyan "*il y a*" or "savage being" would not definitively rise up to a metaphysics of life, because the *offset*, incompleteness, ambiguity, the "polymorphism" of nature/culture, the unachieveability of the chiasm, the evanescent but continual indication of the other than self—all these properly belong to it. It is however fundamentally distinguished from the Heideggerian "*il y a*," to which belongs not a polymorphism, but a *polynomy*, or transcendental polysemy: "Being is said in multiple ways," says Heidegger recalling Aristotle—as time, world, truth, History, language at once. None of these names is completely suitable to it. And so time is only the "prename," the most approximate name of Being. The Heideggerian chiasm—"being is what is proper to man, man is what is proper to being"—is unattainable even in Being. On the other hand, in Merleau-Ponty, Being carries a single name, the flesh, in which the polymorphic differences are ceaselessly "offset" and prohibit linking metaphysical fixation to ontic substantiality. But in order to describe this flesh in the mobility of its non-self-coincidence, *one* of the terms of the differences that "play" in it is revealed each time as *the most appropriate*: it is *silent*, a silence that always "envelopes" speech again (*VI*, 176 and 179) after speech tore it apart ("Sigè the abyss" (*VI*, 179); it is the scattered universal visibility; it is this living spontaneity that obliges saying "it is not I who . . ." It is surely the flesh that makes the diverse sensorial worlds communicate, even though they are incommunicative between them, and form between them "one sole Being."

But the Flesh is flesh "*of* the world." What does Merleau-Ponty understand by *world*? Is it not at first the "natural world," rather than the cultural world, which would be a world of tools since it is not the world in the epochal sense? Or is it once again the ambiguity essential to their chiasm?

THE DIFFERENCES AND THE EFFACED DIFFERENCE BETWEEN THE FLESH AND THE WORLD

If the "world" designates for Merleau-Ponty the ambiguity of what is *both* human and vital, or the intertwining of the social and the organic, if it is the "connective tissue" (*VI*, 174) between humans and between humans and Being, if it designates the "common stuff of which all structures are made" (*VI*, 200) or "the common tissue of which we are made" (*VI*, 203), then it is in this very mixture, which is unacceptable to Heidegger, that Merleau-Ponty's greatest distance with respect to Heidegger would be found. The very possibility of an albeit unattainable reversibility between the natural world and the cultural world is totally excluded for Heidegger. And this is the case because even if we do not affirm the primacy of life, it implies in a Heideggerian perspective the positivity of a subsisting-being enclosed on itself; that is, objectively, it implies the points of identity between being as time, language, humanity, and . . . the *being of life*, which remains obscure and impenetrable to us: it implies an identity between the world that can in its full sense only be human, and the "animal world," the "poor" world, approachable only by analogy with that of Dasein.

The ambiguity of the lived body was that of "a life that behaves as a subject." Is the ambiguity of the "flesh of the world" the *same*? That would mean that it also behaves as a subject, which would bring it dangerously close to an absolute subject or a sensible God. And Merleau-Ponty hesitates to attribute a fantastic auto-affection to it, as we have seen: "[T]he flesh of the world is not a *self-sensing* as is my flesh—It is sensible and not sentient" (*VI*, 250). But in this case, if it senses nothing, "effects" nothing, if it has *fewer* attributes than does my body, how is it possible to read it as a matrix and a universal "milieu," or an "element"? How can we affirm that "my body is made of the same flesh as the world" if this flesh is infinitely poorer than mine? The embarrassment to which the author of this ontology exposes himself, but which he does not perceive, is, on the one hand, linked to his positing of carnal experience as universal, and yet, on the other hand, nothing is less certain than the idea that the essential attributes of "my" flesh (such as dehiscence) could be to the sensible in general. Even if the idea of an eminent, cosmic perceiving being (and thereby of a communion with the unique substance of the world, the *élan vital* or the *duration*) makes sense for Bergson, it is nevertheless so antiphenomenological that it seems that Merleau-Ponty would have to renounce it. However, if the flesh is a "non-sentient sensible," then it cannot carry the structure of dehiscence within itself, and it therefore ceases to have the generality of Being. Merleau-Ponty in some way tries to recapture the principal universality of the flesh at the level of the sole "perceived-being": "[T]he flesh of the world is of the Being-seen, i.e. it is a Being that is *eminently percipi*, and it is by this that we can understand the *percipere*" (*VI*, 250). The *il y a* of the flesh is not an "in-itself, identical to itself, in the night, but the Being that also contains its negation, its *percipi*" (*VI*, 251). But is it not illegitimate to attribute perceived-being to the flesh as *its own internal negation* or as one of the major properties of Being ("Being which contains its own negation")? It seems that we come up against the following alternative or antimony. *Either* the flesh possesses its own dehiscence and contains the model of the world and its constitutive differences (but in this case it hypostatizes itself in a fantastic substance or substrate of the world, which itself is understood as the totality of beings). *Or* dehiscence does not belong to the flesh, but only to the world, which the differences that constitute it in its ambiguity come under (but in this case the world is detached from the flesh, contrary to the expressly followed ontological project). In either case, should not the world in Merleau-Ponty's sense, infinitely richer in difference, be named Being rather than flesh?

Dehiscence and the capacity for sensing are however much more often lent to the flesh than refused to it. Thus, "the flesh . . . is the sensible in the twofold sense of what one senses and what senses" (*VI*, 259)—"the flesh . . . is the dehiscence of the seeing into the visible and of the visible into the seeing" (*VI*, 153). Concerning the touching-touched, the perceiving-being moved, with the "implication thought-language . . . the flesh is this whole cycle . . ." (*VI*, 260). Whence these strange and fantastic propositions concerning the activity of seeing and that of touching being lent to particular things by the bias of the flesh: "If I feel myself looked at by the things" or stranger still, "the things touch me as if I touch them and touch myself: flesh of the world—distinct from my flesh: the double inscription outside and inside" (*VI*, 261). Is this to say that the things touch me *in the same way* that I touch them, that is, by effecting syntheses, etc? This would bring us back to a romantic "soul" of "inanimate objects"! That signifies at any rate that the relation of the outside to the inside does not exist only on the plane of the lived body, but also "absolutely," that is, on the plane of the flesh, to which is lent an interiority! The transfer of the transcendence of the perceiving body to the things is a dream: "[T]he sensible thing itself is borne by a transcendency" (*VI*, 260). Certainly with Heidegger the equipmental thing has its own transcendence, the instrumental with-regard-to, but there are the finalities of the world that constitute the things, and not the inverse. With Merleau-Ponty, "the things . . . are worlds" (*VI*, 218).

The sentient, effective, structuring character of the flesh is evidently the central thesis that is sustained, but at the price of this quasi-naturalist inflection of ontology. The opposed point of view—namely, that the flesh is *non-sentient*—is only rarely evoked and no doubt only as a corrective, as when Merleau-Ponty underlines that the *il y a* is not an "in-itself," even though in a certain sense it is *expressis verbis* as a nonobjective in-itself. However, it seems to us that if the flesh were not itself englobed in a *world*, and in worldly differences (such as the difference between a thing and its particular horizon), it would thus come under a facticity of life, a scattered, unorganized, brute facticity for which the name "wild Being" would only then be all too appropriate. Thus, even though the formula "The invisible is the *invisible of the visible*"—repeated several times (*VI*, 247; cf. also 216)—may allow one to believe it, the flesh is in no way the insurmountable latency of the visible world (its *essentially* hidden aspect—like Heideggerian being—and not provisionally out of view). Since the visible is not an objectively given positivity, the invisible cannot be the inverse of it. The four senses of the invisible are in effect dimensions of the world rather than of the flesh, whose being traverses the difference visible/invisible, since the flesh is, insofar as it is *visibility*, the visible and the "reserve" of the visible:

> The invisible is:
>
> 1) what is not actually visible, but could be . . ." [This aspect is both ontic, the hidden sides of the thing, and ontological, to the extent that it is necessary to perception that it be hidden—but provisionally hidden and linked to the manifested by what Merleau-Ponty calls "the allusive logic of the perceived world." This reference to a world is implicit in all aspects of the invisible.]
>
> 2) what, relative to the visible, could nevertheless not be seen as a thing (the existentials of the visible, its dimensions,

> the non-figurative inner framework). [The strange expression of "existentials of the visible," strange because of the Heideggerian term, designates, it seems, the structures of perception that gather the corporal schema, or in other words the coordination between the visible and the givens of diverse meanings as well as the kinesthetic impressions, all of it making a world of the thing surge forth, that is, a coherent horizon of its diverse possible modes of appearing.]
>
> 3) what exists only as tactile or kinesthetically. [Here on the other hand the visible world in its cohesion suggests other worlds, that of touching, of movement, the sonorous world, such as it is described for example in *Phenomenology of Perception*, 222–23, concerning the invisible space of music different from the space of the concert hall.]
>
> 4) the lekta, the cogito. (*VI*, 257) [This strange subcategory of the invisible refers to the conceptual world of philosophy: the *lekta* are the incorporates of the Stoics; the cogito: in what way are they invisibles of every visible? That is not very defensible—why not say "thought" or "language"?]. (*VI*, 257)

In essence, the flesh is in no way invisible since it is the Visible, the Tangible: yet as such, does it not belong each time to a *world* which gives it meaning? It is in no way in retreat, or *verborgen*, and consequently it is less ontological than the *world*. Is not what is missing from the sensible as such, in order to merit being designated as Being, the capacity to institute a *world*, to introduce *something other* than a vague thickness, that is, an active, dimensional, truly universal meaning—even if it is a matter of partial (and not total) universality, like the visual or the sonorous? The flesh in our view is certainly *elemental*, but alas, also *elementary*.

That the latter Merleau-Ponty was seduced by the thought of being and its overcoming of subjectivity is indubitable. That his ontology falls back, at least partially, into a metaphysic—due to an insufficient deconstruction of the tradition (there is not a metaphysics that has thought "universal being" as a being)—this seems incontestable, in that he names Being a unique ontic dimension, and in that he hypostatizes and universalizes it: "brute or wild being ('perceived world')" (*VI*, 170). In order to be universalizable, even metaphysically, should not the perceived world in effect *close in on all its dimensions?* Yet it is noticeable that it possesses neither History nor Speech. The universality of the sensible becomes as a consequence a metaphysical abstraction: in the reversal of the ancient "soul of the world," the flesh constitutes a *body of the world*, and this body is supposed to determine the world that gives it meaning and figure.

Does not the notion of the "flesh of the world" close in on a supplemental difficulty, to the extent that the two terms comprising it have and do not have autonomous existence, have and do not have essential unity? Are they separated merely for the needs of analysis? It seems that the "sensible in general" does not have signification without a "world," and yet ontology makes a quasi-world or a pre-world of it, by positing it as an original and universal dimension. Would there not be a *possible dehiscence apart from between the flesh and the world*, just as there is both an irreconcilable coordination and a difference between "earth" and "world" in Heidegger? But for that to be the case, it would be necessary to introduce in Merleau-Ponty a principle of conflictuality, of battle or strife, which is totally missing from his philosophy. At the end of the day, what is so *savage* about "savage Being"? The critique of objectivism and of the thinking-from-above is used in a soft, muffled, peaceable way. The Merleau-Pontyan flesh, like his idea of the Earth, is neither strange nor barbaric: "The earth is the matrix of our time as it is of our space: every constructed notion of time presupposes our protohistory as carnal beings co-present to a single world" (*S*, 180). However often it approaches a philosophy of nature—always described as maternal, as quasi-domestic—the thought of the flesh does not therein discover a disquieting and inexhaustible force, a contradictory power of opening and closing on itself. The Earth, Heidegger writes, is the effortless and untiring force of what is there, reduced to nothing (by the contradictory exigency of the world). The earth appears as that which carries all, as that which is self-secluding.[7] The flesh is given neither in this overabundance, nor with this refusal.

Can an ontology arise as much from the excess of the gift as from its restraint [*retenu*]? Does not a carnal *il y a*, without measure and without reserve, without negativity—i.e., as an "element," "matrix," "formative milieu of the subject and object" concerning the dehiscence as well-ordered "fold," or as a "close-bound system that I count on," which is not "chaos, but a texture that returns to itself and conforms to itself" (*VI*, 146), thus perfectly harmonious and transparent—establish itself on an all-too-comfortable forgetting of nothingness? The Merleau-Pontyan nothingness has a full and reassuring figure: "The negative, nothingness, is the doubled-up, the two leaves of my body, the inside and the outside articulated over one another. Nothingness is rather the difference between the identicals" (*VI*, 263). The noncoincidence of the body or hypothetically of the flesh is no doubt the most benign and least redoubtable figure of nothingness in the entire history of philosophy!

NOTES

1. Heidegger, *Fundamental Problems of Phenomenology,* trans. A. Hofstadter (Bloomington: Indiana University Press, 1982), 70.
2. Heidegger, *The Principle of Reason*, trans. R. Lilly (Bloomington: Indiana University Press, 1991), 47.
3. Ibid., 48.
4. Nerval, *Vers dorés*, in *Œuvres complètes I* (Paris: Gallimard), 39. Translated for this essay.
5. Heidegger, *What Is Called Thinking?*, trans. J. G. Gray (New York: Harper and Row, 1968), 6. (The French translation of this passage more clearly places emphasis on the fact that Being is nowise a mere construction of thought: "what gives us to thinking is in no way instituted by us."—tr.).
6. Heidegger, *On the Way to Language*, trans. P. Hertz (San Francisco: Harper and Row, 1971), 133. (Note that "language" here translates the German *Sprache*).
7. On this, see Heidegger, "The Origin of the Work of Art," trans. J. Young and K. Haynes, in *Off the Beaten Track* (Cambridge: Cambridge University Press, 2002), 1–56. See especially the second section ("The Work and Truth") of this seminal essay, as well as Michel Haar's extended commentary in his study *The Song of the Earth: Heidegger and the Grounds of the History of Being*, trans. R. Lilly (Bloomington: Indiana University Press, 1993).

11

Chiasm, Flesh, Figuration

Toward a Non-Positive Ontology

VÉRONIQUE M. FÓTI

> But what is beautiful is taking seriously the idea of the Erwirken of thought: It is really voidness, invisibility—All the fuss about "concepts," "judgments," "relations" is eliminated, and the spirit secret like water in the fissure of being . . . there are only structures of the void—Simply, I want to plant this void in visible Being, to show that it is the reverse thereof.
>
> —Maurice Merleau-Ponty, *The Visible and the Invisible*

Given that the fourth chapter of Merleau-Ponty's posthumous work, *The Visible and the Invisible*—the chapter titled "The Interlacing—the Chiasm"—traces subtle and complex interrelationships in filigree, it is tempting to immerse oneself in the *finesse* of the individual analyses—such as that of the five-note musical phrase possessed of a "withdrawn and chilly tenderness"—rather than seeking fully to grasp the challenging notion of the chiasm. Since Merleau-Ponty responds, in this chapter, to his own earlier painstaking critiques of reflection, dialectics, and intuition as frameworks for philosophical interrogation, so that what the chapter articulates is of the very core of his late thought, it is salutary to resist this temptation. What is needed instead is a tracing out of chiasmatic structure, and of where and how it inscribes itself in multiplicity. Such a study will open in its turn upon Merleau-Ponty's understanding of Flesh, which, in his late thought, comes to displace any classical or positive ontology, and also, in this context, on the interrelationship of vision or visibility with invisibles. From this vantage point one can then raise the question why the philosophical interrogation of art, notably of painting, gains crucial importance for the late Merleau-Ponty. Although *Eye and Mind*, which is contemporaneous with *The Visible and the Invisible*, remains an insightful and scintillating text if looked upon simply as an essay in phenomenological aesthetics, its philosophical bearing is more far-reaching and needs to be approached, if it is to reveal itself fully, from out of an interrogation of the chiasmatic articulations of Flesh.

CHIASMS

What he calls "the chiasm" marks, for Merleau-Ponty, the very movement of phenomenalization; it is not a static relation supervenient upon the prior givenness of its terms. These terms, in their rich diversity, articulate themselves only within the chiastic dynamism of inter-encroachment and differentiation that makes for the "dehiscence" or phenomenal "bursting forth" (*éclat*) that Merleau-Ponty calls Flesh. Hence, as he remarks in a Working Note of November 1960, any analysis that (true to its name) seeks to sort out or disentangle what is here commingled succeeds only in rendering it unintelligible, which implies that a philosophy that recognizes the chiasm hinges on a new sort of intelligibility.[1]

To speak of "the chiasm" is really to hypostatize and singularize a movement and an articulation that, being pervasive, take multiple forms. One can speak, for instance, of the chiasmatic interrelation of sentience and the sensible, of body and world, of the sensory modalities with each other and with motility, of visibility and the invisible, of self and other, idea and flesh, or of speech and meaning. Rather than being variants or instantiations of an archetypal chiasm, these chiasmatic interrelations can be comprised into unity only insofar as they are themselves chiasmatically interlinked (which implies that they cannot be collapsed into any fundamental identity or "coincidence"). As Merleau-Ponty puts it in a Working Note, "in what sense these multiple chiasms amount just to a single one: Not in the sense of synthesis, of an originally synthetic unity, but always in the sense of *Uebertragung,* of encroachment, thus of the radiation of being" (*VI*, 261).

In an earlier Working Note, he reflects that the Sartrean dualism of the For-itself and the In-itself cannot yield the relationship of being to itself ("a relation to Being which would *accomplish itself in the interior of Being*") that, he is convinced, Sartre was in quest of. The thought of the chiasm remedies this failure precisely in that it allows a unitary world to configure itself "across incompossibilities" (such as, for Sartre, my world and the world of the Other, within which I am objectified), without assuaging their oppositional tensions (*VI*, 215). For this reason, he can describe the chiasm as the truth of the Leibnizian preestablished harmony—a truth, moreover, that is not limited to unifying singular monadic perspectives but interlinks "wholes unified in advance by way of differentiation," which is to say, chiasmatic articulations (*VI*, 261).

Whereas the preestablished harmony belongs to a positive or classical ontology, an ontology of *substantia*, the pivot of the chiasm is insubstantial, a "nothingness." It will be instructive here to join Marc Richir in a careful reading of the Working Note of 16 November 1960, in which Merleau-Ponty, having described nothingness paradoxically as "the difference between identicals," resorts to the analogy of the finger of a glove which can be reversed, so that, at the point of reversal, one touches one configuration through or across the other. In this sense, he points out, "For Myself" and "For the Other" are not positive subjectivities that would come to be interlinked; but rather, what is given is just the axis that interlinks them: the "tip of the finger of the glove is nothingness—but nothingness that one can reverse [*retourner*], and where one can then see *things*—The only "place" where this negative would really be is the fold, the application one to the other of the inside and the outside, the point of reversal [*retournement*]."[2]

Richir carries out a difficult analysis of the empty tip of the finger of the glove as horizon, the imminence of which allows both things and the body as *Leib* (not as empirical body or *Körper*) to emerge in inter-encroachment through the reversal or "passage to the other side." He stresses, however, that horizonal latency is not as yet the "true negative" of the point of return:

> And this return [retournement] is a fold; but the folding thereof is itself nothingness. The folding of the fold hence has no existence, cannot be situated; and its operation, beneath the folding, which is to say, reversibility, is "true negativity," open upon the abyss. . . . Merleau-Ponty, better than many others, understood that phenomenology has to do with the fundamental non-positivity of all that is, of all that is practiced and of all that can be thought.

It is not surprising that Merleau-Ponty himself, in a Working Note of May 1960, speaks of the "true negative" in the language of Heidegger as "an unconcealment of concealment" which, in its relucence on Husserlian phenomenology, becomes "an originary presentation of what is incapable of originary presentation" (*VI*, 249). Richir approaches the issue of the negativity of the "operant chiasm" (the chiasm that cannot be construed as an *arkhè*) from out of the context of Merleau-Ponty's remarks on "the other scene" of dream. Since dream accomplishes a spontaneous *epokhè* of the positivity of body and world, it allows phenomenalization to come about in releasement from reification; and, although dream does not give one access to "true negativity" or the emptiness at the heart of phenomenalization, it frequents, as Richir notes, "the edge of being," the jointure "where the multiple entries upon the world intercross." Richir concludes that this very multiplicity of registers of phenomenalization (with which dream—though not uniquely—puts one in touch) orients one away from any substantial ontology.[3]

The chiasmatic interlacing and reciprocal modeling, as Merleau-Ponty calls it, of body and world is then not an interlinking of entities that could ever be fully separated out or else could complement each other in virtue of an ideal reversibility. The sentient body, far from being a subjectivity related to the sensible as its objective counterpart, must incorporate itself into the sensible, making "use of its being" to take part in the being of things;[4] but it is also always already phenomenal and reflexively translucent for itself. The body's sentience and sensibility are, Merleau-Ponty writes, inter-involved or even reciprocally inserted into one another: "[T]here are two circles, or two eddies, or two spheres, concentric when I live naïvely and, as soon as I interrogate myself, the one slightly de-centered with respect to the other" (*VI*, 138). The living body can no more be reduced to a sensible given, however ingenious and complex (such as the Cartesian physiological mechanism) than the sentience and reflexivity that "sustains" it could ever be consummated without any gap or residual opacity.

What holds of the body holds equally of the sensible world: it is not a flat, self-contained datum which could be separated out into the various sensible registers (such as visibility and tangibility) or subsumed under eidetic givens; it is, rather, a field of dynamic latencies in pervasive inter-encroachment. Jacques Garelli indicates here Merleau-Ponty's reinscription of the texture of the Husserlian lifeworld:

> So that, for Husserl, there are no brute diverse sensibles, offered to the activity of the pure a priori forms of sensibility. . . . For, always and already, the originary, pre-individual passivity of the world, in the movement of self-surpassing—the characteristic of passive syntheses, wrought by layers of sedimentation never fully closed upon themselves—offers a field of unities open to meaning in formation, which invests the "pathic" dimension of the world.

As Garelli notes, Merleau-Ponty's originality, in reinscribing these Husserlian themes, lies in his radicalizing these reciprocal inter-encroachments, so as to undercut any reference to fixed significations or eidetic givens. His thought traces the origination of meaning to "a pre-objective, pre-thematic, ante-predicative horizon, itself invested with a sedimentation of meaning, the recovery of which forbids any coincidence in the definitively purified ideality of a self-presence characterized by identity."[5]

In consequence of this radicalization, the chiasm interlinking body and world is itself a chiasm of chiasms. One cannot hope to reach any level of originary simplicity that would underlie the intercalated density of a multidimensional chiasmatic articulation. There is, Merleau-Ponty notes, no pure *quale*; even this patch of red before one's eyes that might seem a mere sense datum is, rather, a tenuous concretion or crystallization of sensible being. In its concise and imperious presencing, it offers, as Merleau-Ponty puts it, "past visions, visions to come, in entire clusters" (*VI*, 135). The sentient/sensible body, in its synergic, prereflexive unity, is likewise not a whole closed in upon itself, nor is it wholly coincident with the empirical body. Even if one considers one's awareness of the empirical body in pain, in illness, or in the grip of terror, one becomes aware that it escapes the "body schema" and the scope of one's possible initiative. One encounters here what Merleau-Ponty, in *The Visible and the Invisible*, likes to call the body as surround or perimeter (*enceinte*), as the vaguely defined but encompassing reach of one's exposure and vulnerability, radiating outward, somewhat like a funnel, from an "inside" core.

Between "inside" and "outside," there is not just a binary interlacing, but what Merleau-Ponty refers to as a "double inscription," where the inside receives "without flesh," although, he is careful to say, not in the manner of a "psychic state." It receives, rather, "as intra-corporeal, the reverse of the outside that my body shows to things" (*VI*, 261). This outside is the sensory presencing brought to pass by the sentient body's engagement with the world; but how is one to think the intra-corporeal, discarnate inside?

Richir offers a subtle analysis of this redoubling, according to which the interior inscription is that of the non-sensible "self" of things within the nonempirical body as *Leib*, which thus encounters, always only in imminence, its own non-sensible "self"—not, once again, as psychic interiority, but in virtue of a kind of figuration that is non-sensible yet is intimately interlinked with sensory figuration. It will be necessary to return to this topic in considering the invisibility that inhabits Flesh.

One can note here the intimacy of the chiasmatic interlinking of inside and outside, which are themselves chiasmatically articulated. The body, Merleau-Ponty writes (and this cannot be just the empirical body) "loosens itself upon [*se détache sur*] things;" yet, in so doing, it also "detaches itself [*se détache de*] from them" (*VI*, 137). The body's "double reference" as sentient/sensible (perhaps also as *Leib* and *Körper*) attests to these intercrossed trajectories which cannot be brought together without a shift or gap.

The inside receives "without flesh"; yet, in virtue of the pervasiveness of chiasmatic articulation, even "pure" ideality is not, Merleau-Ponty argues, entirely discarnate or without horizons. It constitutes a "surpassing in place" of the generality that already "diffuses itself along the articulations of the aesthesiological body" (*VI*, 152). The "reverse" of sensible presencing, intercalated with it throughout, allows for the anonymity and generality that pertain to the very "style" of sensible presencing. Activity and passivity intermesh, so that the seer finds herself not only engulfed by the visible but also, as it were, "seen" by things; her vision takes shape in the in-between of an abyssal mirroring. Merleau-Ponty points out that one touches here upon the deeper meaning of narcissism: "not to see in the outside, as others see it, the contours of a body in which one dwells, but above all to be seen by it . . . to be seduced, captivated, alienated by the phantom, in such a manner that seer and seen reciprocate one another, and one no longer knows who sees and who is seen" (*VI*, 139).

Sensibility is like a wave by which she who senses is carried along, and which is sustained by an inexhaustible vastness and depth. If this wave, Merleau-Ponty reflects, can recoil upon itself here and now, yielding sentience and sensory reflection, it can also do so everywhere, so that the chiastic structure that unifies the synergic sentient body also interlinks sentient beings with one another:

> Why should not synergy exist between different organisms, if it is possible in the interior of each? Their landscapes are mutually entangled; their actions and passions fit together exactly: All this is possible once one ceases to define sensibility primordially in terms of its pertaining to one same "consciousness" and understands it instead as a returning of the visible upon itself, as carnal adherence of the sentient to the sensible, and of the sensed to the sentient. For, as overlapping and fission, identity and difference, it brings to birth a ray of natural light. (*VI*, 142)

The "natural light," for Descartes the defining prerogative of the *res cogitans* who can escape the confines of solipsism only by first validating the infinite and eternal ground of its *cogitatio*, here plays across the undulations of sentience and gleams in its depths like bioluminescence. Rather than seeking to surmount or marginalize difference, intercorporeity foregrounds it, in keeping with the divergence essential to chiasmatic articulation. The Other with whom I am inextricably interlinked is not just, as the French language expresses it forcefully, *mon semblable* (literally, "my similar"), but may belong to orders of sentience remote from the human.

Given that chiasmatic articulation is multidimensional, Merleau-Ponty moves on from the dimension of dynamic vastness or transitivity to consider depth or dynamic verticality, limning his thought of a "vertical genesis" or "surpassing in place." It is not possible here to examine his rather summary discussion of the libidinal reach of sentience and of the emergence of expression, which offers a pathway, via gesture and the reflexivity of phonation and hearing, to the place of language and thought.

What Merleau-Ponty insists on is the shift (*bougé*) or non-closure that remains characteristic of chiasmatic articulation in its spiraling verticality; it is this hiatus that allows the first-order visibility (that of things) to be complemented by a second-order visibility of "lines of force and dimensions" (*VI*, 149). The subtle Flesh or horizonality that is here revealed shows the inextricable bond between ideality and Flesh. *Pace* Descartes, who sought to unveil truth, to strip "naked" his piece of wax, or to soar above the limitations of embodiment, Merleau-Ponty emphasizes that there is no sensuous presencing without a screen, and that certain idealities, such as the notions of light, of voluminosity, or of voluptuousness, would be strictly inaccessible to a disembodied intelligence. At the same time, however, the chiasm does not allow for the reduction of such idealities to mere sensory givens. Echoing Mallarmé's "*la fleur absente de tous bouquets*," Merleau-Ponty remarks that what comes to presence here is "*l'absente de toute chair*" ("the one absent from all Flesh")—a negativity that permeates Flesh and that is not sheer nothingness.

One cannot leave behind or "exit from" chiasmatic organization to lay claim to any positivity, even that of "pure" ideality. Nevertheless, a "rigorous ideality," which Merleau-Ponty also describes as a "cohesion without concept," already permeates fleshly experience, being "of the same type as the cohesion of the parts of my body, or that of my body and the world."[6] While Merleau-Ponty declares himself still unprepared to situate dimensions of ideality such as language, culture, or mathematics definitively within the spiraling vortex of chiasmatic Flesh, he does point out that, far from being primordial, they draw upon the bond between idea and Flesh tied by the "carnal essences." In the intercalation of sound and sense in "operant language," of ideality and language, or of the *ecstases* of time, one encounters anew: "This never achieved differentiation, this opening always to be re-opened between sign and sign, as Flesh, we have said, is the dehiscence of what sees into the visible, and of the visible into what sees."[7] This differentiated opening marks a crossover to the "other side" of sensory configuration; and the vital crossing point of this chiasm of chiasms is a nucleus of emptiness.

INVISIBLE FLESH

The Flesh of the world, Merleau-Ponty writes, cannot be explicated in terms of bodily flesh or physicality. However much the body, in the ordinary sense, may have been neglected by Western philosophy, Merleau-Ponty is not concerned to provide the means for its rehabilitation. Rather, he notes, one's body (*le corps propre*) must itself be understood in terms of the Flesh of the world, if one is to avoid the pitfall of construing it as an in-itself, a primary carnality that would underlie the *ecstases* of sentience, of desire, and of suffering. Not only is such a supposed in-itself unfindable, but carnal being, Merleau-Ponty argues, is itself ultimately "the presentation of a certain absence" (*VI*, 179, cf. 250).

What Merleau-Ponty calls Flesh is the coiling-over [*enroulement*] or inter-dehiscence of sentience and sensibility, encountered as a tissue of latencies, a "mirror phenomenon," or as pervasive horizontality (which he refers to by the Husserlian term *Horizonthaftigkeit*). Sentience and sensibility are here not the hackneyed notions of perception and its objectified correlate (such as the sense datum), but indicate the spontaneity of manifestation shown forth at once, or in indivision, as both φαινεσθαι and φαινομενον, in the union of active and passive perfection that Spinoza first called attention to.[8] In Merleau-Ponty's non-substantialist thought, however, this Spinozan insight becomes centered on the sheer gap or absence at the dynamic core of presencing. He develops this realization more daringly in the speculative shorthand of the Working Notes than in the textual body of *The Visible and the Invisible.* Flesh becomes here the name of, or the placeholder for, the being of beings. Therefore Flesh, as an "impregnation with possibles" [*prégnance de possibles*] is not any sort of actual entity, such as "the bare thing at issue" [*die blosse Sache*], or even, in the programmatic Husserlian phrase, *die Sachen selbst*.[9]

Flesh as a dimensionality marked by both sedimentation and transcendence, by chiasmatic depth structure and by a lateral investiture of existentials, "*ess*ences" or holds sway (*west* in Heidegger's sense).[10] As a "dehiscence" or "bursting forth" (*éclatement*), it refuses to be fixated and possessed; it works a dispossession; and this work is one that philosophy must take up: Philosophy "cannot be total and active grasp, intellectual possession, since what there is to be seized is a dispossession. . . . It is the simultaneous examination [*épure*] of the taking and the taken in all orders" (*VI*, 266). If the insubstantial density of Flesh is constitutive of corporeity, even the empirical body cannot be reified. As Richir emphasizes, dream interests Merleau-Ponty because it brings about a spontaneous *epokhè* of the positivity of body and world; but the distinction drawn between the agile, nonempirical body as *Leib* and the empirical *Körper* (or, as Merleau-Ponty also phrases it, between "the first self" [*le Je premier*] and "the designated self" [*le Je dénommé*]) needs itself to be radicalized or referred back to the root of emptiness. If the designated or empirical body is the objectification of a negativity that is, as such, ungraspable, the objectification or reification will lack any solid basis, however persuasive it is to the natural attitude or the perceptual faith. What "the other scene" of dream reveals, then, is that "the true institution [*Stiftung*] of Being" is, in all the registers of Flesh, without positivity.[11]

The chiasmatic density of Flesh is also constitutive of visibility (the emblem, for Merleau-Ponty, of sensibility as such). The invisibility that is coextensive with visual presencing (that is, as it were, its "other side") attests, once again, to the truth that the world is "in its very fabric not made of actuality." In one of his most succinct and daring formulations, Merleau-Ponty writes that "the invisible is *here* without being *object*; it is pure transcendence without an ontic mask. And the "visibles" themselves, they are, in the last analysis, likewise only centered upon a nucleus of absence" (*VI*, 229).[12] This text focuses on the ontological import of the invisibility that pervades visual presencing; but Merleau-Ponty also takes pains to characterize this invisibility more amply and to sketch out more detailed analyses. Most crucially, visible configuration allows for the presencing, as such, of what is incapable of originary presentation, or of what remains essentially concealed (Merleau-Ponty frequently avails himself of the Husserlian and Heideggerian expressions of an *Urpräsentation* of what is not *urpräsentierbar*, or of an *Unverborgenheit der Verborgenheit*). Such unconcealment does not have the character of representation; it "hollows out" visible presencing rather than being a positive production. At the same time, Merleau-Ponty emphasizes that it "counts" in the world, so much so that the spiraling verticality of presencing that he seeks to outline would not be possible without this abyssal moment. Invisibility pertains to visual presencing as such and therefore does not negate it.

Although Merleau-Ponty likes to say that figure/ground articulation is fundamental to visual perception (whereas some contemporary painting has problematized this articulation, rendering it polyvalent and undecidable), one needs to be aware that his thought of the invisible of the visible divests both figure and ground of their usual identity. In two Working Notes from May 1960, he reflects that every visible, whether or not it is figural, brings with it a nonvisible ground (*VI*, 246–48). This ground is no neutralized and flattened background dominated by the figure; rather, it is ultimately the chiasmatic Flesh out of which the visible emerges, flashing forth along "a ray of the world." In keeping with this astral imagery, the ground is more like a comet's tail than like dark space. The figure or configuration itself is therefore not an objective *quale*; it cannot be fixated by the gaze, nor is it mediated by and explicable in terms of thought. It is glimpsed spontaneously, in a kind of *ekstasis*, in its inherent dynamism and transience, and latently or transparently within the fabric of sensuous presencing. Such a glimpsing contrasts sharply with the ideal of *clara et distincta perceptio* that furnished Descartes with a metaphor for intellectual apprehension.

The seer, Merleau-Ponty writes in a memorable formulation, is "poised upon the visible like a bird, hooked fast to the visible, not *within* it. And yet in chiasm with it—" (*VI*, 261). What the seer, in her tenuous hold upon the visible, does not and cannot see is what allows for sight; and this "blind spot" [*punctum caecum*] underlies the objectifying tendency of the perceptual faith. As a matter of principle, and not of mere misguidedness, consciousness "disregards Being and prefers the object to it." This obscuration, however, is not entirely hopeless; and, in Merleau-Ponty's view, artistic figuration has a certain power to dispel it.

THE WORK OF FIGURATION

Being, Merleau-Ponty notes, demands creation of us, if we are to be capable of experiencing it (*VI*, 197). Philosophy endeavors, through intellectual creation, to achieve an adequation to being (note that "adequation," unlike "coincidence," preserves a differential moment). In this sense, Merleau-Ponty observes that "art and philosophy *together* are precisely not arbitrary fabrications in the universe of the "spiritual" (of "culture"), but [they are] contact with Being precisely in that they are creations" (*VI*, 197). Are art and philosophy then straightforwardly on a par? Merleau-Ponty's meditation in "Eye and Mind" indicates otherwise; but before considering it, one needs to remind oneself that, even apart from art (which is a Western philosophical concept) and philosophy—though at best questionably apart from culture—visual or, more generally, sensory presencing is already creation. There is no Cartesian nakedness of some piece of wax, or of any sensory given. Merleau-Ponty writes that the look can, paradoxically, rejoin the sensible in its independence only by clothing it in its own Flesh (*VI*, 131). This fleshly opening upon the sensible is no sort of production or reproduction; it is, rather, a work of figuration.

Carnal figuration allows for the presencing of a *Gestalt* that is not an *eidos*, for the bodying-forth of an *esse*ntiality, a *Wesen*, that elides thought and reveals itself only in and through sensory presencing. Such presencing is, as already noted, imbued with complex "participations" and supported by an "interior armature" of existentials derived from sedimentation. It is hollowed out by an invisible or insensible "reverse," by what Barbaras calls "an internal negation, a retreat of the visible."

Richir points out that the mirroring proper to Flesh as a "mirror phenomenon" is a figuration of the double ground, invisible/insensible, of the visible/sensible.[13] It could also be understood, somewhat more broadly, as indicating the imaginary, or even illusional, matrix of what is experienced as real. Richir offers a subtle analysis of the "specular extract" or figural *Bild* that is the *esse*ntiality of things. This *Bild* is, as Merleau-Ponty stresses, no sort of image; it is, in Richir's words, "that in which the *Etwas* becomes *Sache* or *Ding*," the figuration of the infigurable. The spontaneous work of figuration allows perception to resurface, as it were, from abyssal horizonality, where otherwise it would lose itself. According to Richir (who maintains his guiding distinction between *Leib* and *Körper*):

> The *Leib* seems to lose itself in the world, so as to find itself in the *Wesen* of things: The *Wesen* or *Bild* is the presentation, always already figured, of "the non-presentable originary." . . . The *Wesen* are so many "specular extracts" of the *Leib*, taken precisely in itself . . . [it] has no figure or face. . . . Henceforward, the *Wesen* of the world . . . which are ever so many figures of the true negative, are ever so many articulations where the body (*Leib*) and the world achieve their reflexivity . . . in non-coincidence.

Richir's analysis traces the double inscription of things in their presencing as sensible within the chiasm of sentience and sensibility, and as insensible and received "without flesh" within the abyssal ipseity of *Leib*, whence they are bodied forth, not as sensibles, but as *ess*entialities or *Wesen* through a work of figuration. These two inscriptions are chiasmatically intercalated and thus indissociable; but they cannot be collapsed into coincidence.

The fundamental reason why the figuration at work in sentience tends to remain hidden is, as Richir expresses it, the "transcendental illusion" that the two inscriptions "coincide in a single intercalation."[14] This transcendental illusion is taken up and carried forward by the perceptual faith, which aims at pure givenness, objectivity, the irrecusable presence of the in-itself, and which in its turn informs varied modalities of thought that tend toward absolutization and totalization. It is here, to counteract this impetus and to disrupt the transcendental illusion, that Merleau-Ponty turns toward artistic figuration.

When the artist—for Merleau-Ponty above all the painter—penetrates to the fabric of inchoate meaning, or to the "wild being" that subtends thought and civilization, s/he does not reach some pristine positivity. First of all, the painter "lends his body to the world"; and this body is not just the empirical body. In its complex intertwinings of vision and movement, activity and passivity, sentience and sensibility, it is closer to Richir's *Leib* which senses "only its *shadow*, its shadow, so to say, carried upon the world itself; and the *Bild* of the thing is thereby also its *Wesen* . . . extracted right away from the visible/sensible. . . . To put it differently, the *Leib* lets *ester* that alone of the world which sees or senses 'itself' across it."[15]

Now, however, this "strange system of exchanges" does not issue just into the sensory presencing that solicits the perceptual faith; for, to the artist, this faith fails to do any justice to "what senses itself in him." What can begin—if only begin—to do it justice is the creation of what Merleau-Ponty calls "a visible of the second power, carnal essence or icon of the first" (*EM*, 164). It does not matter whether or not his icon is figurative. What matters is that it communicates a way of being touched by the world, together with the fundamentally non-positive character of presencing, its refusal of fixity. Insistently and hauntingly, it renders *unverborgen* what nevertheless remains *Verbergung*—the very hiddenness that is discounted by the perceptual faith. What artistic figuration is in quest of defamiliarizes accepted identifications and eludes both presentation and representation in principle; and this defamiliarization and elision is integral to the power of art.

The painter consummates vision as an oblivion of self and as participating "in the fission of Being," the "continual birth" that ultimately allows for his or her own "birth" in reflexivity. If the philosophy still to be created is, as Merleau-Ponty remarks, the one that animates the painter (without being thematized), it might seem, however—given some of his concluding formulations and quotations in "Eye and Mind"—that this philosophy would mitigate the attrition of positivity that the present study has emphasized. Thus, Merleau-Ponty cites Leonardo da Vinci's remark that the soul can rest content in its bodily prison, so long as the body offers it eyes that open upon the radiance of the world; and he claims that the painter cannot but accept the idea of the ocular "windows of the soul," and that s/he cannot consent that visual access to the world should be "illusory or indirect" (*EM*, 186–87). However, the illusion denied here is the intellectualist illusion that casts vision as derivative from or mediated by thought, rather than the transcendental illusion brought about by sentience itself. Artistic figuration does not get caught up in either of these illusions; it exposes them; and it is for this reason that Merleau-Ponty holds that it can guide a reorientation of philosophy. Its guidance leads philosophy, particularly phenomenology, away from the positivity of classical ontologies and enables it, in Merleau-Ponty's view, to rejoin, by a somewhat deviant path, the essential unthought of Husserl's late thought.

NOTES

1. See *VI*, 268. Merleau-Ponty here refers to the philosophical imperative to unravel what is intermeshed specifically to Husserl's *Ideen II*, the Husserlian text that is generally the focus of his engagement with Husserl.
2. See, *VI*, 263ff. See also Marc Richir, "Le sensible dans le rêve," in *Merleau-Ponty: Notes de cours sur l'origine de la géométrie de Husserl; suivi de Recherches sur la phénoménologie de Merleau-Ponty*, ed. R. Barbaras (Paris: PUF, 1998), 239–54.
3. Richir, 251.
4. Ibid., 252ff.
5. *VI*, 137. Compare this passage to his remark at *EM*, 162 that the painter brings his body to the work. See also *VI*, 146.
6. Jacques Garelli, "Héritage husserlien et expérience merleau-pontienne," in *Notes de cours*, op. cit., 102.
7. Ibid., 97.

8. *VI*, 153; compare *EM*, 182: "Here is a proof that there is a system of equivalences, a Logos of lines, of lights, of colors, or reliefs, of masses, a presentation without concept of universal Being."
9. *VI*, 153; on the chiasmatic structure of time, see also the note entitled "Time and Chiasm," in *VI*, 267ff.
10. Baruch Spinoza, *Ethics*, trans. S. Shirley (Indianapolis: Hackett, 1982), Part II, prop. 13, sch.
11. See *VI*, 250. The familiar English translation of the Husserlian phrase is "the things themselves," but this translation ignores the subtle difference between *Sache* and *Ding*. A better translation might be "what is at issue," or "the very issues." In his late thought, Merleau-Ponty renounces not only the *Ding*, but also any delimited *Sache*. On his radicalization of the late Husserl (especially the Husserl of *Experience and Judgment*), see Garelli, op. cit.
12. Merleau-Ponty echoes Heidegger's frequent reminder that *Wesen* is to be understood verbally. See, for instance, *VI*, 229. I have adopted the neologism *ess*ences to translate Heidegger's *west* in such a manner as to call attention to the fact that it functions as a word for being.
13. Compare Richir, 240, and the working notes in *VI*, 246 and 262. See also *VI*, 135ff.
14. Jacques Derrida draws attention to this text as calling for "an entire re-reading" of the late Merleau-Ponty in his *Memoirs of the Blind*, trans. P.-A. Brault and M. Naas (Chicago: University of Chicago Press, 1990), 52.
15. Richir, 244.
16. Ibid., 245.
17. Ibid., 249.
18. Ibid., 245.

12

Phenomenology of the Icon

JENNY SLATMAN

According to Husserl, phenomenology is a philosophy of the *eidos*.[1] With this he places himself directly in the tradition of Western philosophy since Plato. The *eidos* is the essence of something. Phenomenology is not interested in the actual circumstances of things, but sets out to clarify their essence. For Plato, the *eidos* is equivalent to the unchanging idea (*idea*). It is the intelligible form that can be comprehended through contemplation. It is thus the opposite of the ephemeral world of the senses. It is the opposite of what appears to us in the world of the senses: the *phainomena*. For Plato, a phenomenology—the doctrine of the *phainomena*—could never be a philosophical discipline because it is the task of philosophy to try to grasp the *eidos* by means of contemplation (*theoria*), and it will never find that *eidos* in the world of the senses. It was one of Husserl's great merits to have shown that *eidos* and *phainomenon* are not diametrically opposed to one another. In his view, the *eidos* of something cannot be detached from its phenomenal form. The *eidos* does not exist in some "world of ideas," but makes its appearance in our only world: the world of the senses. It is not itself something sensory, but it manifests itself, as it were, along with all of the sensory world that is offered to us.

In his early work Husserl takes the *eidos* to be something static. The objective ideality of number, for example, is something that is impervious to time. In his later work (I have in mind his *The Origin of Geometry*), we see that his view of the status of the objectivity of the ideal has changed. The objective ideality of geometry, even though it is "supratemporal," is not an ideality detached from the effects of time and history. It acquires its objective character precisely in the course of tradition and thus in the course of history. It is known that this crucial late text by Husserl played an important role in the philosophical development of the work of Merleau-Ponty. This is most explicit in one of his last lectures at the Collège de France, which is devoted to Husserl's *The Origin of Geometry*.[2] Merleau-Ponty confronts Husserl's text with one of Heidegger's later texts, *On the Way to Language*. One of the purposes of this confrontation is to link Husserl's notion of ideality—which Merleau-Ponty characterizes as "*idéalité en genèse*"—with Heidegger's dynamic concept of the essence or *eidos* as *Wesen*.[3] I shall not go farther into Merleau-Ponty's attempt to reconcile the views of the two German philosophers here. What interests me is the way in which Merleau-Ponty himself interprets the idea of "*idéalité en genèse*," of ideality as a dynamic *Wesen*. My hypothesis is that this form of ideality can be grasped from an "iconography of vision." The ideality envisaged by Merleau-Ponty can be seen at its clearest in artistic expression. In this essay I shall try to show that Merleau-Ponty's aesthetics can be interpreted as a phenomenology in which the classical *eidos* is replaced by the *eikoon*. As the *eidos* is offered to contemplative thought, the *eikoon* presents itself within corporeal vision: "Seeing is this sort of thought that has no need to think in order to possess the *Wesen*" (*VI*, 247). We shall see that it is particularly the art of painting that invites us to see in this way. This phenomenology of the icon is bound to have repercussions for philosophy itself, because in the last resort it is philosophy—not art—that is out to thematize and express ideality. My final claim is that, in its form of expression, philosophy should be like artistic expression, and that we can find a certain form of iconicity in its discourse.

THE NEGATIVITY OF EXCHANGING LOOKS

Plato's *Politeia* presents a hierarchy of the three different ways in which reality can be grasped. First, as mentioned above, it is the *eidos* that presents the essence of the thing. Second, we may have a representation of the thing, referred to as *eikoon*. Finally, we may also have a representation of something that does not exist, but only appears (*phainomenon*), referred to as *eidolon*.[4] We can immediately recognize the terms *idea*, *icon*, and *idol* here. Philosophers usually situated the ideality or essence of what is at the level of the idea, but one might wonder whether pure *eidetic* inquiry does not lead to *idolatry*. Heidegger claims that Western ontology should be understood as an onto-theology: the meaning of *Sein* is ultimately grasped by deducing it from an ultimate *Seiendes*, a God. Is an ontology of this kind which creates one or more Gods in order to be able to grasp *Sein* not idolatry? Nowhere does Merleau-Ponty speak of "onto-theology," but his critique of the so-called objectivist ontology of the modern era has many affinities with Heidegger's analysis. He comments on modern science that it "still lives in part in a Cartesian myth . . . its concept of Nature is often only an idol to which the scientist makes sacrifices, the reasons for which are due more to affective motives than to scientific facts" (*Nature*, 85). To avoid the idolatry of the eidetic and to be able to deliver a clear criticism of the ontology of representation of modern thought, the ideality or essence should be sought at the level of the icon. It is true that Merleau-Ponty himself nowhere refers to the classical distinction between *eidos*, *eikon,* and *eidolon*, but he does use the term *icon* a few times to indicate the ontological status of the image in art. I shall start from these references to put the first pointers toward a phenomenology of the icon in position.

The first meaning given to icon in *Eye and Mind* concerns the picture as the expression of the "internal equivalent" of the things seen by the painter: in the painting "appears a 'visible' to the second power, a carnal essence or icon of the first" (*EM*, 164). In his lecture notes on "L'ontologie cartésienne et l'ontologie d'aujourd'hui," Merleau-Ponty characterizes a painting explicitly as an icon. The icon is a painting that is the result of the fact that the painter belongs to the visible world because he not only sees but is also seen.[5] The icon concerns the "imaginaire" of the painting. It is like the visible that bears the invisible inside itself. In this capacity it is the opposite of the image that is taken to be a representation of an object. The term *icon* therefore occurs where Merleau-Ponty is criticizing Descartes' representational thought. The image as representation represents the visible by excluding the invisible from it. The representation is the visible as *quale*, as positive visibility. What is more, as we can read in Descartes' *Optics*, (mental) representation does not require any resemblance between the image and the object that is represented. This may also be the reason why Descartes excludes painting from his theory of representation and confines himself to a discussion of copper engravings and drawings where "icons lose their powers" (*EM*, 170). Merleau-Ponty continues his critique as follows: "The etching gives us sufficient indices, unequivocal 'means' for forming an idea of the thing that does not come from the icon itself; rather, it arises in us, as 'occasioned' by the icon" (*EM*, 170–71). So for Merleau-Ponty the icon is a painting, an image that is not simply a representation. There is no question of an external connection between the object and its image. It is precisely because the painting arises within the reversibility of the flesh of the painter's body and the flesh of the visible world that there is an inner connection between painting and world. The icon expresses this inner relation. The icon is the place where the looks are exchanged, the place of the chiasma of seeing and being seen and of the visible and the invisible.

The important point here is to note that the term *icon* does not just refer to images of saints, as in the case of Byzantine and Russian icons. Nor are we dealing with the icon as a semiotic sign distinguishable from the symbol and the index, as in Peircean semiology. In the phenomenological sense, the icon is the image of the visible that bears its invisible with it. To distance himself from the Cartesian view according to which there is no inner relation between the image and what it represents, Merleau-Ponty claims that the icon's capacity lies in the possibility of "resemblance" and "analogy." However, these terms do not mean that there is a relation of identity between image and object. Merleau-Ponty only uses these terms to indicate that, thanks to the senses, people are able to *recognize* a connection between image and visible world, instead of constructing a connection of this kind using the mind's eye. I believe that the analyses of painting contained in Merleau-Ponty's *Eye and Mind* should be understood in the light of this concept of the image. His analyses are intended to bring iconology back into the philosophical fold: "In paintings themselves we could seek a figured philosophy of vision—its iconography, perhaps" (*EM*, 167).

Before going into the way in which Merleau-Ponty thematizes the invisible in art, I shall first briefly deal with a number of motifs from the work of Jean-Luc Marion because he is one of the few thinkers to have given a phenomenological account of the icon.[6] It may prove easier to grasp Merleau-Ponty's brief allusions to the icon in the light of Marion's analysis. In his *L'idole et la distance*, Marion combats the idolatrous metaphysics of onto-theology—which is eventually bound to end in atheism—by elaborating a philosophy of distance that entails a veritable philosophy of the divine. The distance that is constitutive of the "contact" with the divine is manifested in the icon. The icon is thus the opposite of the idol. According to Marion, the icon is not the figuration of a God, but "the visibility of the invisible, the visibility where the invisible appears as such."[7] The affinity with Merleau-Ponty's vocabulary is striking. Although it is obvious that Marion's definition of the icon is particularly inspired by the Christian tradition, he states in *Dieu sans l'être* that his analysis of the icon is neither historical nor religious. The distinction between idol and icon is not based on the distinction between cultures whereby the idolatry of Greek culture is opposed to the iconicity of the invisible god of Christianity. The distinction in question is a phenomenological one, not a factual one: "The icon and the idol determine two ways of being of entities, not two categories of entities."[8] The difference between these two ways of being is determined by the way in which the image is intended. In the case of the icon, it is the invisible that is "intended." While the idol is the result of an intention that is satisfied with something that is visible and in which the intention meets its destination, the icon discloses the invisibility that is inaccessible and beyond the reach of intention (*invisable*) too.

Marion's *La croisée du visible* is an investigation of the two forms of imaging within present-day visual culture. This study is therefore particularly interesting when it comes to Merleau-Ponty's "iconography of vision" as it is operative in art. Marion rejects the so-called idolatry of the visible on which present-day visual culture is based, and argues for an iconography of the invisible based on religious experience such as prayer. Let us first consider how he further articulates the distinction between idol and icon here. The icon is characterized primarily by the exchange of looks. In this way it evades what can be foreseen. The icon gives us the unseen (*l'invu*) that is unforeseen. What the icon presents to us is a void, a hole, a negativity, a privation: a *kenosis* involving the disfiguration of every figure. Such a *kenosis* can manifest itself because the exchange of looks, like Merleau-Ponty's reversibility between the viewer and the visible, never takes place fully. The *kenosis* of the icon is based on the so-called "natural negativity" of seeing.[9] This negativity, which is always present in seeing and being seen, characterizes the invisible—the *punctum caecum*—within the visible. The idol, on the other hand, presents us with nothing but the visible. What it shows is entirely foreseen, and thus leaves no room for the unforeseen unseen. Moreover, idolatry is free from the gaze of the other. Whereas the spectator of the icon is a *voyant*, someone who submits to the gaze of the other, the spectator of the idol is a *voyeur*, someone who "fills him/herself with the most accessible visible," without exposing him/herself to the gaze of the other.[10] The idea of the *voyeur* corresponds to the traditional idea of the spectator or the transcendental subject, whereas the *voyant* in a certain sense corresponds to the visible seer as described by Merleau-Ponty. The *voyeur* is the one who "permits, governs and defines the image," while the *voyant* is open to an unforeseen gift.[11]

Marion regards television as the example of idolatrous voyeurism: "The structurally idolatrous television image obeys the voyeur and produces nothing but prostituted images."[12] The voyeur sees only what s/he desires to see. His/her *libido vivendi* finds satisfaction in "the lonely pleasure of the screen."[13] The voyeur produces idols. S/he only produces what s/he wants to see. In this way, s/he is not involved in the spectacle that is seen. Hence the voyeur, as Marion presents him/her, is the incarnation of what Merleau-Ponty calls "thought as survey," observation from a bird's-eye view (*pensée de survol*). It is vision without a point of view in the world, and thus disembodied vision. Although one may question the adequacy of Marion's analysis of the phenomenon of television, the similarity with Merleau-Ponty's analyses is immediately clear.[14] While Marion sets out to overcome the "muddy tyranny of the visible" or idolatrous voyeurism by means of the effect of prayer that purifies the eyes, Merleau-Ponty opposes painting to "thought as survey." Incidentally, as far as iconicity is concerned Marion does refer to fine art too. His *Dieu sans l'être*, for example, contains an analysis of Dürer's *Melancholia* (1514) to show that melancholy opens up a distance that implies the unconditional love of God (*agapè*) and that transcends the ontology of the entities. The gaze of the central figure in this etching transcends the limits of the visible because it is orientated toward a vanishing point that is absent. Marion wants to show that there is something in this etching that transcends the domain of the visible entities. That is the domain of iconicity. For both Merleau-Ponty and Marion, thus, the icon is an image that transcends the visible of the representational ideology, and this image can be realized in the art of painting.

The comparison between Marion and Merleau-Ponty can be taken a step farther. Marion explains (iconic) seeing in terms of an "exchange of looks." Merleau-Ponty describes the practice of the painter in terms of the reversibility of the gaze. What Marion defined as the *voyant*, in opposition to the *voyeur*, corresponds to how Merleau-Ponty describes the painter. The analysis in *Eye and Mind* begins with the statement that the most important characteristic of the painter is that s/he expresses him/herself in a direct way through his/her body. According to Valéry, whom Merleau-Ponty cites here, the painter's body is involved (*EM*, 162). The painter does not detach him/herself from his/her corporeal position in the visible world; s/he belongs to this world. S/he is the one who sees but is visible at the same time, and thus forms a part of the visible world. When the painter paints, when s/he turns the visible world into a painting, s/he "exhales" (expiration) this world that s/he had previously "inhaled" (inspiration) through his/her body. The practice of painting consists of a "respiration in Being" (*EM*, 168). The painter's body is a part of the spectacle, and the landscape is incarnated in the painting. So the painter accomplishes the chiasma between seeing and being seen, between the seer and the visible. Because the painter's body is implicated, s/he is subjected to the visible. Merleau-Ponty:

"Since things and my body are made of the same stuff, vision must somehow come about in them; or yet again, their manifest visibility must be repeated in the body by a secret visibility" (*EM*, 163). This secret visibility "in the innermost part" of the painter can now manifest itself as an externalized visibility, that is, as something that is also visible for others to see. This externalization of the visible constitutes pictorial expression.

The icon, then, is the result of an interaction between the painter and his/her visible world. In the case of a displayed image, this interaction must be understood as an exchange of looks between the painting and the spectator. It is known that the characteristic of the Byzantine icon lies in the fact that the image of Christ or one of the saints gazes at the spectator. In this case the spectator feels that s/he is not just a voyeur, but also a seen spectator (*voyant*). An interaction of this kind is not confined to religious experience or to the situation in which the looks really do cross. The painting as icon—not just in the Byzantine sense, but in the phenomenological sense—confronts the spectator with the fact that s/he does not stand outside the spectacle, that s/he cannot adopt a bird's-eye view. The spectator is not a *voyeur*, but is implicated in the visible world of the work of art.

Marion's theory makes it clear that the seeing of the painter and of the spectator can be understood in terms of the "exchange of looks," and it enables us to characterize Merleau-Ponty's analysis of the art of painting as a phenomenology of the icon. This iconography is not particularly concerned with religious images in the Christian tradition. In a fundamental way it is a critique of the ordinary notion of seeing and calls for a different way of seeing in order to elaborate a new ontology of the visible. The icon invites us to search for a different manner of Being of the visible beings. Marion's analysis of the icon implies an appeal to religious experience, a return to the divine beyond onto-theology and a rejection of the visual phenomena of our popular culture. Merleau-Ponty's analysis, on the other hand, even though it implies a critique of the idolatry of the representational ideology, and even though it resembles a critique of onto-theology, does not entail an explicit return to the religious. Moreover, his analysis of the visible and of the art of painting does not automatically lead to a rejection of the phenomena of popular culture such as television, film, and multimedia. His critique of the representational ontology does not necessarily coincide with a critique of popular culture. Before going into a number of analyses of works of art, I will now first specify the phenomenology of the icon more precisely as the ontology of the invisible in the visible.

ONTOLOGY OF THE INVISIBLE

The phenomenology of the icon can be understood as an implementation of the "destruction of the objectivist ontology of the Cartesians" (*VI*, 183). This destruction boils down to a critique of representational thought and is aimed at recovering the meaning of so-called wild or vertical Being. As Merleau-Ponty formulates it in a working note: "What I want to do is restore the world as a meaning of Being absolutely different from the 'represented,' that is, as the vertical Being which none of the 'representations' exhaust and which all 'reach' the wild being" (*VI*, 253). This restoration can be implemented on the basis of the analysis of seeing and the image. The most important representative of the objectivist ontology or of the ontology of representation for Merleau-Ponty is Descartes, hence the primary target of the analysis in *Eye and Mind* is the Cartesian visual paradigm. In this text Merleau-Ponty develops an ontology of the art of painting aimed against the representational thought of Descartes' *Optics*, in which seeing is reduced to a "thinking of seeing" (*penser de voir*). The *Optics* marks a rupture with medieval thinking about images. While Scholastic philosophy speaks of a correspondence between the *esse naturale* (the thing outside the soul) and the *esse intentionale* (the mental image), Descartes speaks of a causal link that is constituted by thought.[15] Thought constitutes the mental image by an act of interpretation. It interprets the impressions that are caused by the movement of light. Seeing is thus comparable to the act of deciphering or reading. The visible, the impressions of light in motion, are like signs that can be deciphered by the mind, by which it forms an image. These signs do not resemble the things in reality, they represent them. In this way representation breaks with "the magic of intentional species—the old idea of effective resemblance so strongly suggested to us by mirrors and paintings" (*EM*, 171) and thought produces an idea of the visible that is no longer derived from the "powers of the icon." "Nothing is left of the oneiric world of analogy . . ." (*EM*, 171). In Descartes, free thought has become the measure of seeing. The eye of the *voyeur* as a *pensée de survol* does not provide any account of its own bodily position in the visible. The Cartesian model thus leads to a representation of Being as an absolutely positive being, and the space of the representation as a "space without hiding places" in which the things exist *partes extra partes* (*EM*, 173). Iconic space, on the other hand, is the place where things "encroach upon each other" and where the wild Being deflagrates. The painting as icon is not a re-presentation of Being, it is a *presentation* of its appearance.

The artist is assigned an important role in Merleau-Ponty's ontology of the "wild Being"—the ontology beyond representation. This role is due to the fact that artistic expression, the creation of a work of art (*poièsis*), is always directly linked with sensory perception (*aisthèsis*). The work of the painter is not the product of a *pensée de survol*, but precisely of his or her sensory implication with the visible world. Besides criticizing scientific abstract thought, the art of painting also criticizes profane, everyday seeing. Generally speaking, the aesthesiological roots of seeing are forgotten in everyday seeing. As a result, it fails to see the invisible in the visible. The painter's eye, on the other hand, is trained to distinguish matters that are not actually visible, the so-called phantoms of the visible such as light, reflection, shadows, color, and depth (*EM*, 166). It is precisely thanks to these phantoms that we are able to recognize full visibility, that is, the visible with its invisible: "The visible in the profane sense forgets its premises; it rests upon a total visibility which is to be recreated and which liberates the phantoms captive in it" (*EM*, 167). In other words, we could also say that painting is the performance of the transcendental reduction because it brackets everyday seeing in the profane sense. It disrupts our natural relation with the world in order to put it in a new light. The painting "gives visible existence to what profane vision believes to be invisible" (*EM*, 166). The painting is the "rumination of the world" (*EM*, 161).

According to Merleau-Ponty, of all artists it is the painter who is able to suspend the being of the world to enable it to appear to us in a different way, for, he claims, the painter does not have the "responsibilities of humans who speak," such as the writer or the philosopher. "Only the painter is entitled to look at everything without being obliged to appraise what he sees. For the painter, we might say, the watchwords of knowledge and action lose their meaning and force" (*EM*, 161). The urgency of art is not political or practical but ontological. In giving voice to the visible world, the painter is not the only creator of this "voice of silence." According to Merleau-Ponty, an expression should not be understood to be something that is strictly personal or individual. Artistic expression is "not imitation, nor is it something manufactured according to the wishes of instinct or good taste" (*SNS*, 17). Thus, in "Indirect Language and the Voices of Silence," he rejects André Malraux's idea of "creative expression." Malraux claimed that modern art as the creative expression par excellence is a "passage to the subjective" and "a ceremony glorifying the individual," in which the style of the painter is "the means of recreating the world according to the values of the man who discovers it."[16] Merleau-Ponty argues that this notion of expression fails to do justice to the real meaning of the phenomenon of style, for style is not the unmediated self that the painter incorporates in the canvas: "[S]tyle is not a manner, a certain number of procedures or tics that he can inventory, but a mode of formulation that is just as recognizable for others and just as little visible to him as his silhouette or his everyday gestures" (*Signs*, 53). Style is an interaction with the visible world, it is the way in which people communicate, and therefore it cannot be a private expression. Expression *institutes* a style that is recognizable for others.[17] Merleau-Ponty criticizes Malraux's subjectivist position to emphasize that artistic expression institutes an intersubjective meaning. This intersubjectivity also applies to that art form that might easily be associated with a strictly individual expression: Abstract Expressionism or action painting. Although it is only natural to associate Abstract Expressionism with Merleau-Ponty's aesthetics, this form of painting is equally an intersubjective expression.[18] Even Jackson Pollock's drippings have an intersubjective meaning. The expression is a form of "participation" rather than "action."[19]

The purpose of Merleau-Ponty's observations on art in *Eye and Mind*, *Cézanne's Doubt,* and *Indirect Language and the Voices of Silence* is to explain expression on the basis of sensory perception or *aisthèsis*. It should therefore be remarked that the importance of these analyses is ontological rather than art historical. Merleau-Ponty emphatically presents himself, not as a connoisseur of art, but as a layman who wants to show "how painting enters into his reflections, and to register his sense of a profound dissonance, a transformation in the relationship between humanity and Being, when he holds up a universe of classical thought, contrasting it en bloc with the explorations of modern painting" (*EM*, 179). This confrontation between art and thought is guided by the assumption that the entire history of modern painting has a metaphysical meaning. It is apparently the case that the painter who grapples with depth, color, and light is already caught up in the most cardinal questions. The practice of painting implies the time-hallowed question: What is being?—*tí to on* (*EM*, 178). The painting discloses "carnal essences" (*EM*, 169) by exposing the dimensionality of the visible.

That dimensionality can be discovered in pictorial aspects such as depth, color, line, and movement. These aspects are dimensions of the visible; as such they are not themselves genuinely visible entities. They are invisible dimensions that enfold the visible entities. Thus, a dimension transcends positive visibility, but at the same time it is one of its conditions of possibility. Through the inclusion of its negative side—the invisible—the pictorial dimensions show the level of the ideality. In perception "it is by the same virtue that the color, the yellow, at the same time gives itself as a *certain* being and as a *dimension*" (*VI*, 218). So the perception simultaneously gives expression to the particularity of the visible and to its universality; it is "every possible being" (*VI*, 218). When I perceive this yellow, this particular yellow in front of my eyes is concerned, but at the same time this particularity transcends itself and becomes a dimension for other visible entities within my visual field: "Every visual something, as individual as it is, functions also as a dimension, because it is given as the result of a dehiscence of Being. What this ultimately means is that the hallmark of the visible is to have a lining of invisibility in the strict sense, which it makes present as a certain absence" (*EM*, 187). Since my gaze is intentional and is always directed at something, it does not stop at the positive visible entities present, but goes beyond them. This transcendence of sense perception can be explicated using the example of Proust's "petite phrase," as Merleau-Ponty does in *The Visible and the Invisible*. If you listen to a piece of music, for example Vinteuil's Sonata, you do not hear five separate notes—the only positively given sensory elements—but you hear its "petite phrase" as something that transcends these five notes and confers musical significance on them. After all, what you hear is not notes but a piece of music. This is how Proust determines the notion of the "musical idea." It concerns not an intelligible idea such as the *eidos*, but an idea "veiled with shadows" (*VI*, 150). So within sensory perception we can distinguish sensory ideas: "Literature, music, the passion, but also the experience of the visible world are—no less than is the science of Lavoisier and Ampère—the explorations of an invisible and the discourse of a universe of ideas" (*VI*, 149). The domain of the *eidos* is not opposed to that of the *phainomenon* as an opposition between the *epistèma* of thought and *aisthèsis*. The *eidos* presents itself in the *phainomenon* as *eikoon*. So the ancient opposition is transcended through the description of the invisible (or the ideality) within the visible. The "*voyance*" that Merleau-Ponty says "renders present to us what is absent" is the accomplishment of a "carnal *Wesenschau*" (*EM*, 171) or of a "*Wesenschau* of an eye that listens."[20] And this takes place especially in art. Let us now examine how Merleau-Ponty makes visible the invisible of the visible of a work of art.

THE DIMENSIONS OF ART

Merleau-Ponty discusses four dimensions of visual art: depth, color, line, and movement. To indicate the dimension of pictorial depth, it first has to be distinguished from the classical scientific notion. According to Euclidean geometry, depth is the third dimension that can be derived from height and breadth. The Cartesian view of representation corresponds to this spatial paradigm. According to Descartes, depth appears before our "thought as survey," and according to this way of thinking, people see things not behind one another in space but in accordance with their different widths. From this perspective, the things do not have any relation with one another in depth. They only have a position for a "surveying eye," or as Merleau-Ponty puts it: "We are [as Cartesians] always in the hither side of depth, or beyond it. It is never the case that things really *are* one behind the other" (*EM*, 173). The Renaissance artists to whom Descartes refers wanted to represent the Euclidean depth by representing a third dimension as a "window" of breadth and height through the technique of linear perspective.[21] Merleau-Ponty's analysis of pictorial depth, however, rejects both the idea of projection (by means of linear perspective) and that of "thought as survey" (from Descartes). Of course, this flows from his notion of "aesthesiology." The spectator (*voyant*) is in the visible, and in that capacity he or she cannot simply arrange things tidily before his or her gaze. The things are "rivals before my sight (*regard*) precisely because each one is in its own place—in their exteriority, known through their development, and their mutual dependence in their autonomy" (*EM*, 140). The aesthesiological depth is a "global locality in which everything is in the same place at the same time," it is "a voluminosity we express in a word when we say that a thing is there" (*EM*, 180). A thing is there, not as a visible *quale* or a "sliver" of visibility, but as a being in a depth with a volume and with its shadows and its invisibility. Depth is the dimension par excellence in which things can conceal themselves, and thus in which they can appear as well. On this view, depth is not derived from height and breadth, but these two dimensions are abstractions of the "global locality." Modern art seems to have replaced the positive visibility of space as a third dimension by a "deflagration of Being" in the "global locality" (*EM*, 180). The "shell of space" is fragmented in modern art (ibid.). A good example of this fracturing is Cubism, in which the viewer is confronted by a number of aspects and surfaces of visible things at the same moment. If we look at Pablo Picasso's *Portrait d'Ambroise Vollard* (1910), for example, we see a fragmented portrait consisting of different, contradictory spatial surfaces. It is as if this face bursts apart before the eyes of the viewer. By presenting the simultaneity of the different planes, Cubism immobilizes the natural way of viewing which consisted of looking at things as though they were tidily arranged in space. What could already be seen in Cézanne, but which becomes even clearer in Cubism, is that the space can no longer be divorced from its content (*EM*, 181).

Color is no more a secondary quality than depth is a derivative dimension. Color is not an ornament, but a dimension "which creates—from itself to itself—identities, differences, a texture, a materiality, a something" (ibid.). The genetic force of colors was discovered particularly in the era of Impressionism. The application of the effect of complementary colors (such as red-green) and the abandonment of local colors enabled the artist to create a certain vibration on the canvas. In "Cézanne's Doubt," Merleau-Ponty shows that Cézanne goes farther than the Impressionists because he added warm colors and black to his palette. While the Impressionist canvases only convey impressions or sensations, Cézanne uses black and warm colors to "represent the object, to find it again behind the atmosphere" (*SNS*, 12). Colors hereby acquire a different function in the genesis of visibility: "The object is no longer covered by reflections and lost in its relationships to the atmosphere and to other objects: it seems subtly illuminated from within, light emanates from it, and the result is an impression of solidity and material substance."[22] Let us consider the example of Cézanne's *Les baigneuses* (1894–1905): we see that the forms of the nude female bodies are not clearly demarcated from their surroundings. The black lines are accentuated by blue and green. This sets the line in motion, and it is only through this vibration that the figures take on form. In *Eye and Mind* Merleau-Ponty refers in particular to the work (and writings) of Paul Klee to describe the genesis of visibility through color.[23] The well-known watercolor *Föhn im Marc'schen Garten* allows a dreamy landscape to emerge from the soft colors. The image is constructed without the use of line. There are only differently colored forms, but they merge through the technique of watercolor. It is in these colors that defy delimitation and yet speak clearly for themselves that the visibility of the image is created. We can add an example from the Abstract Expressionism of the 1950s. The colored fields in the canvases of Mark Rothko (1903–1973) have no other purpose than to institute a sort of "harmonic" seeing. Because they appeal directly to our vision, these colors present nothing but themselves and their relations to one another. These examples make it clear that color itself is not a visible thing; it makes visible. Color is the color of the Being that appears. It is like the element fire, which forms the fuse for the deflagration of Being.[24] If we look at colors we see nothing, no spectacle, but the birth of the visible. That is why Merleau-Ponty says that the painting is autofigurative: "The painter contributes his body, that is, his eye and hand. He lets the things live in his body and create there an inner double of the things which is only spectacle of something by being "spectacle of nothing" and "autofigurative.'"[25] The painting as icon is not the image *of* something, but it enables the visible world to appear.

The same is true of the line. It should not be taken to be that which pins down the image by giving it fixed contours either. Merleau-Ponty distinguishes between two notions of the line: a prosaic notion in which the line is taken to be a "positive attribute and property of the object in itself," and a notion according to which the line is "flexuous" (*EM*, 182). When Descartes illustrates his theory of vision in the *Optics* with examples from art, he refers in particular to the technique of sketching and to the copper engraving because they are based on the prosaic conception of the line: the line that delimits the being of extensive things. According to Descartes, only the extensive thing (*res extensa*) can be represented. That is why he rejects painting in favor of the sketch and the engraving.[26] Visual art, for Descartes, is not a presentation of being, but a representation comparable to a text. Merleau-Ponty's critique of Descartes sets out to demonstrate that the line is not just in the service of representation. Not only paintings but also sketches may contain a "flexuous" line, as Leonardo da Vinci had already noted. This "sinuous outline" is not objective, nor is it confined to the visible; it "corrodes prosaic space and its *partes extra partes*," it is the "generating axis" that makes visible (*EM*, 183). Lines are themselves not visible things: "[T]hey are always on the near or the far side of the point we look at" (ibid.). As a dimension, the line penetrates the visible and constitutes a certain emptiness. This dimension may consist of a single line, as in the drawings of women by Matisse, for example, of which Merleau-Ponty says that they "were not immediately women, they became women" (*EM*, 184). But this dimension may also consist of several lines grouped together, as we can clearly see in Cézanne's many apples. As a result of the plurality of lines in these canvases, "one's glance captures a shape that emerges from among them all—rebounding among these—just as it does in perception" (*SNS*, 15). Since the oscillating line renders an account of the emergence of the visible before our eyes, it gives expression to the way in which the seeing body perceives. While for Descartes the line serves the geometric representation of space, the "flexuous line" responds to natural perception. Depth, color, and line are dimensions that together constitute the *logos* of the painter. They form a "system of equivalences" which can bring about "a nonconceptual presentation of universal Being" (*EM*, 182). Since the dimensions transcend the level of the concept, they are able to form an expression beyond representation.

The final pictorial aspect discussed by Merleau-Ponty is motion within the image. The canvas can suggest movement without moving itself. How is that possible? Pictorial movement is not the result of a representation of successive events rendered as "a series of appropriately mixed, instantaneous glimpses along with, if a living thing is involved, attitudes unstably suspended between a before and an after" (*EM*, 184–85). One may think, for example, of the famous photographic series by Muybridge, in which each shot represents a particular pose of a horse in motion. If the series of photographs is followed one after another, the viewer receives the impression that the horse is moving. This notion of represented movement is criticized by Merleau-Ponty. Following Rodin's notion of movement, he claims that "instantaneous glimpses, unstable attitudes petrify movement" (*EM*, 185). Movement only arises in an image if different moments are brought together in it. This is very clear in Rodin's figures. He made them by representing the positions of the different parts of the body as they would never be found in reality in a single moment. The arm, for example, describes a different moment of the movement from the trunk or the leg. The combination of those different moments in a single figure, this "internal discordance," is what sets the figure in motion. The time of the figure is thus not the time of succession, but that of simultaneity. The figure combines the different temporal moments in a single instant. The simultaneity shows that different beings are absolutely together, and that this is a mystery that "psychologists handle the way a child handles explosives" (*EM*, 187). Since the time of succession is shattered, a "deflagration of Being" can take place in the painting. As a result of this explosion, the image is no longer static, as the *eidos* or the *idea* were, but as *eikoon* it has become a "moving image."

When we talk about a "moving image," it is appropriate to refer to film as well. Merleau-Ponty calls film a new way of symbolizing thoughts because it is about a "movement of the representation." In his 1945 article "Film and the New Psychology," he writes that film really fulfills the ideas of *Gestalt* psychology. The cutting, montage, and metrics of the film do not present us with a sum total of impressions, but the film finally appears as a whole, "a temporal *Gestalt*" (*SNS*, 54). The film does not simply show us stories, facts, or ideas, but it gives expression to "that special way of being in the world" (*SNS*, 58). Merleau-Ponty never really developed his theory of film, but we do find a philosophical analysis of film in, for example, Gilles Deleuze.[27] In spite of the fact that Deleuze has a good many bones to pick with phenomenology, his idea of "movement-image" does not seem so far removed from Merleau-Ponty's notion of the icon described above. Deleuze criticizes phenomenology for being the theory of the luminous consciousness that always opens outward in order to be the consciousness *of* something. He is closer to the position of Bergson, who claims that consciousness *is* something and that it may coincide with things.[28] However, I think that the latter view is easiest to reconcile with Merleau-Ponty's idea of the carnal and the intentionality in the innermost of Being. Deleuze's analysis of film, I believe, can therefore be associated with the phenomenology of the icon. The thesis defended by Deleuze in his books on the cinema is that movement is not capable of being represented by "immobile sections" (*coupes immobiles*). Film presents "mobile sections," and these are called "movement-images."[29] According to Deleuze, this moving image corresponds to what Bergson had called the expression of time as *durée*. It is able to express this *durée* because the consciousness of the film is not "luminous" or "surveying." The camera is itself a part of the visible and physical world, it constitutes the specific cinematographic consciousness: "[T]he sole cinematographic consciousness is not us, the spectator, nor the hero; it is the camera—sometimes human, sometimes inhuman or superhuman."[30] The eye of the camera, like Merleau-Ponty's "carnal seer," is itself a part of the things, and in that function it can articulate the chiasma of seeing and being seen, of the visible and the invisible. The correlate of this cinematographic eye is called "movement-image" by Deleuze, but it can also be seen as the incarnation of what I have referred to above as "moving image" or icon.[31]

After analyzing depth, color, line, and movement, Merleau-Ponty comes to the conclusion that the art of painting can offer us a different notion of Being. In the shattering of depth and the simultaneity of movement we recognize a "deflagration of Being." The Being that is always regarded as an identical, stable Being is burst apart by the explosive force of painting. As a "presentation without concept," painting frees Being from its conceptual sedimentations. It gives "mute Being," which had been muzzled by representational thinking, its voice back. The phenomenology of the icon leads us to the "voices of silence."

THE ICONICITY OF THE PHILOSOPHICAL EXPRESSION

Merleau-Ponty's analyses of the art of painting are a part of the research on indirect language. The voices of painting reveal language at the moment of its genesis much better than everyday language usage does. After drawing a parallel between painting and language, Merleau-Ponty says: "In short, language speaks, and the voices of painting are the voices of silence" (*Signs*, 81). Apparently the most important difference between painting and ordinary language is that the former is a silent expression, while the latter is a voiced expression. The paradigm of painting—or of art in general—is that of silence, and that of ordinary language is sound, though it should be noted that the voices of silence are operative not only in visual art but also in literature and poetry.[32] The term *silence* indicates here that the expression will never be complete, will never attain its fulfillment in the final pronouncement. This silence of the expression, this basic incompleteness of an expression, is manifested in the iconicity of the image. The icon is the moving image that can never be pinned down and is never complete. This is not to say, however, that such an expression is nothing at all, because it too sediments in a particular way. After all, it acquires form in a given canvas or work. It institutes itself in a physical and spiritual way within the history of art. To discover exactly how painting plays a role within Merleau-Ponty's analysis of language and expression, we must examine how the work of art sediments and institutes itself and how this differs from the sedimentation and institution of ordinary language.

Like every institution, the institution of the work of art is a sort of incision in the horizontal time of history. The work of art cuts a notch for itself in the history of art, in cultural and human history. The institution is a paradoxical moment because it is simultaneously a continuation of the past and a radical break with it since it produces something entirely new. Institution, as Merleau-Ponty uses the term, is thus both continuity and discontinuity. The difference between language and the work of art, in my opinion, is that the latter form of expression repeatedly shows the "*blessure béante*" of its institution. So the work of art displays in particular the discontinuous character of the expression. Art has that privilege because it can never detach itself entirely from the world of the senses. The difference between the silent and the spoken expression, between silence and sound, can be linked with the distinction that Merleau-Ponty makes between *logos endiathetos* and *logos prophorikos*. Within the institution of the work of art it is not possible to abandon the innermost core of the *logos endiathetos*. In the last resort, art is nothing but a continually present *logos prophorikos* that can never realize itself as such. Let us briefly consider a working note from January 1959 in which Merleau-Ponty goes into the relation between the two *logoi* with reference to the art of painting:

> The "amorphous" perceptual world that I spoke of in relation to painting—perceptual resources for the remaking of painting—which contains no mode of expression and which

> nonetheless calls them forth and requires all of them and which arouses again with each painter a new effort of expression—this perceptual world is at bottom Being in Heidegger's sense, which is more than all painting, than all speech. Than every "attitude," and which, apprehended by philosophy in its universality, appears as containing everything that will ever be said, and yet leaving us to create it (Proust): it is the *logos endiathetos* which calls for the *logos prophorikos*. (*VI*, 170)

The world of the senses, the world of the painter, always tends toward its own expression. The work of art is this movement from "the inside outward." But what it expresses does not achieve the level of articulation of pronouncement. The work of art institutes itself silently and its sedimentation is only imminent. Its institution is never accompanied by shrill cries. Rather, it incarnates the perpetual and painful doubt formulated in such a masterly fashion by Balzac in his *Le chef d'oeuvre inconnu*. After having worked on his masterpiece for ten years, Frenhoffer eventually shows it to his friends Porbus and Poussin, but they see nothing at all on the canvas except for a "delightful little foot." Completely disillusioned by this reaction, Frenhoffer sets fire to all his canvases, and the next day news spreads that he is dead.[33] In this case, the painter's doubt is expressed in total despair. Of course, this need not be the case. In most cases it is expressed as an incessant creative repetition. Doubt provokes *poièsis*—exactly what Merleau-Ponty meant by doubt in his essay "Cézanne's Doubt."

The institution of the work of art takes place in silence and its sedimentation is always provisional. In this way art shows us the structure of the indirect language. This analysis of the indirect language was explicated above by means of a phenomenology of the icon. This clearly brings out the ontological stake of the analysis. After all, it is not just a question of an analysis of the structure of language, but of an analysis of the form of the expression of the meaning of Being. Within direct language ideality manifests itself as an *idée fixe*, as *eidos*. Within indirect language it appears as *eikoon*. The icon is the expression of Being in its wild state. This conclusion is not lacking in consequences for philosophy itself. The question arises of whether the language of philosophy can do justice to this wild Being. Merleau-Ponty asks the same question:

> Hence it is a question of whether philosophy as reconquest of brute or wild being can be accomplished by the resources of the eloquent language, or whether it would not be necessary for philosophy to use language in a way that takes from it its

> power of immediate or direct signification in order to equal it with what it wishes all the same to say. (*VI*, 102–103)

In his preface to *The Visible and the Invisible*, Claude Lefort claims that Merleau-Ponty has never really answered this question. He adds: "We know only that he constantly claimed for it [philosophy] an original mode of expression and by no means thought of substituting for it the language of art or of poetry" (*VI*, xxxi). It is true that Merleau-Ponty did not want to abolish the distinction between philosophy and art just like that, but that does not rule out the possibility that in the last resort his analysis may well require a different form of expression for philosophical discourse. For if philosophy is to be an ontology of wild Being, it must express itself indirectly and silently. Such a change in philosophical expression could change the discourse into a "dis-cours," that is, a discourse that is disqualified, that has no rights, that is illegitimate and obscene, as Maurice Blanchot suggests with regard to Merleau-Ponty's philosophy.[34] By critiquing its own manifest discourse, by interrogating itself, philosophy disqualifies itself.

So we see that Merleau-Ponty's philosophy of the expression calls for a reflection on the possibility and form of philosophy itself. Philosophy that wants to return to the things themselves in their wild state is only possible if it can render account of the fact that this return will always be incomplete and provisional. That is why philosophy should express itself in a way that is analogous to the expression as icon. Philosophy is distinct from art, but that does not alter the fact that they are both a form of incessant creation. They are both a form of *poïèsis*. When Merleau-Ponty writes that "painting is a sort of philosophy: grasping the genesis, philosophy *en acte*,"[35] is he not suggesting that philosophy should come closer to the practice of the work of art? Of course, philosophy does not create images or icons. It is expressed in words. But speaking can have an iconic structure too. My hypothesis is that the iconicity of the philosophical text lies in its metaphorical dimension.[36] The metaphor breaks with the conventional, rusted language usage and sets language in motion. The metaphor is the icon of the text. We can find a similar metaphorical use of language in Merleau-Ponty's writings. We find many terms that at first sight look a little strange within philosophical discourse, such as "flesh," "deflagration of Being," "respiration of Being," "dehiscence of Being," "floating in Being," etc. All these terms indicate that the standard philosophical terms are not really sufficient to put the dimension of wild Being, of the things themselves into words. However, it is not so that Merleau-Ponty uses the terms interchangeably. So there is not a strict opposition between metaphorical and literal language use. The metaphorical dimension lies in the fact that different metaphorical terms are used beside one another as synonyms. A plurality of terms is used to explicate a particular matter each time. The matter is thus not pinned down by a particular term. It is through this metaphorical use of language that philosophy really can get back to the things themselves, to wild Being. And it is precisely through such a dynamic use of language that the work of the philosopher resembles a work of art. Thus the phenomenology of the icon leads to what Merleau-Ponty calls a "figured philosophy." It is a form of philosophy that moves between image and concept, and which can thereby do justice (*parler juste*) to the matter itself.

NOTES

1. The publication of this article has been facilitated by the support of the Royal Netherlands Academy of the Arts and Sciences (KNAW).
2. Merleau-Ponty, *Husserl at the Limits of Phenomenology*, trans. L. Lawlor and B. Bergo (Evanston: Northwestern University Press, 2002).
3. The reference to Heidegger's later notion *Wesen* can be found in *VI*, 115, 174, 179, 203, 206–207, 247; in his 1958–59 lectures on Heidegger in *Notes de Cours 1958–1961* (Paris: Gallimard, 1996), 91–148; and in his 1960 lectures on *Husserl at the Limits of Phenomenology*, op. cit.
4. See Eliane Escoubas, *Imago Mundi. Topologie de l'art* (Paris: Galilée, 1986), 107–12.
5. "C'est ainsi qu'il peut y avoir des êtres qui ne sont pas de l'en soi et qui ne sont pas rien: les tableaux—les icones. C'est le double interne des choses descendant en elles, la vision retournée, ce qui la tapisse intérieurement descendant dans le visible," in *Notes de Cours 1958–1961*, op. cit., 174.
6. See in particular his *L'idole et la distance (*Paris: Grasset, 1977), *Dieu sans l'être* (Paris: PUF, 1991), and *La croisée du visible* (Paris: PUF, 1991).
7. *L'idole et la distance*, 25.
8. *Dieu sans l'être*, 16.
9. Merleau-Ponty claims that the relation between seeing and being seen is never fully reversible. There is always a discrepancy, an *écart*. He calls this "natural negativity." For a more detailed analysis of this, see my "The Psychoanalysis of Nature and the Nature of Expression," in *Chiasmi International* 2 (Paris: J. Vrin, 2000), 207–33.

10. *La croisée du visible*, 91.
11. Ibid.
12. Ibid., 97.
13. Ibid., 98.
14. I have shown that there is a good deal to criticize in Marion's analysis in my article "Tele-vision: Between Blind Trust and Perceptual Faith" in *Religion and Media,* ed. H. de Vries and S. Weber (Stanford: Stanford University Press, 2001), 216–26.
15. As Merleau-Ponty describes it: "In the world there is the thing itself, and outside this thing itself there is that other thing which is only reflected light rays and which happens to have an ordered correspondence with the real thing; there are two individuals, then, bound externally by causality." See *EM*, 170.
16. André Malraux, *La création esthéthique*, 51. Cited in *Signs*, 52.
17. The term *institution* plays an important role in the work of Merleau-Ponty. He uses the term as a kind of substitute for the Husserlian term *constitution.* Constitution stands for the "bringing about" of an object by consciousness. Institution, on the other hand, refers to the fact that something is brought about within a history or a tradition and thus also refers to the intersubjective aspect of every creation.
18. As Wayne Froman does, for example, in his "Action Painting and the World as Picture" in *The Merleau-Ponty Aesthetics Reader*, ed. G. A. Johnson (Evanston: Northwestern University Press, 1993), 337–47.
19. See Dominic Willsdon, "Merleau-Ponty on the Expression of Nature in Art" in *Journal of the British Society for Phenomenology*, 29: no. 2 (May 1998): 213.
20. Mauro Carbone, *La visibilité de l'invisible. Merleau-Ponty entre Cézanne et Proust* (Hildesheim/Zurich/New York: Georg Olms Verlag, 2001). Carbone stresses that the *voyance* is not confined to visual art. Poetry and literature can have this function too. Unlike Carbone, however, I will not deal with literature and poetry here, but confine my analyses to visual art.
21. In his *De Pictura* (1435), Leon Battista Alberti presents the window as belonging to the technique of linear perspective (Book K, section 19).
22. *SNS*, 12. The analysis of Cézanne's work by Merleau-Ponty in his "Cézanne's Doubt" follows the so-called double critique of his *Phenomenology of Perception*, in which he criticizes both empiricism and intellectualism simultaneously. In his essay on Cézanne, he compares Impressionism with empiricism and Realism with

intellectualism. Cézanne's work is an attempt to reconcile the two perspectives.

23. Galen Johnson emphasizes the importance of Klee for the later Merleau-Ponty. As Merleau-Ponty was writing *Eye and Mind*, Klee's writings had just appeared in French. See Galen Johnson, "The Colors of Fire: Depth and Desire in Merleau-Ponty's *Eye and Mind*" in *Journal of the British Society for phenomenology* (January 1994): 53–63.
24. Ibid., 60.
25. *Le peinture apporte son corps, i.e., son oeil et sa main, il laisse les choses vivre dans son corps et y susciter un double interne qui n'est spectacle de quelque chose qu'en étant 'spectacle de rien,' 'autofiguratif.'* See Notes de cours, op. cit., 170.
26. "For Descartes it is self-evident that one can paint only existing things, that their existence consists in being extended, and line drawing alone makes painting possible by making possible the representation of extension." See *EM*, 172.
27. That Merleau-Ponty's phenomenology is eminently suitable for an analysis of the cinematographic experience has been developed in exemplary fashion by Vivian Sobchak in her *The Address of the Eye* (Princeton: Princeton University Press, 1992). See also Gilles Deleuze, *Cinema I: The Movement-Image* (London: Athlone Press, 1992) and *Cinema II: The Time-Image* (London: Athlone Press, 1989).
28. See for example the following critical passage: "Phenomenology was still squarely within this ancient tradition: but instead of making light of an internal light, it simply opened it on to the exterior, rather as if the intentionality of consciousness was the ray of an electric lamp ('all consciousness is consciousness *of* something . . ."). For Bergson it is completely the opposite. "Things are luminous by themselves without anything illuminating them: all consciousness *is* something, it is indistinguishable from the thing, that is from the image of light. . . . In short, it is not consciousness which is light, it is the set of images, or the light, which is consciousness, immanent to matter. . . . The opposition between Bergson and phenomenology is, in this respect, a radical one." *Cinema I*, 60–61.
29. "In short, cinema does not give us an image to which movement is added, it immediately gives us a momentimage. It does give us a section, but a section which is mobile, not an immobile section + abstract movement," in *Cinema I*, 2.
30. Ibid., 20.

31. Deleuze also uses the term *icon*, but in a Peircean sense.
32. "Like a painting, a novel expresses tacitly," in *Signs*, 76.
33. Honoré de Balzac, *Le chef d'oeuvre inconnu* (Paris: Flammarion, 1981).
34. Maurice Blanchot, "Le discours philosophique," *L'arc* 46 (1971): 2.
35. "La peinture est donc une sorte de philosophie: saisi de la genèse, philosophie en acte," in *Notes de Cours*, op. cit., 58.
36. I have elaborated this thesis more fully in the last chapter of my *L'expression au délà de la représentation. Sur l'aisthêsis et l'esthétique chez Merleau-Ponty* (Leuven/Paris: Peeters-Vrin, 2003).

13

On the "Fundamental of Painting"

Chinese Counterpoint

JACQUES TAMINIAUX

During the spring of 1995, the British Museum organized an exposition of the work of Zhu Qizhan, the Chinese painter and calligrapher born in 1892, who lived and worked his whole life in Shanghai. In a review of this exposition, the *International Herald Tribune*'s art critic Souren Melikian wrote on March 11 of the same year that the work of Zhu Qizhan was one of the best examples of a very particular accomplishment, in that it seemed to resolve the contradictions between the Occidental and Chinese traditions. There are of course other examples that overcome this apparent contradiction, other examples of attention both to the Occident and to the Chinese traditions, as I was able to note during a brief stay in Taipei in 1994. Unfortunately, there are also examples of pure and simple submission to the Occident, to its fashions, to its advertising slogans, to the speculative caprices of the art market, examples that abound in the latest sales catalogs from Sotheby's—documents that are like a hymn to the most literal and omnipresent hyperrealism. Be that as it may, we could say that Zhu Qizhan's work, rather than being subjugated to the Occident, is a happy testament to what we today call *transculturalism*, the phenomenon that implies neither the absorption of one culture by another, nor the reduction of either to the lowest common planetary denominator, but rather a complicity between two cultures. But what does this complicity mean?

Obviously, so that Zhu Qizhan could be open, at a certain point and in a certain way, to an encounter with the Occident, he had to recognize in Western painting some form of correspondence or agreement with what he took to be the appeal of the Chinese tradition. In other words, he had to recognize in Western painting a certain form of response to the properly *pictorial* questions that aroused in him his own attention to the persistent appeal of the Chinese tradition.

But what must we understand here by Western painting? The extension of this title is immense, since it covers the long Byzantine period, the Trecento, the Quattrocentro, the glorious periods of Flemish and Dutch painting, the Italian Renaissance, the Age of Baroque, French Classicism, Romanticism, Naturalism, Impressionism, Cubism, Expressionism, Abstraction, etc. Does Zhu Qizhan discover in all of these temporal phases of Western painting some form of correspondence or agreement with what he takes to be the persistent appeal of the Chinese tradition? Not at all. In fact, a bit like the way that the Chinese literati of the Qing Dynasty reacted when, thanks to Italian Jesuits such as Giuseppe Castiglione, they discovered Renaissance painting and its procedures (linear perspective, the science of signs that gives the illusion of volume, of movement, of forms, of tactile values, of materials), so too did Zhu Qizhan react when he became informed of the history of Western painting—politely, but in no way enthusiastically. Apparently, all this history was for him the object of distant curiosity—it did not concern him in its own right, it did not challenge him. The academic tradition issuing from the Renaissance, its variations and metamorphoses notwithstanding, left him indifferent. Even the Impressionists left him cold. But then what about this transcultural factor I mentioned a moment ago? In reality, this factor began to emerge in the framework of his own experience and his own painterly project with respect to only three Western works—those of Cézanne, Van Gogh, and Matisse—which he felt intimately called out to him. Why this privilege—in some way transcultural—for these works? This question guides the remarks that I wish to make here. In Cézanne, Zhu says that he admired an exceptional sense of volume. In Van Gogh, he admired the power of the traits. And he says of Matisse that "he was capable of being born, emerging from the original form of objects."

Since I am but an amateur, I in no way have the required competence to analyze the way that these three conjoined admirations exercised themselves in Zhu's work. I think however that his reactions have a signification that extends beyond his artistic biography. In effect, it would be relatively easy to find analogous reactions expressed by other Chinese painters of this century. (Zao Wou Ki would be a good example of one.) This suggests that Zhu's reactions are not just personal, and that the three objects of admiration that I've just evoked point toward a domain of convergence between certain potentialities inherent to the tradition of Chinese painting, and to certain Western developments that begin to emerge late, or at least fully came to light only in the last decades of the nineteenth century, developments that include such names as Klee, Miro, and Giacometti. My major purpose here is to characterize *the domain of this convergence* itself, which perhaps explains—I again cite the critic Melikian—that "China today is probably the only country in the world where contemporary art keeps narrow links with its past."

In my eyes—and I hope that it's not a professional deformation—the approach to this domain of convergence has a philosophical stake, not only because the domain concerned raises some philosophical questions, but above all because its exploration requires specific philosophical tools. I think that the teachings of phenomenology are particularly useful for delimiting the domain in question. Phenomenology is in effect a manner of philosophizing, which according to the famous catchphrase of its founder Husserl, demands "a return to the things themselves," that is, to phenomena, beyond all obedience to the results of the positive sciences, beyond all ideological biases, beyond every metaphysical school. Its concern is neither to explain nor to edify a system, but only to describe. I will specify right away that in the vast field of phenomenological research, the most precious teaching appropriate to the matter before us is, in my opinion, procured from the long meditation that Merleau-Ponty, that phenomenologist of perception, devoted to painting, and notably to the Western painters who called out to Zhu Qizhan, notably Cézanne. This meditation is, so to speak, condensed in a brief essay "Eye and Mind," written by Merleau-Ponty the year before his death.

Of course, this essay does not treat Chinese painting, but only Western painting since Cézanne. But I would like to try to show that what Merleau-Ponty discerned at the very heart of Western pictorial methods is in no way foreign to the tradition of Chinese painting. On the contrary, we could say that there is a sort of narrow affinity between what he calls (concerning the Cézannian heritage) the "fundamental of painting" and the very principles that govern Chinese painting. Merleau-Ponty was a philosopher of perception par excellence, a philosopher of incarnation, of the flesh, of humans belonging to the world of perceived appearances. It is in relation to our primordial and carnal insertion in the perceived that he tried to delimit the major traits of what he called the "fundamental of painting" (*EM*, 161). I would like to suggest, at my own risk, how the themes that characterize this "fundamental of painting" in relation to the Cézannian heritage are, according to Merleau-Ponty, not only transposable to Chinese painting, but have also always been capital for it, even though they had remained more or less hidden in the Western tradition for a long time, emerging into the foreground in the West only in recent works.

The first theme is gathered in a verb: *habiter*—to live in, to inhabit. Merleau-Ponty writes at the beginning of *Eye and Mind* that "science manipulates the things and gives up living in them" (*EM*, 159). This method is inventive of increasingly artificialist models that ultimately propagate the idea that the world is nothing other than an artificial support that permits transforming it. This method creates the illusion of being without place, without habitat, engendering the thinking-from-above that Merleau-Ponty argued "must return to the *il y a*, which underlies it; to the site, the soil of the sensible and opened world such as it is in our life and for our body—not that possible body which we may legitimately think of as an information machine but that actual body I call mine, this sentinel standing quietly at the command of my words and my acts" (*EM*, 160). Yet it is at this site, which is strictly correlative of the lived body, at the "fabric of brute meaning" which constitutes it, from which the painter draws, according to Merleau-Ponty, even though scientific artificialism wants nothing of it. Painters such as Cézanne, Van Gogh, and Matisse testify to the fact that before being delocalized pyrotechnicists, we are inhabitants of the world.

Obviously, we could object right away—and Merleau-Ponty would have recognized the pertinence of this objection—that painting living in the world is a phenomenon altogether recent in Western painting. Historically, the tradition of Western painting lived for years under the distant influence of Plato, who proclaimed that we do not really belong to the common world of perceptible appearances offered to our bodies, that, rather, we belong to a world of essences, forms, ideas, a world that transcends the world which we perceive and in which we appear to one another. This is the famous dual-world theory that, taken up in the Christian framework, for a long time prevented Western painters from fully living in "the sensible world . . . such as it is in our life and for our body" (*EM*, 160). Byzantine art is probably the prototype of this dualist schema, which consists in taking for granted that this world where we live carnally is not the true world, and which in turn imposes on the artist the duty of orienting the community of believers to a superior reign of grace and benediction by transforming and purifying the perceived world in order to make it the symbol of a superior world. There is no trace of this sort of symbolism found in the Chinese tradition.

George Rowley, who was a professor at Princeton and conservator of the Chinese collections of this university's museum, notes in his book

Principles of Chinese Painting that "[t]he Chinese approach avoided every pictorial invention that could direct the imagination toward another world, exactly the inverse of Byzantine art."[1] And according to him, the reason for this avoidance of all duality of heaven and earth is that in the Chinese tradition, the Tao of heaven belongs equally to the earth, which means that the chasm between mind and matter, soul and body, inherent to the Western tradition since the late Middle Ages, had never been a principle of the Chinese tradition. On the contrary, the very notion of Tao as cosmic principle, which is, according to Rowley, the touchstone of Chinese painting, allows Chinese painters to concentrate on "the notion of one sole power animating the entire universe, instead of insisting on the Western dualism between spirit and matter, creator and created, animate and inanimate, human and non-human." In a recent analysis of the principles of Taoist aesthetics, Wai-Lim Yip recalls that it developed from the writings of Laozi (the *Dao De Jing*) and of Zhuangzi (the *Zhuangzi*) composed between the sixth and third centuries BC, in reaction to a hierarchical and universally englobing system of denomination (The Naming System) imposed by the Zhu dynasty, whose keystone was the emperor called "Son of Heaven." This system is called Kingly or Heavenly Dao, and Laozi attacks it and makes it break apart when, at the beginning of the *Dao De Jing,* he posits that "the speaking Dao [way] is not the Constant Dao. The namable Name is not the Constant Name" (ch. 1). And he specifies concerning the Dao: "Dao as such / is seen, unseen / seen, unseen/ this is, in it, something forming / Forming, unforming / there are, in it, things" (ch. 21). This proposition means that phenomena extend beyond all human pretensions to define, subject, or classify them as hierarchies or oppositions. As it is said in the *Zhuangzi*: "[N]ot to discriminate this and that as opposites is the essence of Dao . . . there you attain the Central Ring to respond to what is endless . . ." (66). On this, Wai-Lim Yip comments in these terms: "Thus, only when the subject retreats from its dominating position, taking the 'I' from the primary position for aesthetic contemplation, can we allow the Free Flow of Nature to reassume itself. Phenomena do not need "I" to have their existence, they each have their own inner lives, activities, and subordinate, are categories of superficial demarcation. Subject and object, consciousness and phenomena interpenetrate, inter-complement, inter-define, and inter-illuminate, appearing simultaneously, with humans corresponding to things, things corresponding to humans, things corresponding to things extending throughout the million phenomena" ("Daoist Aesthetics," *Encyclopedia of Aesthetics*, Oxford University Press, 1998, volume I: 504–505). In light of these conceptions, it would not be an exaggeration to say that the Chinese pictorial tradition, at least since the Five Dynasties, is a tribute to what Merleau-Ponty calls "living in the things." It is this aptitude to live in the things that is noticeable in the attention that painters since the Sung epoch bring to the way that the most modest perceptible entities appear starting from themselves: to leave a fish to its fish-being, so that it marries the river, to leave a rock or a stone to their rocky, stony existence, to rejoice in the ludic flight of wild birds, to capture a prune branch in its own way of flowering, or a bamboo shoot in its particular adjustment to the movement of the wind.

At this point, one could object—and here again Merleau-Ponty accepts the objection as pertinent—that the Byzantine symbolism, with its insistence on a neat hierarchy between earth and heaven, constitutes only the first stage of Western painting, a stage that painters of the Renaissance leave behind. But the objection tends to forget that painting is reborn of itself, as Panofsky clearly demonstrated in his admirable studies on the Florentine painters (Michelangelo and Titian); this Renaissance painting was itself inspired by a particular type of Platonism that had played a decisive role in the invention of linear perspective, such that these painters were less interested in celebrating appearances for themselves than in purifying and arranging them in reference to ideal structures that were supposed to testify to a superior ontological region and to theological essences, in the proximity of which we do not live because our profane bodies are not adapted to it.

Once again one could object that after a certain time, a process of secularization is produced that was aimed at replacing the doubling of the world with a deliberate attention to this world in Western painting. But here again, it is easy to reply to this objection that post-Renaissance painters, apparently dedicated to the celebration of this world, were not really engaged in the task of "living in the things" or of bringing to painting the co-belongingness of humans and nature. The dualist framework, so typical of all forms of Platonism from Pseudo-Dionysus to Marcilio Ficino, does not disappear following the triumphant irruption of the modern *cogito*, associated with the intellectual revolution in physics and to the Cartesian methodology. The substitution of the gaze of the *cogito* for the gaze of a divine spectator did not mean that we belonged to appearances, nor that we were "in the world" as its true inhabitants. It meant only that those appearances provided the occasion for this new center of reference (the cogito—in relation to the medieval creator) to affirm its preponderance, either as its power over nature and thus of rational structures that it projects, or as its impressions or its sensible humors.

Here we find a good example in the pictorial genre dating from this period, which the French significantly call "dead nature," while the English refer to it as "still life." This genre was illustrated for the first time by the Dutch and persisted, through multiple avatars, until French Cubism; it is a genre that makes a strong case for the elements of nature (fruits, vegetables, flowers, drinks, meats, and fish) and is associated to the tools of everyday life (plates, vases, glasses, etc.). This genre, as Rowley underlines, is entirely omitted from the Chinese rubrics of classification for paintings. And the reason for this omission is no doubt that in the "dead nature" concerned, flowers, fruits, animals and natural entities in general lose their proper presence in order to be subordinated, as decoration, to a strictly human center, which consequently makes them into means for the human's joys or daily activities. The famous series of six *kakis* painted by Mu Ch'i are on the contrary nowise mere decoration, not even a gracious spectacle—they impose a presence that is their own.

Another example is furnished by the comparison between the painting of landscapes in the Western tradition and the Chinese landscape paintings, the most ancient of which date to the epoch of the Five Dynasties, that is, before the year 1000 AD. It is probably significant that the first landscapes to appear in Western compositions, in Piero della Francesca or Mantegna for example, are views of Tuscany as the background for human scenes painted according to the rules that were then seeking their proper articulation in linear perspective, rules according to which a monocular and immobile vision imposed a single vanishing point and a single horizon line. The fact that the Italian landscape was not worthy in itself, but instead was valued as the entourage of a human scene, confirms this anthropological centering. Except in very rare examples, it always seems as if the Western landscape had preserved its subordination to an anthropological center. There are mountains, lakes, and rivers in many Flemish paintings from the fifteenth and sixteenth centuries but always as the background of a scene (often religious), forming the center of the panel, for example, the flight from Egypt, Moses saved from the waters, the deposition of Christ, etc. Equally in the Baroque age, the landscape is just decoration for mythological scenes—Diana the huntress, the three Graces and so on. Even in the Romantic epoch, in Turner for example, when mountains seemed to be worthy in themselves, in reality they serve as support for the strictly human expression of affects: nostalgia for simplicity, aspiration to authenticity, rejection of social conventions, etc. The pictorial enterprise is once again governed by a dualism: that of nature and human artifice. Only with Cézanne is the mountain painted for itself in its particular density, in its being-mountainous. And in this regard, Merleau-Ponty notices that the thingly density concerned is not the correlate of a solitary immobile vision, but rather that it goes together with a plurality of mobile views, profiles, or sketches (as Husserl would say). It is not an object for a knowing subject. This could clarify Zhu Qizhan's interest. In effect, what Cézanne discovered in his own way, by rejecting both classical naturalism (which signals things already known but does not explore them in the, say, way that the living body does) and Impressionism (in that it dissolves the density of the things into the flux of lived experience) is that to which the Chinese landscapists were always attentive.

This is why their landscapes, which one gradually unfurls laterally, never refer to one sole immobile point of view that would be the sign of the mastery of a subject over an object; rather, they leave a plurality of points of view emanating from the perceived itself. When in the eleventh century the famous Fan Kuan painted his famous caravan of voyagers crossing mountains and rivers, the mountain is not for him a mere decoration for the scene. The concern, he said, was to seize the "very bones of the mountain," a metaphor that we find again in Cézanne's writing. But to understand nature according to its own rules means (for the Sung painters or for the successive generations of the letterers during the Yuan, Ming, and Qing dynasties inspired by their works) that it was a question of minimizing the human factor to the benefit of nature or of increasing the power of nature to the detriment of the human's. The stakes were rather to rejoin an equilibrium between the natural and the human, an equilibrium inherent to the very notion of inhabiting, understood as the co-belongingness of natural appearances and the perception to which it relates. In this regard, it seems to me extremely significant that even though they painted mountains, waterfalls, and lakes for their rocky or watery being, the Chinese letterers inspired by the Sung heritage almost always introduced one or several observers or walkers into their landscape, as well as the emplacement of a possible point of observation such as a straw shelter, a house, a hermitage. By proceeding in this way, they evade altogether the Western dualist structure (natural decoration versus human scene) and the lack of equilibrium inherent to it. But inversely, they also avoid the romantic temptation to celebrate the sublime superpower of nature. The famous waterfall at Lushan, painted by Shi-Tao, incontestably testifies to the power of natural elements. But unlike the romantic conception, it is not a superpower that the human would valorize at the same moment that the human is wiped out by it. On the contrary, in the scene that Shi-Tao shows, there are two peaceable spectators, one seated, the other standing on the summit of a promontory, neither very certain of the immensity of the waterfall, but who observe its power without fear.

The second theme that occupies me in Merleau-Ponty's essay is what he calls the *chiasm*, or *reversibility*. With these words, he aims at certain very concrete modalities of *encroachment*, or of the cross-checking deliberately ignored by both Platonic and Cartesian dualism. From a Cartesian point of view, for example, not only do the body and mind have opposed properties (extension on the one hand, thought on the other), but moreover that which moves itself in space is not that which looks and observes, just as that which sees is not at the same time that which is seen. We find the legacy of these Cartesian dualisms once again in the Sartrean distinction of the in-itself and the for-itself, as well as in the Sartre's famous analyses according to which that which sees freezes what it looks at, and what is seen is frozen by what looks at it. Against the grain of all dualism of this kind, Merleau-Ponty insists on the radical ambiguity of perception. He writes: "[M]y mobile body makes a difference in the visible world, is a part of it; this is why I can direct it in the visible. But it is just as true that vision is suspended in movement. . . . What would be vision without the movement of my eyes? . . . all my displacements in principle . . . are recorded on the map of the visible. Everything I see is in principle within my reach . . . recorded on the map of the 'I can'" (*EM*, 162). And he adds: "[T]his extraordinary encroachment . . . forbids us to conceive vision as an operation of thought that would set up before the mind . . . a representation of the world. . . . Immersed in the visible by its body, itself visible, the seer is not appropriated by what he sees" (ibid.). This encroachment, this chiasm of vision and movement calls the classical dualism of contemplation/action into question, as well as simple alternatives such as seeing/visible, seeing/touching, touching/touched, etc. We must say both that my body is one of the things and that the things are a prolongation of my body, that they are "encrusted in its flesh" (*EM*, 163). According to Merleau-Ponty, this is what Western painting became conscious of with Cézanne.

I believe that these encroachments on which Merleau-Ponty insists are attested to by Chinese painting from the beginning, and have been meditated upon and underlined in diverse ways by the Chinese letterers. Of course, their teaching was assisted in this regard by their philosophical tradition, in which we vainly seek the equivalents of diverse dualisms which traverse the history of Western philosophy; for Taoism and Confucianism, whatever their differences, have in common the quest for the dynamic fusion of opposites. But even independently of this favorable philosophical context, we can say without exaggeration that the Chinese pictorial tradition is a constant and always renewed tribute to what Merleau-Ponty calls chiasm or encroachment. Merleau-Ponty underlines that all the problems that Cézanne confronted are linked to this chiasm. When he described his own experience, Cézanne was already accustomed to saying that not only was he looking at the things, but that the things were also looking at him. This way of speaking underlines a major aspect of encroachment: the seer is himself visible. This encroachment explains the frequency of self-portraits in the work of artists who were not particularly narcissistic, from Velázquez and Rembrandt to Cézanne and Van Gogh. But when Cézanne in Aix or Van Gogh in Arles painted their own faces, they also un-painted themselves as visible, but not as inscribed in the englobing look that is the visible world. Cézanne did not paint himself into the landscape of Sainte-Victoire. On the other hand, it seems to me exemplary of the Chinese painters' profound sense of the chiasm as analyzed by Merleau-Ponty that a Shi Tao should paint himself into the middle of the landscape. We find testimony to the same encroachment of seer/visible in Chu Ta, who paints insects or birds while they are in the midst of looking at their spectator. Closer to us, with Shi-pai-shi, admirer of Chu Ta, the shrimp have a gaze.

Another aspect of the chiasm is the seeing/moving encroachment that I spoke of a moment ago. Merleau-Ponty underlines that the properties of the perceived as perceived are inseparable from the echoes that the visible sustains in our bodies, and he suggests that the creative painter is the one capable of making these echoes reemerge pictorially. He writes: "[Q]uality, light, depth, which are there before us, are there only because they arouse an echo in our bodies, and because the body welcomes them. This internal equivalent, this carnal formula of their presence that the things excite in me: why would they not in their turn sustain a still visible trace where every other look will retrieve the motifs that excite its inspection of the world? Thus there appears a 'visible' of the second power, a carnal essence or icon of the first. It is not a faded copy or a trompe-l'oeil" (*EM*, 164). In the same context, he claims that "interrogation of painting . . . aims at a secret and feverish genesis of things in our bodies" (*EM*, 167). These formulae (carnal essence, icon, secret genesis) are destined to suggest that the *trompe-l'oeil* had never been the true stake of Western painting. But of course, it is in contemporary works—Cézanne, Klee, Matisse, Giacometti—that Merleau-Ponty recognized the best testimonies of it.

I think that the whole Chinese tradition testifies to this carnal essence, which is at antipodes with the *trompe-l'oeil.* Is not this carnal essence aimed at when Shi Tao writes, "50 years ago, I had not yet been born from the landscape. Not that the landscape could be neglected or left to itself. Now that the landscape is born from me and me from it, it charges me to speak for it. The spirit of the landscape and my spirit have met and consequently transformed, in such a way that the landscape is indeed in me, Ta-ti" (cf. Francois Cheng, *Souffle-Esprit*, 30–31). Is this not a marvelous manner to express what Merleau-Ponty calls the "feverish genesis" of the things in our bodies? We find another when T'ang Tai, of the Qing Dynasty, writes, "[T]he concern is not to imitate nature, but to take part in its very process" (Cheng, 50). Or again when La Ta-Ching, in the Sung Dynasty, relates the story of Ts'ao Wu-I who excelled in the painting of insects and notably crickets: "[W]hen I was young, I put crickets in cages in order to observe them, day and night without a break. Then, mindful of the truth, I observed them in their natural milieu, in the grass. It was there that I began to grasp their profound nature, to the point of identifying myself with nature. In such a way that, at the moment of painting, I no longer know if it is me who has become cricket, or it is the crickets who have transformed themselves into me the painter" (Cheng, 92–93).

Let us note moreover that Merleau-Ponty, when he tried to characterize what he called the "carnal formula of things in our bodies" (*EM*, 164), reveals that this formula gives place to a trace, a sketch, or a "generative line" in the painter—that which the painter's body brings, as Valery says. The very facts that the Chinese tradition of painting—as calligraphy—is narrowly linked to the movements of the brush and to the simple material of ink place it in a more favorable position to grasp these generative lines and their carnal equivalents than is oil painting. In the Western tradition, the gesture of the hand that holds the brush never totally condenses the very act of painting—the act that is, so to speak, always divided anew between the concept and its implementation, between spirt and its incarnation, which made Da Vinci say that painting is *una cosa mentale*, and made Michelangelo the Platonist say that it is something other than the eye that judges and the hand that executes. This scission is absent from the Chinese act of painting, which gathers both in what Shi Tao called the "unique trait of the brush."

We could still draw out from Merleau-Ponty's notion of chiasm many fecund glimpses of the relation between the old and the new, which would allow us to avoid applying the simple alternative of fidelity-to-nature and fidelity-to-tradition to Chinese painting. But to conclude, I would like to take up a third theme that seems to me of great importance: the mixing of the visible and the invisible. Nietzsche, in *The Gay Science*, related the anecdote of the girl who asks her mother if it is true that God sees everything, and who, after receiving a positive response, replies to her mother that she finds this indecent. Nietzsche's corrosive irony aside, it is not unfair to claim that at the very root of the Western pictorial tradition—that is, at the source of the Christian reappropriation of Platonism—we find a relation to an ultimate spectator, to a visual foyer in front of which the visible world entirely unfurls itself. This is the idea of a full and complete visibility (of the spiritual and not the sensible order) without any invisible counterpart. It would be useless to say that, from a phenomenological point of view, a visibility defined in this way would signify the ruin of perception. Husserl already underlined that the density of the perceived is in solidarity with the fact that the perceived presents itself through its profiles, which consequently hides other profiles. Merleau-Ponty, in agreement with Husserl on this point, underlines that it is essential for the perceived world as such to include hidden horizons, be they interior or exterior. The visible always has an invisible framework. A thing entirely visible from all sides at once is a concept, and not a perceived thing.

In the admirable pages on Descartes' *Dioptrics*, Merleau-Ponty notes that Cartesian extension is a "space without hiding places, which in each of its points of view is neither more nor less than what it is" (*EM*, 173), that it is a "wholly positive being, beyond all points of view, beyond all latency and all depth, without any real thickness" (*EM*, 174), and that for Descartes, "the encroachment and the latency of things do not enter into their definition . . . they are only thoughts that I form and not attributes of things" (*EM*, 173). Such a notion of extension in no way corresponds to the space in which we move about carnally and that offers itself to our perception. Merleau-Ponty notes concerning Cézanne that in the implicit philosophy that animates Cézanne when he paints and when he thinks about painting, space is not the same space of which Descartes' *Dioptrics* speaks: "It is no longer . . . a network of relations between objects such as would be seen by a witness to my vision would see it, or by a geometer who reconstructs and surveys it from the outside; it is rather a space reckoned starting from me as the zero point or degree zero of spatiality. I do not see it according to its exterior envelope, I see it from within, I am immersed in it. After all, the world is around me, not in front of me. . . . Vision takes its fundamental power to show forth from itself" (*EM*, 178).

If living perception grasps things by sketches or by profiles, then the Cartesian concept of space is not adapted to our visual field. This field is not the addition of entities defined once and for all. In it, the distinction of the whole and its parts is not operative. It is not *partes extra partes* because each of its parts is the announcement of a horizon, or as Merleau-Ponty says, a "total part." This is what is at the heart of Cézanne's efforts to capture the Mountain at Saint-Victoire. Of Cézanne's implicit philosophy, Merleau-Ponty writes that "essence and existence, the imaginary and the real, the visible and the invisible—painting confuses all our categories by deploying its oneiric universe of carnal essences" (*EM*, 169). It seems to me that this implicit philosophy animating Cézanne's practice is also that which is at the heart of the characteristic traits of Chinese landscape painting. To express it in negative terms, it would evidently be vain to look for the equivalent (however remote) of the Cartesian cogito, or of the notion of a mastery and possession of nature by a *mathesis universalis* from which issues the Cartesian definition of space, in the legacy of Taoism and Confucianism that inspires the Chinese pictorial tradition. Likewise, still in negative terms, it is probably vain to seek a pictorial echo of the Cartesian concept of space in the Chinese landscape tradition.

On the other hand, it is not vain to look for the virtualities or the echoes of Cartesian concepts in the Western tradition since the Renaissance. After all, by considering the theoretical work that grounds the invention of the linear perspective in Italy (even if this work remains Platonist) we have the right to suspect that the concept of wholly positive extension without latency developed in the *Dioptrics* is anticipated by these theoretical works. Certainly, linear perspective refers by definition to a point of view. This point of view is not that of a living body, but rather of an ideal construction, a geometrical projection. Certainly this point of view is finite and limited by definition. But the very finitude of the perspectivist point of view is itself the refraction of a spatial system that de jure is beyond every point of view, in that it tolerates an infinite substitution of points of view. That alone would suffice to explain why, when they were confronted with the paintings of Father Giuseppe Castiglioni (who as a good missionary wanted to paint like a Chinese while respecting the rules of linear perspective), the members of the Imperial Court of China did not succeed in recognizing them as truly Chinese. This painting is grounded on the wholly positive concept of space, which is diametrically opposed to the Taoist principle of the fusion of opposites (i.e., of being and non-being, and with respect to painting, to the visible and the invisible).

Permit me, then, to cite some significant passages from the *Dialogues* of Pu Yen-t'u on the mind of the painter, such as François Cheng relates them: "[A]ll things under the sky, and not only the landscape, include their double aspect visible/invisible. The visible incarnating what is manifested to the outside, falls under the Yang; the invisible concealing what is hidden on the interior, falls under the Ying. Their complementary nature contributes to the law formulated in the famous adage 'one Ying, one Yang, the Tao.'" And Pu gives examples. The first of these examples is a little like a metaphorical condensation of what Merleau-Ponty articulates in his own way: "Let us suppose a dragon who leaves its aquatic lair and flies up into the sky. If he shows himself entirely naked, what mystery will he enclose? The spectator who lifts his head to observe the dragon will have quickly detailed it: here is the head, there is the tail, the beard, the claws . . . once his curiosity is satisfied, he will be disinterested. A true dragon always dissimulates itself behind the clouds . . . sometimes he makes a few of his scales shine, sometimes he lets a bit of his tail hang out. The fascinated spectator . . . will never be able to get his head around it. Thus it is by its visible-invisible that the dragon exercises its infinite power of fascination."

Here is the extraordinary symbolization of what Merleau-Ponty calls the "fundamental of painting," understood in its explorative work in opposition to the simplistic views of a trivial naturalism, which would give painting some task other than signaling the already-seen. And here is what Pu writes concerning landscape painting: "How can a landscape composed of mountains and water inspire a painter if its peaks, forests, bridges, and habitations are presented as frozen samples without secret? This is why a true mountain possesses in its heights inviolable summits and in its depths unfathomable abysses." A little farther on: "the landscape that fascinates a painter must thus include both the visible and the invisible. All the elements of nature which seem finite are in reality related to the infinite. In order to integrate the infinite in the finite, in order to combine the visible and the invisible, it is necessary that painting know how to exploit the game of Full-Empty of which the brush is capable, and of concentrated-diluted of which ink is capable."

Pu wrote in the eighteenth century, and the landscape painters he admired were the Sung masters of visible-invisible such as Kuo-Hsi, Fan K'uan, Li T'ang, and their heirs in the Yuan Dynasty, such as Wu-Chen, Ni Ts'an, Wang Meng, Huang Kuang-Wang. But is it not significant that what he tries to express of the spirit of this landscape tradition is clearly very close to what Merleau-Ponty tried to articulate concerning Cézanne, when he underlined that at the heart of his thought and practice of painting, there is this: "[W]hat is proper to the visible is to have a lining of invisibility in the strict sense, which it makes present as a certain absence" (*EM*, 187)? Whatever the case, it seems to me that this convergence can contribute to elucidating the transcultural complicity to which I made allusion at the beginning.

NOTES

1. G. Rowley, *Principles of Chinese Painting* (Princeton: Princeton University Press, 1959).

14

Variations of the Sensible

The Truth of Ideas and Idea of Philosophy in the Later Merleau-Ponty

MAURO CARBONE

The last courses that Merleau-Ponty held at the Collège de France focus on the "concept of Nature," on the one hand, and the "possibility of philosophy today" on the other. Merleau-Ponty brings together under the first heading both the courses of 1956–1957 and the course of 1957–1958—which, centered on "Animality, the Human Body, Transition to Culture," purports to be the "continuation" of the former. In 1959–1960, Merleau-Ponty uses his last course to discuss the further issue of "Nature and Logos: the Human Body." As for Merleau-Ponty's reflections on "the possibility of philosophy today," one can trace these not only to the 1958–1959 course, where that expression actually appears (*Themes*, 99), but also to the last two courses left unfinished by Merleau-Ponty's unexpected death ("Philosophy and Non-Philosophy Since Hegel," and "L'Ontologie cartésienne et l'ontologie d'aujourd'hui"), and to the second course of 1959–1960, entitled "Husserl at the Limits of Phenomenology."[1] What is the connection between these two foci of attention toward which Merleau-Ponty's last reflections converge? Undoubtedly, the connection lies within the problem of what he called "new ontology"—and more precisely, the problem of its configuration and of its philosophical formulation.[2]

As is well known, Merleau-Ponty's project to elaborate this "new ontology" found its roots and its reasons in the "ontological rehabilitation of the sensible" (*Signs*, 167), which he announced in his 1959 essay "The Philosopher and his Shadow." The human body—at the same time sentient and sensible—reveals how this very body holds a carnal relation with the sensible world, which therefore shares its ontological status. It is exactly this rehabilitation that implicates, according to the summary of the course concerning *Nature and Logos: The Human Body*, "a philosophy of the flesh as the visibility of the invisible" (*Themes*, 178), a philosophy that—in light of this rehabilitation—rethinks the relation between the sensible and the intelligible, that is, the very notions of idea and concept. On this subject, the preparatory notes of one of the two courses abruptly ended by Merleau-Ponty's death are of particular interest. From the course notes to *L'ontologie cartésienne et l'ontologie d'aujourd'hui*[3] emerge more clearly the developing lines that Merleau-Ponty wanted to follow in reconsidering, according to his new ontological perspective, the relation between the sensible and the intelligible, that is, between existence and essence. We underline that Merleau-Ponty considered these developing lines to be *operating*—even if they are not made philosophically explicit—in contemporary ontology.

At the very center of these developing lines is finally thematized a notion that had often, but only implicitly, been present in the later texts of Merleau-Ponty (it is formulated only once in "Eye and Mind" [see *Pri*, 171]). This notion is *central* in reconsidering the relation between the sensible and the intelligible, and is designated with the term *voyance*.[4] This French word literally indicates "clairvoyance," the "gift of double sight," but—in view of the misunderstandings that might occur if such a notion were given a Platonistic acceptation—we shall continue to employ the original French term. In an effort to fully understand the import of this notion, we shall turn to it after briefly reviewing the overall project of the course in which it appears. The task of this course is to try (in part through a direct contrast with Cartesian ontology) to give a philosophical formulation to contemporary ontology, which, according to Merleau-Ponty, has until now found its expression in art and in literature.

The first stop that he envisions for his journey is thus a survey of the landscape of "contemporary ontology," as it has spontaneously and implicitly been delineated in art and in literature—"especially in literature," as he emphasizes at one point (*NC*, 391). This is worth noting for those who claim that the last phase of Merleau-Ponty's thought refers exclusively to painting. Merleau-Ponty's discussion of the *artistic* domain does indeed concentrate on painting, following the path already traced out in "Eye and Mind." But when it comes to the recognition of the *literary* domain, here Merleau-Ponty intends to examine the work of

Proust as well as investigating Valéry, Claudel, and other authors of "recent literature" (*NC*, 191) exemplified by Saint-John Perse and Claude Simon.[5] And although it is unmentioned in this program of research, there is another literary reference that assumes a theoretically central position in the definition of the contemporary ontological landscape in Merleau-Ponty's view. This reference is Arthur Rimbaud's *Lettre du voyant.* Merleau-Ponty arrives at this reference via a statement by Max Ernst that identifies the present task of the painter with the precise task that Rimbaud's manifesto assigns to the poet: "Just as the role of the poet since the famous *Lettre du voyant* consists in writing under the dictation of what is being thought, of what articulates itself in him, the role of the painter is to grasp and project what is seen in him."[6] Both have to bring to expression, as it were, what, following Merleau-Ponty, we might call "the passivity of our activity" (*VI*, 221), that is, the reflexivity of the Being itself.

From this perspective, *voyance* ends up baptizing that "new bond between the writer and the visible" (*NC*, 190) which Merleau-Ponty sees as enforced by the research he calls "modern" (though we have argued that it should be understood as contemporary), and which can rediscover the "Renaissance beyond Descartes" (*NC*, 175). As he explains, "The moderns rediscover the Renaissance through the magical idea of visibility: it is the thing that makes itself seen (outside and inside), over there and here" (*NC*, 390). While on the one hand Merleau-Ponty contends that "da Vinci vindicates the *voyance against* poetry" (*NC*, 183)—which, unlike painting, da Vinci considers to be "incapable of 'simultaneity'" (*NC*, 175)—at the same time Merleau-Ponty also notes that "moderns make of poetry also a *voyance*" (*NC*, 183). Therefore, they show that poetry is indeed "capable of simultaneity." The frequent effort to bring simultaneity to expression is thus, according to Merleau-Ponty, one of the characteristic traits of contemporary ontology.[7]

At this point Merleau-Ponty departs from Descartes' view of vision, which had reduced vision to a kind of *thought*—the kind stimulated by images, just as thought is stimulated by signs and words. In contrast, Merleau-Ponty conjectures that the "unveiling of the '*voyance*' in modern art—a *voyance* which is not Cartesian thought—might have [an] analogue in the arts of *speech*" (*NC*, 182–83; emphasis added). He suggests that "[p]erhaps we should, instead of reducing vision to a reading of signs by thought, rediscover in speech, conversely, a transcendence of the same type that occurs in vision" (ibid.). Indeed, it is precisely to this that he thinks Rimbaud has contributed in a decisive way.

Voyance—which, in the mutual referring of perception and imaginary, "renders present to us what is absent" (*Pri*, 41)—therefore characterizes seeing in Merleau-Ponty's conception. As Heidegger reminds us, seeing is not a *vor-stellen*, that is, it is not "to represent by frontal positioning," which would be "to subject."[8] Seeing should instead be regarded as "complying with"—a verb that expresses the indistinguishability of activity and passivity. With *voyance*, we discover that seeing is a complying with the showing of the sensible universe itself, within which we find ourselves and through which runs the power of analogy.[9] In virtue of this power, bodies and things recall each other, establish new relations, invent lines of force and of flight, and, in the end, draw what Husserl expressed as a "*logos* of the aesthetical world."[10] This expression of Husserl's is often used by Merleau-Ponty precisely because of the reconsideration it suggests of the relationship between the sensible and the intelligible.

By offering this characterization of seeing, *voyance* helps to characterize that "mutation of the relationship between humanity and Being" (*Pri*, 63; trans. modified) that in "Eye and Mind" Merleau-Ponty confesses to feeling "when he holds up a universe of classical thought, contrasting it en bloc with the explorations of modern painting" (ibid.). This same mutation, which a dense working note in *The Visible and the Invisible* finds manifest in "atonal music" (which is in fact assimilated to "paintings without identifiable things, without the *skin* of things, but giving their *flesh*"),[11] therefore, consists in a *carnal* configuration of the relationship between humanity and Being. This mutation is obviously not expressible in the language of consciousness, of representation, of the modern frontality of subject and object. This is why Merleau-Ponty judges contemporary literature as linking, with the visible, that "new bond" which might be configurable as *voyance*.

After having examined the conception of language that Descartes expressed with regard to the idea of a universal language,[12] and after having seen in this conception "the equivalent of the theory of perspective" (*NC* 183),[13] Merleau-Ponty turns to the contrasting contemporary conception of language, which—according to him—characterizes language "not as an instrument in which thought would be as the pilot in his boat—but as some sort of substantial union of thought and language—Language not governed, but endowed of its own efficacy" (*NC*, 186). The *Lettre du voyant* becomes an emblem of this contemporary conception, since there the autonomy of language is pushed to such a point that poetry is supposed to be *voyance*. This is why Merleau-Ponty considers Rimbaud "a fundamental milestone within a development of literature which began before and continues after him" (*NC* 187).

Echoing that "mutation of the relationship between humanity and Being" which "Eye and Mind" sees expressed by painting, Merleau-Ponty writes that "it might be the case of a change of the relationship with the Being in the writer starting from Romanticism" (*NC*, 187). As we have already seen, the change he has in mind is a change of the relationship between the visibility of the first and the speech of the other, which—instead of aiming at designating meanings (*NC*, 189)—mixes with things and, just as, for Rimbaud, "the wood . . . finds itself a violin," it becomes a sensible emblem of the sensible itself.[14]

Merleau-Ponty sees another manifestation of this change (while claiming that this very manifestation entails a sketch of a non-Platonistic theory of ideas)[15] in the pages of the first volume of Proust's *Recherche*, pages to which he returns again and again throughout the course of his reflections. These pages are those in which Proust distinguishes "musical ideas"—as well as literary ones, and also "our notions of light, of sound, of perspective, of physical pleasure, the rich possessions wherewith our inner temple is diversified and adorned"—from the "ideas of the intelligence." The former are "veiled in shadows" and therefore "impenetrable to the human mind, but none the less perfectly distinct from one another, unequal among themselves in value and significance."[16] Thus, the preparatory notes we are considering have an additional point of interest, insofar as, when we newly examine those pages of the *Recherche* that *The Visible and the Invisible* was commenting on when it was interrupted by its author's sudden death,[17] they suggest what the developments of that commentary might have been.

The Visible and the Invisible defines as "sensibles" the ideas described by Proust (*VI*, 151), for they appear to be inseparable from their sensible presentation. It is to our sensible finitude, therefore, that they are offered. The course notes proceed to consider, in their own right, the grounds on which such ideas had been assimilated by Proust into his notion of light in particular. In fact, as Merleau-Ponty explains, the encounter with these ideas, just like the one with light ("visible light," he specifies [*NC*, 194]), and just like the one with the sensible, is an "initiation to a *world*, to a small eternity, to a dimension which is by now inalienable—Universality through singularity" (*NC*, 196).

Moreover, the notes continue, "here just as there, in light just as in the musical idea, we have an idea which is not *what* we see, but is behind it" (ibid.). If, on the one hand, this transcendence restrains us from possessing such ideas—from conceptually grasping them, as light is likewise ungraspable—then on the other hand, it compels them to show themselves (again, just as light does) in what they illuminate. Something similar happens to the idea of love in the *petite phrase* of

Vinteuil's sonata that had once been the "national anthem" of Swann and Odette's love.

Therefore, it is toward such transcendence that the sensible finitude is an opening: that very "transcendence of the same type that occurs in vision," which, as we have seen, Merleau-Ponty rediscovers in speech and which he recognizes in Rimbaud's poetics of *voyance*. It is, precisely, the transcendence of *voyance*: not "second sight" directed to the intelligible, but rather a vision that sees the invisible in the visible and thus allows us to find, within the very veil of music or of literary speech, the invisible of the idea that shines through—as Proust has taught us. Thus, we find here an explanation of the sense of the question—at first glance a surprising one—that appears in a Working Note of *The Visible and the Invisible* dated November 1959: "Generality of things: why are there several samples of each thing?" (*VI*, 273, trans. modified). Judging by what we have said up to now, the sentence that immediately precedes this question seems to give it an answer: "[T]the things are Essences at the level of Nature" (ibid.).

In other words, each thing as generality is a sensible idea. Of course, it certainly is not an idea in the Platonistic sense, which, as Merleau-Ponty emphasizes, would remain "outside time" as well as outside space: an idea that would be presupposed as an *originary* by its samples. On the other hand, neither does it have the sense of an empiricist inductive generalization,[18] which inevitably would take place a posteriori with respect to the samples. Rather, it is a generality that, as "trans-temporal and trans-spatial element" (*Nature*, 230), shines through ("trans") its samples. In fact, these samples are what provide us with an *initiation*, which, as Merleau-Ponty explains in *The Visible and the Invisible* while commenting on Proust's thought, "is not the positing of a content, but the opening of a dimension that can never again be closed, the establishment of a level in terms of which every other experience will henceforth be situated. The idea is this level, this dimension. It is therefore . . . the invisible *of* this world, . . . the Being of this being" (*VI*, 151).

The sensible idea is, therefore, a "dimension" which opens up simultaneously with our first encounter with its samples, thus offering to us an anticipation of knowledge that "can never again be closed." The sensible idea thus turns out to be marked by a temporality—to which also the term *initiation*[19] refers—which is similar to the one that marks the rhythm of a melody. In fact, in one of the "Two Unpublished Notes on Music" published in the third issue of *Chiasmi international* Merleau-Ponty writes: "While listening to beautiful music: the impression that this movement that starts up is already at its endpoint, which it is going to have been, or [that it is] sinking into the future that we have a hold of as well as the past—although we cannot say exactly what it will be. Anticipated retrospection—Retrograde movement *in futuro*: it comes down towards me entirely done."[20]

Thus, the sensible idea does not claim to be outside time, nor is it subjected to the law of temporal succession. Consequently it avoids the separation between the sensible and the intelligible, existence and essence, sensible variations and ideal theme. Thus, the ideal theme only exists *together* with the sensible variations that on the one hand deny it—being variations—but which by this very negation indirectly affirm it. Hence, mediated by the description given by Proust of the musical idea, Merleau-Ponty's perspective seems to characterize the ideal theme as the *absent,* which only its own sensible variations can indirectly make present,[21] and which is therefore *inseparable* from and *simultaneous* with them. The variations themselves constitute the theme, without however exhausting it: they constitute it as their own excess,[22] as it were.

Moreover, it is in these sensible variations that we can find at work the "*original distortion* of the phenomenon"[23] that Marc Richir believes to be of decisive importance in order to avoid conceiving—still in a Platonistic way—the intuition of the essences as a frontal and discarnate vision, and therefore in order to avoid deeming the truth intrinsically separable from illusion,[24] while the latter is part of the truth, precisely because phenomena present themselves to us in an original distortion. In fact, as Richir specifies, the illusion "becomes truly illusionary only if it is rendered autonomous onto itself—if it separates itself from the phenomenon in order to erase it."[25] Merleau-Ponty, in turn, synthesizes this in the following way: "What there is then are not things *first* identical with themselves, which would *then* offer themselves to the seer, nor is there a seer who is *first* empty and who, *afterward*, would open himself to them—but . . . things we could not dream of seeing 'all naked' because the gaze itself envelops them, clothes them with its own flesh" (*VI*, 131; emphasis added).

We are thus bound to connect this statement with an important point of Friedrich Nietzsche's, included in the "Preface to the Second Edition" (1886) of *The Gay Science*, the pages of which were also pointed out by Merleau-Ponty in the preparatory notes of the course on "Philosophy and Non-Philosophy Since Hegel." There, Nietzsche wrote: "We no longer believe that the truth still remains truth, if one removes the veils that cover it, we have lived enough to believe in this. Today, for us, it is only a question of decorum to not want to see everything in all its nakedness, to not want to interfere in everything, to understand everything and to 'know' everything. . . . Perhaps truth is a woman who has reasons for not letting us see her reasons."[26]

It is in this light that the sensible idea itself, in relation to its own samples, finds its definition. The notion of *voyance*, which for Merleau-Ponty asserts its rhythm in simultaneity, allows us to rethink the relation between the sensible and the intelligible: in our vision, the particular, while offering itself as such, *contemporaneously* dimensionalizes itself and becomes a universal, like "a note that becomes tonality."[27] In other words, the particular becomes an "element" to which we are *initiated. Voyance* thus enables us to trace the genesis of the sensible idea—or, in other words, the sensible genesis of the idea—in the vision of the individualities *among* which the generality takes its shape, and—like "something which is not contained in any one of them and which binds them together internally"—it radiates throughout these very individualities, eliciting the glimmering of an anticipation of knowledge.[28] The sensible idea, then, should not be conceived as an abstract substitute for what is perceived, as though it were its imprint and, as such, separable and therefore graspable. Rather, it should be understood—as we mentioned above—in terms of an *absence*, which is for this reason always *missed* in every attempt to grasp.[29] It is an absence indirectly presented by its samples.

Voyance—which, on the analysis that we have so far proposed, sees in a given entity the shaping of its own Being, and which therefore cannot separate existence and essence—comes to manifest itself as *Wesensschau*. However, it does not consist in the operation of a Subject that is *Kosmotheorós* in a modern sense, but rather in a thought that is one with that sensible seeing which we have proposed to define as *"complying with," from within*, the showing of the sensible itself. This is thus a thought that works through a *carnal Wesensschau*,[30] which, precisely for this reason, is a *synaesthetic* one.[31] To use the brilliant expression appearing as the title of Paul Claudel's book (to which Merleau-Ponty himself refers in his lectures on the "ontology of the day"),[32] we might say that this is the *Wesensschau* of a *listening eye*: an expression that, synaesthetically, refuses any analytical separation between the sensory fields and more particularly between the presupposed activity of seeing and the presupposed passivity of listening.

Moreover, the epochal "mutation of the relationship between humanity and Being" (which we have seen Merleau-Ponty trace in the bond that, in his opinion, both the writer and the artist ties up with the visible) requires also an adequate philosophical expression. But he deems that this, in turn, requires us to reconsider the very idea of philosophy. In the light of what these course notes indicate, this reconsideration does not at all mean abdication, but rather an availing itself of the experiences by virtue of which modern art and literature—prior to philosophy—were able to give a full expression to that mutation. In a Working Note to *The Visible and the Invisible* intended to "elaborate an idea of philosophy," Merleau-Ponty writes that the latter "shows by words. Like all literature" (*VI*, 266). According to this idea, therefore, philosophy, as well as literature, tends to tie a "new bond" with the visible.

How, then, does Merleau-Ponty envision this "showing by words" that, as we have seen, characterizes the proximity of philosophy to literature? In order to clarify what *The Visible and the Invisible* calls (with a term that is consciously inadequate) the "object" of philosophy, Merleau-Ponty explains that the "effective, present, ultimate and primary being, the thing itself, are [*sic*] in principle *apprehended in transparency* through their perspectives, offer themselves therefore only to someone who wishes not to *have* them but to *see* them, not to hold them as with forceps, or to immobilize them as under the objective of a microscope, but *to let them be* and to witness their continued being—to someone who therefore limits himself to giving them the hollow, the free space they ask for in return, the resonance they require" (*VI*, 101, emphases added).

In this dense passage, the attitude of philosophy in relation to its "object" is discussed in terms of "seeing," which is understood, as we said above, as a *complying with*. Characterized in this way, the attitude of philosophy implies the renunciation of the claims to an intellectual possession of the *Begriff*; and becomes instead a "letting-be." This last expression—which is not the only one inspired by Heidegger—is repeated a few lines later to designate perception itself, where the latter is significantly defined likewise as an "interrogative thought": "It is necessary to comprehend perception as this interrogative thought which *lets* the perceived world *be* rather than posits it, before which the things form and undo themselves in a sort of gliding, beneath the yes and the no" (*VI*, 138/102; emphases added).

In this light, we can therefore assert that in the characterization of philosophy as a "showing by words," the seeing implied here[33] has to be understood as an "apprehending in transparency," the thinking of the sensible—the *logos* of the aesthetical world—*letting it be* and thus giving back to it—in a never-ending phenomenological reduction[34]—precisely "the resonance it requires." As "showing by words," language is indeed the resonance of the silence in which the sensible dwells, and upon which language itself feeds. Thus, language cannot claim to observe from the outside, it cannot claim not to be implicated, because not even philosophical language "reabsorbs its own contingency, and wastes away to make the things themselves appear" (*Signs*, 78). Rather,

Merleau-Ponty assigns to philosophical language the duty "to accompany" (*VI*, 165/124) the break-up of the originating. Therefore, we have to understand philosophy's "showing by words" in the sense that we have already mentioned: the sense of "complying with" from within—through the work of creation of those words—the showing of the sensible *logos*.[35]

As we have already seen, Merleau-Ponty judges that modern art and literature—prior to and more effectively than philosophy—have succeeded in expressing the "mutation of the relationship between humanity and Being" that he finds in our epoch. In other words, Merleau-Ponty seems to mean that modern art and literature—prior to and more effectively than philosophy—have begun to *comply with*, from within, the showing of the sensible, *letting be* its peculiar "logic of implication or promiscuity" (*Themes*, 118). Complying with this logic in which "every relation with being is *simultaneously* a taking and a being taken" (*VI*, 266),[36] modern art and literature do not superimpose upon the sensible the antithetical logic of representation, which for the most part has dominated philosophy. The logic of seeing conceived as "representing by frontal positioning" is precisely what underlies the notion or concept according to which the subject *grasps* in thought the universal representation of the object positioned in front of it.

In the last page of "The Philosopher and his Shadow," Merleau-Ponty provides the emblem of this logic of representation: the (supposed) representative frontality found in Renaissance perspective (*Signs*, 181). On the other hand, he assimilates the being of the sensible to a "Baroque world."[37] In this world, in fact, Merleau-Ponty sees a "configurational meaning which is in no way indicated by its 'theoretical meaning'" (or rather, by its *kosmotheoretical* meaning), even if—as Merleau-Ponty emphasizes—it is precisely this "brute mind" that is going to be "asked to create culture anew" (*Signs*, 181).

In "Everywhere and Nowhere," also collected in *Signs*,[38] Merleau-Ponty states, with Husserl, that "our"—epochal—"philosophical problem is to open the concept without destroying it" (*Signs*, 138). Note that Merleau-Ponty is concerned with "opening" not only the concept, but also all the other categories underlying Western thought, and note also that by "opening," he means rediscovering "the source from which they derive and to which they owe their long prosperity" (*Signs*, 139). It is in this way that Merleau-Ponty tends to "resignify" the concept. On the one hand, he aims to reactivate the concept's motivations in order to conserve its "rigor" (*Signs*, 138). On the other hand, he aims to abandon (as Proust's description of sensible ideas teaches),[39] the pretense to the "intellectual possession of the world" (*Signs*, 138) that the concept seems always to exhibit.

We must therefore "resignify" the concept (to use our terms above) along the lines of the Baroque configuration of the sensible—in which every taking is simultaneously a being taken and feeling is in reality a letting-be. In this way, we would renounce the claims of the *Begriff* to take "intellectual possession of the world" and we would enable conceptuality to speak, at last, about "the passivity of our activity." Perhaps this is exactly what Merleau-Ponty meant by his phrase "to open the concept without destroying it." Certainly, such a "resignification" (which takes into consideration, as hyper-reflection teaches, the bond between conceptuality and conceptlessness, between conceptuality and the sensible as itself *invisible*—that is, the always *carnal* configuration of sense)[40] also implies the "resignification" of metaphoricity, which is traditionally opposed to conceptuality. Such a "resignification" of metaphoricity would lead us to recognize the deepest metaphorical origin of the concept.[41] Or better, it would lead us to recognize a common source of the concept and metaphor as "styles of being,"[42] which therefore plant their roots in the polymorphism of Being itself, in the "oneiric world of analogy" (*Pri*, 132), in short, in the excess of the sensible, not only in the excess of language.

Thus, it seems no accident that it is precisely in a discussion about a theorist of the Baroque that we are reminded that the term concept, in its Latin etymology, had a certain semantic halo whose traces one can discern in the "aphilosophical" thinking toward which Merleau-Ponty tends. In an essay on the Baroque Spanish theorist Baltasar Gracián, we read: "Twentieth Century philosophy usually considers the term 'concept' as the translation of the German word *Begriff*. This last word came to the attention of philosophical reflection because of the enrichment of a speculative complexity by German philosophers from Kant on. It happens, then, that we say 'concept,' but we think *Begriff*, what escapes us is that the word of Latin origin has an opposite semantic orientation to that of the German word."[43] Specifically, conceptus differs from *Begriff* in the following way: while the etymology of the latter, via the verb *greifen*, refers to grasping (the exact English equivalent of *greifen*), the etymology of the former refers to an entity that is concave, and that, being concave, can function as a basin. This feature of meaning underlies not only the use of the verb *concipio* in which it means "to be pregnant," but also the use that indicates "receiving something into one's spirit, one's thought, one's sense." This latter use is the source of the Latin meaning of "concept" as "mental conception."

Concavity, or hollowness, is therefore a crucial feature of the basic meaning of *conceptus*. On the other hand, we know that Merleau-Ponty frequently uses, in his last reflections, the term *hollow* [*creux*].[44] Furthermore, above we have seen Merleau-Ponty employing that term precisely to characterize the relationship between thought and Being. In this light, the connection between Merleau-Ponty's thinking and the Latin *conceptus* becomes more evident. The meaning of *conceptus* evokes the gesture of "welcoming" rather than the gesture of "grasping." Rather than the attitude of "subjecting," it evokes the attitude of "complying with." According to the meaning of *conceptus*, "to conceive does not mean to take possession of anything, but rather to create space for something."[45] And the direction of Merleau-Ponty's thinking seems to be exactly along these lines.

NOTES

1. The summaries, prepared by Merleau-Ponty himself for these and the other courses that he conducted at the Collège de France, are brought together in the Themes of the courses. In addition, the notes—considered particularly reliable—that anonymous auditors took throughout the first two cycles of courses devoted to the "concept of Nature," have been published together with the notes that the philosopher himself drafted in preparation for the third course: see Nature. The preparatory notes of these last courses are published in M. Merleau-Ponty, *Notes des cours au Collège de France 1958–1959 et 1960–1961*, préface de C. Lefort, texte établi par S. Ménasé (Paris : Gallimard, 1996) (designated hereafter as *NC* in the body of the text). We have examined and discussed the notes of the two uncompleted courses in our *The Thinking of the Sensible. Merleau-Ponty's A-Philosophy* (Evanston: Northwestern University Press, 2004), to which the reader can refer. The preparatory notes of this course on "The Origin of Geometry" are published in M. Merleau-Ponty, *Notes de cours sur 'L'origine de la géométrie' suivi de Recherches sur la phénoménologie de Merleau-Ponty, sous la direction de R. Barbaras* (Paris: P.U.F., 1998), 3–92, Engl. trans. by L. Lawlor with B. Bergo, *Husserl at the Limits of Phenomenology* (Evanston: Northwestern University Press, 2001).
2. Moreover, this is implicitly confirmed by the summary of the course, whose English title is "Philosophy as Interrogation." In this summary Merleau-Ponty announces: "[W]e have decided to postpone until next year the continuation of the study we began on the

ontology of nature, and to devote this year to some general reflections on the meaning of this inquiry and the question of the possibility of philosophy today" (Themes, 167). See also the corresponding *NC*, 37–38.

3. In fact, the preparatory notes devoted to *Philosophie et non philosophie depuis Hegel*, before their publication in *NC*, had been published in *Textures*, no. 8–9 (1974): 83–129, and no. 10–11 (1975): 145–73, edition by C. Lefort, Engl. trans. by H. J. Silverman; "Philosophy and non-philosophy since Hegel," in *Philosophy and non-philosophy since Merleau-Ponty*, ed. H. J. Silverman (New York: Routledge, 1988), 9–83. On the contrary, the documentation concerning *L'ontologie cartésienne et l'ontologie d'aujourd'hui* was limited to eight pages of notes taken by A. Métraux, who published them, exclusively in German, in the book, which he introduced and edited himself: see M. Merleau-Ponty, *Vorlesungen* I (Berlin/New York: De Gruyter, 1973), 229–36.
4. The English translation renders *voyance* as *visualization.*
5. See *NC*, 391–92. Merleau-Ponty synthesizes briefly below: "All considered Proust: the carnal essences; Valéry: the conscience is not within the immanence, but within the life; Claudel: the simultaneity, the most real is beneath us; St J Perse: the Poetry as an awakening to the Being; Cl. Simon: the zone of credulity and the zone of the sensible being.

   "There is an overturning of the relationships between the visible and the invisible, the flesh and the mind; a discovery of a signification as nervure of the full Being; an overcoming of the insularity of the minds."
6. G. Charbonnier, *Le Monologue du peintre I* (Paris : Julliard, 1959), 34. Max Ernst's statement is already echoed in *VI*, 208, and quoted in *Pri*, 167. On this subject, the reader can refer to our *La Visibilité de l'invisible. Merleau-Ponty entre Cézanne et Proust* (Hildesheim: Georg Olms Verlag, 2001), 110–18.
7. Thus, in its entire ontological pregnancy, it is necessary to understand the meaning of "simultaneity" established by *L'oeil et l'esprit*: "beings that are different, 'exterior', foreign to one another, are yet absolutely together" (*Pri*, 187). Regarding the literary expression of simultaneity, Merleau-Ponty considers it, in particular, in the conclusive sentence of the Recherche (about which, see *NC*, 197) and also, as the quotation in our footnote 34 indicates, in the pages of Claudel (*NC*, 198ff) but also in those of Simon (*NC*, 204ff).
8. *NC*, 170 and 173, as well as *L'oeil et l'esprit*, where it is emphasized that the "extraordinary overlapping [*empiétement*]" between

vision and movement "forbids us to conceive of vision as an operation of thought that would set up before the mind a picture or a representation of the world" (*Pri*, 162). Christine Buci-Glucksmann points out that, by the notion of *voyance*, Merleau-Ponty elaborates "a Seeing which excesses the sight, a visual freed from the only optic-representative frame" (C. Buci-Glucksmann, *La folie du voir. De l'esthétique baroque* [Paris: Galilée, 1986], 70).

9. As we know, Merleau-Ponty significantly defines the sensible universe as "the oneiric world of analogy" in *Eye and Mind* (*Pri*, 132).
10. See E. Husserl, *Formale und transzendentale Logik. Versuch einer Kritik der logischen Vernunft*, ed. P. Janssen, in Husserliana, vol. XVII (the Hague: Martinus Nijhoff, 1974), 257. Originally published in *Jahrbuch für Philosophie und phünomenologische Forschung,* X (1929). It ought to be remembered that Rimbaud, in turn, came to theorize the becoming voyant of the poet "by a long, immense, and systematic derangement of all the senses" (A. Rimbaud, Lettre du voyant [to Paul Demeny, written May 15, 1871], in A. Rimbaud, Oeuvres-opere, ed. I. Margoni, 3rd ed. [Milano: Feltrinelli, 1971], 142), upon which Merleau-Ponty comments: "This does not mean not to think any more—the derangement of the senses is the breaking down of barriers between themselves in order to find again their undivision—*And therefore not my thinking, but theirs*" (NC, 186; emphasis added).
11. *VI*, 218. Here, the specific reference is to Paul Klee's painting, as we can conclude from *NC*, 56, where Merleau-Ponty again uses the expression "skin of things," this time speaking precisely of Klee. As for the parallelism between contemporary music and painting, Merleau-Ponty develops it in NC, 61–64. See esp. 61–62: "Generalization (and 'purification') of music as well as of painting: there were some privileged forms of tonality. . . . All this [is] not physically suppressed, but rather reintegrated into [a] wider range of musical possibility, according to which the privileged structures constitute only a few of the possible variants of the 12-tone series."
12. See the letter written to Mersenne on November 20th 1629, in R. Descartes, *Œuvres philosophiques*, ed. F. Alquié (Paris: Bordas, 1998), vol. I, 227–32.
13. This equivalence was previously claimed in *OE* 44n.13/389n.22: "The system of means by which painting makes us see is a scientific matter. Why, then, do we not methodically produce perfect images of the world, arriving at a universal art purged of personal art, just as the universal language would free us of all the confused relationships that lurk in existent languages?"

14. See *NC*, 186, and about the quotation from Rimbaud, see the letter À Georges Izambard (May [13], 1871), considered a draft of the *Lettre du voyant*, in Rimbaud, *Oeuvres-opere*, 334.
15. Regarding this, he asks himself: "Is it not a general conception of ideas?," and shortly below: "They said platonism, but these ideas are without an intelligible sun" (See NC, 193 and 194).
16. For the reference here and hereafter to the Proustian pages, see *R* I, 349–50, 379–81.
17. We already discussed the commentary that *The Visible and the Invisible* develops on these pages in the fifth chapter of our *La Visibilité de l'invisible*, to which the reader can refer.
18. "We are not here proposing any empiricist genesis of thought: we are asking precisely what is that central vision that joins the scattered visions, . . . that I think that must be able to accompany all our experiences. We are proceeding toward the center, we are seeking to comprehend how there is a center, what the unity consists of, we are not saying that it is a sum or a result" (*VI*, 145).
19. With this term Merleau-Ponty translates the Husserlian concept of *Stiftung*, which, in his opinion, designates "the unlimited fecundity of each present which, precisely because it is singular and passes, can never stop having been and thus being universally" (*Signs*, 59), exactly because once and for all that present inaugurated a dimension pregnant with promises and anticipations.
20. M. Merleau-Ponty, "Deux notes inédites sur la musique; Two unpublished Notes on Music," trans. Leonard Lawlor, *Chiasmi International*, no. 3 (2001): 18.
21. In reference to the theories of E. S. Russell and R. Ruyer, and even to those of Uexküll, Merleau-Ponty synthesizes: "One can, therefore, speak about a presence of the theme of these realizations, or say that *the events are gathered round a certain absence*: so, in the perception, the vertical and the horizontal are given everywhere, and are present nowhere. In the same way, the totality is everywhere and nowhere" (*Nature*, 239–40; our emphasis). Furthermore, we have already seen Merleau-Ponty compare the "orientation" that underlies animal behavior according to Uexküll, with that "of our oneiric conscience toward certain poles which *themselves are never accessible to a direct view*, but which are direct occasions of all the dream elements" (*Nature*, 233; our emphasis).
22. This excess is indicated by Proust emphasizing that "[w]hen he [i.e., Swann] had sought to disentangle from his confused impressions how it was that it [i.e., the little phrase] swept over and enveloped

him, he had observed that it was to the closeness of the intervals between the five notes which composed it and to the constant repetition of two of them that was due that impressions of a frigid and withdrawn sweetness; but in reality he knew that he was basing this conclusion not upon the phrase itself, but merely upon certain equivalents, substituted (for his mind's convenience) for the mysterious entity of which he had become aware . . . when for the first time he had heard the sonata played" (M. Proust, *Du côté de chez Swann*, II, cit., 189, Engl. trans., 380). For Merleau-Ponty's commentary on this passage, see *Le visible et l'invisible*, cit., 197, Engl. trans., 150, as well as *NC* 193–95: in this passage, both texts find the description of the relationship between "sensible ideas" and "ideas of the intelligence." Therefore, Proust seems to describe here a double excess: that of the "sensible ideas" with respect to their presentation, but also with respect to their conceptualization.

23. M. Richir, "Essences et 'intuition' des essences chez le dernier Merleau-Ponty," in *Phénomènes, temps et êtres. Ontologie et phénoménologie* (Grenoble : Millon, 1987), 78.
24. In virtue of the "*distorsion originaire du phénomène*," Richir explains, "il y a . . . bien, en un sens, intuition des essences (*Wesensschau*), tout comme il y a, *indissociable* de celle-ci, intuitions des faits. Néanmoins, cette 'intuition', qui n'est pas vision désincarnée, n'est ni tout simplement vraie ni tout simplement fausse (illusoire), car *l'illusion fait partie intégrante de sa vérité, tout comme la vérité fait partie intégrante de son illusion*" (ibid.).
25. Ibid.
26. F. Nietzsche, *Die fröhliche Wissenschaft*, "Vorrede zur zweiten Ausgabe": "Wir glauben nicht mehr daran, dass Wahrheit noch Wahrheit bleibt, wenn man ihr die Schleier abzieht; wir haben genug gelebt, um dies zu glauben. Heute gilt es uns als eine Sache der Schicklichkeit, dass man nicht Alles nackt sehn, nicht bei Allem dabei sein, nicht Alles verstehn und 'wissen' wolle. . . . Vielleicht ist die Wahrheit ein Weib, das Gründe hat, ihre Gründe nicht sehn zu lassen?" 20. Engl. Trans. taken from M. Merleau-Ponty, "Philosophy and Non-Philosophy Since Hegel," 11–12.
27. P. Gambazzi, "La Piega e il pensiero. Sull'ontologia di Merleau-Ponty," *Aut Aut*, no. 262–63 (1994): 28.
28. For the characterization of the relationship between sensible and intelligible that we have synthesized here, see in particular the working notes of *The Visible and the Invisible* entitled "The 'senses'—dimensionality—Being" and "Problem of the negative and of the concept, Gradient," respectively dated November 1959 and

February 1960, *VI*, 217–19 and 236–38.

29. "We do not possess the musical or sensible ideas, precisely because they are negativity or absence circumscribed; they possess us" (*VI*, 151).
30. On this subject, we are reminded of the critique of Husserl's "myth" of a disincarnated *Wesensschau* operated by a "pure spectator"—a critique that Merleau-Ponty develops in the previously quoted chapter "Interrogation and Intuition" of *The Visible and the Invisible* (see *VI*, 116). Moreover, in a Working Note to the same text, he writes: "[S]eeing is this sort of thought that has no need to think in order to possess the *Wesen*" (*VI*, 247).

    Thus, if Buci-Glucksmann wrote that "the voyance—which renders present to us what is absent—defines at the same time *the place of art and the access to Being*, the simultaneous arising of an aesthetics and of an ontology" (Buci-Glucksmann. *La Folie du voir*, 71), at the same time we can also see a gnosiology emerging here, for Merleau-Ponty also defines by *voyance* a *Wesensschau* of carnal essences: "a *totally virtual Wesensschau* and, at the same time, *always already working* in the intuition (or in the vision, or, more generally, in the apprehension) of this or that phenomenon" (see Richir, op. cit., 79).
31. In relation to the synaesthetic configuration of *Wesensschau* that Merleau-Ponty seems to propose, we should not forget that he also characterizes it "as auscultation or palpation in depth" (*VI*, 128). In addition, as to the problem of the unity of the senses, it should be pointed out that to conceive such a unity does not imply the presupposition of their original indifferentiation, but instead points out that *Transponierbarkeit* for which "each 'sense' is a 'world', i.e. absolutely incommunicable for the other senses, and yet constructing a something which, through its structure, is from the very first open upon the world of the other senses, and with them forms one sole Being" (*VI*, 217).
32. This deals with *L'Œil écoute* (Paris: Gallimard, 1946). Regarding Merleau-Ponty's observations, see *NC*, 198–201.
33. In this case "to show" is the translation of the French expression "faire voir."
34. "This is to be understood not as an imperfection . . . but as a philosophical *theme*: the incompleteness of the reduction . . . is not an obstacle to the reduction, it is the reduction itself, the rediscovery of vertical being—" (*VI*, 178).
35. In this sense, that work of creation, as Merleau-Ponty writes in a Working Note to *The Visible and the Invisible* significantly entitled

"Philosophy and Literature," "is hence a creation in a radical sense: a creation that is at the same time an adequation, the only way to obtain an adequation" (*VI*, 197).

36. See also another often quoted passage from *The Visible and the Invisible*: "He who sees cannot possess the visible unless he is possessed by it, unless he *is of it*" (*VI*, 134–35). This confirms, moreover, how (unlike Heidegger) Merleau-Ponty's problem does not lie in revoking every will to possess, but rather in recognizing the original and ineradicable reciprocity of possession. This same opinion is maintained by Barbaras: *"Il n'y a pas d'alternative . . . entre saisir activement une chose et être dépossède par elle"* (Barbaras, "La puissance du visible: Merleau-Ponty et Aristote," in *Le Tournant de l'expérience*, 19).
37. Christine Buci-Glucksmann, particularly, thematized the closeness between the aesthetical ontology of the "last" Merleau-Ponty and the ontological aesthetics of the Baroque. See C. Buci-Glucksmann, *La folie du voir. De l'esthétique baroque* (Paris: Galilée, 1986), esp. 73 and 85–86.
38. "Partout et nulle part" is composed of six sections which constitute the preface and the introductions to five chapters of the collective work *Les philosophes célèbres*, edited by Merleau-Ponty (Paris: Mazenod, 1956). It was later published in *Signs*.
39. "We do not possess the musical or sensible ideas, precisely because they are negativity or absence circumscribed" (*VI*, 151).
40. "There is no other meaning than carnal, figure and ground" (*VI*, 265).
41. Arendt is a scholar who recognizes this deepest metaphorical origin of the concept. Significantly, in her discussion, she refers to the relationship of "symbolical exhibition" between ideas of reason and aesthetical ideas, outlined by Kant and defined in the §59 of the *Critique of Judgment* (see "Language and Metaphor," in Arendt, *The Life of the Mind*, vol. 1, 98–110).
42. Barbaras also reaches this conclusion in the paragraph entitled "La métaphorique du monde" in his *De l'être du phénomène. Sur l'ontologie de Merleau-Ponty* (Grenoble: Millon, 1991), 224 ff. That paragraph provides a valid examination of the working note of *The Visible and the Invisible* dated November 26, 1959, which is devoted to the metaphor. Barbaras emphasizes how Merleau-Ponty criticizes the traditional conception of the metaphor as a simple transfer of sense from one entity to another. Along the same lines, see also J. Garelli, "Le lieu d'un questionnement," *Les Cahiers de Philosophie, nouvelle série*, no. 7 (1989): 131–33.

43. M. Perniola, "Presentazione" of B. Gracián, *Agudeza y arte de ingenio* [1648]; *L'Acutezza e l'Arte dell'Ingegno*, It. trans. Giulia Poggi (Palermo: Aesthetica, 1986), 19.
44. "In short: nothingness (or rather non being) is hollow and not *hole*" (*VI*, 196). Another working note adds: "The soul, the for-itself, is *a hollow and not a void*, not absolute non-being with respect to a Being that would be plenitude and a hard core. The sensibility of the others is 'the other side' of their aesthesiological body. And I can surmise this other side, *nichturpräsentierbar*, through the articulation of the other's body on my *sensible*" (*VI*, 233).
45. Perniola, "Presentazione" of B. Gracián, *L'Acutezza e l'Arte dell'Ingegno*, 19. See also the comparison between Merleau-Ponty and Gracián made by Buci-Glucksmann, *La Folie du voir*, cit., 85.

15

The Body of Speech

FRANÇOISE DASTUR

In the late text on "The Origin of Geometry"—which we know Merleau-Ponty had read very early, as it is already mentioned in a note in *Phenomenology of Perception,* and of which he would later give a close and careful commentary in a course at the Collège de France in 1959–60,[1]—Husserl, marking a surprising reversal of his previous position, comes to see in language [*langage*] the condition for the possibility of ideal objectivity, from which it "procures, so to speak, its linguistic flesh [*Sprachleib*]."[2] He implies that the objectivity of truth (in this case, that of geometrical ideality) can be constituted only by its inscription in the sensible, which would not disturb the ideal purity of meaning, but would on the contrary allow it to come to light. Spoken-language [*langue*][3] is thus here considered as this living body from which ideality is born, rather than as the inert instrument of the idea's communication. Husserl thus posits the premises of a wholly other thinking of spoken-language and of body, but without fully developing them.

To snatch spoken-language away from its instrumental status, to give back to speech its body-of-flesh and its native opacity, which a long tradition had tried to reduce to the phantom of a "pure language" that would interpose no more than a spectral and transparent body between the things and us, and which would thus manage to forget itself—this is precisely one of the tasks that Merleau-Ponty assigns himself as early as *The Structure of Behavior.*

We know that in the period following *Phenomenology of Perception* (i.e., during which he worked on the incomplete text *The Prose of the World*), Merleau-Ponty is decisively opened to "the mystery of language" and to the phenomenon of expression by leaving the massive oppositions of reflexive philosophy behind him. But we must nevertheless remember that beginning with his first book, he had profoundly called into question the understanding of the relations of body and soul, an understanding that takes as its model the traditional representation of spoken-language as the adjoining of a sound and a meaning (*SB*, 208–11). But what must be taken into account is what allows for *both* the union *and* the distinction of the body and the soul—that is, the *birth* of meaning and the *coming into the world* of mind. The recourse to the notion of *Gestalt*, insofar as it implies the "*joining* of an idea and of an existence which are indiscernible" (*SB*, 206), allows him to think the relations of matter and form differently than do materialism, spiritualism, and criticism; and it also allows him to see these relations not as relations of exteriority, but rather as relations of inherence, and to see their connection as in no way empirical, but rather as grounded on an "originary operation" by which a meaning comes to "live in" [*habiter*] a fragment of matter (*SB*, 209). Merleau-Ponty thus invites us to understand the "metaphor" of inhabitation—which from the first work onward is called upon to take the place of the classic metaphor of animation (for a long time favored by Husserl) in order to signify the nonsubstantial duality of body and mind, and moreover, we are invited to understand it according to a language that is both Hegelian and Husserlian at once, starting with the dialectic of the constituted and the constituting.

The body thus loses its thingly massivity in order to appear as the ensemble of the already-constituted powers of the subject, and in this sense, all of the body's habits could already be considered as the "impalpable body," through which the self raises itself from its current state to a new meaning. Merleau-Ponty writes that "mind does not use the body, but rather realizes itself through it at the same time transferring the body outside physical space" (*SB*, 209). It is this "originary operation" of the *transference* from the physical to the spiritual—which he will subsequently name "primordial expression" (*PW*, 78)—that he must take into account with the aid of the notion of structure and of a new, not exclusively intellectualist understanding of the transcendental.[4] If, as he specifies in *Phenomenology of Perception* in opposition to Marcel, he prefers to give to the relation of being only its intraworldly predicative sense to the benefit of the relation of *having* (understood in its strong sense, which is still visible in the etymology of the term *habitude),*[5] which indicates "the relation of the subject to the term in which it projects itself" (*PhP*, 202), this preference is because it permits understanding inherence *as* transcendence. This "transcendence in inherence" constitutes the very matrix of intentionality for Merleau-Ponty—an intentionality that is not simply "objectivating" but also "operative" in Husserl's terms, because it is the fact of a consciousness that projects itself in both the physical world and the cultural world, and which would be conceived originarily not as an "I think" [*je pense*] but rather as an "I can" [*je peux*] (*PhP*, 159). We must go back to this primordial "operation" or "expression" if we want to understand the relations of body and soul, as well as those of signifier and signified: "[W]e can compare the relations of body and soul to those of the concept and the word, but on the condition of glimpsing, beneath the separated products, the constituting operation which joins them, and of retrieving, beneath empirical languages, the exterior accompaniment or the contingent clothing of thought, the living *speech* which is the sole effectuation of it, in which the meaning is formulated for the first time, and thus establishes itself as meaning and becomes available for subsequent operations" (*SB*, 210).

Already in 1942, Merleau-Ponty had uncovered "living speech" at the origin of the old opposition of the body and soul of spoken-language, and he thus appeals to the very effectivity of *life* and to its power of adjoining[6] in order to disentangle the apparent separation of thought and language—a separation that has the paradoxical result of making spoken-language the "contingent clothing" of a thought, which, consequently, can no longer be understood except as the true "body" of signification. The idea that "beneath" the contingent diversity of empirical languages there reigns an empire of identical significations is not just a naive view of spoken-language, but nevertheless it also orders the phenomenological theory of signification from the beginning.

If in the introduction to the *Logical Investigations*, Husserl notes that the phenomenological research preparing the elaboration of a pure logic must not neglect the analysis of the connection of the sensible face of language to the act of signifying that animates it, and if he also affirms that "it is essential to keep in mind the grammatical side of logical experiences,"[7] he nevertheless continues to view linguistic expressions as the "grammatical *clothing*" in which all significations (the true objects of a pure logic) are first given.[8] Consequently, it is hardly astonishing that in the first *Investigation*, wherein he affirms that the pure expression of all indication takes place only in the soliloquizing self-presence in which words are only "represented" without being effectively proffered, Husserl posits that in principle there is truly language only where signification is disengaged from the body of spoken-language and thus decrees its independence with respect to the contingency of signs.

This conception, which sees spoken-language as the contingent superstructure of signification, is not only the consequence of the early Husserl's logicism, of his project of a "pure grammar" or an "eidetic of language" (which in the end, as Merleau-Ponty rightly underlines (in *PW*, 16), consists in elaborating the theory of a "language without words"), but also organizes the Heideggerian approach to signification in *Being and Time*. In 1927, Heidegger still considers that if signifiability does indeed constitute the very structure of the world and the condition of possibility for the opening of being-in-the-world to significations in the logical sense, then "these in their turn found the possible being of the word and of speech" (*BT*, 82). Speech still appears as a phenomenon "founded" on signification, according to a strictly Husserlian perspective, as the use of the verb *fundieren* indicates. It is thus not astonishing to find a remark in Heidegger's personal copy of his book (which he used at Todnauberg, namely, the famous *Hüttenexemplar*) apposed to this phrase; the remark reads: "False. Speech does not form a supplemental stage, but it is on the contrary the originary deployment of the truth as There."[9] We will, however, have to wait several years before he discovers (in his summer semester course on logic in 1934) that in this meditation on the *logos*, he was in fact looking to pose not the logical question of signification, but rather the question of the unfurling of speech,[10] which alone constitutes the truly originary phenomenon.

Yet it is indeed this originary phenomenon of the unfurling of speech that Merleau-Ponty has in mind in the chapter devoted to the body as expression and to speech in *Phenomenology of Perception*. There, it is first of all a matter of valorizing "this simple remark that *the word has a meaning*" over against the empiricism that reduces language to a pure physiological phenomenon, as well as against the intellectualism that sees in it only a pure categorical operation (*PhP*, 206). The kinship that Merleau-Ponty discovers between intellectualism and empiricism comes from their common incapacity to grasp the phenomenon of speech as a whole: intellectualism considers the sonorous emission as the simple "envelope" of the interior operation that is authentic speech, while empiricism on the contrary sees the sole reality in the verbal image. Both thus agree that speech is a phenomenon submitted to a physiological or psychological mechanism. To each one, Merleau-Ponty opposes a wholly different conception of the word, which does not make it into a simple inert envelope or a purely physical phenomenon, but rather sees in it an *exis*, a *habitus*, a permanent disposition, and gives back to it the interior power that allows it to inhabit things and to be the vehicle of signification (*PhP*, 206–207). It is true that

Merleau-Ponty is careful to underline, on two occasions (in *PhP*, 207n4 and 208n5), that the power that the word has both to accomplish thought and to make the thing surge forth (and not simply just to signify the thought or the thing) is effective only in the authentic or originary speech which formulates *for the first time* what is thought or perceived, and not in ordinary language in which we must see a "second-order expression" or a speech about speech which German suggestively calls *Gerede*, the piling-up-on-itself of discourse—i.e., verbosity, chatter, gossip, the "as they say." In the framework of an analysis of everydayness, Heidegger is led to emphasize this "positive phenomenon" which constitutes the already-expressed being of spoken-language and the already-interpreted being of existence. *Gerede* is a positive phenomenon, because it is not a question for the being of speech (which is human being) of freeing itself from "the everyday way of being interpreted into which Da-sein has grown initially," and "it is not the case that a Da-sein untouched and unseduced by this way of interpreting was ever confronted by the free land of a 'world,' merely to look at what it encounters" (*BT*, 159). Nevertheless, such a modality of speech is "fallen," in that it does not have a direct relation to that of which it speaks, but rather consists simply in transmitting and repeating itself, "gossiping and passing the word along" (*BT*, 158). We thus cannot remain at this level in order to take account of the being of language. We must appeal to the more originary modality of speech, which Heidegger will find in poetry in the 1930s.[11] It is thus from the poetic experience of spoken-language that the famous definition of language as the house of being is issued: in the 1946 conference dedicated to Rilke on the occasion of the twentieth anniversary of the poet's death, Heidegger goes as far as to say that "if we go to the fountain, if we go through the woods, we are already going through the word 'fountain,' through the word 'woods,' even if we are not saying these words aloud or have any thoughts about [spoken-] language."[12]

By distinguishing "speaking speech" from "spoken speech" (*PhP*, 229) or "instituting speech"[13] from "instituted speech" (*PhP*, 213), Merleau-Ponty likewise discovers this fundamental opposition between two modalities of speech, one of which refers to "the significative intention of its nascent state," and the other to the "sedimentation" of speech-acts and to the "fall" back into being of what is beyond being, namely, meaning (*PhP*, 229). In Merleau-Ponty, who takes up the Husserlian geological metaphor of sedimentation, we find the idea that the expressive act, and more precisely the speech act, has the virtue of opening "empty zones" in "the thickness of being," by which human being escapes from its enclosure in nature. But, as Merleau-Ponty underlines, this kind of *escaping*, which alone could be used to define the human and which characterizes the ensemble of expressive behaviors, manages to constitute itself in the depths of available significations only in the particular case of spoken-language: "[W]hat alone is true—and justifies the particular situation that we make ordinarily of language—is that alone of all the expressive operations speech is capable of sedimenting itself and of constituting an intersubjective acquisition" (*PhP*, 220). The operation of sedimentation in no way refers to the possible conservation of speech in writing, which Merleau-Ponty sees as an operation that is not different from speech, but rather is only "an essential mutation of speech" (*Themes*, 187). The operation refers rather to a process internal to speech itself, by which "it forgets itself as contingent fact" and can thus rest on itself, giving us the persistent illusion of a "thought without speech," of a pure meaning, which is nothing other than what we call Reason (*Themes*, 187). The specificity of the expressive operation that is speech is itself constituted by its possibility of *indefinite reiteration*, which allows speaking about speech, and thus also runs the risk of leaving the "soil" of primordial expressive experience. This internal power of reiteration is thus at the origin *both* of the signifying power of speech *and* of its petrification into available signifiers: "Such is the function that we divine through language, that reiterates itself, depends on itself, or that like a wave reassembles itself and retakes itself in order to project itself beyond itself" (*PhP*, 229). This "essential power" that Merleau-Ponty recognizes in speech is nothing other than what comprises the very essence of *Sprache* according to Humboldt, that is, that it "is not a made work [*ergon*] but an activity in the midst of becoming [*energeia*]."[14] It is, however, not a matter of understanding this activity of speech simply as the work of placing the world and humanity into an external relation, but rather and more profoundly as the work of an internal productivity by which spoken-language is constituted as the result of itself, in the image of the human soul such as it is defined by Aristotle in *On the Soul*, that is as *epidosis eis auto*, as growth starting from itself.[15]

Now we better understand Merleau-Ponty's formula: "Speech is the *excess* of our existence over natural being" (*PhP*, 229). This excess is nothing other than that of history or of culture whose growth continues (by conservation and overcoming that which had been conserved) and opposes itself to the simply repetitive form of Nature, as Gadamer underlines with respect to Droysen.[16] If, however, it is in the particular case of spoken-language (and not in every expressive operation as such) that this historicity manages to accumulate in a real manner, to form what Saussure rightly called the "treasury" of spoken-language,[17] it is because, of the many expressive operations, spoken-language is the only one able to take itself as an object, and it can do so only because it constitutes itself as its own object (as opposed to music, for example, which receives its object from the outside). Merleau-Ponty very rightly takes notice that in music, artists must, by means that remain their own, recommence the task at its beginning and appropriate the exteriority of sonorous matter, but in the case of speech, the alliance of the phonetic element and of signification is the result of a long tradition that ends up at "the idea of a thought without words whereas the idea of a music without sound is absurd" (*PhP*, 221). If language seems to us to be more transparent than does music, it is because we have formed a ground with instituted speech, which we give ourselves right away by detaching available significations from their historical provenance, forming an autonomous intelligible world, whereas in the case of music, the meaning seems necessarily linked to the empirical presence of sounds (*PhP*, 218–19). We can understand from this that the very existence of the word may become virtual, since the word has never had a properly real status except in an inadequate representation of spoken-language, and that it has never played the role of an exterior "sign" of thought, in the sense that it would be the announcement or the indication of thought (*PhP*, 211). On the contrary, it is the reciprocal envelopment of speech and thought that constitutes in itself the operation of expression: this must not be understood as the worldly exteriorization of a wholly interior meaning, but rather as that which makes a meaning exist and gives it life, in such a way that it is the meaning itself which *is there* and which, as in the case of musical or theatrical art where "signification devours signs," tears them from their empirical existence in order to make of them the very presence and the flesh of the idea (*PhP*, 212).

It is thus possible to retrieve the pertinence of the distinction that Husserl makes in the first *Logical Investigation* between indication and expression. There is, however, an important difference in the way that Merleau-Ponty sees communication. Whereas for Husserl, "the expressive functions in communication essentially rest on the fact that they operate indicatively,"[18] with words serving as signs of the lived psychical experiences of the other, for Merleau-Ponty communication constitutes an "enchantment" or a sort of possession, wherein the listener is decidedly not in the position of a translator constrained to conceive thoughts appropriate to the emitted signs, and the speaker herself in no way represents the words that she employs; both the listener and the speaker are immersed in the *presence* of a meaning that is everywhere, but that is nowhere posited in itself (*PhP*, 209). On the other hand, Husserl describes with exactitude the phenomenon of expression when he notes that "expression seems to direct interest away from itself and towards its sense" and that "when we live in the understanding of the word," the word consequently appears to us as indifferent and thus loses its status as an "indicative sign," which it must take on in communication.[19] The neutralization of the existence of the word[20] is for him the foundation of the expressive operation, and for this very reason it takes place only in the solitary discourse, since this is in no way assimilable to a dialogue with oneself, and in which we content ourselves with represented words instead of real words. There is thus expression only where the word serves as a pure *vector* of meaning: Husserl here opposes to the act of indicating [*Anzeigen*], which implies a mediation and a position of existence, the act of designating [*Hinzeigen*], thus recognizing a pure function of *monstration* in the linguistic sign.

Yet it is exactly the same motif that leads Merleau-Ponty to see in speech a gesture, since the gesture, as he underlines, *does not amount to thinking about* the lived psychical experience of which it is the expression, and, far from referring to a psychic fact that would be hidden behind it, the gesture *is* on the contrary this lived psychic experience itself (*PhP*, 214). But for Merleau-Ponty, it is this very monstration or gesticulation that should not be reserved to the soliloquy alone, but rather placed at the foundation of communication with the other. Husserl defines indication as a passage from one actual knowledge (that of the existing sign) to another inactual knowledge (that of another existence indicated presumptively by the existence of the sign).[21] To see indication in communication implies that communication is understood as an operation of cognition that consists in the act of intellectual interpretation of a factual given. This is the thesis that Merleau-Ponty recuses by invoking the necessity not of the interpretation of a given, but of the understanding of an intention: "[T]he meaning of gestures is not given, but understood, that is, grasped again by an act of the spectator. The whole difficulty is to conceive this act and not to confuse it with an operation of knowledge. Communication or the understanding of gestures is obtained by the reciprocity of my intentions and the gestures of the other, of my gestures and the readable intentions in the behavior of the other. Everything happens as if the intention of the other *lived in* my body or as if my intention *lived in* his" (*PhP*, 219; my emphasis). It is thus not necessary for Merleau-Ponty to understand communication with the other as the operation that would consist in compensating for or getting around the abyss that separates us from the other, and which would thus be similar to that operation which procures for us the knowledge of beings different from us; on the contrary, we must "restitute the experience of the other deformed by intellectual analyses," just as much as we must "restitute the perceptual experience of the thing" over against the same kinds of analyses that see knowledge in perception (*PhP*, 215). For here, as a very old doctrine says, the like likes the like,[22] and the alterity of the thing and the other rises from the ground of identity, which is precisely what must be retrieved. Just as there is a *co-existence* of my body and things that make of perceptual experience not the construction of a scientific object but rather the test and proof [*l'épreuve*] of a corporeal presence, so too is there between me and the other a *reciprocity* that allows the intentional meaning to live in more than one body and to emigrate from one body to another. It is because I can take into account the (corporeal) gesture of the other that I can understand her, and this implies that the spectacle given to me has meaning for me only if it is met with possibilities that are my own and that are aroused in virtue of it. But the gesture can do this only because it is not given to me in the same way as the thing; rather, it is given only as an invitation or a question, according to the inchoate style proper to that which is only *gesture*, or more exactly, to that which is *in gestation*, in the midst of becoming, and not a "ready-made or finished thing." The meaning of the gesture is thus not "behind it," as Merleau-Ponty underlines, as if it were a hidden signification that we would then have to decode, but rather it is immanent to the gesture (*PhP*, 215). And it is no different for the linguistic gesture.

Merleau-Ponty's concern was thus to show what speech has in common with other phenomena of expression in order to make its specificity appear more clearly. Yet this specificity is truly detectable only at the level of this first speech, which is that of the child, of the writer,[23] of the philosopher, or even of the "first man who spoke" (*PhP*, 208n5). Merleau-Ponty thus does not renounce posing the question of the origin of language, "a still pressing problem, even though psychologists and linguists agree in order to recuse it in the name of positive knowing" (*PhP*, 216). Humboldt himself refused to respond to this question, considering that "spoken-language bursts from deep layers of humanity, which forbids us from ever seeing in it a simple work and a creation of peoples themselves"; we must see in it "not a product of voluntary action, but rather an involuntary emanation of spirit, not a work that nations have fashioned, but rather a gracious gift that granted them their most intimate destiny."[24] It is impossible to conceive of the genesis of language as the process that would consist in designating objects with words in order consequently to assemble them into a discourse, since neither words nor objects exist prior to the act of that spoken-language, the act which, on the contrary, must be thought as the simultaneous formation of thought and speech, world and meaning. The origin of language remains an unsolvable problem, since we must always posit the existence of a language before language in order to take account of it. We can thus not compare spoken-language to a code, which is, however, exactly what Saussure does when he affirms that "the vocal organs are just as exterior to spoken-language as are the electrical appliances used to transmit Morse code to the alphabet."[25] As Merleau-Ponty rightly underlines, we can appeal to the principle of the arbitrariness of the sign, which supposes the conventional nature of linguistic signs, only in order to take account of the "conceptual and terminal meaning" of words (*PhP*, 217). By ceding to a retrospective illusion, we thus try, with the aid of the terminal products of history of language (namely, the concept of the sign and the vocable) to explain the genesis of the language. The opposition of nature and convention cannot be invoked here, because it presupposes an already established communication. We must come back from it, from beyond the conceptual and terminal meaning of the word, back to its original, emotional, and gestural meaning, which is both constrained and free, both entirely natural and entirely cultural. We could consider the gesture and emotional mimicry as natural signs only if they were narrowly determined by our biological organization. Yet as ethnology teaches us, the use that humans make of their bodies differs according to societies and "is transcendent with respect to the body as a simply biological being" (*PhP*, 220). The whole of "the natural" is in reality *instituted* in the human being, which implies that human behaviors (which are certainly dependant on determinant, biological conditions and thus "weighted by a coefficient of facticity") are invented (*Themes*, 112). But such an invention is, however, nothing arbitrary, since it consists in the taking-up and renewal [*l'assomption et la reprise*] of the determinant possibilities that are opened by our corporal organization. The thought of *institution*, the central character of which cannot be underestimated in Merleau-Ponty's philosophy,[26] thus supposes the creation of significations that both transcend their conditions of appearance and remain immanent to the behaviors that lead to them: it implies an alliance of spontaneity and receptivity, an "exchange" between consciousness and its object which constitutes a "remedy for the difficulties of the philosophy of consciousness" and an alternative to the thought of constitution (*Themes*, 111).

If all invention were indeed the institution of a *communication* between past and future,[27] between subject and object, between me and the other, then this would mean that all institution rests—in an unobvious way no doubt—on this institution of spoken-language that Merleau-Ponty never treated thematically, but to which he refers in an anticipatory way at the end of his 1953–54 course on "The Problem of

Speech" (cf. *Themes*, 87–94), and to which he makes allusion in his inaugural course at the Collège de France. There, after having recalled the impasse in which the alternative of idealism and realism, of things and consciousness, traps us, and which must be overcome, it is explicitly said that "living language [*langage vivant*] is this concretion of spirit and of thing that causes difficulty" (*Praise*, 54). This language, or rather this living speech, is that which we must rejoin, beyond instituted speech, in order to understand the operation of its institution. Can a "theory of the sign such as linguistics elaborates" really allow this (*Praise*, 54)? To respond to this question would require engaging in a precise analysis of the interpretation that Merleau-Ponty gives of Saussurian linguistics. It will perhaps suffice to indicate briefly that Merleau-Ponty's reading of the *Course on General Linguistics* does not seem so rigorous: he seems rather to be looking for a "synchronic linguistics of speech," which would be distinguished from a "diachronic linguistics of spoken-language," even though the opposition of synchrony and diachrony belongs only to spoken-language in Saussure (*Signs*, 86).[28] Merleau-Ponty's principle interest in Saussure is the idea that "language is less a sum of signs . . . than a methodical means of discriminating signs from each other and of thus constructing a universe of language" (*PW*, 31), and that "signs one by one do not signify anything, that each of them express less a meaning that marks a divergence of meaning between itself and the others" (*Signs*, 39). It is by this diacritical conception of the sign that Saussure rejoins Humboldt's ideas about language, and more precisely, his idea that a spoken-language expresses a world and that a universe of language corresponds to a universe of thought (*Themes*, 91). But we can wonder whether the Saussurian theory of the sign as a psychic entity with two faces and as combination of the signifier and the signified,[29] a theory that considers these latter as two equally *given* elements, can be compatible with the Merleau-Pontyan idea of a *reciprocal enveloping* of thought and speech. And we can also wonder whether, with this dichotomy of signifier and signified, the Humboldtian idea of a double process of formation of thought and speech implied in the idea of "internal linguistic form" [*innere Sprachform*] is not lost. In order to stick uniquely to *Phenomenology of Perception* here, let us note that Saussure is not cited, but that Merleau-Ponty finds support in Goldstein's analyses (*PhP*, 226ff), which certainly give to "categorical behavior" a preponderant role in the formation of language, but which already prefigure the other works in which Goldstein will more neatly link signification to speech and the categorical attitude to articulated language, thus encountering Humboldt and his internal linguistic form once again.

Even if "Humboldt's ideas on language" are not often cited by Merleau-Ponty, they are nevertheless closer to him than are Saussure's, whom he invokes many times in texts published after the *Phenomenology of Perception*; this proximity attests to his own conception of the origin of language. For what characterizes the Humboldtian conception of *Sprache*, *la parole*, speech,[30] is the accent placed on the originally corporeal character of the articulatory phenomenon and on the impossibility (when we consider the being of language in its birth and not in its result) of distinguishing, otherwise than abstractly the semantic articulation from phonetic articulation. For Merleau-Ponty, knowing a word is certainly not reducible to a "preestablished neural network," nor is it the persistence of a "verbal image," but rather the possession of an "articulatory and sonorous essence" which is like "one of the modulations, one of the possible uses of my body." It thus consists in a practical idea, which cannot be represented but only acted, in an ideal *habitus* that "takes part in my equipment" (*PhP*, 210). Merleau-Ponty's concern is just as much to return language to the body as it is to pull the human body out of the order of things in order to open it to the order of the symbolic: "[W]e thus do not reduce the signification of the word and not even the signification of the perceived to a sum of 'corporal sensations,' but we say that the body, insofar as it has 'conducts' or behaviors, is this strange object that uses its own parts as a general symbolic of the world and by which consequently we can 'frequent' this world, 'understand' it and find a signification for it" (*PhP*, 275). The body is not only a thing, that is, "a complex of *sensible* qualities among others," but also an "object *sensible* to all others," which implies that it welcomes them, that it prepares itself to receive them, and that it thus draws their forms by itself (*PhP*, 275). It is thus "our permanent means to 'take on attitudes' and to 'communicate with time and with space" (*PhP*, 210). We clearly see, therefore, that this "natural power of expression" that Merleau-Ponty recognizes in the human body comes from its general capacity to gather in itself that which exceeds it, and it is this ex-pression[31] of being, starting from beings, that is the true origin of ideality and of speech. If we want to respond to the question of the origin of language, Merleau-Ponty specifies, we would have to make the emotional and gestural meaning of the word enter into account, that is, we would have to return to the poetic use of spoken-language, and then "we would find that the words, vowels, phonemes are just as much ways of singing the world and that they are destined to represent objects not, as one believes with the naive theory of onomatopoeia, by reason of an objective resemblance, but rather, because they extract from it and in the proper sense of the word *express* the emotional *essence* of it" (*PhP*, 217; emphasis mine).

"To give its true physiognomy back to the act of speaking": such was Merleau-Ponty's objective in the chapter of the *Phenomenology of Perception* (*PhP*, 211). The word *physiognomy* already implies by itself a certain corporeity of speech. Merleau-Ponty declares that it is necessary that "the word and speech cease being a way of designating the object or thought, in order to become the presence of this thought in the sensible world and not its clothing, but its emblem or its body" (*PhP*, 211). To see in speech the very body of thought is, however, to renounce both the idea of a transparency of language and this ideal that we secretly venerate, a language "which in the last analysis delivers us from itself by delivering us to the things" (*PW*, 4). It is this ideal of the expression of a "Nature without man" that guides philosophy and science from their beginnings, and which sustained the algorithmic dream of a universal language and thought (*PhP*, 218). We must take account of these "enlightenments" born of the revolt against the given language and the uprooting of speech from history, and submit reason itself to its own critique, as Kant already wanted (*PW*, 5). This critique, which consists in exhibiting the irrational ground of reason itself, took on with Heidegger, but also with Merleau-Ponty, the decisive form of a "critique" of language. The exact sense of this critique for Merleau-Ponty was a matter of beginning by limiting the claims or pretensions of spoken-language to be something other than a particular case of "this irrational power that creates significations and that communicates them" (*PhP*, 220). Yet it was to try to rejoin what the poets know obscurely of language and what one among them knew how to explain, namely, that its secret resides precisely in monological nature.[32] For "clarity is established on a dark ground, and if we push the research far enough, we will finally find that language, too, says nothing other than itself, or that its meaning is not separable from it" (*PhP*, 219).

NOTES

1. The note in question is in *PhP*, 208. The résumé of the course can be found in *Themes*, 181–91. The course notes are available as Merleau-Ponty, *Husserl at the Limits of Phenomenology*, trans. L. Lawlor and B. Bergo (Evanston: Northwestern University Press, 2002).
2. Edmund Husserl, "The Origin of Geometry," trans. D. Carr in Jacques Derrida, *Edmund Husserl's 'Origin of Geometry:' An Introduction*, trans. J. P. Leavy (Lincoln: The University of Nebraska Press, 1989), 161. [Note that the German term *Sprach-*

leib derives from two roots: *Sprache*, speech, from the verb *sprechen*, to speak, and *Leib*, a living body (which Merleau-Ponty initially translates as *le corps propre* in *PhP*, and later as *la chair*, flesh, in *VI*), related to the verb *leben*, to live. Hence the term could be translated literally as "speechbody," or "the body of speech," and is thus the origin of the title of this essay—tr.]

3. [From the French, both *la langue* and *le langage* can simply be translated as "language," but to do so ignores the multiple distinctions and resonances the French words convey, which are especially pertinent when the author's argument makes use of these distinctions. *Le langage* is generally understood as language in the formal-logical sense, i.e., as the structures that exist independently of any particular language, or a universal grammar. *La langue*, on the other hand, refers to "the tongue," i.e., that (with) which one speaks—not just the organ, but also (as in the Saussurian sense) the available sedimented significations that we use for ordinary communication, or language as it is embodied. Translation complications arise when we understand that both the French terms also translate the German *Sprache*, the verbal form of which is *sprechen*, to speak, or in French, *parler*, which refers us again, but differently, to the lived aspect of language as expressive articulation. As Dastur notes, *Sprache* (at least in the way that Humboldt uses it) should be translated into French as *la parole*, which consequently prohibits us from translating *la langue* simply as "speech." Instead, we have elected to translate *la langue* as "spoken-language," in order to maintain its distinction from *le langage*, *die Sprache*, and *la parole*; these distinctions are central to Merleau-Ponty's meditations on language and to Dastur's argument concerning them—tr.]
4. This is the direction in which the last lines of *The Structure of Behavior* point. See *SB*, 224.
5. [The *Oxford English Dictionary* makes clear the etymological relation to which Dastur is alluding. The English word *habit*, like the French *habitude*, is derived from the past participial form (*habit-*) of the Latin verb *habere*, which, through coherent deformations over the course of time, becomes, e.g., *avoir* in French, *avere* in Italian, *haben* in German, and *to have* in English. Through this development, "habit" comes to mean the way in which one holds or has oneself [hence, demeanor, dress, disposition, or way of dealing with things]. Moreover, the past participial form *habit-* becomes the root of the verb *habitare* [to have dealings with, possess, cohabit, dwell, inhabit], from which derives the French *habiter*. Once one acquires

a *habit*, one *has* it, it *inhabits* one's way of being (a habit may be hard to break, so we might be inclined to say that it *abides* in us, but in fact this verb comes from a wholly other, Teutonic etymology), and determines not only "the relation of the subject to the term in which it projects itself," but also the manner in which the subject will project itself: this is the "strong sense" of the "relation of having" to which Dastur refers. The citation from *PhP*, 202, refers us to Gabriel Marcel's important study, *Being and Having*, trans. K. Farrar (London: Dacre Press, 1949), which takes up these connections and their implications in greater detail, and to which Merleau-Ponty is critically responding—tr.]

6. A muffled echo, perhaps, of *Lebensphilosophie* (Klages is cited in the same pages) and of Dilthey's *Zusammenhang des lebens* (the cohesion of life) evoked by Heidegger in section 77 of *Being and Time.*
7. Edmund Husserl, *Logical Investigations,* trans. J. N. Findlay (London: Routledge and Kegan Paul, 1970), 257. This page of the English translation refers to Volume II, Part One, Section 4 of the introduction to the German edition. The section bears as a title "It is essential to keep in mind the grammatical side of our logical experiences."
8. Ibid., 250; my emphasis.
9. *BT*, 82. Heidegger's marginalia are reproduced at the bottom of the page in the edition printed as *GA* 1. [The French edition translation, which I have translated into English here, differs slightly but noticeably from Stambaugh's, which reads as follows: "Untrue. Language is not imposed, but *is* the primordial essence of truth as there [*Da*]"—tr.]
10. See for example Heidegger, *On the Way to Language*, trans. P. D. Hertz (San Francisco: Harper and Row, 1971), 7–8.
11. See for example Heidegger's Winter Semester 1934–35 course, wherein he says that poetry is the origin of language and where the essential unity of poetry and spoken-language is affirmed. See *GA* 39: *Holderlins Hymnen 'Germanien' und 'Der Rhein.'*
12. Heidegger, "Why the Poets" in *Off the Beaten Track*, ed. and trans. J. Young and K. Haynes (Cambridge: Cambridge University Press, 2002), 232–33. Although it is hard to guess from the title, this volume is a translation of *Holzwege.*
13. This phrase appears only in *PW*, 121.
14. Wilhelm von Humboldt, *Über die Kawi-Sprache auf der Insel Java, nebst einer Einführung über die Verschiedenheit des menschlichen*

Sprachbaues und ihren Einfluß auf die geistige Entwickelung des Menschengeschlechtes, in Wilhelm von Humboldt, *Gesammelte Werke* (Berlin: B. Behr, 1903–1936), VII: 418.

15. Aristotle, *On the Soul*, 417 b 5. On the subject of this interpretation of Humboldt's thought, allow me to refer to *Telling Time: Sketch of a Phenomenological Chrono-logy* by Françoise Dasur, trans. E. Bullard (London: Athlone Press, 1999).
16. Hans-Georg Gadamer, *Truth and Method* (New York: Crossroads Publishing, 1975), 184. Droysen himself cites Aristotle's declaration according to which the soul is *epidosis eis auto*.
17. Ferdinand de Saussure, *Course on General Linguistics*, ed. C. Bally et al., trans. W. Baskin (New York: McGraw-Hill, 1959),14–15. "It is a treasury deposited by the practice of speech in the subjects belonging to the same community, a grammatical system existing virtually in each brain, or more precisely in the brains of an ensemble of individuals; for language is not complete in any one individual, it exists perfectly only in the mass." Translation modified.
18. *Logical Investigations*, 278 (First Investigation, section 8).
19. *Logical Investigations*, 279.
20. Husserl underlines this: "The non-existence of the word neither disturbs nor interests us, since it leaves the word's expressive function unaffected." *Logical Investigations*, 279.
21. *Logical Investigations*, 270 (First Investigation, section 2).
22. Cf. F. W. J. Schelling, *Philosophical Inquiries into the Nature of Human Freedom*, trans. J. Gutmann (Lasalle, IL: Open Court Press, 1936). Speaking of this "very ancient doctrine," Schelling relates that it is said to have come from Pythagoras, from Empedocles, and that we also find it in Plato. Goethe takes it up again as well. It is interesting to note that it is in the framework of the *Naturphilosophie*, with which Merleau-Ponty has so many affinities, that such a doctrine can be invoked.
23. We must underline once again that writing is not here considered otherwise than as a mutation of speech, such that the writer *speaks*, that is, is himself only a *speaking* arousing in us the primordial experience of expression on this side of our habits of language.
24. Humboldt, op. cit., in *Gesammelte Werke*, VII: 17.
25. Saussure, *Course*, 18. Translation modified.
26. I refer you to the excellent and yet unpublished thesis by Koji Hirose, *Problématique de l'institution dans la dernière philosophie de Merleau-Ponty*, defended in 1994, as well as his article "L'institution de l'oeuvre de Merleau-Ponty," in "Merleau-Ponty, le

philosophe et son langage," *Recherches sur la philosophie et le langage* 15, Grenoble (1993).

27. *Themes*, 108: "We understand by the concept of institution...those events in experience which endow it with durable dimensions, in relation to which a whole series of other experiences will acquire meaning, will form an intelligible series or a history—or again those events which sediment in me a meaning, not just as survivals or residues, but as the invitation to a sequel, the necessity of a future."
28. Saussure, *Course*, Part One, Chapter III, 81, 90–95.
29. Saussure, *Course*, Part One, Chapter I, 65–70.
30. We normally translate the German term *Sprache* by language, either *langue* or *langage* in French, even though it is the substantive formed from the verb *sprechen*, which means *parler*, to speak. I have constantly translated it here as speech, *la parole*, in order to avoid the trap of identifying Humboldtian *Sprache* with Saussurian *langue*, which refers not to the act of language, but to the treasury of available significations, and thus implies this sedimentation which is at the origin of what Merleau-Ponty calls "spoken speech."
31. This term should be understood in the sense of extraction, as when, in French, "*on exprime le jus d'un citron*," one extracts juice from a lemon.
32. Cf. Novalis, "Monolog," cited by Heidegger in *On the Way to Language*, 111.

16

Body, Flesh

CLAUDE LEFORT

"It is that as yet mute experience . . . which we are concerned to lead to the pure expression of its own meaning": we are tempted to use Husserl's formula, which Merleau-Ponty cites and comments on in the "Preface" to his *Phenomenology of Perception*, as an exergue for the whole of Merleau-Ponty's book, because it summarizes its intention and gives to the heir the ambition attributed to the founder, namely, "to make reflection equal the unreflected life of consciousness." Yet it is true that Merleau-Ponty accomplishes this return to experience and discovers what sustains and animates the operations of reflection by a path that separates him from Husserl, since he denounces the vanity of an enterprise whose goal is to install the philosopher in the principle of all things and to reveal the secret of the constitution of essences, a pretension to which he opposes the ultimate virtue of description. Merleau-Ponty argues that this path was already opened by Husserl, who refused to follow it to the end; but he also thought he found in Husserl's later work the passage that would lead him to his own philosophy. We must designate this site of access, for such is the place that Merleau-Ponty will first have had to abandon, and then will have rejoined, in order both to understand the impossibility of occupying it and to disabuse himself of the illusion of the pure restitution of experience.

THE THINKING BODY

In the *Phenomenology of Perception*, the analysis of the body requires a new status of knowledge. To admit that there is a knowledge of the body (and even scattered in it a knowledge of organs, of the eye and the hand) means that we must renounce the model of a consciousness transparent to itself, and instead pursue in the most nimble forms of thought the signs of an attachment to the sensible. Instead of being freed from this model by means of the fiction of a transcendental *affection*, we will rather be devoted to the description of the paradoxes of existence-in-the-world.

Merleau-Ponty certainly does not propose to transfer to the body the origin that modern philosophy had situated in consciousness. To attribute this intent to him would involve a concerted effort *not* to read him. The *Phenomenology of Perception* seeks its ground in a new theory of the cogito, temporality, and freedom, to which the last part of the book is devoted. In what is undoubtedly the most explicit chapter, "The Natural Thing and the Human World," Merleau-Ponty firmly marks the limits of psychological description. After establishing the thing as a correlate of the body, Merleau-Ponty confronts the enigma of its transcendence, welcomes the contradiction of Being in-itself and for-us, and tries at least to think (if not resolve) this contradiction by returning to the experience of temporality and to the effect of ambiguity that marks the position of every subject. However, even if he forbids us from situating the genesis of the sensible world and of its representation in the body, he no doubt finds in the body the power to go toward the originary—that originary named mute experience or the unreflected life of consciousness. To know the difference between the body and the material thing (i.e., that the body is neither inside nor outside of space and time, and that all spatiality and all temporality implicate the body, without its figure being inscribed there by us) is to scrutinize its exchanges with the world (where it institutes itself in the movement of incorporation and where simultaneously something happens [*advient*]), and finally it is to lose the points of reference that distinguish subject and object. We are thus constrained to leave the metaphysical confine, the borders of which Husserl had extended only in order to better defend the fortress of the cogito. The body thus opens the passage to a thought that nothing subsequently restrains in its movement of exploration. Or, in order to remain faithful to the formulae of the "Preface" (and if we want to learn a truth that metaphysics had covered over, a truth concerning speech and knowledge themselves), then let us say that the body represents par excellence the mute to which it is appropriate to restore speech, or that it represents the unknown from which we must free knowledge.

Whence comes this privilege accorded to the body? The question seems vain. Does it not suffice to describe perception without prejudice, in order to go directly to an experience that marks the shortcomings [*défaults*] of the philosopher's categories? But more vain still would be the response. It would take account neither of the force of the prejudice nor of that which allows for its removal. How can we say that experience teaches itself without immediately having to add that it also lets itself be ignored, and without being obliged to think this other experience that would be the work of its discovery?

We would like to avoid this difficulty by invoking the progress of science. The possibility of allowing the testimony of the senses, in itself mute, would be linked to the constitution of instruments susceptible to making known the properties that make the body incomparable to the machine. This would then be not the prejudice, but rather the weakness of the means of knowledge that had prohibited Descartes from conceiving what he, as a human being instructed by life, could not ignore. Given the place that Merleau-Ponty gives to the findings [*données*] of psychology and psychopathology, we should at least agree that science organizes the elaboration of a new status of the body. The argument would, however, lead back to the least sustainable version of empiricism if it let us reduce science to the mere accumulation of instruments, or let us suppose that an experience is gradually opened up by the natural effect of the use of these tools. Or, if we were required to relate these instrumental operations to their conditions of possibility, if we had to seek the principle that organizes their discovery, then we would be led directly back to the very question that we had wished to dismiss. How could we support the claim that psychologists' observations teach Merleau-Ponty the meaning of his procedure? He uses psychology deliberately, either to denounce the artifices that unknowingly maintain psychological description in the framework of a mechanism, or to show that these artifices lend to the body abilities that are decidedly incompatible with the status of an object. This use of psychology surely allows us to recognize a divergence between, and a mutual modification of, theory and praxis in science, such that the articulated alternative is partially defused. But the science of perception nevertheless does not furnish phenomenology with its ground, nor does the philosopher propose to sift through and sort out all of its statements simply in order to attain exactitude. If that were the case, then whence would come his authority to refute, correct, or to take hold of these statements, unless he makes the norms of scientific activity his own? The truth is that Merleau-Ponty does not address psychology in order to learn from it what the body is, because he knows that psychology itself does not hold the key to the representation of the body, having instead received it from metaphysics. If he questions psychology, it is because it accomplishes the destiny of its principles and allows this destiny to be read outside of psychology, in a discourse entirely committed to "what appears." Psychology (or more generally, science) instructs, because it does not tolerate the reserve of metaphysics, because it marks its return in front of things (in the forgetting of the movement that made it possible and was inaugurated by a retreat), and because in particular, it would not guard the place of an unthinkable of the body, of an experience of life hidden to consciousness. But it also instructs, as we have suggested, because its involvement or being-carried-away [*emportement*] in the object exposes it entirely and does not allow it to keep watch over its principles, and because its madness for a language where everything may be said also carries the incessant passion of transgressing what is permissible to say, thus unintentionally muddling the limits of its domain.

To the question "whence comes the well-known privilege of the body?" we must answer: from the function that Merleau-Ponty thinks metaphysics assigned it, a function that makes of it the object par excellence of its denial [*dénégation*] and, as such, gives it the status of an object of science. We could no doubt then wonder how the ability to know this denial comes to the philosopher—to Husserl first of all, though he does not develop all of the consequences of his critique, and then to his heir. But we must agree that such an ability does not estrange Husserl and Merleau-Ponty from their forebears, but rather that they inherit it from them; and we agree that we need not oppose what condemns an experience taken in-itself to ignorance to what condemns it to knowledge. Since denial is not simply a shortcoming [*défaut*] of knowledge, and since it supposes a process of interpretation, the failure of which it only testifies to and signals, then consequently, to think the object of this denial would be to return to the past of metaphysics. It would not be to cancel metaphysics to the benefit of an experience that has not yet been given expression, as if we possessed a capacity of seeing denied to others. It would, rather, be to make good use of metaphysics, to admit that metaphysics had always been an enterprise of discovery and that as such it had always given over to reflection that which had been poorly known in the shared representation of mankind, and, finally, it would be to grasp what had been covered over by metaphysics during its movement of discovery. This task is made possible by scrutinizing the object of the denial as an object that denial produces without being able to include it in its own discourse.

We must be wary of interpreting the formulae with which we began in a naive manner. "To return to mute experience," "to make reflection equal to the unreflected life": we should judge whether this program arises from Cartesianism or from Kantianism, rather than leading it back toward a "this-side" of metaphysics, since to bring mute experience and the unreflected life to expression would be to free them from the weight of representation, beneath which they are dissimulated, and since metaphysics begins by taking on this task.

It is thus not astonishing that the *Phenomenology of Perception* articulated in one sole argument the critique of the metaphysical idea (such as it is elaborated by scientific psychology) and the discovery of the experience of the body (where mute experience is indicated). In fact, we can read the entire work under the title given to its long introduction: "Traditional Prejudices and the Return to Phenomena." The same operation that destroys the prejudices also makes appear what the prejudice prohibited from being seen. The trial of idealism and realism rigorously orders the interpretation of bodily behaviors. In its very construction, the work [*PhP*] follows the lines of the model elaborated by the Tradition, as if it were only a matter of establishing—on property received as inheritance, or on the site of a ruined building—an edifice of the same proportions as the previous one.

This conclusion, however, is troubling. One is right to doubt the freedom of a critique that, in wanting to be radical, remains narrowly subjected to the form of an inherited knowledge. Must we not recognize that under the cover of their trial, these metaphysical theses are nevertheless still in command? Must we not wonder if the description of the body does not leave its author a prisoner of these theses in a manner that escapes him? Merleau-Ponty follows a path of discovery by way of a return to the phenomena of the body, but does he not wholeheartedly keep faith in metaphysics by supposing that what it denies is what it covers over? Is it not this faith that launches him on a quest for an originary [experience], at the moment when he shows that philosophy lapses into the imaginary by ceding to the vertigo of a sovereign consciousness? Is it not this faith that makes him seek, on this side of essences, an ultimate text in mute experience? This text no doubt seems of the sort that we will never finish deciphering, because with temporality, the register of the world and of our own experience remain indefinitely open. But if it is necessary to lose the knowledge of the origin, at least an origin of knowledge is preserved, an origin with respect to which the guarantee of truth is made.

Since our purpose here is only to scrutinize the limits of an enterprise that, in its very principle, tends to break open a passage beyond the metaphysical tradition, we must unjustly pass over in silence all that transgresses these limits. It will thus suffice to bring our questioning to the point where the contradiction of the *Phenomenology of Perception* is revealed—where what is denounced in Descartes returns as an inverted sign. Just as we could not make of reflection the model of consciousness unless the means for this were given by the unreflected, thus depriving ourselves of knowing the trace of it, so too does it seem impossible to form a ground on the unreflected unless the power of referring to it has been conquered and unless we have been deprived of making it rational. And so too do we again probe these formulae that Merleau-Ponty takes up in order to free phenomenology from Husserlian idealism. To want "to make reflection equal the unreflected life of consciousness"—was this not to expose oneself to restoring what must be destroyed, namely, the fiction of a de jure coincidence of being and thinking? To want "to lead mute experience to the pure expression of its own meaning"—was this not to imagine a silence just as full as the word of god, or to install a language before language, such that the second language is but an echo of the first?

We sense ourselves on firmer ground to denounce this equivocation, which Merleau-Ponty signals in the working notes of *The Visible and the Invisible*. We learn from him again to glimpse the failure of *Phenomenology of Perception*, to rid ourselves of the illusion of a prereflexive cogito or a tacit cogito (that would retain the meaning of the Cartesian cogito), and to understand that "the very description of the silence rests entirely on the virtues of language."

We can only draw from his auto-critique a consequence that had remained implicit by observing that the body does not retain the status conferred to it in his first works. In light of this critique, the possibility of finding the formula of experience in it (from which consciousness would draw its life) evaporates, because it is not what the descriptions claim to rejoin, or because to describe it is also to inscribe it on a register opened by the exercise of speech, or because the return movement toward that which limits itself to this side of thought is effected in the movement proper to thinking. We must understand the discovery in a wholly new sense when Merleau-Ponty says: "Being is what demands of us creation so that we have the experience of it." What does it mean to discover in this case, if not to be committed to an expression that finds in itself the sign of an impression, or to confide in a speech that bears witness, in the being of language, to that of which it can speak only because it is the speech of it? This discovery may be that of vision or of thought, but never in the sense that it would attain something, least of all the ground of things, since it lives in a divergence from every term, and since every term is offered to it only at the price of an incessant detour of expression. Such is the enigma, which is neither that which we want to circumscribe in the space of consciousness or the body in order to undo or to produce it, nor that from which we want to draw the response to every question. In the distance of what is given to knowing, or of what is already opened to us, in this secession wherein to think is to undergo an ordeal [*faire l'épreuve*], we are at each moment led to a place and joined to an event—either to the locality of the body and to the event of vision, or to locality of the psyche and to the event of thought. Yet this enigma is neither outside of him who thinks, nor inside of him as his own—the enigma of human being. And the thinker cannot overstate how he conceives of the enigma; while thinking, he is traversed by this enigma and speaks it like a native language. With the extreme choice of thinking thinking itself, the advent [*avènement*] of self-thinking [*le penser à soi*] wherein all things are made thinkable (which is the choice of philosophy) never ceases, but rather is the adventure [*aventure*] that demands of us creation so that we may continue to experience it. Thus, at the most, we can say that philosophy responds uniquely to this demand with its decided welcome of interrogation. But philosophy would make itself the master of interrogation only by forgetting its birth, its inscription in the thinking that it thinks, in the Being of thinking—an inscription already operating both in the time of the secession of thinking, and in the time of its own secession as philosophy. Such is philosophical interrogation which, in its exercise (where the terms of both the origin and the achievement are effaced, and where thinking comes to know its element in the interminable) must always liberate its own sign from that which it interrogates. Its work is such that every mode of expression is revealed to be taken up in the work of the question—the modes of vision or of speech, of painting or of literature, but also of the technical or the political.

How to appeal to the unreflected against reflection? If we must preserve these words, it is only on the condition of replacing them in the living milieu of language where they refer to one another. Merleau-Ponty makes us understand that reflection contains its own unreflected. If freed from the fiction of a consciousness defined as self-transparency, what then does it designate if not the power of thought (in its continued, successive, and simultaneous emigration in everything that it thinks) to be turned back on itself here and now, as if to grasp itself from within. We cannot say of the fact that thought lives outside of itself and toward itself that thought therefore concerns two contrary properties whose alliance would not put the realist division of an *inside* and an *outside* in question. There where thought ignores itself, we must agree that it is not separated from itself since it still carries the possibility of a return-to-self. And even there where ignorance is such that the lacuna will never be filled and such that we must leave "unconscious thought"—this separation signals the trace of the relation-to-self, because, as Freud suggests, a destiny of our thought is formed from its own effect, and because there is a tilting-back of thought on thought or on the institution of a space where their work is done. Thought is not outside of itself when it ignores itself in public things—those things to which we attribute a reality and that would happen without our participation. As anonymous, the time and space of the dispersion of thought are also those of its collection and recollection; even when it is torn apart, the world of thought remains that of exchange, the world of culture, one sole world. Nor is thought outside of itself when it keeps to the abyss of personal history, because although the I fails to think it, each thought [of mine] is nevertheless taken up in it. Likewise, there where reflection can take place, there is no coincidence of thought with itself and no canceling of the difference of Being and of thinking. What we name reflection is only the trial-at-the-limit of the relation that it maintains with itself, the actual instantaneous self-contact in which the *I* lights up, where the spark supposes the fusion of "thinking-being." This is a limit-experience in the sense that on its surface, by making surface, thought casts its shine (the *I*), and in the sense that in its signal, in the infinitesimal distance of the "I:think" there is revealed the internal division of thinking and its continued escape into the depth.[1]

To think is to make an experience and an ordeal of secession. Merleau-Ponty misses no occasion to recall it: vision is not the thought of seeing. Thinking is neither sensing nor doing, but neither is it to leave the living being behind. Secession is the incessant work of secession and its exile from thinking for itself, just as much as its exile from the living. Yet if in its escape thought is referred to itself, then its attachment in its place is its attachment in all places, and the description of its own place is also the description of the place of vision, which completes its description of its unique movement; the advent of self-thinking carries the memory of the advent of the vision of the living. Just as it could not be a matter of returning to the experience of the body—as if this experience had a positive status, or as if the body limited itself to some thinkable distances—so too was it necessary to discover the body there where it is, operating on this side of consciousness. Vision is not surprised by the retreat that thought would arrange for us on its threshold. But no longer is the task to transfer what we discover in one register to another, or to draw from the experience of thinking a model that the experience of vision would then read, or from the latter a model for the former. If thought thinks vision, it is because vision lives in it, because the thought that forces its limit does not free itself from it, and because thought itself unfurls a landscape, tests the soil, disperses and rejoins itself, encounters itself, knows the surface, depth, and direction; and because thinking, following its own fashion, has a spatiality and a quasi-materiality like the visible. And also, vision is not entrenched in a confine, and seeing means (much more than having a view on something) frequenting the invisible; it means being open according to the dimensions and the horizons of the perceived, which are nowhere, neither in the visible nor in the seer, and which form the framework of ideality, the texture or the matrix of thinking.

Must we judge that the critique to which Merleau-Ponty submits his first attempts consummates his rupture with metaphysics? It is true that what metaphysics covers over would not take on the figure of what it denies. Neither the body nor mute experience offers the representation of what covers it over: it is still representation—and discovery is not appropriation of the hidden. We must also say that metaphysics does not conceal anything if not its own movement, in which thought as vision is ignored like every other experience. However, the knowledge of what is ignored is not foreign to metaphysics— it is possible knowledge that carries the ignorance of itself with it insofar as it advenes. With it is woven an as yet unexpected link. Interrogation of *what is* is henceforth not separated from the interpretation of *what is thought*, as the interpretation of interrogation. Undoing the Tradition in which the movement of metaphysics is ignored is possible only by an effort [of interpretation] on the working of finished works [*un travail sur le travail des oeuvres*] which, each in its time and place, was undoing the Tradition—the work of Descartes, of Husserl, or of every other work in which metaphysics is offered for reading.

Reading the later writings teaches us that Merleau-Ponty does not stop looking in the past for the announcement of his own enterprise. If this requires a rupture with the Tradition—with what he named the philosophy of consciousness (for it is a remarkable fact that he spoke only exceptionally of the tradition, whether Greek or Eastern, and only under the pressure of circumstances)—then this is accomplished only in the quest for signs already produced by its advent. The knowledge of the experience of metaphysics, rather than gathering itself outside of itself, is always first a knowing of what it does not know in-itself, germinated as its non-knowledge, designating its wild region. It is thus more than ever from the depths of Husserl's work—from the hollows of the unthought where the appearance of thought swells—that the ability to think what demands to be thought arises. The critique of the Tradition, operating in the critique of the myth of originary consciousness, does not unfold without the questioning of its works from which arises (in the rigor of metaphysical thought) the question of the origin, or without the ordeal of philosophy as the strangeness of a perpetual beginning. And such is the enigma that, in its questioning and in its ordeal or proof, is given the impossibility of deciding the distance of some *one* to *another*, of the place where they take hold of each other, of that which begins here and elsewhere. Such is the enigma wherein the point of origin, once separated, returns insistently as the question of origin, in relation to the work of thought, beneath the sign of the "interview" and of the "interruption."[2]

How to think a relation such that what joins *one* to the *other*, and thus holds them together, belongs to a rupture? How to think the differentiation of terms and a non-difference outside of identity and of difference? How to think, in the interview and the interruption, under the sign *between* [*entre*], the fluttering [between] being [and] nothing? If this is what becomes of the question of the origin, then it is born nowhere, neither in thinking nor in metaphysics. At best, it is a matter of the question. With it, every question is stated. When we ask,"How to think a relation such that . . . ?" we already slide into an imposture, letting it be believed that someone could ask after its place, even though we are taken up into the question, and returned by it, expelled, carried along in the wave of its expression. If this is what becomes of the question of the origin, then it is confused with that of the advent . . . a question in which "the before" always comes to encounter "the before"; a question in which the fantastic figure of the primordial carries the rift of vision that describes it, and the vision that inaugurates is extracted by an explosion, by a breaking of something visible and already there; a question in which every opening to Being redoubles an opening to Being, such that nothing happens, nothing has happened, and such that the opening is distant to itself, inactual, reflected, Being in suspense.

Merleau-Ponty writes in *The Visible and the Invisible* that "the originary explodes and philosophy must accompany this explosion, this non-coincidence, this differentiation." To say that the originary explodes is thus not to renounce philosophy, but rather to lead it back to the question that makes it live, the question of the origin, which is still named a question of Being, a question of nothing, a question of truth. It is rather only to leave the confine of the philosophy of consciousness, wherein this question finds its shelter. It is true that such an abandonment supposes a risk whose consequences do not escape us. For to want to accompany the explosion of the originary is to welcome the explosion of its own discourse, to renounce grasping its origin, to be forbidden from occupying the position that would allow taking all things in the same expropriation, to be devoted to discord. It is even to be deprived of circumscribing the question of Being as the question of its explosion, since in doing so, one would rejoin the imaginary center of a pure radiating; it is also perhaps to be exposed to the risk of losing the language of metaphysics and the security of the concept, the securities of the towers that hide it, without pausing to borrow its law—since this language is closed in on the tumult of the savage mind or else frees it in a manner unknown to itself or despite itself; it is, finally, consenting to speak here and now, to say the event, to extract it from the collective discourse that nourishes our own, with no resource but interpretation, by keeping empty the place where the other will come in order to read [to] us. But in the assumed risk of explosion, of noncoincidence, of differentiation, it is also true that interrogation refers to itself, and that its movement, as Plato or Socrates already said of philosophy, does not stop describing the Same, does not stop abolishing the distinction which, however, does not stop places, positions, and moments from being produced in it.

THE SENTIENT FLESH

These are events where the internal indivision and division of the space of metaphysics, of the space of thinking, speech or vision—and also their mutual unfolding and refolding—are made and unmade, which Merleau-Ponty summarizes in his last writings under the name of flesh. Flesh, the "interiorly worked over mass," he writes—is not substance, but "element," not positive being but "latency," "dimensionality." A tissue of difference, the continuous advent on itself in a "dehiscence," a scission such that the self as the originary is "always elsewhere," such that what has come forth is always marked by its expulsion, by its rejection, by its amputation, riveted here and now, at a distance from another rivet, turned toward something by the effect of a re-turning that creates its own absence, opens itself in two by the movement that opens it to the outside. What is given to us to think is what the writer designates as the "ultimate notion," as "that which has no name in any philosophy." A more elaborate version of mute experience, or of the ultimate text that was otherwise deciphered through the body is not offered to us with this notion of flesh. Rather, it is by the destitution of this text, by the defeat of the body's image, that we are led to interrogate flesh as the ultimate notion. Ultimate in the sense that it gives a name to that which is without figure, which resides nowhere and belongs to no hidden ground, does not suppose the reference to a subject who would unconceal it or who would operate the movement of the discovery. It is in this sense that it carries the enigma of differentiation and reflection, of history and repetition.

It is necessary to say more, precisely because the phenomena of the body no longer have the privilege of giving access to the originary that the flesh is not born in one place, and that it is necessary for speaking about its birth to take it as a resource starting from its "element." It is precisely because all flesh is the development of a flesh and the envelopment of another that it becomes possible to interrogate the sensible and to resume the intention of *Phenomenology of Perception*, in such a way that we free the question of the origin from it. It is a fact that in the essays in *Signs*, in "Eye and Mind," and in *The Visible and the Invisible*, Merleau-Ponty seeks the beginning of his own discourse in this interrogation. When he writes that "the sensible world is older than the universe of thought," or that "the child perceives before thinking . . . begins by placing his dreams in things, his thoughts in others . . ." and that "these facts of genesis can not be ignored by philosophy in the name of an intrinsic analysis," these propositions do not give way to equivocation. The question of origin is stated only by positing the terms of a genealogy. If in this genealogy, "the before" always encounters "the before," if the difference in time effaces itself with the positivity of the terms that sustain it, then this effacement itself is not nothing. How is it forgotten? How is the weight of the before forgotten and subtracted from time? We would be freed from genealogy, by referring it to the order of the empirical, only by misunderstanding that what we name as such demands to be thought, and forms the milieu of our life, the temporal difference of which we could not economize, once difference *in* time is erased, lest it lapse into phantasm.

To start from the sensible is, for Merleau-Ponty, to justifiy the necessity that leads toward a beginning, in order to know the trial of its effacement. Yet this necessity that is to be unveiled there, and that has to be installed in the universe of language or of thought, is such that we risk ceding to the fascination of an order, risk expurgating the history that passes through it, and losing the power to interrogate. The illusion would be to find a key in the operation of the senses that would open to the operations of speech or thought, since every analysis brings more than mere presuppositions into its domain, namely, a work already in the form of signs and significations. And thus it is true that the beginning of philosophical discourse is deprived of necessity, that the notion of flesh excludes it, that in this sense the beginning is made here and there, or to follow the expression of the writer, that philosophy is *everywhere and nowhere.* We must only agree that the efficacy and the dignity of the beginning is attached to the power that it gives to raise the question of the origin (of being or of the truth) in a place, and to attain there all that asks to be thought—and at the same time, to make thought slide elsewhere by effacing the points of reference that would circumscribe this place as the place of the real. Such is the power conquered in *The Visible and the Invisible.* The body no longer retains access to a passage toward the originary. Its description does not in the end require a displacement beyond its frontiers: the discovery of consciousness as temporality, which would alone be of a nature to liberate us from psychology. To interrogate the relation of the seer and the visible, to know in interrogation the ordeal of description and inscription that makes the seer, like the very ordeal that institutes speaking and thinking, Merleau-Ponty says *everything*, or if one prefers, he immediately gains the register of the interminable, a register that he could not abandon in order to look in another for the key to his reading. It is thus not the operation of the senses that it comes again to charge anew with a virtue of which the philosopher would want to know nothing. It no longer suffices for him to follow the movement that makes the thing into a correlate of the body, and at the same time, makes of the body's organs a collection of responses solicited by the sensible; it no longer suffices for him to describe an internal history of each sense, the encroachment of the modes of vision or touching and their common history, the mutual encroachment of vision and touching, the advent of sensibility of the world across a differentiation and a corporal reflection.

The enterprise is related to a beginning that it ignores, to its beginning henceforth incessant, when, with the notion of flesh, it confronts the enigma of the reversibility of the seer and the visible and of the double *dehiscence* of the visible in the seer and of the seer in the visible, and when it makes the mutual advent of terms and their passage into each other into a passage to and advent of nothing. So, Merleau-Ponty does not address the senses as if their residence were known, as if we had only to explore the body, where we had learned that it is—that we are—thanks to a familiarity that makes it superfluous to interrogate its identity. The senses become strange, senses of something by their power to detach from that which they make sensible; openings of a body that does not pre-date them, which is discovered as the space of their work, the time of their working, which is held together, stands up, and behaves only to the extent that the *dehiscence* of the sensible is accomplished through it. We could say, paraphrasing Michaux, that among the number of senses, he counts one that modifies the rest, namely the sense of lack. It is impossible to wonder if this sense of lack is lodged in the body or elsewhere; it is without locality and, taken in its vibration, vision and touch no longer reside anywhere. However, this sense of lack makes our establishment, it accompanies the draining of being, it is the organ of presence. Michaux says again: "I touch it and palpate it like wood." As an organ, it is not a stranger to differentiation; just as each sense allies several simultaneous proofs, Merleau-Ponty observes, so too does vision or touching inscribe the sensible on several "leaves" at once. This organ, even if indeclinable like them, is, however, supported by the unthinkable conjunction of the lack of self-seeing, of the visible-to-itself and of the lack of visibility, of a pure diffusion, of an indifference of Being, of nothing.

We are always led back to asking, as if for the first time, What is seeing? What is touching?—and being seen? and being touched?—What is the initiation to the world in sensing? Merleau-Ponty, however, does not speak of what we are accustomed to circumscribing with the fact of vision, of touching, of sensing. He asks: What is this sinking into being, and this detaching from being? What is this primordial cutting-up of an *inside* and an *outside*, such that from the inside all of "what is" becomes surface, and that from the outside all of "what is" folds itself back into its depth?

We can interrogate vision only by thinking an ultimate divergence that prohibits us from finding support in an edge of being, in order to attend to the separation from the other. We do not know how to conceive this divergence, because it would be to cede to the illusion of a retreat outside of the space of our emergence, to place this space under a new eye, to engender a new divergence, for which we have yet to give a reason. To interrogate vision requires that we renounce looking for where and how it operates, and that we consent to the division of speech. The divided speech says: divergence is vision itself; vision is neither in the seer nor in the visible, but it is the act of seeing and seeming, two events in one. In divergence, the seer and the visible are not only disjoined, but are disjoined in such a way that in the passage from one to the other, there is no assurance for either, and in such a way that each is carried into the other, the seer into the place of the visible, the visible there where it is seen. The divided speech says again: divergence is the invisible itself, this difference of figure and ground that is not the de facto unperceived, but escapes perception or the product in principle; the de facto visible and the de facto invisible are shared, but visibility and invisibility do not let themselves be shared. The absolute visible, without restriction, is the invisible. The visible—in its restriction, the figure appearing against a ground; the invisible—in its restriction, the ground pressing down on this side of the figure—these imply seeing in its restriction, the circumspection of the seeing. The segregation of the figure in the field is simultaneously its exhibition, its birth to the outside. The going-outside-of-itself of the visible is simultaneously its return-to-self, returning on itself, a taking up again of being in the gaze. The seer belongs to the advent of the visible; the sharing of the invisible and the visible is the same as the sharing of the seer and the visible. The divided speech says again: in this sharing, the seer is itself shared out, made visible, exhibited and looked at—but returned on itself in the returning of the visible on itself, and as such visible to itself, seen. And yet, the seer is seen and does not see itself seeing, is looked at by another, but does not see the other looking at it. Reflection does not accomplish itself, neither for me seeing myself, nor for us seeing ourselves—it is only imminent and always differed. Such is the seer-visible: circumscribed, it does not rejoin itself, it is open—or "built," as Merleau-Ponty once says, around vision—its borders are not covered over. It exists only in virtue of an internal differentiation that accompanies the differentiation of the visible from whence it emerges—which is not outside of it, but on the inside of it, in the very moment when it is the exteriorization of it. And so, the seer is both invisible and visible to itself, is separated from itself. But its invisibility is not the contrary of its visibility, nor the limit where visibility fails—it is in the invisible that it encounters itself. It is by its internal divergence, its internal opening, that it can see and make itself visible—a divergence, an opening that is not beneath any eye, to which we could not give any form, and that we must think only as the possibility of diffusion. The pure seer, seeing without restriction, is the annulation of vision, indivision, the impossible non-diffusion without diffusion, the fusion of the seer and the visible, the impossible indifference of the invisible. But the divided speech must then follow up: the invisible is at once the pure difference that makes visibility, the sharing out of the visible and the seer, and pure indifference. To see is not to see what makes seeing possible. To see is to misperceive the divergence of the figure and the ground, the interior and exterior horizon of things, as Merleau-Ponty notes, and is simultaneously to cede to the mutual involvement [*emportement*] of the visible and the seer. The restriction takes place in the involvement, but the two movements do not work without each other. The restriction is thus always menaced by the forgetfulness of that of which it is the restriction, by the fascination of the *seen*, by an unreserved adhesion to the figure, by a grasping of the difference that subverts it while degrading it in the perceived as its de facto misperceived. And the involvement is always menaced by the forgetfulness of the involved division, by the passion for indifference, by the impossible accomplishment of what Merleau-Ponty calls "the narcissism of vision." Vision is never assured of its movement; the visible is always on this or that side of itself. To their indetermination is tied the adventure of appearance, of illusion, of memory, of dream, of phantasm, of the work. To interrogate vision in the end demands saying vision as interrogation, since it is never assured of itself, never accorded to the visible, or since its fantastic assurance, its indefectible attachment to what are given to it in-itself, or since the seer is always taken up in the growth of the visible, or in the quest for its remainder—always exceeded or deceased in its own movement.

Interrogation does not install us in the place of vision, in the place of the body; such would not be interrogation. We do not have to displace ourselves in order to rejoin this other place of the body, which would be desire, or to make a path toward the territory of speech, and then of thought. In *Phenomenology of Perception*, it is true, the image of such a path still fooled us. But in his last writings, Merleau-Ponty recognizes his task as an "ascension on the spot." The discourse wraps itself in the effect of what Merleau-Ponty names—and what makes—the flesh of the work. The discourse unfurls itself, loses itself as it suits it to be lost from the beginning, in the unending. Vision, as the writer never stops asserting, is the opening to Being. But what is this opening that calls for the breaking of speech, its irruption into the visible, and the breaking repeated by the speech of its own closure, always necessarily and vainly raised? What is such an opening, with the impulse always oriented forward, and every thing offered as debris, rejection in its wake?

Must we not rather say: the opening to Being is vision, speech, desire? That the unsealing [*descellement*] is the history of their multiple event? Should we not name "work" [*oeuvre*] all that is open, produced, and has neither its beginning nor its end outside of itself? Or rather "myth"—this primitive spacing where the difference between being and nothing is effaced, where history, the event of vision, of speech, and of desire, are before history, before the event? But the *oeuvre* and the myth are a travesty of the invisible and the unthinkable, the figurative enigma of what is without figure. The *oeuvre* and the myth carry the trace of the seeing, speaking, desiring being, who is inscribed in vision, speech, desire, and always trapped in the rolling-up of flesh, always returned, committed in this position to the "indirect and upturned grasp of all things," who does not see the Opening, who dreams it—for whom the Opening, as Merleau-Ponty notes, is "the invisible of vision, the unconscious of consciousness" . . . "the other side or the reverse (or the other dimensionality) of sensible being."

With the "ultimate notion," which has no name in any philosophy, Merleau-Ponty leaves thinking near the unthought. Is it this reserve that wakes in us the memory of a speech close to that of *The Visible and the Invisible*, of a speech where the dream of the open is freed from metaphysical language—the speech, if ever there was one, reserved for a poet? In the eighth *Elegy of Duino*, Rilke writes:

> With all their eyes all creatures gaze into
> the Open. Only our eyes, as though turned in,
> on every side enframe it
> like traps encircling its free outgoing
> What is without we know from the face
> of animals alone, for even the youngest child
> we turn around and constrain to look backwards
> at forms and not at the openness that
> lies so deep within the face of animals. Free of death
> [. . .]
>
> Turned always towards creation, we see there
> only the reflection of what is free
> obscured by us. Or how a silent animal
> looks at us and silently looks us through and through
> This we call fate: to be facing
> and nothing but that, always facing
> [. . .]
>
> And see the half-security of the bird
> who from its origin nearly knows of one and the other
> as if it were the soul of an Etruscan
> issued from a dead man, that space received
> but with his resting figure forming a cover.
> And how troubled one is, born of the womb
> and forced to fly. As if afraid of himself,
> he furrows the air, just as a crack
> traverses a cup. The way the wing
> of a bat cracks the porcelain of evening.
>
> And onlookers, always, everywhere,
> turned towards all things and never outwards!
> It overflows us. We order it. It falls to pieces.
> We organize anew, then we ourselves decay.

And who has turned us so about that we,
whatever we may do, must have the air
of someone who departs? And just as on
the final hill, where the whole valley is shown
once again to him, he returns, stops, lingers—,
And so we live and forever take our leave.

NOTES

1. [This passage is especially difficult to translate, because Lefort is playing semantically and visually with the "I" of "I think," suggesting that it is not the subject that produces the action (the I that does the thinking) but rather the action that produces the subject (the thinking that makes the I). The I is thus the object or product of the internal division of thinking, of thought thinking itself, the surface or the signal of the contact or fusion of thinking and being. And each thought "of mine" is consequently not my own, but instead belongs to the thinking that I am. Hence the spatial or typographical distance between the subject-I and thinking is infinitesimal, and Lefort tries to mark this non-distance graphically by more or less eliminating the space between the two graphemes; thus, "I:think"—tr.]
2. We borrow these terms from Maurice Blanchot who gave them a meaning that is henceforth unforgettable. See Maurice Blanchot, *The Infinite Conversation*, trans. S. Hanson (Minneapolis: University of Minnesota Press, 1993). See, e.g., "Interruption," 75–79.
3. Rainer Maria Rilke, *The Duino Elegies*, "Eighth Elegy," trans. S. Garmey and J. Wilson (New York: Harper and Row, 1972), 61–64. Translation modified.

CONTRIBUTORS

RENAUD BARBARAS is Professor of Philosophy at the Université de Paris I—La Sorbonne, and has written widely on Merleau-Ponty, phenomenology, and contemporary philosophy. His book-length study of Merleau-Ponty's philosophy, *The Being of the Phenomenon,* is translated in English (Bloomington: Indiana University Press, 2004). His essay appears in his book *Le tournant de l'expérience* (Paris: Vrin, 1997).

MAURO CARBONE is Professor of Philosophy at the Università di Milano in Italy. He has translated Merleau-Ponty's work into Italian, and has authored many works on the philosopher's relation to art and literature, including *The Thinking of the Sensible: Merleau-Ponty's A-philosophy* (Evanston: Northwestern University Press, 2004). His piece was written especially for this volume.

FRANÇOISE DASTUR is Emeritus Professor of Philosophy at the Université de Nice. Prior to her appointment there, she taught at the Université de Paris, XII (Créteil), and at the Sorbonne. She is well-known for her work in phenomenology, having published many books on the topic, including *Heidegger and the Question of Death* (Prometheus, 1998), *Telling Time* (Athlone, 2000), and *Phénoménologie en questions* (Seuil, 2005). Her essay first appeared in her book *Chair et langage: essais sur Merleau-Ponty* (Paris: Encre Marin, 2000).

BERNARD FLYNN is Professor of Philosophy at the SUNY-Empire State, and regularly offers seminars on Merleau-Ponty's thought at the New School. He has published on contemporary political thought, notably *Political Philosophy at the Closure of Metaphysics* (New Jersey and

London: Humanities, 1992) and *The Philosophy of Claude Lefort* (Evanston: Northwestern, 2006). His essay was first written in English, then appeared in French in R. Barbaras and F. Robert (eds.), *Notes de Cours 1959* (Paris: PUF, 1994).

WAYNE J. FROMAN is Professor of Philosophy at George Mason University, where he served as Department Chair from 1989 to 1999. His extensive publications in phenomenology and contemporary European philosophy include the book *Merleau-Ponty: Language and the Act of Speech* (Lewisburg, Pa.: Bucknell University Press, 1982). In 1995–1996 he held a Visiting Senior Fulbright Research Professorship at the Hegel-Archiv, Ruhr-Universität, Bochum.

VÉRONIQUE M. FÓTI is Professor of Philosophy at Penn State University. She has written widely on phenomenology, painting, and tragedy. Her books include *Vision's Invisibles* (Albany: SUNY Press, 1993) and *Epochal Discordance: Holderlin's Philosophy of Tragedy* (Albany: SUNY Press, 2007). Her essay was written especially for this volume.

The late MICHEL HAAR was Professor of Philosophy at the Université de Paris I—La Sorbonne, and was well known for his work on Heidegger, including the book-length studies *Heidegger and the Essence of Man* (Albany: SUNY Press, 1993) and *The Song of the Earth* (Bloomington: Indiana University Press, 1993). His essay first appeared in Barbaras and Robert (eds.), *Notes de Cours* 1959 (Paris: PUF, 1994).

CLAUDE LEFORT was Merleau-Ponty's assistant, a member of the editorial board of *Les Temps Moderns*, a co-founder of Barbarism, a Professor at the École des Hautes Études in Paris, and editor of many of Merleau-Ponty's manuscripts. He is well known for his many works in political philosophy, including his classic study of Machiavelli's political thought, and his recent *Complications: Communism and the Dilemmas of Democracy* (New York: Columbia University Press, 2007). His essay first appeared in his book *Sur la colonne absente: essais autour de Merleau-Ponty* (Paris: Gallimard, 1978).

DAVID MICHAEL KLEINBERG-LEVIN is Professor Emeritus of Philosophy at Northwestern University. He is the author of many books, including *The Body's Recollection of Being* (New York: Routledge, 1990), *Modernity and the Hegemony of Vision* (Berkeley: University of California Press, 1993), and most recently, *Before the Voice of Reason: Echoes of Responsibility in Merleau-Ponty's Ecology and Levinas's Ethics* (Albany: SUNY Press, 2008).

MARC RICHIR is associated with the Belgian National Research Fund, and with the Center for Philosophy and Psycholoanalysis at Université de Paris VII. He has published and edited many books on Husserl and phenomenology, and has translated Husserl's work into French. His essay originally appeared in the volume he edited with Etienne Tassin, *Merleau-Ponty: phénoménologie et expériences* (Grenoble: J. Millon, 1992).

PAUL RICOEUR was one of France's leading philosophers in the twentieth century, and a major exponent of hermeneutics as a practice of reading, his work on which is well known around the globe. The two essays appearing here in translation for the first time were published in *Lectures 2* (Paris: Seuil, 1992).

JENNY SLATMAN is Assistant Professor of Philosophy at Tilburg Universiteit in the Netherlands. She is the author of *L'expression au-delà de la représentation. Sur l'aisthêsis et l'esthétique chez Merleau-Ponty* (Paris: Vrin, 2003) and writes on the mediation of the body and the body-image in relation to self-understanding and the question of identity.

JACQUES TAMINIAUX is a well-known Belgian philosopher and phenomenologist and the author of many studies of contemporary European philosophy. He was a Distinguished Visiting Professor at Boston College and a Professor at L'Université de Louvain until his retirement. His many books include *Heidegger and the Project of Fundamental Ontology* (Albany: SUNY Press, 1991), *The Thracian Maid and the Professional Thinker* (Albany: SUNY Press, 1998), and the seminal *Nostalgie de la Grece a l'aube de l'idealisme allemand: Kant et les Grecs dans l'intineraire de Schiller, de Holderlin et de Hegel* (The Hague: Martinus Nijhoff, 1967).

ROBERT VALLIER, formerly a Chercheur Associe at the College International de Philosophie, is currently Assistant Director of the Honors Program at DePaul University. He works on contemporary French philosophy. He is completing a book-length study on the concept of institution in Merleau-Ponty's work.

INDEX

action, 2, 19–21, 38–41, 57–58, 70, 134, 159, 188, 205–206, 229, 265, 292n1
anonymity, 98, 107, 109, 114n13, 125, 159, 171, 173, 188
Arendt, Hannah, 254n41
atonal music, 240

Balzac, Honoré de, 214, 219n33
barbarous source, 8, 158–61, 163
Being, 3, 5–11, 13, 15–16, 22, 26, 38, 44–57, 59n12, 65–56, 69, 117, 121, 126–27, 130–33, 136–37, 148, 161–63, 165–70, 173–81, 182n5, 183–84, 191–93, 195, 196n8, 202–204, 206–12, 214–15, 239–42, 244, 246–48, 249n5, 252n28, 253n30–31, 255n44, 276, 280–82, 284–85, 288, 290
Being and Time, 4, 14, 25, 28, 63–64, 67, 161, 166, 173, 260, 271n6
Bergson, Henri-Louis, 2, 4–5, 8–9, 33–58, 58n1, 59n10, 59n12, 59nn14–15, 60nn21–23, 131–32, 136, 150n4, 175, 178, 212, 218n28
Bernet, Rudolf, 125, 128n4
Blanchot, Maurice, 215, 219n34, 292n2
body, the, 8, 15–16, 19, 22, 38–40, 43, 66, 84–86, 88, 92, 94, 96, 99, 103–105, 110–11, 114n12, 126, 135, 138–39, 151n10, 157, 170–75, 181, 185–89, 190, 193, 195, 203, 211, 230, 258–60, 268, 275–83, 285–88, 290
Buci-Glucksmann, Christine, 250n8, 253n30, 254n37, 255n45

Cartesian Meditations, 42, 119, 128n2
Cézanne, Paul, 12–13, 209–10, 217n22, 222–24, 228–31, 232–34
Cheng, François, 231, 233
chiasm, the, 63, 68, 171, 176, 183, 184–87, 189, 194, 229–30
child, the, 89, 93, 95, 98, 107, 265, 286
Claudel, Paul, 14, 28, 239, 244, 249n5, 249n7
Confucianism, 230, 233
Cogito, the, 3, 25–6, 39–40, 126, 180, 226, 276, 280
 tacit Cogito, 3, 16, 26, 27, 280
consciousness, 3–6, 18–19, 26–27, 29–30, 33, 47, 50, 53–54, 62–65, 81–82, 87, 90, 93, 100–101, 104, 117, 119, 123–25, 130, 151n13, 155–61, 163, 166–67, 173–75, 188, 192, 211–12, 217n17, 218n28, 225, 240, 259, 266–67, 275–76, 278–84, 287, 290

da Vinci, Leonardo, 210, 231, 239
dehiscence, 4, 9–11, 30, 66–67, 172–73, 176, 178, 181, 184, 190–91, 207, 215
Deleuze, Gilles, 8, 157, 164n2, 211–12, 218n27, 219n31
Derrida, Jacques, 81, 87, 112, 113n9, 115n24, 133, 150n7, 155–56, 164n1, 196n14, 269n2
Descartes, René, 2, 14, 117–18, 122, 189, 192, 199, 204, 208, 210, 218n26, 232, 239–40, 250n12, 277, 280, 283
Dilthey, Wilhelm, 271n6
Droysen, Johann Gustav, 262, 272n16

Eye and Mind, 11, 13, 184, 193, 195, 199–209, 218n23, 223–24, 238, 240–41, 250n9, 286

Fan Kuan, 228
Ficino, Marcilio, 226
flesh, the, 2, 5, 7–11, 15–16, 22, 66–68, 70, 72, 74, 82, 84, 86–87, 94–96, 99, 101–8, 112, 121–22, 127, 129–33, 137, 139, 145, 147–49, 157, 166, 170–77, 178–81, 191, 200, 224, 238, 249n5, 263, 286, 290
Foucault, Michel, 117, 157
Francesca, Piero della, 227
Freud, Sigmund, 105, 113n9, 115n21, 282

Gadamer, Hans-Georg, 262, 272n16
Garelli, Jacques, 186–87, 195n6, 196n11, 254n42
Geraets, Theodore, 33–34, 58n2
Gestalt, the, 14, 36, 122–23, 167, 193, 211–12, 258
Giacometti, Alberto, 223, 230
Goldstein, Kurt, 35, 267
Gracián, Baltasar, 247, 255n43, 255n45

Hegel, Georg W. F., 49, 71–72, 123, 132, 158, 258
Heidegger, Martin, 2–4, 8–11, 14–5, 22, 25–31, 37, 63–64, 67, 76, 85, 118, 122, 125, 133, 143, 148, 151n8, 152n17, 153n21, 157–58, 161, 165–81, 182nn1–2, 182nn5–7, 185, 191, 196n12, 198–99, 214, 216n3, 240, 245, 254n36, 260–61, 269, 271n6, 271nn9–12, 273n32
Heracleitus, 161
human sciences, 3, 19
Humboldt, Wilhelm von, 15, 262, 265, 267–68, 270n3, 271n14, 272n15, 272n24, 273n30
Husserl, Edmund, 2–5, 7–9, 11, 14, 16, 19, 25–38, 41–46, 51, 61–66, 69, 73–76, 82, 87–88, 92–93, 95, 99, 117–21, 123–24, 126, 128n2, 129, 131, 138, 143, 146, 152n20, 157–60, 164, 164n4, 166–67, 173, 185–87, 190–91, 195, 195n1, 196n11, 197–98, 217n17, 223, 228, 232, 237, 240, 246, 250n10, 251n19, 253n30, 257–61, 263–64, 269n2, 271n7, 272n20, 275–76, 278, 280, 283

Ideas II, 137
il y a, 9, 59n12, 166, 168, 176, 178–79, 181, 224, 252n24
institution, 6, 12, 14, 71, 73, 75–76, 80, 126, 162, 191, 213–14, 217n17, 266–67, 273n27, 282. See also *Stiftung*
intentionality, 3–5, 26, 29–31, 35, 87–88, 93, 99–100, 113n6, 169, 212, 218n28, 259
intercorporality (or intercorporeality), 6, 92, 94–95, 97–99, 105, 107
intersubjectivity, 61–63, 65–67, 70, 73–74, 92, 100
intuition, 5, 28, 36, 38, 41, 45–47, 50–52, 54–56, 158, 166, 172, 183, 243, 252nn23–24, 253n30

invisible, the, 11, 13, 22, 45, 53, 58, 64–69, 74, 86, 123, 127, 150n5, 155, 166, 176, 179–80, 184, 191–92, 199–201, 203, 205–207, 212, 231, 233–34, 238, 242, 249n5, 283, 288–91

Kant, Immanuel, 4, 7, 28, 30, 38, 75–76, 80, 82, 117, 124–25, 168, 247, 254n41, 269
khôra, 130, 133, 139, 143–48, 150n7, 152n19
Klee, Paul, 209, 218n23, 223, 230, 250n11

La Ta-Ching, 231
Lacan, Jacques, 95, 113n9
Laozi, 225
Leibniz, Gottfried, 125
Levinas, Immanuel, 2, 6, 67, 79–83, 85–86, 91, 93, 95, 97–99, 99–112, 112n1, 113nn2–3, 113nn7–8, 115n16, 115nn18–20
logos, 64, 103–104, 134, 152n19, 168, 196n8, 210, 213–14, 240, 245–46, 260
Lukács, Georg, 164n3

Mallarmé, Stéphane, 189
Mantegna, Andrea, 227
Marion, Jean-Luc, 2, 12, 200–203, 217n14
Marx, Karl, 2, 20–21
Matisse, Henri, 210, 222, 224, 236
metaphysics, 5, 16, 45–46, 48–49, 52–56, 87, 88, 91, 106, 111, 114n11, 131–32, 157, 164, 167–68, 175–76, 180, 200, 276–79, 283–85
Michaux, Henri, 287–88
Michelangelo, 226, 231
Miro, Gabriel, 223
Mu Ch'I, 227
Muybridge, Eadweard, 211

naturalism, 9, 36, 119, 124, 127, 163, 172, 222, 228, 234
Nietzsche, Friedrich, 173, 231–32, 243, 252n26
Nothingness, 2, 5, 10, 20, 45–53, 55–56, 59n12, 59n14, 59n19, 131–32, 136, 181–82, 185, 189, 255n44

Opening, the, 290

Panofsky, Erwin, 226
Parmenides, 132, 136
perception, 1–2, 6–7, 15–16, 18–20, 22, 27, 29, 35–36, 38–41, 52–57, 85, 88–91, 95, 114n10, 119–20, 122, 125–26, 155–57, 161, 165–70, 173–75, 179–80, 190, 192–93, 205–207, 210, 223, 228–29, 232, 240, 245, 251n21, 265, 276–77, 288
Perniola, Mario, 255n43, 255n45
Perse, Saint-John, 239, 249n5
phenomenological reduction, 7, 9, 35, 40, 44, 47, 121, 124–25, 245
phenomenology, 4, 6–7, 10–11, 15–16, 19, 22, 25–31, 33–5, 38, 41, 44–46, 48, 52, 61, 80–81, 86–88, 91–102, 107, 109, 111–12, 119, 130, 155, 160, 167, 185, 195, 197–99, 203–204, 211–12, 214, 216, 218n28, 223, 277, 280
Phenomenology of Perception, 2–4, 9, 14–16, 18, 20–22, 25–27, 34, 40–41, 43–44, 50, 54, 84–85, 109–10, 114n10, 121–22, 125–26, 139, 151n10, 156–57, 166, 173, 180, 217, 257–58, 260, 267–59, 275–76, 279–80, 286, 290
Plato, 2, 7, 125, 130, 133, 150n3, 152n16, 197–98, 224, 272n22, 285
politics, 2, 19, 21, 105
Politzer, Georges, 35–36, 58n5
pre-human, 57–58
pre-personal, 92
pre-Socratics, 2, 158, 161

Proust, Marcel, 14, 207, 214, 239, 241–43, 246, 249n5, 251n22
Pseudo-Dionysus, 226
psychologism, 118–19
psychology, 19, 35–36, 42–43, 96, 119, 211, 277–79, 287
Pu Yen-t'u, 233

Rembrandt, 230
reversibility, 12–13, 94–98, 105, 114n10, 130, 157–58, 161, 171, 177, 185, 186, 200–202, 229, 287
Ricoeur, Paul, 2–3, 10
Rilke, Rainer Maria, 261, 291, 292n3
Rimbaud, 14, 239–42, 250n10, 251n14
Rodin, Auguste, 211
Rothko, Mark, 209
Rowley, George, 224–25, 227, 235n1

Sallis, John, 133, 135, 150n7, 151n9, 151nn14–15, 152n16, 152n19
Sartre, Jean Paul, 2, 5, 9, 20–21, 30, 33, 47, 49, 95, 132, 167, 184, 229
Saussure, Ferdinand de, 262, 266–68, 272n17, 272n25, 273nn28–29
Savage mind, 5–6, 69, 70–79, 285
Schelling, Freidrich W. J., 2, 8–10, 130, 158, 161, 175, 272n22
Schopenhauer, Arthur, 9, 175
sedimentation, 3, 5, 57, 63–64, 69–70, 72–76, 186–87, 191, 193, 212–14, 261–62, 273n30
Shi-Tao, 228–29
Simon, Claude, 239, 249n5, 249n7
Socrates, 133, 285
speech, 15, 17, 22, 62, 64, 71, 104, 134, 138, 161, 168, 174–76, 180, 184, 214, 239, 241–42, 257, 259–69, 270nn2–3, 272n17, 272n23, 273n30, 276, 280–81, 285–86, 288–91
Spinoza, Baruch, 102, 190, 196n10
Stiftung, 70–72, 162, 191, 251n19. *See also* institution
Structure of Behavior, The, 3, 13, 14, 22, 35, 40, 122–23, 151n13, 257, 270n14
symbolic, the, 6, 65, 69, 71, 73, 75–76, 268

T'ang Tai, 231
Taoism, 229, 233
temporality, 3–4, 25–31, 56, 81, 83, 86, 101, 106, 112, 167, 242, 276, 279, 287. *See also* time
time, 2–4, 8–9, 26–30, 37–39, 41, 54, 56, 62, 74, 81–3, 87–88, 101, 121, 167, 172, 176–77, 190, 196n9, 212, 242–43, 268, 276, 286. *See also* temporality
Titian, 226
trace, the, 80–87, 92, 99, 103–104, 106–10, 112, 113n9, 175, 280, 282, 290
transcendental subjectivity, 5, 45, 63, 65

Uexküll, Jakob von, 13, 251n21

Valéry, Paul, 14, 202, 239, 249n5
Van Gogh, Vincent, 222, 224, 230
Velázquez, Diego, 230
Visible and the Invisible, The, 1, 5–7, 11, 14–16, 17, 34, 43, 47, 50, 61, 86–87, 97, 109, 114n10, 121, 124–31, 138–39, 151n13, 155–61, 165, 173, 183–84, 187, 190, 207, 215, 240–42, 245, 251n17, 252n28, 253n30, 253n35, 254n36, 254n42, 280, 286–87, 291
voyance, 13–14, 207, 217n20, 238–40, 242, 244, 249n4, 250n8, 253n30

Wild Being, 126, 128, 180, 194, 204–205, 214–16
Wittgenstein, Ludwig, 8

Zhu Qizhan, 12, 221–23, 228
Zhuangzi, 225